Phaenomenologica

Series Founded by H. L. Van Breda and Published Under the Auspices of the Husserl-Archives

Volume 245

Series Editors

Julia Jansen, Husserl-Archives, Leuven, Belgium

Stefano Micali, Husserl-Archives, Leuven, Belgium

Editorial Board

R. Bernet, Husserl-Archives, Leuven, Belgium

R. Breeur, Husserl-Archives, Leuven, Belgium

D. Lories, CEP/ISP/Collège Désiré Mercier, Louvain-la-Neuve, Belgium

U. Melle, Husserl-Archives, Leuven, Belgium

R. Visker, Catholic Univerisity Leuven, Leuven, Belgium

Advisory Editors

R. Bernasconi, Memphis State University, Memphis, USA

D. Carr, Emory University, Atlanta, USA

E.S. Casey, State University of New York at Stony Brook, Stony Brook, USA

J.F. Courtine, Husserl-Archives, Paris, France

F. Dastur, Université de Paris, Paris, France

K. Düsing, Husserl-Archives, Köln, Germany

J. Hart, Indiana University, Bloomington, USA

K. Held, Bergische Universität, Wuppertal, Germany

K.E. Kaehler, Husserl-Archives, Köln, Germany

D. Lohmar, Husserl-Archives, Köln, Germany

W.R. McKenna, Miami University, Oxford, USA

E.W. Orth, Universität Trier, Trier, Germany

C. Sini, Università degli Studi di Milano, Milan, Italy

R. Sokolowski, Catholic University of America, Washington, USA

B. Waldenfels, Ruhr-Universität, Bochum, Germany

SCOPE: Phaenomenologica is the longest running phenomenological book series world-wide. It was originally founded as a companion series to the Husserliana, and its first volume appeared in 1958. To this day, the series publishes studies of Husserl's work and of the work of related thinkers, investigations into the history of phenomenology, in-depth studies of specific aspects of phenomenology and phenomenological philosophy, and independent phenomenological research by scholars from all over the world. This unique series now unites several generations of phenomenologists, including Emmanuel Levinas, Jan Patočka, Eugen Fink, Roman Ingarden, Alfred Schutz, Bernhard Waldenfels and Marc Richir.

Initial inquiries and manuscripts for review should be sent directly to the attention of the Series Editors at phaenomenologica@kuleuven.be.

Andrew D. Barrette

The Origin of the Question: Phenomenological Philosophy after Edmund Husserl

 Springer

Andrew D. Barrette
Department of Philosophy
Boston College
Chestnut Hill, MA, USA

ISSN 0079-1350 ISSN 2215-0331 (electronic)
Phaenomenologica
ISBN 978-3-032-13568-1 ISBN 978-3-032-13569-8 (eBook)
https://doi.org/10.1007/978-3-032-13569-8

© The Editor(s) (if applicable) and The Author(s), under exclusive license to Springer Nature Switzerland AG 2026

This work is subject to copyright. All rights are solely and exclusively licensed by the Publisher, whether the whole or part of the material is concerned, specifically the rights of translation, reprinting, reuse of illustrations, recitation, broadcasting, reproduction on microfilms or in any other physical way, and transmission or information storage and retrieval, electronic adaptation, computer software, or by similar or dissimilar methodology now known or hereafter developed.
The use of general descriptive names, registered names, trademarks, service marks, etc. in this publication does not imply, even in the absence of a specific statement, that such names are exempt from the relevant protective laws and regulations and therefore free for general use.
The publisher, the authors and the editors are safe to assume that the advice and information in this book are believed to be true and accurate at the date of publication. Neither the publisher nor the authors or the editors give a warranty, expressed or implied, with respect to the material contained herein or for any errors or omissions that may have been made. The publisher remains neutral with regard to jurisdictional claims in published maps and institutional affiliations.

This Springer imprint is published by the registered company Springer Nature Switzerland AG
The registered company address is: Gewerbestrasse 11, 6330 Cham, Switzerland

If disposing of this product, please recycle the paper.

For Anthony Steinbock, who continues to serve as a mentor…
…οὔ τοι ἔπειθ' ἁλίη ὁδὸς ἔσσεται οὐδ' ἀτέλεστος.

—*Homer, Odyssey, Book 2, from ll. 267–280.*

Preface

> Philosophy is indeed, as it has so often been said, the science of the last and highest questions.[1]

In this book, I take Edmund Husserl as a model and guide for a phenomenological philosophy. I take him as a model insofar as his inquiry persists throughout his life, putting even the most self-evident and long-standing matters into question, allowing only adequate evidence to fulfill his striving for answers. I take him as a guide as he reflectively explicates inquiry, elucidating its various manifestations and their criteria for success. By taking after Husserl, this work takes up an intergenerational invitation to find and to live according to the methical demands of the questioning spirit that he uncovers and exemplifies. Indeed, there appears here, in the interpersonal and socio-historical horizon, *the origin of the question.*

Through the chapters, I aim to show *that* and *how* Husserl investigates inquiry. As there has not yet been a sustained treatment of this theme in the literature, I show *that* it is, in fact, present in his work. To do so, though, I also show *how* he treats inquiry, not only by asking his own questions, but by taking up motifs from other inquirers. This shows, in turn, how we take after his way of phenomenological inquiry in our investigation of phenomenological philosophy.

Following these aims, I expound four basic accounts of inquiry in Husserl's lifework. The first tends to focus on the *foundation* of question-expressions in intentional acts. The second, static account, coming after his so-called transcendental breakthrough, discovers the *source* of these acts as found in the immanent pure ego as it transcends itself in its *horizon* of the world. The third goes back to the *origins* of the activity, accounting for the genesis of inquiry in the subject's living in the

---

[1] Hua Mat IX, pp. 6–7. In the following, *Husserliana: Gesammelte Werke* shall be abbreviated as Hua, Hua Mat, for the *Materialienband*, or Hua Dok, for the *Dokumente* followed by volume, section or page numbers. Translations are my own, unless otherwise noted.

world. Finally, the fourth goes back to the socio-historical *roots* of inquiry, explicating how it stems from the generative world-horizon in which it participates. With these, I sketch the structures and historicity of the very *ways* of inquiring—especially in their practical, theoretical, and phenomenological appearance—without reducing them to historical happenstance.

Indeed, I find Husserl discovers inquiry as *given* and *given across generations* with his peculiar sort of "historical-teleological" phenomenological inquiry.[2] This way of inquiring reveals the dimension of *generativity*—a term which is found to denote at once a process of becoming *and* a socio-historical dimension to that process which extends across generations.[3] By inquiring-back into generativity, Husserl discovers the generative world-horizon as a peculiar *transcendental* condition of inquiry, at once delimiting questions by referring to previous achievements and giving conditions for new and novel questions in history. In this respect, even transcendental phenomenological inquiry appears as irreducible to the individual inquirer. For, as Husserl realizes, "the phenomenologist and phenomenology itself stand in this historicity!"[4] Thus, phenomenology, once established, comes to be passed on as a *task (Aufgabe)* that is *"given over"* (*aufgegeben*) to future phenomenologists, as the German compound noun suggests—*die Aufgabe*: from *auf-* ("over" or "up to") and *geben* ("to give").

In this task, Erazim Kohák emphasized that Husserl directed others to "See!"[5] To that, I add that he also implored us to "Ask!" And these directives are given, not as *impositions*, but rather as *invitations*. They are invitations, extended across generations, to inquire-back into oneself and into the world in order to discover the very ideals according to which we and our inquiry operate. By taking up this invitation to

---

[2] See, for example, Husserl (1970) pp. 3 fn. 1 and 102.

[3] Most significantly and substantially in Steinbock (1995).

[4] A phrase so emphasized by Steinbock, found at Hua XV, p. 393: "Aber der Phänomenologe und die Phänomenologie stehen selbst in dieser Geschichtlichkeit."

[5] See, Kohák (1978), pp. xi–xlli. Kohák translated Husserl's to Arnold Metzger, in Husserl (1981), p. 363, in which Husserl says, "Finally, with respect to method, perspective, and areas of work of the *Ideas*, I can say but a single word, 'See!' I truthfully believe that I can say it, in full awareness of my responsibility. This does not in any way preclude the possibility that much could be improved, that here and there may be and is something false in the book."

know ourselves and to live according to the ideals of knowing and acting, phenomenological inquirers become bound together in a sort of "historical communication," as Husserl puts it.⁶ To do this is to philosophize together—συμφιλοσοφεῖν.⁷

---

⁶ See, for example, Husserl (1970), pp. 17–18: "…we must inquire back into what was originally and always sought in philosophy, what was continually sought by all the philosophers and philosophies that have communicated with one another historically; but this must include a critical consideration of what, in respect to the goals and methods [of philosophy], is ultimate, original, and genuine and which, once seen, apodictically conquers the will;" consider also Husserl (1970), p. 280: "These are the men who, not in isolation but with one another and for one another, that is, in interpersonally bound communal work, strive for and bring about *theôria* and nothing but *theôria*, whose growth and constant perfection, with the broadening of the circle of coworkers and the succession of the generations of inquirers, is finally taken up into the will with the sense of an infinite and common task."

⁷ I mean this as Aristotle uses it in the *Nicomachean Ethics*, Book IX, 1172a5. For Husserl's uses of this term, see Hua Brief. II, pp. 78 and 253; Hua Brief. III, p. 457; Hua Brief. IV, pp. 76, 129, 187, and 484; and Hua Brief. VI, p. 239. With this point in mind, let me thank all those who helped in the long process of finishing this work. A special thank you is due to the current Director of the Husserl-Archives, Prof. Julia Jansen for permission to consult the *Nachlass*, to quote from the published and unpublished manuscripts, and to provide translations of Husserl's writings. I am also grateful to the previous Directors, Prof. Dr. Ullrich Melle and Prof. Dr. Rudolf Bernet, for their permissions and helpful guidance.

Contents

1 Introduction 1
   1.1 Sense of the Work as a Whole 1
   1.2 Turning to Husserl 4
   1.3 Outline of the Work 7

2 The Act and Intentional Essence of Inquiry 9
   2.1 Preliminary Remarks—Toward a Logic of Question–Answer
      with the Transcendental Question 9
      2.1.1 Classical Logic and the Place of Questions 10
      2.1.2 Preparatory Sketch of Husserl's Campaign Against
          Skepticism 19
   2.2 Toward the Essence of Inquiry via Intentional Analysis 24
      2.2.1 Beginnings and Breakthroughs of Phenomenology 25
      2.2.2 Objectivating and Non-objectivating Acts
          and Relevant Relations of Foundation 29
      2.2.3 The Act of Inquiry as Mediating Fulfillment: The
          Logic of Question–Answer 32
   2.3 Concluding Remarks: The Interior and Exterior Voice 37

3 Toward the Source and Horizon of Acts of Inquiry 41
   3.1 *Preliminary Remarks—The Radicalization
      of the Transcendental Question* 42
      3.1.1 An Elucidation of δόξα and ἐπιστήμη vis-à-vis Inquiry 43
   3.2 Natural and Transcendental Questions 49
      3.2.1 Metaphysics: The Transcendental Question
          and a Demand for Absolute Cognition 50
      3.2.2 Doubt Compared to Inquiry 53
      3.2.3 Inquiry in the Intuitive Method of Transcendental
          Phenomenology 57
   3.3 Natural Inquiry Within the World 63
      3.3.1 The Pure Ego as Source of Inquiry 64

		3.3.2	Inquiry in the Natural Practical Attitude	66
	3.4	Concluding Remarks: Correlation Analysis and the Regressive Procedure		71
4	**The Genesis of Inquiry**			75
	4.1	Preliminary Remarks—Toward a Transcendental Logic of Question and Answer		75
		4.1.1	Aristotle's "Analysis": Questions in Science as About Causes and Origins	76
		4.1.2	The Appearance of the Demand for a Regressive Procedure in Correlation Analysis	82
	4.2	Husserl's Discovery and Description of Genesis from the Regressive Approach		85
		4.2.1	Passivity and Activity	88
		4.2.2	Normativity as a Theme of Genetic Phenomenology	92
	4.3	Inquiry as a Multi-layered Striving for Determination and Differentiation		95
		4.3.1	The Origin of Inquiry in Passivity	96
		4.3.2	*Intellectus Agens*: The Noetic Activity of Inquiry	100
		4.3.3	Interested and Disinterested Inquiry and the Constitution of Inquiring Attitudes	107
	4.4	Concluding Remarks: The Need for Further Genetic Analysis		112
5	**Knowing, Valuing, and Further Reflections on Inquiry and Method**			113
	5.1	Preliminary Remarks—Ethics as a Practical Science		114
		5.1.1	The Unity of the Sciences and Their Unifying Principle	115
	5.2	The Relationships of Knowing and Valuing		117
		5.2.1	Objectivation and Values	118
		5.2.2	The "Why and Because" in Philosophical Ethics	126
	5.3	Some Senses of Method		138
		5.3.1	Methods and Techniques	138
		5.3.2	*Leitfaden* and *Leitmotifs*: Clues Appearing In and Obtaining Between Methods	141
	5.4	Concluding Remarks: Toward a Generative Analysis of Inquiry		142
6	**The Generative Roots of Inquiry**			147
	6.1	Preliminary Remarks—The Question of History		147
		6.1.1	Principles and Givenness	149
	6.2	Preliminary Sketch of Some Generative Themes		156
		6.2.1	The Home/alien Problematic in the Question of Generativity	156

	6.2.2	Instinct and Reason	161
6.3	The Generation of World-Inquiry as Participating in the World-Horizon		164
	6.3.1	Birth, Childhood, and the Development of Instinct Toward Inquiry	165
	6.3.2	Instinct, Imitation, and the Original Question of History—Why?	170
6.4	From Myth to Philosophy: A Transformation of the "Why" Question		178
	6.4.1	Myth: Meaning and Value Relative to the Homeworld	178
	6.4.2	The Meeting of Mythical Worlds and the Appearance of Wonder in Greece	181

7 Concluding Overview: From Latent to Patent unto Manifest Reason 189

Appendices 197

References 215

Index 225

Chapter 1
Introduction

Augustin: nur die Liebe macht sehend—für Wert und Ideal
Nemo cognoscitur nisi per amicitiam.[1]

1.1 Sense of the Work as a Whole

Inquiry seems familiar enough. It is given with the questions of our practical problems, our theoretical wonder, as well as our communicative life. But do we attend to it straightaway? Not at all. We are instead captivated by the world in which we live, absorbed in our questions. Quite naturally, we take inquiry for granted, naively presuming questions will arise where they need answers. To be sure, we recognize and rely on this fact. After all, we train scientists to observe closely and we trust educators to guide rightly, so that where we have yet to inquire, we might still. But this is not yet a disengaged inquiry into inquiry itself. To that end, I pursue a *phenomenology of inquiry*.

The sense of such a task is not self-evident, of course. Even if inquiry spontaneously appears in experience, methodological reflection upon it—and so, too, the motives, results, and benefits of this reflection—does not. One could pretend to strike it out alone in their reflection, exploring how inquiry emerges, operates, and transforms. Sooner or later, though, one must face the facts of collaboration and cooperation, of inheritance and indebtedness, even within one's own inquiry. Indeed, without some understanding of these dimensions, an account of inquiry is doomed, not only to that incompleteness intrinsic to most investigations, but to an inadequacy to both the matter and the method. In other words, without attention to socio-historical horizons, an inquiry into inquiry would fall short of the task at hand.

---

[1] Edmund Husserl, from an unpublished section of manuscript E III 10/2. The passage comes from St. Augustine, *De diversis quaestionibus octoginta tribus*.

After all, one does not have *ways* of asking and answering sorted out all at once. Spontaneous though questions may be, inquiry develops only as one inquirer follows after others. Questions are put within and to a world that is built, in no small measure, by prior questions and answers. And these previous achievements sketch the horizons from which questions emerge and in which inquiry operates. Now, to be sure, one might ask new and novel questions. But these, too, appear from those horizons to which one's answers contribute. What is more, in these questions, one still cooperates with others insofar as one's way of asking shares, not just a personal style, but also the goal of realizing certain values and ideals. Thus, along with Anthony Steinbock's elucidation of how we take "after" others chronologically and methodologically, I add how we strive "after," or "reach up to" others that "bring us up."[2]

To clarify, let me mark, albeit in a provisional manner, a few ways the Husserlian phenomenologist goes "before" inquiry. In the first place, the phenomenologist suspends any position-taking in the world by way of an ἐποχή and performs a *phenomenological reduction* to "go back" ("reduce," in its literal sense of *re-ducere*) before matters of fact to how they appear. After disengaging with the ready world, with its developed ways of inquiring and already acquired answers, the phenomenologist can ask how matters become meaningful and valuable at all. So, in the second place, the phenomenologist may aim toward grasping *a priori*, essential structures of possible instances of, say, questions and inquiry, in an *eidetic reduction*. Still more, with these insights into the "how of givenness," the phenomenologist can give a *constitutive* account of how matters appear *as* such and so in experience while also accounting for the degrees of accordance of actual operation to ideal possibilities. Thus, for example, we can give an account of how matters appear *as* questionable while also accounting for how various possible ways of inquiry might meet or really do respond to such questionability. This also points to how the phenomenologist may also understand a lawfulness of experience from insights into givenness, rather than imposing abstract ideals onto experience or treating norms as merely relative to the one experiencing. It is possible, for example, to clarify the sense of "good questions" and "good answers" in the measure that they meet the demands given in their very appearance and operation. Thus, in the third and final place, phenomenology finds how subjects stand "before the law" which is meant for each subject. In other words, phenomenology seeks to give the possibility of a radical *self-responsibility by yielding the insight needed for living in accord with demands and norms of subjectivity*. Failing to do so means not living up to the laws of reason before which we are.[3]

---

[2] Although this notion may be seen throughout Steinbock's writings, it is perhaps most succinctly formulated in, Steinbock (2017), p. xii: "In *Home and Beyond: Generative Phenomenology after Husserl*, I introduced what I called 'generative phenomenology' as 'after' Husserl to mean both according to Husserl in the prepositional sense, and temporally following him, as a conjunction." It is evident, I hope, that the present work would not be possible without Anthony Steinbock's continued insights, direction, and friendship.

[3] Husserl (1970), p. 16; Hua VI, p. 14: "Ist es nicht sogar die der 'faulen Vernunft,' welche dem Ringen um eine Klärung der letzten Vorgegebenheiten und der von ihnen aus letztlich und wahrhaft rational vorgezeichneten Ziele und Wege *ausweicht*?" See also, Hua XXVIII, p. 339.

1.1 Sense of the Work as a Whole

At the confluence of these senses of "before" and "after," appears a clarified sense of the *ideal of presuppositionlessness* in Husserl's phenomenological method. That ideal *does not* mean a counter-sensical negation of position: the phenomenologist does not simultaneously pretend to deny themselves any position while nevertheless taking one, as if wiping away the horizon without standing on some ground. Rather, taking up that ideal means setting as a goal a sort of critical reflection that brings to question all positions and position-takings in order to become aware of them, to understand them, and, if necessary, to replace them with ones that have more adequate evidence.[4] Taken in this sense, presuppositionlessness is an ideal which Husserl clarifies and exemplifies such that each phenomenological philosopher might at once take after him, stand before it, and appropriate it in their own activity.

Once again, then, Husserl does not mean for phenomenological philosophy to impose ideals and values. He himself does not claim complete authority from mundane grounds, nor does he suggest anyone should do so, as if one human person or group has an encompassing monopoly on the true, the good, and the beautiful. Nevertheless, from Husserl, there comes a *bequest* of achievements, with which we work as apprentices, trying to understand for oneself even while sharing values and ideals.[5] Indeed, the above already begins to clarify the phrase from Augustine, found in Husserl's manuscripts, and set as the heading of this work: "Only love makes us see—for value and ideal. No one knows except by friendship." I take it as a complement to the more well-known Augustinian tag, taken from the *De vera Religione,* at the end of the *Cartesian Meditations*: "Do not wish to go out, but to go back within, for truth dwells in the interior man."[6] Taken together, I understand that a turn inward may discover, not a *solus ipse*, but community.

With this in mind, I follow, throughout this book, a way in which "reason returns to itself," as Husserl puts it, through the intergenerational activity of inquiry.[7] In so doing, I find a movement through history from *latent* reason to *patent* reason, and then to *manifest* reason. In latent reason, inquiry is *hidden* from itself, as it operates in a horizon restricted to the world relative to the subject. In patent reason, inquiry *opens* to the world *in itself* but remains also *problematic* as it lacks an adequate account of *how* this is so. In manifest reason, finally, is the reason that asks how inquiry *appears at all*, differentiating and setting in order ways of inquiry. Thus, Husserl understands phenomenological philosophy as *realizing* a possibility latent yet pressing in the earliest emergence of reason. Indeed, he eventually *inquires-back* into the appearance of phenomenology itself—undertaking, in other words, a "phenomenology of phenomenology," as Eugen Fink, Husserl's last assistant and collaborator, would identify it—with which he discovers that "transcendental inquiry

---

[4] An early formulation of this in §7 of the "Introduction" to Volume II, of *Logical Investigations*; see Husserl (2001a), pp. 177–180. It also appears later, for example, in the "Principle of Principles" of §24 of *Ideas I*; see Husserl (1982), p. 44.

[5] For the suggestion, see Husserl (2019), p. 5.

[6] Husserl (1960), p. 157; see Hua I, p. 183: "*Noli foras ire in te redi*, sagt Augustin, *in interiore homine habitat veritas.*"

[7] See Hua XXXVII, p. 225; and, again, Husserl (1970), p. 339.

is itself a world-historical process insofar as it enlarges the history of the constitution of the world…"[8] As this work also participates in that world-historical process by inquiring into inquiry, a few more words about the history of its theme in Husserlian phenomenology may serve to motivate it.

1.2 Turning to Husserl

To be sure, inquiry is not a usual Husserlian theme. Despite a few articles and a surfeit of mentions in the literature of its general importance, there has not yet been a systematic, phenomenological treatment of it.[9] While this study aims to fill that lacuna, it is also important to note that its existence is due more to the situation surrounding Husserl's writings than to their content and method. That much of his work was left unpublished during his lifetime is well-known. With the manuscripts accessible only to the few that could read them, the next generation of phenomenologists became torchbearers of the new science. As they taught its new way of approaching matters, they introduced their original works. This initiated a period of expansion during which phenomenological themes were set. As a result, inquiry became something of a suspiciously *un*-Husserlian theme.

On this point, the work of Martin Heidegger comes to mind. Around 1926, amid a growing personal rift, Heidegger published the first part of the monumental *Sein und Zeit* in the *Jahrbuch für Philosophie und phänomenologische Forschung*. This work begins, of course, not just by announcing a renewal of the question of being—the *Seinsfrage*—but also by implicitly challenging the abstract yet "foundationalist" Cartesianism that was supposed to constitute the whole of Husserl's work. For, unlike the Cartesian absolute pure *ego* that is abstracted from any world in which and to which questions may be asked, the meaning of Heidegger's *Dasein* is inextricably constituted by inquiry of the world and of itself, as it is, "in its very Being, that

---

[8] Husserl (1970), p. 264. For more on this point, see Džanić (2023), especially the first chapter, "Husserl and Fink: From Philosophical Systematics to a 'Phenomenology of Phenomenology,'" pp. 17–45. As Džanić says, in footnote 23 of that Chapter: "With regard to the phrase 'phenomenology of phenomenology', see [Sebastian] Luft's remark (Left, 2002: 16). He challenges the opinion that this phrase is, at its core, a very un-Husserlian one, introduced into phenomenology by Fink. Husserl's own use of the phrase dates from 1930 (Hua XXXIV, p. 176), and it therefore cannot be established who used it first. However, even if not in letter, the phrase is fully consistent with Husserl's earlier discussions of a critique of a critique in spirit. In this respect, Fink's use of the phrase in the *Sixth Meditation* is continuous with this goal."

[9] One can find recent recognition of its methodological importance, for example, in the work of C. Struyker Boudier (1983), Witold Plotka (2012), and, perhaps most recently and persistently, Daniel Sobota (2020 and 2021). The work of Joel Hubick (2024) also argues for the significance of questioning in phenomenology, in general, while showing its presence in Husserl's thought. It also appears as a theme in the early collaborations of Eugen Fink and Ludwig Landgrebe with Husserl himself. I address these throughout the work. My aim is to show the appearance and operation of inquiry at all, while setting it into relation to phenomenology as a way of inquiry.

1.2 Turning to Husserl

Being is an issue for it."[10] Given the apparent methodological abstraction from this concreteness, not only did Husserl have little to say about inquiry as a matter of fact, but his phenomenology *could not* say much.

The view that Husserl's work was deficient with respect to its analysis of inquiry neither begins nor ends with Heidegger, of course. For example, two decades prior to *Sein und Zeit*, Johannes Daubert, a student and confidant of Husserl, critiqued and developed the phenomenological analyses of questions.[11] Later, Eugen Fink also stressed the need for making inquiry methodologically explicit. Rather than addressing these critiques and developments directly, however, I show that he took inquiry as a theme, while parsing his rich and complex reflections on how the matter appears. With this, a reasonable comparison with the work of others as well as a responsible decision which, if any, is most adequate to the matters themselves becomes possible. In truth, though, if we follow after Husserl's sense of phenomenological philosophy as collaborative, the goal is to understand the matters rather than pit thinkers against each other.

So, through the chapters. I show Husserl's developing investigation of inquiry. What becomes clear is that he does not understand inquiry as one-sidedly "founded" on the subject at all. Indeed, he certainly does not take the question, "Why does inquiry appear?" as adequately answered with "because the *subject* asks" or even "because the subject *can* or *might ask*." Rather, for him, the inquiring subject is given to itself as in a questionable world. Still, one might object, all this is under the shroud of immanence, yet founded on the subject. But this objection overlooks the *correlation* of subject-world, especially as the subject stands within the generative world-horizon which gives the range and sense of questionability at all. To clarify these points, the phenomenologist inquire-back into that correlation, into the source and origins of inquiry itself.

Still, the *way* Husserl works presents a unique challenge for our investigation. He "zig-zags" through analyses, answering this or that question, only to later, after further study, realize he is either out ahead on still another question or that he had an earlier analysis somewhere in a manuscript that he himself had not yet adequately appreciated but which changes the sense of some previous answer.[12] And rather than merely crossing-out or throwing-away less than adequate analyses, he questions how the difference was possible and how these possibilities relate, in order to help guide others through the labyrinth. For the explorer, there are no wrong turns, only fuller maps, whereas the tourist, easily exhausted, wants direction only to the highlights and the gift shop. This is the essential benefit of following him on his explorations: being led toward fuller answers by setting them into relation to those less so. It is also true, though, there is a need for those following after to take stock of how they will approach the whole.

---

[10] Heidegger (1962), p. 32.

[11] It is worth noting that Heidegger's interest in inquiry came quite earlier, evidenced by a longer extant piece "Question and Judgement" from 1915; see, Heidegger (2000), p. 25. Also, Daubert was working on his "Question Essay" as early as 1911.

[12] Husserl (1970), p. 58.

The interpretive approach I take in this book thus relates to Husserl in a particular way. To explain, let me clarify by contrast. On the pages of Husserl's personal copy of Heidegger's *Sein und Zeit*, there is the old Aristotelian gloss in Husserl's handwriting: "*Amicus Plato, sed magis amica veritas.*" In these faint pencil-markings, there appears, not the words of a defiant hero, but the lament of one who felt the loss of philosophical friendship. With this in mind, it makes sense that Husserl also inveighs against Heidegger's espousal of a "violence of interpretation," writing the following response: "I differentiate what they say [that is, their words] and what they [that is, the authors] ultimately aimed at and wanted to say as they said them."[13] I understand Husserl to mean here that, while he tries to understand another without imputing something they did not say, he nevertheless takes seriously that they also seriously strive to the truth. In fact, he accepts this as, in a way, more important than where they may have fallen short of that goal. For, taken this way, even the false-starts and apparent dead-ends give a clue to the mind at work and to the truth it seeks, which is that which you also seek. To be Plato's friend, then, means taking seriously that Plato himself is asking you to join him in seeking the truth which exceeds him. Further questions and answers—even those which would clarify or correct him—appear in the light of seeking together for the truth. Where the seeking together is dropped, then violence enters—where one only works for oneself, one sets oneself up to work against others. In contrast to this, I take Husserl's as asking others to follow along with him in order to find out together what is truly the case.[14] This is, in fact, how he read others and even how he read himself—and it is how I venture to read him and others.

In sum, if inquiry indeed appears in experience, it is a matter for phenomenological investigation. What is more, it is *operative* in the *doing* of phenomenology, that is, it is "at work" in it, even if it is not made an explicit theme.[15] Even if it is left unthematic and conceptually implicit, it is essential to the activity. So, unless we are prepared to defend that the phenomenologist asks no questions, we must face the strange circumstance that, though we have long felt the directive, "Back to the matters themselves!" we have not yet clarified *how* questioning is essential to this return. With this call, I claim, Husserl himself reestablishes the demand to bring inquiry to question. And this means, for the present inquiry, participating in an intergenerational task of philosophy.

---

[13] In fact, Husserl marks-off this phrase in a way that, as far as I can tell, is the upper limit of emphasis in his marginalia, namely, three exclamation points and three question marks. See Husserl, (1997a), p. 453, where Husserl underlines Heidegger's phrase, "every interpretation necessarily has to use violence," putting in the margin, "!!!???".

[14] Thus, Husserl speaks to his teacher of the joy and peace of working with a like-minded person. See Appendix A.

[15] On this point, I am indebted to Eugen Fink's insights into the "*Operative Begriffe*" of Husserl's thought. I follow Fink's argument that an operative concept is one that is *at work*) in the thinker's analyses even if it is not made an explicit theme of analysis; see Fink (1981).

1.3 Outline of the Work

This work traces Husserl's developing analysis of inquiry through five chapters.

The Chapter 1 considers Husserl's treatment of inquiry in his earlier analysis of intentionality. I begin with how question sentences fall outside classical formal logic, since they do not take a position on the truth or falsity of a state of affairs, that is, are not apophantic. Then, I show his phenomenological account of how questions, despite not having a truth-value, are meaningful. The questions, Husserl finds, emerges within the intentional life of thinking such that the expression gives voice to the intentional acts of inquiring. By founding the question expression and sentence in intentional life, Husserl places inquiry within a broader understanding of "logic" which includes the full range of thinking, thought, and said.

The Chapter 2 turns to the appearance of inquiry in the earlier formulations of Husserl's transcendental project. If the previous chapter shows how he investigates the logical problematic of meaningful sentences and expressions, this chapter shows how he discovers the pure ego as the source and the world as the horizon of inquiry. Further, there appears, in the methodological development of phenomenology, a basic distinction between transcendental phenomenological inquiry and natural inquiry. Where natural inquiry leaves the source and horizon unquestioned, transcendental phenomenological inquiry proceeds under suspension of any positing—an ἐποχή—in order to understand how any position taking appears at all. From this methodological development, I also consider some aspects of his analysis of practical inquiry, which serves to bring to question the limitations of a phenomenological method that does not account for the genesis of matters.

The Chapter 3 thus takes up how Husserl accounts for the emergence and operation of inquiry by going back to its origin in individual facticity. More exactly, his genetic account of inquiry discovers how it appears within a striving for determination and differentiation in the intentional life of the individual. I also bring to the fore here an important distinction between interested and disinterested inquiry, wherein the latter detaches from interests in relation to the ego in order to strive to determine and to differentiate matters in themselves and in relation to each other. This distinction is essential for understanding science and, indeed, phenomenological science, insofar as these disinterestedly inquire into the "things themselves." It also raises the question about why and how such inquiry would arise at all, which is more directly considered in the next chapters.

The Chapter 4 then considers some of Husserl's reflections on the relationship of cognizing and valuing, investigating especially how inquiry appears therein. Along with raising the question of the judgment of value, I pay special attention to Husserl's analysis of the question of the will, in which there is a deliberation about the best possible choice and what should be done. I also bring to the fore the intelligible relation of motives, in what Husserl identifies as the "Why" and "Because." By inquiring into these relations, the phenomenologist can understand the lawfulness of *reasons why*. Finally, then, I make clear a few senses of method in Husserl's thought, especially with respect to how and why they appear at all. From these points, an understanding of phenomenological ethics as a practical science emerges, insofar as it makes clear which actions should be done and why.

The Chapter 5 reconstructs Husserl's inquiry-back into the generation of inquiry. In the first steps of this, I expound the emergence of inquiry from childhood curiosity. The original question about *why* appears within the home, in order to answer *why* the homeworld has particular meanings and *how* to navigate it practically. From this, I turn to the transformation of inquiry from within the curiosity of myth to philosophical wonder, as the latter breaks from relative truth and establishes theoretical science, the ideal of which is in determining the universal truth which is true, not just for those in this homeworld, but as true for everyone everywhere. As the instantiations of this ideal following from Greek philosophy tends to the objective pole, the correlation of the subject-world is left unquestioned. So, there arises a demand for the further inquiry of phenomenological philosophy, to which I turn next.

In a **Concluding Overview**, I provide a brief reconstruction of Husserl's account of the development of reason and inquiry (represented in the figure at the end of the main text). Especially significant, in this respect, is his eventual explication of the phenomenological inquiry-back into the emergence of sense, meaning, and value, as it makes manifest reason to itself. Indeed, it raises awareness to inquiry as essential in making the best possible world together.

Finally, in the **Appendices**, I provide translations of a few letters which give a glimpse into Husserl's personal communication about the range of inquiry. These span from the years just after his breakthrough to phenomenology to the year before the end of his life. They at once show the consistency of his mind and its development within the context of other persons.

Chapter 2
The Act and Intentional Essence of Inquiry

Abstract This chapter presents Husserl's treatment of inquiry in his early intentionality analyses. I first show how question sentences come to fall outside classical formal logic, since they do not take a position on the truth or falsity of a state of affairs, that is, are not apophantic. Then I show the way in which Husserl gives a phenomenological account of how questions, despite not having a truth-value, are meaningful. The meaning of questions emerges within the intentional life of thinking such that the expression articulates or "gives voice to" intentional acts. The expression can be formalized, as in classical logic, but this abstracts from the intentional life to which it refers. As such, Husserl can take up inquiry within a broader understanding of "logic" that includes the full range of meaning.

Keywords Act phenomenology · Intentionality · Inquiry · Interiority · Logic

2.1 Preliminary Remarks—Toward a Logic of Question–Answer with the Transcendental Question

Too often neglected—if noticed at all—is the fundamental role of inquiry in Husserl's work, especially surrounding the seminal *Logical Investigations*. In fact, here, he both takes it to be among a "just as important as it is difficult disputed question" and brings this apparently "inconspicuous" matter *in question*.[1] In this chapter, I thus clarifies the problematic of inquiry in this work while elucidating it as operative in the nascent science of phenomenology. To meet these aims, I take two main steps:

1. After introducing Husserl's understanding of classical formal logic and its exclusion of question-sentences, I explicate his breakthrough to a more adequate account of cognition via phenomenology, including the beginning analyses of the act of inquiry;

---

[1] Hua XIX/1, §68, esp. p. 737. Findlay renders the phrase "ebenso wichtigen wie schwierigen Streitfrage" as the "most important and most difficult points at issue." I suggest that Husserl's use of *Streitfrage*, which Findlay glosses as "point as issue" should be taken as a point *in question* or a *disputed question*.

2. I then readdress the sense of a logic of the interior life, which also serves to highlight how the method of phenomenological inquiry itself emerges *with* these investigations.

Meeting these aims yields a preliminary understanding of the phenomenological sense of "logic," now taken, as Husserl puts it later, in the original sense of λόγος—as "thinking, thought, said."[2] From this sense, phenomenology accounts for the meaning of questions insofar as question expressions are founded upon inquiry which intends answers. To prepare this analysis, let me begin by presenting his earlier understanding of the appearance of philosophy in Greek culture, which helps clarify his understanding of logic and the need for renewed logical investigations.

2.1.1 Classical Logic and the Place of Questions

Husserl tends to consider the development of logic from the context of Greek philosophy. This is especially true in relation to his own attempt to recover and realize logic as a "theory of theory,…science of the sciences."[3] It is thus worthwhile to trace, in increasing detail through this book, some aspects of his account of this historical path.

About the early stage of science in Greece, Husserl notes, in an 1896 lecture given while a *Privatdozent* at University of Halle: "The skeptical attacks against the possibility of all cognition caused the building of science to falter. In order to secure the efforts of serious science, one had to make indubitable distinctions between strict cognition and sophistic semblance."[4] These skeptical attacks found in claims to knowledge an insecure edifice, an uncritical belief in what counts as evidentially true. Indeed, where one natural philosopher claimed the fundamental element to be water, another claimed it was fire, still others number, mind, the indefinite, and so on, none offered an account of what justified one position to be more adequate than another. Upon detecting that lack, skeptics began to erode any claim to truth. In the midst of this, Husserl finds the appearance of a basic philosophical question—which he calls, a few years later, the "transcendental question"—namely, "How is cognition possible at all?"[5]

Before turning directly to the first answers to the transcendental question, let me underscore how Husserl takes skepticism, more generally, as pressing further

---

[2] See Husserl (2001a), pp. 1–38, especially 8. Also, the later summary of the *Logical Investigations* in Husserl (1975), p. 59: "to get at the primary presuppositions of the sense of '*logos*' and thereby of all science, and to clarify these presuppositions in specific analyses."

[3] See, for example, Hua XVIII, 244. And Husserl (2001b), §66b, p. 152.

[4] Hua Mat I, p. 304. Some of Husserl's inspiration for this reading appears in the Q-manuscripts, the extant notes from lecture courses, especially from Franz Brentano and Carl Stumpf on the history of philosophy, as well as in his reading of Wilhelm Windelband. I find that this way of constructing the history of philosophy remains basically intact through his life, even if its interpretation develops.

[5] Hua Mat III, p. 82: "So how is cognition possible at all? This transcendental question continues to press in the development of philosophy."

2.1 Preliminary Remarks—Toward a Logic of Question–Answer …

questions to be answered.[6] For him, skepticism is a motor thinking, at least insofar as it is *searching, watchful*, as the Greek word, σκεπτῐκός, suggests. Through its watchfulness, it discovers unanswered questions, unresolved issues, weak points and lacunas in reasoning. Of course, the *sophistical skeptic* no longer seeks out true reasons, seeking instead to show any reason to be merely apparent, "mere semblance," as Husserl puts it. In any case, to skeptical probing, philosophical thinking responds.

Husserl presents, for example, two influential philosophical responses to the earlier sophistical skepticism in the Greek world. On the one hand, there is the exaggerated dynamism of a Heraclitus, who concedes the flux and diversity of experience even while recognizing the need for the identity of speech and truth. On the other hand, there are the Eleatics, who, in their positing of a fixed object of cognition, deny the possibility of change and so any cognition of diversity, as Parmenides did so on his "way to truth."[7] Both of these struggle to answer the transcendental question about the possibility of cognition. Yet, the unresolved tension between them—between being and becoming, as it were—only fueled further skepticism about the possibility of knowing the truth at all.

Indeed, in the wake of the unresolved tension, later sophistic skeptics pressed on the way—seen but refused by Parmenides—of *opinion* or δόξα.[8] They engaged, not so much with speculative visions of truth, as with "everyday experience," as Husserl puts it.[9] In some sense, this engagement was in line with the traditional teachers of virtue in Greek culture, those original *sophists*—the σοφοί or "wise ones." However, this later iteration of sophists, without offering an answer to the now explicitly raised transcendental question, held fast to the differences in estimation and evaluation readily found amongst people. The breakthrough to theory did not end everyday, practical life, after all. So, these sophists strengthened their resolve by borrowing terms from theory, showing the varying positions of everyday experience to preclude any identity of speech and truth, thinking and being. To demonstrate this, such a sophist might say, one need only listen to the various answers that multiple people give to the same question, for example, about the meaning of "hot" and "cold" or "short" and "tall." So, it was evident that, as Protagoras eventually

---

[6] As he will put it later, in Hua Mat IX, pp. 20–21 fn. 1: "By the way, a beautiful and well-understandable teleology in the historical development shows up here. In the image one could say: The worst enemies are those who can attack from the back, so the investigating gaze must not merely be directed straight at the things, but ⟨must⟩ also be directed retrospectively at the consciousness, at the form and method of cognition. And indeed, the skeptical attacks of sophistry and all later skepticism of science have grown to salvation…."

[7] Thus, in Hua Mat III, p. 82 continued from above. This is reworked but essentially repeated in Hua IX, pp. 191–192, though here he adds the essential importance of *logos* for Heraclitus.

[8] A rare sighting of this use in Husserl's early works is found at the end of the second volume of the *Logical Investigations*, which I discuss in the first subsection of the next chapter. It becomes, in his later thought, an all-important word to understand in relation to ἐπιστήμη or scientific knowledge.

[9] Hua Mat III, p. 81: "The theoretical consideration of the world immediately leads to contradictions with the common everyday experience. Instead of enhancing and enriching it, it seems to have to negate it." The *seems* here is a key, as it does not really do so—but how so is a main question for us.

claimed, human subjects were themselves the measure of truth.[10] Having conflated theory and practice, they taught that their inquisitive dialectic and rhetorical flair, which manipulated opinion, as the way to navigate the world.

Such sophistry had its effects, of course. It led some in Greek culture to dismiss philosophy, to label philosophers as charlatans, impractical, imprudent, stuck in the clouds. Nevertheless, the "transcendental question" pressed upon the mind of philosophical persons. For Husserl, it is especially the personality of Socrates—at least as Plato represents him—appears as resisting the reduction of truth to opinion by trying to clarify the *"function of concepts."*[11] He does so, however, not so much by casting aspersions upon interlocutors, but by transforming them via his maieutic art. Through conversation, in fact, he shows the sophist that investigation must not stop at the expressed concept—that is to say, that which is *said*—but instead must continue to inquire into how the concept *functions* as an expression of *thinking*. As any expression already evidences a position-taking, one cannot really be a radical skeptic who refuses the possibility of any cognition at all.[12] What is more, Socrates, with his sort of inquiry, invites others to discover in their thinking *a demand for living toward and according to the truth*, offering, not so much "wisdom," σοφία, as an invitation to a φιλο-σοφία, a friendship with wisdom.

Yet, if that which is said indicates thinking, what is *thought* in this thinking, that is to say, what is the *content* of thinking? With respect to such questions, Husserl moves from Socrates and the *concept* to Plato and the *ideas*. Admittedly, there is a conspicuous dearth of direct references to Plato in Husserl's extant early writings, though the influence is indirectly present.[13] For Husserl, the *idea* is the *content of understanding*,

---

[10] See Hua XVIII, p. 122. Husserl later turns more often to Gorgias, whose nihilistic claims give impulse to philosophical reflection upon the subject. In each case, though, there is a relativistic consequence of anthropologism.

[11] Emphasis is my own. This is what Husserl calls a "transcendental problem," in connection to the "transcendental question," for example, at Hua Mat III, p. 82. He also links this later with the "method of definition," which I do not take up directly in the "function" of concepts here. I instead focus upon the, perhaps more Platonic, interpolation of desire, as expressed again, for example, in Hua Mat IX, p. 28. Also see the invocation of Socrates and Plato to describe the subsumption of particulars into a general concept, a "paradigm" or *Inbegriff*, at Hua Mat I, p. 89, which is something Husserl does, in fact, in various points of the manuscript from which this selection came (K I 19).

[12] See Hua Mat IX, pp. 7–9.

[13] Peter Varga has shown this indirect influence. See Varga (2013). This is evident in Husserl's course work as student and his readings of authors like Hermann Lotze, Wilhelm Windelband, and, later, Paul Natorp. For example, let me refer to the follow works: Hua XIX/1, 138 and in Hua XX/1, pp. 414–415; or, again, somewhat earlier, in 1903, *Zeitschrift für Psychologie und Physiologie der Sinnesorgane*, Vol. 31, pp. 287–294, republished in Husserliana XXII, pp. 152–161. He places all these in relation to Brentano, saying, "Incidentally, my 'Prolegomena' are not directed against you and your students. I believe that there are no such great differences between us in these most general questions, I only consider the stress of individual distinctions, which you believe to be able to do without. I must also say that all mystical-metaphysical employment of 'ideas,' ideal possibilities and the like is completely far from me. Also, Bolzano does not realize his 'representation' and sentences 'in themselves.' These conceptions of Bolzano have had a strong impact on me, as did Lotze's reinterpretation of Plato's theory of ideas. However, I cannot call Bolzano a 'teacher' and 'guide' with respect to what I have presented in my *Log <ische> Unters<uchungen>*. What I offer

and so that which yields the formal cause for true speech.[14] This sets an ideal of a purely theoretical grasp of the possibility of cognition at all, of λόγος *via* λόγος *itself*—that is to say, an understanding of thinking, thought, said, in their essential relations. In brief, in response to the transcendental question, Plato finds the *idea* of reason, which is a reason why Husserl comes to identify him later as the "Urvater" of strict science and so, too, logic.[15]

Now, to be sure, Husserl consistently takes Aristotle as the "father" of logic.[16] The difference between the monikers is important: Aristotle's continuation of the campaign against sophistical skepticism follows after the "path breaker" Plato but goes beyond it by establishing scientific logic as an independent science.[17] Given this line of development, Aristotle knew the path of *practical* "performative contradiction" which was already present in the Socratic way of getting the skeptic to speak in order to elucidate the actual tendency of thinking, however tacit, toward affirming being. He also knew the *theoretical* response to skepticism in Plato's understanding of the idea of reason, that is, of the *a priori* relation of thinking, thought, and said. Yet, he was also keenly aware that skepticism continued, emboldened by the apparent failures of philosophy to give an adequate answer to the transcendental question. So, the genius of Aristotle responded, as Husserl finds, with a *strict formal science* in distinction to *sophistic semblance*.

---

are fragments of a theory of cognition and a phenomenology of cognition. Both are foreign to Bolzano. He was an eminent mathematical and logical mind, but the finest conceptual analyses and formal-logical theories are compatible with an almost naive theory of knowledge. There is no trace of the idea of a purely phenomenological elucidation of cognition in him (as in Lotze). But I do not want to claim an unheard-of originality; I have learned from many, among the contemporaries from nobody to such an extent as from you! I still feel and call myself your student. I hope that you will not count me among those who are completely undisciplined and for whom the effort you made was not worthwhile." See also Hua *Brief.* VI, p. 460, where he refers to Lotze, in a letter to E. Parl Welch. Husserl seems to have been familiar with Natorp's work already around 1902, as in his letter to Natorp of that year, in *Hua Brief.* V, p. 91.

[14] I expound these points further in the below, taking on board the point of Burt Hopkins about the "pillars of the ancient precedent to pure phenomenology," in Hopkins (2010). I agree with and expound upon his point that the grasp of essential structures, properly understood, is essential to phenomenology and, in fact, leads Husserl to his *pure* phenomenology.

[15] See Hua Mat IX, p. 28.

[16] Hua XXVIII, p. 37, where he says he is the *Vater* of logic; for a similar sentiment, see, Hua Mat I, p. 22; and Hua XXVIII, p. 291.

[17] See Hua Mat I, p. 304.

Indeed, in the face of what Husserl calls a "mysticism of concepts," Aristotle develops his logic.[18] To better understand that phrase, recall that Aristotle's predecessors already encountered how, as Husserl puts it, "some serious difficulties arise from the ambiguity and diversity of linguistic expression."[19] As language did not emerge with the rigor of theory but rather as a symbolic system with practical aims,[20] the same expressed concept could have a diversity of definitions: again, the expression "cold" need not mean the same for one as for the other, and words like "bad" or "good" might acquire different meanings in different practical perspectives and contexts, as rain, for example, might be good for the farmer and bad for the shepherd, and so on. Furthermore, as theory involves the search for more exact and strict definitions, concepts become a focal point of argument: an expression such as, say, "human," to one, might mean a "featherless bi-ped," to another, "animal with speech," or, somebody else again, "a rational animal," and then each of these words have their own arguments supporting their taken meaning, and so on. It was, thus, not difficult to spiral within what Husserl identifies as "the frivolous games of sophistical dialectics," in the sense of putting various concepts in relation to one another in order to argue in circles and to mystify their meaning.[21] In response, Aristotle does not only take the method of performative or practical contradiction, as the Platonic-Socratic

---

[18] For example, consider Hua Mat I, p. 6: "Today one usually calls it *Erkenntnistheorie*, but it is essentially identical, or identical after a part, with the time-honored metaphysics, the 'First Philosophy' of Aristotle. But one likes to avoid a name that has received a bad taste from the hollow erroneous teachings of our century … The sciences therefore need a metaphysical foundation for the time being. This means nothing less than a dialectical spinning out of the concrete results of these sciences from an abstract mysticism of concepts, but, much more modest and fruitful, a sober clarification and examination of the general prerequisites that make the real sciences above the real being, and in further scientific work the production of the most mature and last knowledge of the real being, of its elements, forms and laws, which allows the respective state of the individual sciences, the δεύτερα φιλοσοφία, as Aristotle puts it. However, this metaphysical foundation is not sufficient to achieve the desired theoretical completion of individual sciences…." Let me also mention here how Husserl distinguishes a *naive mysticism* from a more "positive" mysticism. The former refuses evidence as a standard for knowledge. See the relevant passages at Hua Mat VII 7, p. 46. Also, Hua Mat IX, pp. 9, 11, and 50; later, in Hua XXXV, pp. 473–74.

[19] I again give a translation of the passage, as it suggests that language does not emerge with theoretical pretense, at Hua Mat II, p. 104.

[20] For some remarks on language as a system *of symbols*, see Hua Mat I, p. 19.

[21] See Hua Mat I, p. 279.

2.1 Preliminary Remarks—Toward a Logic of Question–Answer ...

dialectic so brilliantly does, but he *also* explicitly formulates the *theoretical countersense* of skepticism.[22] And he does so by explicating the *idea* or *form* of thinking itself—*formal logic*.

To that end, Aristotle's formal logic abstracts from the material content of an expressed statement. That abstraction yields the *form of expression* or, as Husserl will also say, purely formal "sentences" or "propositions" (*Satz*).[23] So, a statement like "Socrates is a human" abstracts from "Socrates" and "human," to the *form*, expressed symbolically as "S is p." This sets the *ideal formal significance of the statement*. Moreover, Aristotle shows how sentences *relate to each other*—an essential point to the properly *theoretical* response. In fact, to answer the "transcendental question," he makes use of that essential distinction between "things in relation to us" and "things in relation to each other," which Husserl notes in the Greek, "the πρότερον πρὸς ἡμᾶς is not the πρότερον καθ' αὐτό."[24] By inquiring into how the sentences relate to each other, he discovers the various familiar laws of formal logic, for example, the law of non-contradiction, the excluded middle, and so on. From these laws of relation, he shows *conclusions* as *formally necessary*, that is, that they *must* "follow" or be "consequent" from each other by the very sense of their relation. Thus, Aristotle develops, in Husserl's phrase, a "science of conclusions."[25]

A skeptical refutation of such a science of conclusions demonstrates its principles and laws. By thinking and speaking, the skeptic is caught practically in counter-sense. Still more, to engage in a theoretical disputation with formal logic would mean to engage in it, and so, again, practically confirm, however implicitly, its validity. To give but one usual example, to conclude that truth could not be known was to affirm that at least that truth could be known. Of course, a skeptic could ignore the fact that they were being counter-sensical or even remain silent, as Cratylus. Formal logic

---

[22] He does so especially in later lectures on ethics, Hua XXVIII and XXXVII. This refutation is sometimes called the argument to *retorsion*. Put simply, one cannot claim something like "there is no truth" without implicitly affirming the truth of at least that statement, and so speak against the claim one makes and speak for the truth: it is, therefore, *contradictory*, both in the sense of the formal logical law of non-contradiction, wherein something cannot both be and not be, and in the more literal sense of *contra-dicere*—to speak against. But such a refutation does not, by itself, give insight into how the claim is counter-*sensical*, that is, how it speaks in a way against and inadequate to the norm of its own operation. Instead, it takes its stand upon a *formal* law. To clarify the difference, I must turn to the *formalization* of logic by Aristotle and its relation to science. For Aristotle's point about the impossibility of demonstrating first principles, see his *Metaphysics*, 1006a: "ὅλως μὲν γὰρ ἁπάντων ἀδύνατον ἀπόδειξιν εἶναι εἰς ἄπειρον γὰρ ἂν βαδίζοι, {ὥστε μηδ' οὕτως εἶναι ἀπόδειξιν}" ["For it is wholly impossible for there to be a demonstration of all things, {as there would then be an aporia such that there would be no demonstration.}"] This point will be addressed, to some degree, in Chapter 3, where I find that the operation of intelligence, as seeking middle terms in logical analysis, yields evidence of first principles.

[23] See Hua Mat I, pp. 304–305.

[24] Hua Mat III, p. 81: "That cognitional critique historically grew up as transcendental philosophy is easy to understand. The transcendental questions were the closest to the cognitional reflection. Here, as elsewhere, the concrete and dependent enters earlier into the circle of vision of cognition as the first and fundamental by its nature. To speak with Aristotle: the πρότερον πρὸς ἡμᾶς is not the πρότερον καθ' αὐτό."

[25] See Hua Mat I, p. 32.

could only serve to make clear the lawful relationship of sentences. As Aristotle knew, the skeptic must move out of skepticism by asking and answering questions for themselves.

However, question sentences are excluded from such classical formal logic. This is because they do not make a truth claim—they are not *apophantic*.[26] Of course, questions can be transposed into an affirmative or negative statement, and so then be included in a science of conclusions. For example, the question "Is the house red?" can be transposed as "The house is red" and so "Is X y?" could become "X is y," and so on. But questions, by themselves, do not declare a position on the relation of subject and predicate. After all, without a transposition of the question to a judgment, there is no conclusion.

The status of questions in philosophy became an issue in a variety of ways. Without enumerating all of these, there is an illustrative example in the later skeptic, Sextus Empiricus. He employs, almost as a methodological principle, the incessant transposition of positions to questions in order to avoid position-taking altogether. He finds that a skeptical ἐποχή, which is a suspension of position taking, still allows questions because they do not declare anything. And once one recognizes that questions do not declare anything, one need not be disturbed by them. In other words, if there is no ἀποφαντικός—no position taken upon (ἀπο) that which appears (φαῖνον)—one could reach a freedom from disturbance (ἀταραξία). Of course, this overlooks, as I aim to show in this book, with Husserl, the fact that inquiry itself arises from a position in the world.

Despite the persistence of skepticism, now more, now less explicit, the formal logic of Aristotle stood for centuries, Husserl notes, as "self-evident."[27] Husserl also detects, however, an eventual historical "degeneration" in the way that formal logic becomes taken as a "finished discipline."[28] By this he means it becomes increasingly isolated as a separate science, and so estranged from its original task as a science of science, theory of theories. Where the path diverges, there appears what he identifies

---

[26] Husserl a few years later clarifies his own use in relation to Aristotle at Hua IV, p. 71: "We call the range of these categories the apophantic categories, following the Aristotelian expression ἀπόφανσις as the sentence. And we understand by apophantic logic the concept of essential laws which belong to the idea of apophansis, that is, the sentence. According to what has been said, this is a region of laws that constitute the most general and absolutely indispensable foundation for the norm of thought. And apart from the norm, they are laws without which all talk of truth and falsity, of following and not following, of presupposing and inferring, that is, of 'yes' and 'no,' of 'if' and 'so,' of 'either' and 'or,' and so on, would no longer have any possible sense."

[27] Husserl (2001b), p. 279: "According to these considerations, the justification of a logic as a is something so clear and self-evident that only one thing is astonishing: however, there could have been a dispute on this point. From the need for a practical theory of cognition logic has also historically grown out of the need for a practical theory of knowledge."

[28] Consider the following passage from Hua Mat I, pp. 23–24: "But no sooner does the tender seedling begin to grow than Greek culture and philosophy fall into degeneration. What remains of it in scientific relation, solidifies in the forms of scholasticism. And this is also the case with logic. As an untouchable legacy of Aristotle it is taken up and considered as a finished discipline. For the purposes of the school, it underwent a dogmatically rigid systematization, which gave it the appearance of skill and completeness that was so dangerous for the following times, especially with regard to its main piece, the doctrine of conclusions."

as another "ancient question," namely, "Is logic a practical or purely theoretical discipline, a technique or a science in a concise sense?"[29]

The question arises, in part, because of the way philosophy itself appeared and developed. As Husserl understands, humans are first and primarily practical.[30] In other words, they concern themselves with things as they relate to themselves, with the "concrete and dependent."[31] It makes sense, then, that early theoretical questions have to do with that which humans *actually* face and navigate, namely, "actuality" or "reality." Indeed, this interest persists through Aristotle's distinction between "first philosophy" or metaphysics and the "second philosophies," from which the ancient question about logic emerges.

"First philosophy," for Aristotle, gives the foundation for science.[32] To explain, it is helpful to understand that "second philosophies" or the sciences of beings (τὰ ὄντα) deal with certain *categories* (τὰ λεγόμενα) or with what comes to be known in Latin as *"praedicamenta"*—*"that which may be declared."* That which may be declared are predicates which are *about being*. But being qua being is neither some particular being, nor some particular predicament, nor even a highest genus; rather, "being," as Aristotle puts it, "is said in many ways" (τὸ ὂν πολλαχῶς λέγεται).[33] A science of being qua being is distinct insofar as it asks about causes and principles of reality, that is, about being itself, not about beings. It is also "first" insofar as it clarifies that which all the others have in common, namely, being. Logic, for its part, investigates reason and reasoning, which operates in all the sciences.

To understand the situation of logic coming from Aristotelian philosophy, it is important to note that it is not Aristotle who labels his work as "logic." In fact, the collection of six distinct logical writings (the *Categories, On Interpretation, Prior* and *Posterior Analytics Topics*, and *On Sophistical Refutations*) first became known as the *Organon*. While the arrangement of the texts is probably from Andronicus of

---

[29] Hua Mat I, p. 34.

[30] Hua Mat III, p. 81: "Humans stand in the world primarily as an acting and evaluating being and only secondarily as a thinking one. One's whole practical interest is turned towards this empirical reality, in which one places one's as a single member. Actuality stands before one as a given fact; and because one feels practically bound to it with all the fibers of one's being, one wants to investigate it as soon as theoretical interest has awakened, and it gives one, as soon as the first beginnings of scientific theorizing have been accomplished, the first cognitional-theoretical problems, and these are precisely transcendental problems."

[31] See Hua Mat III, p. 81.

[32] Hua Mat III, pp. 230–233, especially 233: "For him it is that discipline on which all others depend, in which all others are founded, the science of the first principles and causes (*arche, aitia*) of all being in general." For a summary of the preceding paragraphs, and a preparatory justification of the next sections, see also, Hua Mat I, pp. 304–5: "However, the purely theoretical point of view of the logical form has never completely come through. From the beginning, logic was mixed with metaphysics, and up to the present day the indispensable separation of the two disciplines has not been fully accomplished. On the other hand, the practical intentions pursued with logic, namely, to make it an organon of scientific knowledge, had an essential influence on the content of its teachings, especially on the scope of the forms to be considered. Only since the last century, partly under the influence of a highly developed formal discipline, arithmetic, new efforts to bring to the fore this theoretical point of view more purely have appeared."

[33] See Aristotle, *Metaphysics*, 1003a33 and 1018a35, respectively.

Rhodes in the first century A.C.E., the delineation of them as "logical," nearer to the sense of an independent science, is often ascribed to the second century A.C.E. commentator Alexander of Aphrodisias.[34] Setting aside for the moment the meaning of *analytics*, which signifies much of the guiding sense these texts, the choice of the later title, *Organon* (Ὄργανον), is noteworthy, in the current context.[35] Indeed, the term itself can mean "tool," in the sense of an implement, and so, in that sense, a *technique* or *"practical discipline."*[36] In this respect, in the effort of avoiding fallacious reasoning or to assist in effective reasoning about being, a thinker would rebuild stepwise relations between sentences of each argument, demonstrating how reasoning otherwise would be at odds with logical laws. Even the metaphysician, in the science of being qua being, would be beholden to such laws in their reasoning. As the influence of Aristotle waned, the stoics took logic as an integral part of philosophy—its vital "organ." Just as the removal of an organ would disrupt the whole, so would the loss of logic disrupt the art of living (ἄσκησις), for it meant removing reason as the ruling power (ἡγεμονικόν) of one's life, a point to which I return in subsequent chapters.[37] Logic remained, for them, a distinct science but as within a whole philosophy of life. In short, there came a question about the sense of logic, growing from the roots of what Husserl calls Aristotle's "tender plant."[38]

Husserl's investigations into logic have that "ancient question" in mind. In this respect, he understands, in a nod to Plato, logic to give an insight into the *"a priori* laws of authentic thinking," which should, in turn, ground practical technique. Further, like Aristotle, he finds essential the formulation of the theoretical dimension of this logic insofar as one will need to pay attention to thinking in order to grasp *how* it operates, *how* it *must* operate in order to be successful, that is, all *the relations of acts necessary for operation*. In fact, like both, Husserl also aims to realize logic as normative technique. However, this must be broached in an entirely new way—in a way that takes thinking, thought, said on its own grounds, that is, according to its *own givenness*.

In that way, Husserl's phenomenology demands an "unnatural" (*widernatürlichen*) way of intuiting and thinking.[39] By this he means, rather than taking for

---

[34] For a brief overview of this history, see Kneale (1971), pp. 23–24. Also, Bochenski (1961), §6–9. For reference to this point in Husserl, see Hua Mat III, p. 239.

[35] For a more exact treatment of the meaning of the term in Aristotle, see Byrne (1997).

[36] Again, see Hua Mat II, p. 279: "And essentially practical, logic remained well-founded in the period that followed. In the Middle Ages, Aristotelian logic, or what was understood by it, was considered the organon of scientific thinking." See also Kneale (1971), p. 139.

[37] Husserl will later reestablish the Stoic term ἡγεμονικόν, which means to suggest a ruling of reason in one's life, as I broach especially in the fourth chapter. With respect to the practical concerns of the stoics, it makes some sense that they would introduce the *conditional* way of analyzing statements so important for the development of material logic, as much of practical reasoning consists in *if/ then* statements, for example, *if* I do this, *then* this will happen, and so on.

[38] Hua Mat I, p. 22: "But no sooner does the tender little plant begin to grow than Greek culture and philosophy fall into degeneration."

[39] Hua XIX/1, p. 14.

granted actual awareness, turning attention to the *intentional* dimension of consciousness, that is, to the relatedness between the being aware and the object of our awareness. From this attention, the phenomenologist aims, not to merely describe their different actual occurrences, but to grasp the *essence* of acts of consciousness and their relations. Moreover, such an understanding yields the possibility of thinking in accord with the essential laws of thinking itself. If one understands, for example, what inquiry is, one can better ask questions, avoid mistakes in inquiry, set conditions for better answers, and so on. Thus, Natorp notes, in one of the few initial reviews of the *Logical Investigations*: "The inquiry begins (ch. 1) with the question, whether logic is a normative science. The answer is in the affirmative: logic is the technology (*Kunstlehre*) of scientific knowledge."[40] However, the project does not conclude with that, as Natorp continues: "But now first arises the further question (ch. 2) regarding the theoretical foundation of this technology."[41] It is here, in the further question of a theoretical foundation, that Husserl faces that particular form of skepticism, *psychologism*. For it resists a theoretical account of cognition by reducing logic to real psychological events.

To make further sense of this issue, let me turn, in the next section, to the various forms of skepticism, and how they mistake spheres of ideal and the real. This is especially important to set the stage for a proper 'interior' understanding of conscious operations—a phenomenology—that would yield immanent ideal norms of consciousness rather than a mere description of what is really happening. For Husserl, this expands and clarifies the sense of logic as a science of science, theory of theories, in which inquiry has an essential role.

2.1.2 Preparatory Sketch of Husserl's Campaign Against Skepticism

To reiterate, for Husserl, skepticism is an essential motif in philosophical development. This may seem strange, at first blush, if skepticism is taken as an end-position, namely, as a denial of the possibility of knowledge. However, if skepticism is instead taken, with Husserl, as a *counter-sensical* position—that is to say, a position in *conflict* with the normative operation of reason itself—then it is taken as rousing further questions. In this sense, skepticism motivates a thinker to a more adequate account of that which is the case.[42]

---

[40] In Mohanty, J.N. (1977), p. 56. *Kunstlehre* may also be rendered "technological discipline," in order to retain the sense of "art" (*Kunst*) and "teaching" or "doctrine" (*-lehre*), or also "practical discipline," for reasons I discuss further in Chapters 3 and 4.

[41] See In Mohanty, J.N. (1977), p. 56.

[42] Hua Mat III, p. 85: "In der Skepsis tritt die Vernunft in Widerstreit mit sich selbst, das ist ihr Charakteristikum....Aber sie verzweifelt an der Möglichkeit, die objektive Leistung und Geltung der betreffenden Wissenschaften zu verstehen." ["In skepticism reason enters into conflict with itself, that is its characteristic....But it despairs of the possibility of understanding the objective performance and validity of the relevant sciences."].

An example of such a philosophical encounter with skepticism is in the "Prolegomena" of the *Logical Investigations*, where Husserl attempts to navigate through psychologism. For Husserl himself, the impetus to do so may have appeared as much in response to trends in current thought as in response to the counter-senses he found at work in his own thought.[43] In any case, such conflicts of reason motivated him to ask further questions. Indeed, he aims to get beyond *any* skepticism, not only psychologism. Of special interest, this respect, is his understanding of three general positions on *ideas* and how they lead to skepticism. In the first place, there is a *metaphysical hypostatization of ideas*, wherein an idea is taken to be *really exterior* to the thinker. In the second place, there is a *psychological hypostatization of ideas*, wherein an idea is taken to be *in* the thinker. In the third and final place, a general *nominalism* that transforms what is universal in object and act of thought into what is individual.[44]

First, let us consider the metaphysical sense of hypostatization. It is, for Husserl, basically a formulation of the so-called old "Platonic realism," wherein the ideal really exists externally to thought, "before" actually being thought.[45] We need not venture into the discussion here of whether this is truly Plato's meaning. The point is that, in this philosophical position, ideas are taken as subsisting on their own, as "really real" (ὄντως ὄν), set beyond (as the term *hypo-stasis* suggests) the pale imitations in this actuality.[46] The seeds of a dualism here are evident, as some sort of encounter with beings which are somehow already actual, "ideas," occurs in understanding. As such, there is an emphasis on the striving toward the idea as well as the asymptotic grasp of the idea, which tends to take cognition as never really clear in this life.

Such metaphysical hypostatization is opposed, in a sense, to the psychological sort, which asks, "How can we talk about something if it does not at least exist *in our thought*?"[47] Basically, this suggests an understanding of the ideal as subsisting in the mind, either somehow there prior as "innate" or from an impression of external data. Since I consider his critique of the innatist position later (with Descartes, for

---

[43] Husserl's encounter with Gottlob Frege apparently helped him understand his own psychologism. Indeed, Husserl reportedly said later that Frege had "hit the nail on the head" with his critique, according to the notebooks of W.R. Boyce Gibson. For this, see, Dermot Moran's note in his "Introduction" to the reedition of Husserl, *Logical Investigations*, pp. xli–xlv. There seems to be no first-hand account of Frege's impact on Husserl, though there are second-hand accounts. For the review, see, Mohanty (1977), pp. 6–21. For a more extensive and recent account of his struggle with psychologism, see, Davidson (2021). With respect to Frege, see Føllesdal (1982), pp. 52–56 and Huemer (2004), pp. 199–214.

There are various ways Husserl himself formulates the position. For example, in a 1903 review of Melchior Palagyi "Der Streit der Psychologisten und Formalisten in der Modernen Logik," in Husserl, (1993), p. 204: "The basic error of psychologism consists, according to my view, in its obliteration of this fundamental distinction between pure and empirical generality, and in its misinterpretation of the pure laws of logic as empirical laws of psychology."

[44] See Husserl (2001b), p. 305.

[45] See Husserl (2001b), p. 248.

[46] For the phrase and reference, see the later Mat Band VII, p. 166.

[47] Mat Band VII, p. 166.

example), let me now focus upon the, so to speak, its "impressionistic" or "representational" construal. Once again, we need not address why such positions are also often attributed to Plato, though Husserl himself tends to focus on Locke, at least in the *Investigations*. Locke, according to Husserl, understands *universal objects as thought unities* and the *unity of presentations as particular acts of thought*.[48] To him, though, only individual things really exist, for in actual reality, a universal does not exist, strictly speaking. Without expounding distinctions between simple and complex ideas, those from sensation and reflection, the "ideas" are taken here as "in" the mind, as representations of the "real" thing "outside" the mind. So, in order to account for how the knower comes to something like an ideal, he turns to how we relate these representations. Put otherwise, he takes this as a process of "understanding" things to "look like" or resemble each other. It is, therefore, a matter of "attention," or, we might say, *looking* toward them in order to *abstract* and *associate* that which is common to other things. Thus, according to such a position, the mind cannot really know the fundamental being or "substance" of external actuality but only representations of it.

Again, in the Lockean position, "ideas" originate in sense experience which triggers a process of relating representations.[49] The idea of "triangle" is understood, insofar as one sees these shapes that look like each other—that both have three sides, three angles of 180 degrees, and so on. From such a process of seeing, there come "universal ideas," which are "thought unities," not existing other than as mental representations of objects perceived in particular perceptual acts. And so, too, "triangle" names other objects that look like this one, insofar as one can relate it to other triangles. Thus, the ideal is obviously a content of thought, whereas the real is the external object, ready-made, as it were. With this, the way is paved for the skepticism of Hume, where, at least, the inadequate account of these relations collapses under its own weight: for why should one suppose that there is any "actual reality," any objectivity to which ideas relate at all? How would one get beyond anything beyond one's own fictitious constitution of that data? Such skeptical questions persist, in other words, without an adequate answer.

Now, before turning directly to nominalism and psychologism, it is important to clarify further the confusion of the real and ideal in the above positions. For that, it is essential to distinguish, as Husserl does, the *content* of the act of understanding from the *real* act. For, he finds, the content is neither a real part of psychological data, that is, nor really "*inside*" the mind, nor as really "*outside*" as metaphysical data. Instead, *ideation* yields a novel sort of object—an "idea," which has *ideal* rather than *real* being. Now, this novel object is *not* a representation of sense perception, as Locke would have it, but a peculiar achievement of understanding something

---

[48] See Husserl (2001c), 294.

[49] For more on how Husserl distinguishes the *idea* from a *concept*, see Hua Mat III, p. 63: "Origin of a concept (an *idea*, as I prefer to say) is not the origin of a psychic phenomenon. 'An idea arises,' what does this unclear expression mean? The idea is general. A general can be symbolic, in the way that every symbolic meaning does. However, a symbol is like change that is only worth something if it can be redeemed." As I address further in the next chapter, the *concept* is the symbolic formulation of the idea, for Husserl.

about the data. Of course, it is possible to constitute similarities in the association of perceptual data, as one thing can be associated with another as "looking similar," for example, someone can see a particular shape, or a certain number of particular shapes, and have its perceptual sense constituted *as* similar. However, the grasp of such "similarity" does not mean one has an *understanding* of *what a triangle is* nor does it mean one has correctly judged *this* to be *what* one understands it *to be*.

In the Investigations, Husserl relates the first process to the classical language of "abstraction." The term *abstraction* must not be imagined either as drawing out features from an object, nor as *away* from a thing *into* mind, nor still, as mere fictions of the mind. Rather, by it is meant a procedure that follows upon an active, intelligent relating of parts of presentations such that are set within a "unified fulfillment."[50] To continue the example from above, when one understands what a triangle is, one understands that there *must* be a certain relation of parts to be what it is as a whole—for example, the sides must be three, must relate such that there are 180 degrees and so on—which "*abstracts*" the essential from the incidental. One cannot, by act of perceptual attention, grasp the necessity of these relations: no matter how long or carefully one looks does one understand these relations, for the idea does not "float as a picture before the mind," as he says.[51] Rather, grasping the idea is an organization of data by understanding, through which one *abstracts* the essential and, so to speak, "gets the idea."

Moreover, from abstraction, Husserl finds how it is possible to judge an instance *to be such and so*. One can judge, for example, that *this is* a triangle—as it has three-sides, and so on. Furthermore, in the judgment, there comes a relation of the ideal and the real in thinking such that the essential structures may be construed as that which determines the *possibilities* of it being such and so. In this sense, the ideal is "a priori," giving the range of possibilities for the real, which I qualify throughout the chapters of this book. At present, what is significant is that Husserl also distinguishes the *act* of understanding from the *content* of understanding and the act of judgment

---

[50] See, for example, Husserl (2001b), pp. 202 and 309.
[51] See Husserl (2001b), 252.

as it relates to the content of understanding.⁵² With these distinctions, he prepares the ground for rejecting nominalism and psychologism, to which I turn briefly now.

Nominalism, in general, according to Husserl, "seeks to transform the universal into what is individual."⁵³ In other words, the ideal is again confused with the real, but in a particular way. A key to understanding this is how the *conceptual content* is confused with the *content of an act of understanding*—the "said" with the "thought," we might say. *Nominalism* understands universal meanings as a given name, as from the Latin *nōminālis* suggests. As Husserl puts it, "[Nominalism] one-sidedly prefers the generality which belongs to concepts in their predicative function, as a possibility of associating the same concept predicatively with several subjects. Being blind to the logically ideal character of this possibility...it puts psychological associations in its place...."⁵⁴ To understand his point, let me restate the provisional distinction between the *idea* and the *concept*: concepts, as expressed, as stated or said, are given as actual, really being so; and one can grasp the relation of concepts, but this is not another concept, but precisely an *idea*, in the sense sketched above. Such confusion of this with the ideality sentence, the ideal meaning grasped by ideation, is a hinge of nominalism that takes the *name*, the concept, as a mark of the real.

It is not difficult to detect in the above three positions the foundations of a sort of *psychologism*. This holds, broadly, that logical laws were based upon particular, empirical events rather than ideal relations of intentional acts and contents.⁵⁵ The confusion of the relation of the real and the ideal appears here especially insofar

---

⁵² The many and complex ways one might confuse these, of which I have only indicated some, are perhaps part of the reason why Husserl struggles early on with Aristotle's genus and species distinction and its relation to the universal. It was "bound to fail," as he puts it, even though he already understood the "strict identity of the universal and the existence of universal objects," for he had not understood clearly how the universal object was abstracted from the data, how it became itself an object of understanding, and yet still belonged to the object. See Ms. A III 1/43a, and at Hua 41, Nr. 5, pp. 83–89, on the "strict identity" or, "an der strengen Identität des Allgemeinen und an der Existenz allgemeiner Gegenstände." There he says, "Meine Bemühungen um die Feststellung des Aristotelischen Gattungsbegriffs mussten notwendig misslingen, weil ich das Verhältnis $\neq$ und $\in$ verwechselt habe. Die Hauptsache ist einfach die, dass die Arist <otelesche> Gattung von Arten beziehungsweise von Arten als Gegenständen ist. Die generelle Aussage ist mehrdeutig. Sage ich, der Mench ist sterblich, so heißt das, Mensch =/sterblich. Was ein Mensch ist, ist auch sterblich. ["My efforts to establish the Aristotelian concept of genus necessarily had to fail, because I confused the relation $\neq$ and $\in$. The main thing is simply that the Arist <otelian> genus is of species respectively of species as objects. The general statement is ambiguous. If I say the man is mortal, it means man $\neq$ mortal. What a man is, is also mortal"]. The issue also appears at, Hua Mat I, pp. 128–129, on subsumption und subordination. It is worthwhile to note this realization carries back, for Husserl, into his understanding of Plato's distinction between μέθεξις and κοινωνία, which, he thinks, has to do with the relation of parts and wholes, with respect to the universal and the individual, genus and species. A detailed analysis of these points goes too far afield of our present task, however. I should also recognize the present lack of distinction between the meaning of the terms "essential," "idea," and "ideal," which I further differentiate and determine, following Husserl, below.

⁵³ Husserl (2001b), p. 248.

⁵⁴ Husserl (2001b), p. 266.

⁵⁵ Husserl distinguishes between *real* and *reell*, where the former refers to a transcendent (that is, a spatial or temporal object) object. The latter, by contrast, refers to the immanent contents of the intention.

as the investigator misunderstands their own grasp of the acts and laws of thinking. Again, "blind" to ideality, they replace them with real psychological associations. In contrast, Husserl goes to great lengths to differentiate and clarify logic as a science of science might deal with the ideal laws of thinking. To clarify this point, however, let us finally turn to the problem of "origins" of knowledge by way of intentionality analysis, then back to the role of questions and inquiry therein.[56]

2.2 Toward the Essence of Inquiry via Intentional Analysis

> The immense task of the critique of cognition, especially of the phenomenology of cognition, consists precisely in pointing out all the essential relations that prevail here [in the matter of objectivation], in elucidating the teleology of the intellective phenomena from the ground, and through it in giving final evaluation to all logical laws in the broadest sense.[57]

Husserl's early "logical" work gives an account of the relation of acts necessary for meaningful expression. With this, he also seeks to answer that ancient transcendental question about how knowledge is possible at all. To do so, he goes back to the *origins* of meaning in consciousness. Put in line with the theme at hand, he recovers the meaning of a question by *inquiring into how inquiry is intentional*—that is, is *about* or *of* something, as the word *intendere* (to "stretch toward" or "point to") suggests. In so doing, he is able to give an account of its role in the life of *logos*.

Husserl does not dedicate any section of the *Logical Investigations* to an analysis of inquiry, however. It is necessary, therefore, to expound his position within broader issues, which I do through the following three subsections:

A. I first review some relevant points in the emergence of Husserl's phenomenological project as an inquiry into consciousness;
B. then, I attend to the distinction of *objectivating and non-objectivating acts*, including how question-expressions refer back to question-intentions which intend answers;
C. finally, I present how Husserl's analysis of inquiry answers that aforementioned "disputed question" about questions in logic.

Through these three subsections, there appear some basic terms and relations in an intentional analysis of inquiry, which are worth summarizing at the outset. In the first place, Husserl finds how each instance of inquiry is founded upon an *objectivating act*, insofar as it asks *about some given*. The question expression itself is a *non-objectivating act*, that is, the expression does not make a judgment about the inquiry but rather "gives it voice." In the second place, the act of inquiring itself appears within a conflict of presentations such that there arises an attempt to mediate via an

---

[56] Hua Mat III, pp. 59–85. This section is followed by another on "Skepticism as method," which finds its place in Husserl's way *through* to phenomenology. The point is also sketched in Aguirre (1970), though the focus here is on the later, genetic approach.

[57] See, for example, Hua XXVIII, p. 341.

answer. So, in the third place, the *sense* of the question is in its range of fulfillment, in its possible answer; indeed, the answer is "pre-figured" by the situation in which some questionable matter appears and so, too, by the evidence that would appropriately fulfill it. In the fourth place, the answer itself is a further objectivating act; it fulfills the inquiring-intention. To reach this, the inquirer "weighs" presented possibilities, accepting or dismissing them; if the former, the question is answered, if the latter, one might either seek more evidence or dismiss the entire question as counter-sensical. Finally, in the fifth place, inquiring as *mediating objectivation* also *mediates the unity of intentional life itself*. Human beings live amid the possibility of further inquiry, readied, as it were, for further fulfilling evidence, and answers build upon themselves such that even further questions appear as possibilities. In sum, by treating inquiry within the interior dimensions of *logos*, phenomenology takes up its role in logic and its place in the response to the transcendental question.

With this overview, let me finally turn to Husserl's properly phenomenological work, as it begins this analysis in its breakthrough to intentionality.

2.2.1 Beginnings and Breakthroughs of Phenomenology

Husserl's style of working is exemplified in the work within and surrounding his monumental *Logical Investigations*. The text itself was worked and reworked for decades, from the time of its inception, in the early 1890s to his apparently final attempt at significant revision in the mid-1920s. Through this process, he reflects on its meaning in relation to the rest of his work, writing significant introductions not only to the 1900/01 edition but also in 1913 and 1921–5. These give testament to his manner of inquiring and provide clues to matters into which we inquire.[58]

In a 1913 "Introduction," Husserl calls the *Logical Investigations* a "beginning or rather a breakthrough."[59] He says this "breakthrough" work was not written "for anyone satisfied with his prejudices."[60] Indeed, the oft-repeated rallying cry emanating from this early work, "Back to the things themselves," marks an openness, even a willingness to question that which seemed settled. With that spirit, Husserl sets

---

[58] It is worth noting that Husserl was apparently not always so industrious. When a young man at school, he did not stay on task, seemingly bored, reading off curriculum. At risk of failing entirely, he was set to studying intensely—a fateful moment, perhaps, that set him on his path. See, Hua Dok I, p. 3.

[59] For this phrase, see, Husserl (1975), p. 59: "The *Logical Investigations* signify, therefore, if I view things correctly and if my entire subsequent life's work has not been in vain, indeed a beginning or rather a breakthrough." For further historical information see the "Translators Introduction" at Ibid., xi–xxx. These phenomenological beginnings have their pre-history in Husserl's mathematical work, as a matter of course. To trace these in relation to the breakthrough, and then follow them throughout his work would make for a more complete account of his inquiry and development, to be sure; but it would result in a different work altogether.

[60] I Husserl (1975), p. 59.

presuppositionlessness as a guiding principle of phenomenology.[61] That means that the phenomenologist must not set-out in advance (not to prejudge or pre-sup-pose: *Vor-aus-setzung*) any position but only accept one with *evidence*.

By evidence is meant, however provisionally, how the intending subject *means* an intended object as *meant*, that is, *as* such and so. An intention is fulfilled as meaningful if that which is given accords with or is congruent to that which is meant. Take a perceptual example: while standing at the frontside of a house, one can intend the backside emptily, that is, as not given "in the flesh" (*leibhaftig*) but nevertheless meant *as* being there. Now, one may walk around the house, see the back-side, and so fulfill the intention. However, it could also happen that, upon walking around the house, one realizes the front of the house was a façade, thereby disappointing one's intention, as the given comes into discord with one's meaning of it. Of course, even the empty and disappointed intention is not without meaning, insofar as they become constituted *as such* and *so*, but to be meaningfully fulfilled, strictly speaking, there must be a coincidence of the given and the meant—this, broadly construed, is what Husserl calls *evidence*.[62]

Toward differentiating some of the grades and types of evidence, it is important to note that the fulfillment of an intention is characterized by what Husserl calls an *intuition* (*Anschauung*). This can occur in a *perceptual* act, like seeing the front side of the house, but it can also occur in *categorial* acts, like ideationally grasping *what* a house is or judging a house *to be* there. With this, Husserl grounds *truth* in evidence or, more exactly, in intuitive evidence, while also avoiding abstracting the process of taking a position on truth from a relation to perception. Instead, perception –as a literal rendering of the German *wahr-nehmen* or truth-taking suggests—is the origins of the truth, as it relates to further possible determination by the "understanding" or what he also calls intelligence. Intelligence, for its part, brings to question that which is given in perception as well as other positions taken by the subject. It seeks to take intelligent positions on true being. Of course, positions are also sometimes uncritically "taken-up" or accepted by the subject. This happens, for example, when a subject accepts positions from traditions or culture, in what Husserl calls a "blind or vague opining," which is accepting validity without bringing the evidence for it to question.[63] In contrast, a philosophy which aims to be "presuppositionless" is thus *critical* insofar as it means to question how there is position-taking in cognition at all, *including its own*.

---

[61] See, for example, Husserl (2001b), pp. 177–180.

[62] Evidence is to be distinguished from mere intending, then. See Hua I, §24: "In the broadest sense, evidence designates a general primal phenomenon of intentional life; opposite to other consciousness—which can be apriori empty, pre-meaning, indirect, inauthentic—the quite excellent mode of consciousness of self-appearance, of self-presenting, of self-giving of a thing, a fact, a generality, a value, and so on, in the final mode of the self there, immediately turned on '*originaliter* given.'" Furthermore, he later makes a distinction later between "passive" and "active evidence," the latter of which requires an act of identification of the intuitive *act* and the signification *act*. For more on these points, see Bernet (2003).

[63] As he puts it later at Hua XVII, p. 28: "…a certainty which we have to separate in a familiar manner from the blind conviction, from the vague and however firmly decided opinion, if we are not to fail on the cliffs of extreme skepticism."

2.2 Toward the Essence of Inquiry via Intentional Analysis

In short, it means to be a *self-justified critique of cognition* (*Erkenntniskritik*) toward an answer of that "transcendental question" about the possibility of any cognition at all.

Taken in this respect, the "breakthrough" of the *Investigations* is to *interiority*.[64] That means that the phenomenologist reflectively attends to *how* matters appear *in consciousness*, rather than straightforwardly living in that which is given through perception. Although this phenomenological reflection demands an "unnatural" way of intuiting and thinking, it is *not* an introspection that somehow severs consciousness from givenness. It is, rather, a matter of attending to consciousness, not in terms of a "look" at one's mind, but rather a raising of awareness to the data of consciousness. Upon doing so, the phenomenologist can describe the essential rules and conditions of appearance, formulating the *a priori* structures necessary for meaning and cognition at all. Again, such a process would be interior insofar as it is understanding of one's own consciousness, without reducing the grasp of ideal structures to one's real events.

It must be stressed, however, that the term "consciousness" (*Bewusstsein*) is not univocal in Husserl's work. As Dorian Cairns points out, its meaning varies from a pregnant sense of "being present in any experience whatever" to a restricted sense of "actual advertence."[65] Generally, however, one is *present as conscious* in any intentional act *even if* one is not reflecting upon the act. This is similar to Brentano's reading of Aristotle's *De Anima*, where he found notion of ἐν παρέργῳ, the *nebenbei* or being "nearby" oneself knowing, that is to say, the sort of conscious "presence" of intentional relations in being-aware-oneself (*Bewusst-sein*).[66] Of course, this more basic sense of "awareness" or presence in any consciousness-of may need to be modified according to spheres of acts—for example, in perceptual, intellectual, volitional acts, and so on—but it is nevertheless a *quality* of them *as conscious*. In other words, there is a difference between awareness *of* an *object* and that proper *to* a *subject*, sometimes construed in the distinction between object-experience (*Erfahrung*) and lived-experience (*Erlebnis*).

---

[64] This way of speaking becomes clearer to Husserl later, though it is present already in the *Logical Investigations*; see, for example, the final "Introduction" to the *Investigations* at Husserl (2011), pp. 282–283; "Of special importance is what one has recognized only very late, that reflective experience, the so-called 'inner' (experience) has many steps and dimensions of depths and is very difficult to be carried out if one strives beyond the most superficial. One did not at first have an idea of the depths and mediations. One did not see that the inner experience is not a simple reflection that easily conducts to the concretion of the respective individual inwardnesses [*Innerlichkeiten*, or "interiority"], but that this concretion can be grasped as a whole only within many steps of reflection, that the inner experiencing is a process that is a revelation that is accomplished by ever new reflection...." I prefer the rendering "interiority" for *Innerlichkeit*, if only in an attempt to avoid *imagining* a turning *to* the inner *from* the outer.

[65] This will, of course, be a point of contention and divergence for interpreters. For a more detailed discussion, See Cairns (1972), pp. 19–21.

[66] This does not mean, again, being-aware-*of*-oneself, in the sense of a reflective objectification of oneself, but rather a primitive self-presence, as discussed above.

Indeed, Husserl finds inner, subjective "being-aware" as more "original."[67] There is an awareness *present* in the "aboutness" of consciousness, without which there would not *be* the luminosity of consciousness at all. Indeed, with it comes the possibility of "waking up" to an *interior life of subjectivity* via its intentionality analysis: by "objectifying" one's own consciousness via phenomenology, one discovers a peculiar sort of givenness, namely, of the subject to the subject or the givenness of consciousness itself. So, from a phenomenological perspective, though immediate interior presence may be further mediated by reflection, objects of external perception are given *essentially inadequately*. That is to say, as these matters appear as extended in space and enduring through time, they are given in adumbrations and moments and so never completely, at first blush. One does not perceive at once each side of the house, for example; the house as a whole is given, rather, from this side, then the next, and, even if I anticipate or expect the other sides as to-be-given, they are not given at once as *originally* as "there in the flesh." Of course, implicit in this account is how these adumbrations and moments of the object are synthesized into a unity within experience. As I move around the house, my intention of the other sides is fulfilled or disappointed through further evidence. In this way, an ideal of adequacy, of complete fulfillment, is mediated by continual "surplus" of givenness in experience. There is a play, in fact, between givenness in fulfillment within *apperception*.[68] These phenomeological facts describe *essential* structures to perception and the perceptual object.

As such, Roman Ingarden's point is well-taken that, if Husserl sought an *adequate* (or even *apodictic*, as we shall see) grounding of science, it could not be on the objects of apperception.[69] Since these are given essentially inadequately to consciousness, they would provide only a contingent and relative ground on which to build. Moreover, if the sciences remained in such an objectively oriented perspective, *naïve* of intentionality, they could proceed as if they were self-contained, not somehow unified: for example, botany would seem unrelated to history, simply because of their different objects of study. However, since the knower is conscious, and since

---

[67] In what Husserl calls *"Das 'innere' Bewußtsein,"* an *"inner consciousness" or "inner awareness,"* about which he says, in §6 of the second volume of *Logical Investigations*, that "It is unmistakable that the second concept of consciousness is the more 'original' one, namely the one that is 'prior in itself.'" Admittedly, Husserl does not directly attend to the *pre*-reflective or *pre*-intentional self-presence until his later foray into time-consciousness. Doing so will complicate his position on the possibility of an adequate, reflective grasp of consciousness. Nonetheless, he does not take consciousness merely as the objectification of intentional acts but the *awareness in those acts*. For a more detailed discussion on related points, see Zahavi (2003), pp. 157–180.

[68] Hua XIX/1, p. 399: "Apperception is for us the surplus that exists in the lived-experience itself, in its descriptive content compared to the raw existence of the sensation...The sensations and likewise the acts "apprehending" or 'apperceiving' them are experienced here, but they do not appear representationally; they are not seen, heard, perceived with any 'sense'...." As I discuss below, there is an *apperception* of the ego-cogito, insofar as its content exceeds any singular intuition.

[69] See Ingarden (1975), p. 10.

2.2 Toward the Essence of Inquiry via Intentional Analysis

consciousness is necessarily *intentional*, the understanding of it would found all knowing, unify all activity of knowing.[70]

Immanent reflection yields a different sort of evidence than external perception. With it, there is a consciousness of the acts of consciousness. As such, there is a unity of the act of reflecting and the object of consciousness *as* reflecting. Now, not all objects of immanent perception are given adequately, for Husserl. *Remembering*, for example, is a *re-presentation* (*Vergegenwärtigung*) rather than an evident *presentation* (*Gegenwärtigung*): it is a *mediated* experience of the previously present, re-presented after the break or lapse of time between an experience in the present, which differs from than the immediacy of reflecting upon myself as intending in the moment. Both are a sort of "self-contained" evidence—*self-consciousness*—but qualitatively differ. The phenomenologist utilizes remembering but aims toward evident presentation of conscious data. In so doing, the phenomenologist raises awareness of *both* the activity of knowing *and* the sphere of a new possible science.

So, with the breakthrough work of the *Logical Investigations*, Husserl begins his analyses of the intentional dimensions of consciousness. Rather than describing *what* objects are, he describes and inspects *how* objects are constituted *as* an object or how they are *objectivated*. In this respect, he makes a basic, "all-important" distinction between *objectivating* and *non-objectivating acts*, to which I turn now.

2.2.2 Objectivating and Non-objectivating Acts and Relevant Relations of Foundation

Now, to begin clarifying these terms, by *act* Husserl means, in general, a process of consciousness that correlates with an object.[71] Taken as such, an *objectivating act* is an act wherein an object is *presented* to consciousness.[72] In such a presentation, the object may be intended as existing, in a *positing* act, or as merely presented, that is, as without taking a stand on existence, in a *non-positing* act. Simple sensuous perception, for example, is a positing act, as the seen is posited immediately as existent in sight; fantasy, on the other hand, is a non-positing act, as one's fantasy of

---

[70] Husserl later says that this discovery, "[A]ffected him so deeply that my whole subsequent life-work has been dominated by the task of systematically elaborating this *a priori* of correlation." See also the note at the end of the *Crisis*, Hua VI, §48: "The first breakthrough of this universal correlation apriori of object of experience and modes of reality (during the elaboration of my *Logical Investigations* approximately in 1898) shook me so deeply that since then my entire life's work has been dominated by this task of a systematic elaboration of this a priori correlation."

[71] Again, laying out the details of the way in which Husserl distinguishes his meaning of this term from Brentano's is beyond our current task. Suffice to say Husserl attended to the difference between *real* and *intentional* contents, whereas Brentano, he thought, only attended to the former. The description of the real content is a matter of empirical psychology; intentionality analysis, on the other hand, describes the intentional. On these points, see, for example, Hua XIX, pp. 377–391.

[72] Melle, U. (2020), pp. 193–208. See also Hua XIX, p. 499.

a centaur does not intend its existence but only its presentation.[73] The objectivating act, though, is a basic act needing no additional act for an object to be given or presented.

By contrast, a *non-objectivating act* does need an additional act for a presentation. It is, in fact, often a modification of an original presentation. This includes, in what becomes Husserl's usual list, "wishes, questions, volitions."[74] As I discuss further below, these non-objectivating acts are not themselves originally presentative acts, but rather, *objectivating acts allow non-objectivating acts to have an intentional structure*. Before explicating further, let me clarify how Husserl understands such acts as *founded*.[75]

The concept of *foundation* is presented especially in the "Third Investigation" with respect to the relation between parts and wholes.[76] Broadly, if A cannot exist without B, A is *founded* upon B; conversely, B is *founding* for A. It is also possible for such a relationship to be *reciprocal*, where A and B require each other within a larger unity, like extension is required for color and *vice versa*. The relationship could also be *one-sided*, where the founded can be removed without affecting the founding, as in the relationship between a complex judgment and a simple perception. These are intelligible relations, not a mere physical or even perceptual relation.

So, in a similar respect, Husserl presents a complex *categorial* act founded upon the simple *sensuous* act. The difference between these acts, in Husserl's well-known example, is between simply seeing white paper and grasping *that* the paper *is* white. Both are achievements of consciousness; the latter, however, is a matter of constituting the given object *as such*, as a complex state of affairs and is achieved by *intelligence*. Indeed, such evidence is determined as *being true*, that is, is *verified*, in an *intuitive judgment*, in the "*adequatio rei et intellectus*" that is, as we saw, the "source" of rational position taking on being. Accordingly, a categorial *intuition*, which is the *fulfillment* of the categorial act, is not an "addition" to the perceptually given object but rather constitutes it *as* a state of affairs, knowing *that* it *is*. The categorial intuition thus goes beyond the simple perception that it is founding for it while determining it in cognition as known to be. Once again, we can *understand* this *relation* of foundation, which, in turn, gives a grasp of the *motivation* of acts.

To that end, note first the way Husserl describes the relation of these acts, namely, in *motivation*.[77] He does not mean, then, something like one thing bumping into another, causing its movement, as a mistaken understanding of efficient causality might have it. Although this is how the term is often used in everyday speech, this is simply incorrect on a phenomenological understanding, at least following Husserl.

---

[73] With the transcendental project, Husserl will differentiate this further, as the mode of fantasy becomes *quasi*-positional and so must be suspended.

[74] Understandably, Melle tends to focus upon the discussion of valuing and willing as non-objectivating, leaving out inquiry; this is a point which I take up at length in the fourth chapter of this book.

[75] See Hua XIX, p. 519.

[76] This discussion occurs especially in the "Third Investigation," §14–25, of the *Logical Investigations*.

[77] See Husserl (2001b), pp. 184–186.

By way of analogy, a conclusion is *motivated* insofar as it follows from the premises. So, to say, *mutatis mutandis*, that a question is "motivated" means that there is an intelligible relation of acts, *not* that some chain reaction strictly "necessitated" the question.[78] From this clarification, one can also more readily understand the import of foundation in terms of a relation.

Consider, for example, Husserl's example of joy to illustrate the relationship of foundation. Joy, he says, is only possible if something is given to be joyful *about*: "The joy is not a concrete act in its own right …without some such foundation, there could be no joy at all."[79] Even where one is joyful, where one has a joyful disposition, there is some foundation for that joy, whether it be the nice weather, a nice expectation, the generally good life here-below or anticipated beyond.[80] It is not that this act of joy necessarily posits either the truth or existence of the object it is about—I can be joyful about a mere fantasy or wrong about that which I enjoy—but that there must be something upon which complex acts build. There is a *motivation* for the joy, as it appears in relation to the data and acts.

Non-objectivating acts can become founding as well, however. Where this occurs, there are more complex layers of foundation: one can be joyful about wishing, for example, as a child's joy on Christmas morning builds upon the wishing for a new toy.[81] In this, there is a further depth, so to speak, to the founding; there is, at the foundation, an objectivating act: the joy stands on the wish which, in turn, stands on the objectivating act of fantasizing the toy. The joy is "genuine," "true," in the sense as fulfilled and not merely an anticipation, though there is also an anticipatory dimension to the wish. In any event, though the situation becomes increasingly complex, the basic point about the relation of acts remains.

Also with the above distinctions, some further differentiation within the intention itself is in order. I note that in the unity of an intention, or in the *intentional essence*, there is a distinction between act-*quality* and act-*matter*: the former determines the kind of act, for example, the perceiving, inquiring, judging, enjoying, wishing, and so on; the latter is that to which the quality of the act refers, for example, the percept, questionable matter, state of affairs, value, and so on. With this, the intentional *content* can then be distinguished as the object *which* is intended and *as* it is intended, its "interpreted" sense as meant. Yet, these are in such a *relation* that the *intentional*

---

[78] This distinction is especially important when, in the latter regressive-inquisitive procedure: herewith, Husserl takes an accomplishment and inquires back into the acts necessary for it, that is, for its *motivation*. There has been much discussion, for example, about the motivation of the reduction and the suspension of positing, but this is most concretely understood from a grasp of the *unity of acts* through history. In other words, to describe that motivation would be to describe the historical tension, the "struggle," the "conflict" in its unity and unifying activity—*that is the questioning spirit of human being*.

[79] Hua XIX, p. 419. Husserl will also call this an "act-quality," further distinguishing it from an act-content or matter.

[80] Psychological conditions wherein one shows signs of joy, if even apparently without anything about which to be joyful, may still have motivation, even if these are not "reasonable."

[81] Hua XIX, p. 418: "Again, judgments, be it assumptions or also doubts, questions, wishes, acts of will and the like can found; and likewise also vice versa, acts of the latter kind can appear as foundations. Thus, there are manifold combinations in which acts combine to form total acts."

essence carries its sense. Thus, for example, a wishing-intention has its sense in relation to the wishing/wished-for, the inquiring-intention has its sense in relation to an inquiring/questionable. But this relation holds not *merely because* the object is questioned, as if the object has no other possible interpretation, but *insofar as it is of the question*. That is to say, the interpretation does not exhaust the matter, else even an answer would not be possible, since being "questionable" would deplete its possible sense.

All this serves to prepare an understanding of the relation between inquiry and the question expression. In the following section, I present how Husserl takes the question expression as a non-objectivating act, appearing upon a more original presentation and, indeed, a *conflicting* presentation. From this, inquiry appears as asking *about* that which has appeared *as* questionable. These may then be expressed in a question, founded upon the inquiring-intention. They will be fulfilled, further, in an additional objectivating act, that is, an *answer* that "fits" or "fulfills" this original intention—mediating the original conflict, which I take up after this next section. Before considering Husserl's analysis of inquiry, however, a brief restatement of problems regarding questions in logic, then a short account of some positions in the modern logic of Husserl's time serves to set the sections of an already rather lengthy chapter in order.

2.2.3 The Act of Inquiry as Mediating Fulfillment: The Logic of Question–Answer

As we have seen above, in classic formal logic, questions are excluded from analysis because they are not *apophantic*. It is true, of course, that, for Aristotelians, expressions relate—or "coordinate"—to various acts of psychic experience.[82] Nevertheless, in the "finished science" of formal logic itself, remains with the declarative judgment and, indeed, to the "said" in terms of an abstract, formal concept. In contrast, some modern logicians hold that questions express a meaningful judgment. This occurs, for example, in the work of Bernard Bolzano, which is, in general, important for the work surrounding the *Logical Investigations*, as Wolfgang Künne clearly shows.[83] With respect to the matters at hand, Bolzano thinks that including a question sentence in logic is a matter of determining it as a "sentence in itself" (*Satz an sich*). This is because a sentence carries a sense which may or may not be true and, once this is achieved, he claims, it may be treated within a logic, since it is *apophantic*.[84] The question, he holds, asserts nothing about the object into which it inquires, but rather

---

[82] I explicate this coordination in more detail in later chapters, especially as Husserl begins to think more about the relationship of the "Why" and "Because" of the question and answer, already evidenced in Aristotle's *Posterior Analytics*. See below, in the third chapter, especially in the discussion of Aristotle, *Posterior Analytics*, 89b36–90a34.

[83] Künne (1997), pp. 203–240.

[84] Benoist (2002), pp. 41–49.

2.2 Toward the Essence of Inquiry via Intentional Analysis

asserts a *desire*. So, one can determine the truth of the question sentence, if the desire is true, and falsity, if not.

To further clarify the point, Bolzano argues that the truth or falsity of the question can be accounted for in its *"informational"* meaning. It is not a matter of the content (for example, the proposition "The ball is green" is true if the ball is green); nor is it a purely *formal* matter, since a transposition of the sentence to a judgment would no longer retain the grammatical form (say, from Is S P? to S is P). Rather, and again, a question can be true or false insofar as "I may or may not really want to know about what I am asking."[85] This "informational" meaning can be related to the position of Christoph Sigwart on "sincerity," where, if one does not really want to know, if the question is insincere or rhetorical, then it is no longer considered as a question and no longer assertive of a position.[86] In both cases, even if slightly different manners, the question "in itself" is reduced to declarative or apophantic sentences, thereby taking them up into a logic.

Something of a counter to these thinkers appears in the work of Gottlob Frege. Frege recognizes that it is possible to abstract the propositional content from the activity of thought, as Bolzano's *Satz an sich* does. But doing so is precisely *abstract*. He finds, as Jocelyn Benoist notes, that "propositional content...is neither assertive nor interrogative by itself," so, it is true, the mere content of the question has no truth value.[87] However, the thought or the act of the question that seeks *whether* it is true or false must be put into relation to this content. Since there must be an "act" which asserts it, such an act must be accounted for in a logic that would account for the question. Frege thus takes the question-sentence as containing the same possible *content* as an assertion but precisely does not *actively assert* the content. So, the question-sentence carries the sense of an apophantic proposition but does so with a different "force," as he calls it later; in other words, its *quality* is an interrogative rather than assertoric one.[88] This leads Frege to recognize that the question as *expressing* a *thought* may be true or false but the statement *per se* is non-apophantic. His position is near to Husserl's, at least in this respect, but with some important qualifications.

For Husserl, an expressed *question* is founded upon an experience that appears as *questionable* and is *put in question*. Questionability appears where straightforward

---

[85] Benoist (2002), p. 42, where he refers to Bolzano's *Wissenschaftslehre*, Band I, §22.
[86] For more on this, see Picardi, Eva, and Coliva, (2022).
[87] Benoist (2002), p. 43.
[88] See Dummet (1999), especially p. 67.

certainty is called into question.[89] This happens where intention is duplex,[90] when two or more *apprehensions* or "interpretations" of a presentation "conflict" in a way that neither is determinable as being such and so.[91] As such, there is a relation between the conflicting interpretations, *unified* as *conflicting*.[92] The *quality* of the intention transforms to *inquiring* such that the matter gets put *in question*. An example is in order: as I walk to my classroom in the art building, I perceive something on top the of the stairs; then, along with this presentation, I see it *as* a classmate, but in such a way that I am unable to determine *if* this is so, say, due to the poor lighting in the hallway. A duplicity occurs as my attention "swings to and fro," as Husserl says, between two or more possibilities of this single presentation: classmate or something else. I take this conflict as questionable, perhaps even setting up the other possibility, asking, "Is it a classmate or…a mannequin?".

The *disjunctive* character of inquiry is perhaps seen most clearly in such a 'Yes' *or* 'No' question. In this respect, Husserl himself tends to speak, at least around the work of the *Logical Investigations*, of the question of the being of something. For example, if I ask, "Is that a mannequin?" I am asking *whether* it is thus and so *or* not: either it is *or* it is not. But this "either yes or no" is also implied in any question, insofar as a question determines whether options are or are not: "Yes to this possibility," "No to this one." Note, again, that it is not the *disjoining* but the *disjunctivum*, not the inquiring but the unity-in-question that is the matter here, that is to say, again, the inquiring-intention is duplex, aiming, so to speak, at both possibilities without

---

[89] Husserl, in later revisions of the *Logical Investigations*, and in later works, calls this a *modalization* of being-certain in intentional experience. Also, in his later note, from about 1912, Hua XX/2, p. 466: "Of course, it is not 'predicated' as when I said 'It is questionable, uncertain, indeterminate, doubtful whether…' After all, I do not perform an act of certainty, an act of being. True, the question is there for me, a being-inquiring: But it requires first a new attitude and the execution of a 'positing of certainty,' in order to become certain of a being (here of the being of questionability), in order to grasp the question, or to grasp that and in it a questionable thing." In the next chapters, I discuss further the sense of "attitude," in which there comes a distinction between an overarching attitude under which specific attitudes or "habits of willing acts" occur. Indeed, without some clarification of what is meant by "will," through which the relation of means and end are set, matters remain somewhat abstract and vague.

[90] Hua XIX, p. 465: "Where the consideration [*Erwägung*] is one that swings up and down, completely corresponding to the image of the scales, where question turns into counter-question and this again into that (is it so or not?), there the intention is also a conflicting one, and the entire experience of consideration finds its fulfillment through each of the two possible decisions: it is so - it is not so."

[91] Hua XIX, p. 459: "…[T]wo perceptive apprehensions, respectively two appearances of things interpenetrate each other, according to a certain content of appearance congruent, so to speak. And they interpenetrate in the way of the contradiction, whereby the attentive look can turn to the one, soon to the other of the appearing, but in being canceling objects."

[92] Hua XIX, p. 575: "The synthesis of cognition was consciousness of a certain 'agreement.' But the agreement corresponds as a correlative possibility to the 'disagreement,' the 'conflict.' The view does not 'agree' with the intention of meaning, it 'disputes' with it. Contradiction 'separates,' but the experience of the contradiction puts into relation and unity, it is a form of synthesis."

yet determining either.[93] Inquiry intends the evidence of each possibility in order to come to an answer, that is, to a judicative decision. So, on the one hand, it points beyond itself, insofar as it seeks fulfillment: it aims to determine which possibility is correct, which is "true," in Husserl's renewed sense of *adaequatio* as evidential intuitive fulfillment.[94] In this way, the question needs a further, objectivating act for fulfillment. On the other hand, on the way to this fulfilment, inquiry "weighs" the evidence, returning to the given, to the presentation. Although Husserl spends far more effort in understanding this important dimension in his later work, which I take up below, already he finds it in the intention of that which is *evidently* so.

Inquiry seeks fulfilling evidence. For example, in my asking about the figure on the stairs, I could consider all manner of possibilities. Along with the sense "classmate," I could include "tree," "piano," "rhinoceros," or even an abstract concept like "freedom," and so on. But to determine which is the case, I must attend to data; I must return to the given and "weigh" that which speaks in favor of it, if there is any "motivation" for such a judgment. Now, note that, while this motivation is in relation to the perceptual given, it is *not reducible* to it. That is to say, it is the understanding, the intellect that weighs the data, relating it to the possibilities presented. So, the "absurdity" or, better, *counter-sense* (*Widersinn*) of some of the examples only appears because they *continue to conflict with the given as it is given*, in the sense that they *do not fulfill the conditions set by the inquiry*. More exactly: the range of what counts as an answer is anticipated by the very question—yet, we might also say that, in a way, the answer guides the inquiry! In that respect, the answer is, as Husserl puts it, a "fulfilling unit of *response*."[95] By this is meant that the answer "*fits*" the question such that as an *assent* would mean to the possibility that is most adequate to the question, it is the "reasonable response."[96] In this, then, there is an *identification* in the fulfilling response, a moment of union, as Husserl later says.[97]

With all this in mind, inquiry appears as directed toward determining the object as such and so. It is not directed toward itself, as some modern logicians held, but rather. The question is *given as in relation to the judicative decision*. Importantly, however, this judicative decision, as bringing to term or fulfilling the inquiring-intention, is a *further act*, building upon the previous acts of perception and inquiry. From the relation of these acts, there begins to emerge a "normative" dimension to *logos*, insofar as the very operation of inquiry yields its own law. The relationship of

---

[93] This analysis "... carries over to manifold disjunctions which are not limited to a 'Yes' and a 'No'." See Hua XIX, p. 465.

[94] Hua XIX, p. 648: "And the *adaequatio* is realized when the meant objectivity is given in the conception in the strict sense and is given exactly as that as which it is thought and named."

[95] Hua XIX, p. 465: "...und in dieser Erfüllungseinheit der Beantwortung..." ["...and in this fulfillment unit of response..."].

[96] Hua XIX, p. 465: "...die Antwort passt auf die Frage, die Entscheidung sagt: So ist es, genau so, wie es in der erwägenden Betrachtung vor Augen stand" ["...the answer fits the question, the decision says: that's the way it is, just the way it was in contemplation."].

[97] In the earlier edition of the passage, Husserl calls this instead a "*Gestaltqualität*." I include the phrase "*Einheitsmomentes*" because it indicates the moment of identity and is consistent with his ways of speaking, even in the *Investigations*.

these acts set what "counts" as inquiry. Where inquiry operates in accord with this immanent law, it succeeds in fulfilling the question-intention in the response.

Indeed, the response, Husserl says, is also the "resolution to a kind of tension."[98] That tension is the lack of unity which the inquiry seeks to overcome: it is that tension of conflicting presentations, of not yet having the fulfillment of an intention. In other words, *inquiry is mediating* the fulfilling unit of response. In order to have such a fulfillment, to continue the example, I must return to the figure in the stairwell; I must attend more closely, gather more data, weigh the possibilities, decide and give the most adequate assenting judgment. The answer "piano" does not meet the contours of the question, does not fit the situation sketched by the very intentional essence. The inappropriateness of such an answer thus also leaves a tension—a "good enough" lingers as a not quite "good enough." To explain these points a bit further, and to conclude this section, let me turn back to the problem of those "grammatical forms" in the opening quote of the chapter.

For Husserl, the *expressed question* by itself is non-objectivating. Such an expression is neither a judgment about the state of affairs nor does it take a position on its own activity. Rather, the inquiring is a modification of the original presentation as "conflicting"—a presentation that is taken as *questionable*.[99] So, if I ask a question, there must be something "about which" I ask, otherwise it has *no foundation*, and so no *sense*. Moreover, the inquiring-intention requires fulfillment in a further, objectivating act. This fulfillment *refers back* to the original presentation that has become questionable: the question "Is the ball green?" will only be answered upon attending to the evidence of *whether* the ball is green. Likewise, then, the sense of an answer lies in the objectivating act. Without an account of the relation of these, in a broader logical investigation, any treatment of the grammatical forms in question will remain abstract and inadequate to the matter.

So, unlike Bolzano and Sigwart, for Husserl, the *question expression* is built, so to speak, upon an objectivating act.[100] The presentation has been called into question, that is, a "simple" presentation is taken up into a "complex" *question*. Here, one need not make a judgment about the informational content or sincerity of the question; for, if that was needed in order for it to make sense, why not have to make a judgment about that, and that, and so on *ad infinitum*? Also, while Husserl, like Frege, distinguishes the abstract formal question from the thinking or the inquiring, he takes the question as an expression *founded in an intentional experience*. More exactly, the question

---

[98] Hua XIX, p. 465: "Manifestly, in this lived-experience of fulfillment related to the question under consideration, in this resolution of a kind of tension, also lies the original source for the speech of approving judgment."

[99] See Hua XX/2, p. 466: "Das Unbeschriebensein ist vorgestellt und steht in Frage, steht als fraglich da. Eine Modifikation des Seins, Fraglichsein…" ["The being-undescribed is imagined and is in question, stands there as questionable. A modification of being, being-questionable"] Also at Hua XIX, p. 468: "Als-fraglich-erscheinen konstituiert [constituted as-appearing-questionable.]".

[100] For more on this, see Künne (2003).

proposition is the expression of an inquiring intention which, in turn, is founded upon an original presentation that has been taken *as* questionable.[101]

Husserl's position has a more complex relation to the so-called "Aristotelians."[102] For both Husserl and Aristotle, judgement is essential to knowledge. It is also not reducible to relation of concepts but is rather an activity, the coming to term of a process of cognition. Thus, a question can express inquiry, but not its *full meaning*, for the full meaning of inquiry is in its fulfilling unit of response. However, for Husserl, not only are the expressions of these acts *not* judgments on those acts but they are also not taken as *coordinated* to those acts. Instead, he treats them with respect to a relation of foundation between objectivating and non-objectivating acts. Taken thusly, it is not the question expression itself but the *intention* and *intuition* which *confers* meaning. In other words, the *meaning* of the question is situated in a fuller range of *logos*, insofar as it plays a mediating role in *meaningful* experience.

The latter point is an essential one. The distinction between objectivating and non-objectivating acts gives an account of the full breadth of logos, as it has been conceived so far in the history of logic. These distinctions serve to give logic a normative character insofar as the meaning of non-objectivating acts are shown to fit within cognition *ideally*. The later acts are not sense or meaning conferring, at least in themselves, but they do give sense to experience. In the case of the theme at hand, that which is given as "questionable" is the *lived* experience, *makes sense*, as it were. This latter dimension needs further comment, however.

2.3 Concluding Remarks: The Interior and Exterior Voice

Since the expression is set into one with the intuited interior lived-experience in the manner of a cognition, a complexion arises having the character of a self-enclosed phenomena. To the extent that, in such complexion, we live principally in an act of the question, with which

---

[101] This point, I find, is misunderstood by John Bruin in his remarks on Husserl's theory of questioning. He thinks that, for Husserl, a *question* is an addition of a certain 'quality' to an act already equipped with meaning." There is a confusion here, I find, with the meaning of *act*, *meaning*, and *quality* that may be addressed by understanding that the objectivating intentional act is *foundational* for the quality of questionability upon which the question builds. The *meaning* of a question is upon the *intending-intended* relation. See Bruin, J. (2001), p. 19.

[102] Husserl admits that this is a change from an earlier position. Evidence of this earlier position is sparse, at least as far as I can tell. Some remnants seem to be preserved, however, in his review of Hans Cornelius, then in Frankfurt. This review, in Hua XXII, pp. 136–142, bears the title, "*H. Cornelius, Versuch einer Theorie der Existentialurteile,* (München 1894)." Here, there appears an interest in existential judgments, affirmations and negations, and questions. Husserl makes the point that, for Cornelius, perception is basically the same as noticing content in consciousness. So, Cornelius understands the posed question to communicate the content which is then to be compared in the judgment. It is evident that Husserl has yet to have worked out the relation between objectivating and non-objectivating acts.

an expression merely fits in, and to which it gives articulate voice, the whole complexion is called a question....[103]

In this chapter, we found that Husserl's phenomenological inquiry finds a priority in original "interior awareness."[104] This original awareness, to which phenomenology means to give voice through its inquiry, founds meaningful expressions. Indeed, the question expression itself is founded upon what he calls a "complexion" of interior acts in the lived-experience inquiry. Of course, as Husserl recognizes, it is also possible that a question-expression is, so to speak, "empty," that is, the expression can be *merely uttered*. I can "mechanically" ask, for example, "Is it hot?" without intending or meaning a fulfilling act.[105] But I can also "live-in," as he says, the question by really meaning it, by really intending the answer.

A living inquiry is unified—"set into one," as Husserl says—within interior experience through a series of acts. When one intends an answer for oneself, for example, there is a sort of "monologue."[106] This monologue can be the sort of "talking with oneself" that appears in the acts of discursive thinking. In this, inquiry sets into a reflection upon whether weighed possibilities are the case, whether or not this or that is what it is, what should be done, how it should be done, and so on. Of course, there is not only monological inquiry, but also dialogical inquiry or what I call "interrogation," drawing on the sense of *inter-rogare* as there is an "inquiring between" two subjects who are present to themselves.

In interrogation, in this sense, the other gives or presents the other something to bring into their own inquiry. That may mean that one subject linguistically expresses a question to another, but it may also be expressed through a bodily gesture or some other sign. As the both share an in the lived-experience of the inquiry, so do they share in the intention toward an answer. For example, I can, upon seeing that another is seeking to find a more comfortable position, begin seeking along with them, offering a hand or a pillow to adjust their posture. The inquiry is not originally mine, but I take it up as mine, as we seek an answer. Thus, the full term of that communication is the answer.

Communication with others is not always easy, of course. This is exemplified, as Husserl points out, in the experience of needing to repeat oneself, as when someone asks, "What are you saying?" and "Could you say that again?"[107] The tension that arises wells-up to the point where we *request*, not so much further data, but *the same data again*. When the repetition occurs, the sense of it stands-in for the original presentation so that it can be considered, lived-in, even if the one who repeats it no longer says the expression with the same conviction and the one who requests it consideres it with renewed attention and with the added meaning of having heard

---

[103] Hua XIX, p. 747.

[104] See Husserl (2001c), pp. 81 and 87–89.

[105] This is how he puts it in a 1914 reworking of the *Investigations*, at Hua XX/2, p. 382.

[106] LI II, 332.

[107] For example, in Hua XX/2, p. 386.

2.3 Concluding Remarks: The Interior and Exterior Voice

it multiple times.[108] Furthermore, living-in a question does not mean that one need to "go along with" or "ask-with" the other person, as one need not go along with another's *interior conflict*. If someone asks me whether I see a woman or mannequin in the hallway, the other need not also be "confused" or in conflict but might rather recognize my confusion. In any case, inquiry is communicated between inquirers.

What is more, one might ask about motivations—about why something appeared, why it became questionable, and so on. As Husserl puts it in later reworkings of the *Investigations*: "But let us note there are depths. One can go back into motives, ever deeper. Question back into more and more operations, validity, value—to answer the horizon of the asker must be understood more and more, never perfectly."[109] In short, the way to understand more about oneself and about one's meaningful and valuable world is through inquiry. In fact, this is suggestive of the way Husserl inquired-back into meaning and sense of logic and science itself, as well as how he explicates this as essential to his phenomenological method, which I take up in subsequent chapters.

To conlude this chapter, then, the breakthrough to phenomenology set Husserl on a path to a new science of science, in which inquiry was essential. Nonetheless, the *Investigations* was, for Husserl, a beginning. He had still more questions to answer to fulfill its task. Most famously, of course, comes his development of the transcendental method of phenomenology. With this, he means to radicalize the presuppositionlessness of phenomenology by explicitly suspending the positing of being. In fact, I find Husserl treating his radicalization of the transcendental question as precisely a radicalization of *inquiry*, to which I turn now.

---

[108] Hua XX/2, p. 386: "So we have a double mode, in which the meaning-intentions and the unified act of the propositional meaning (of the certain belief, as we want to presuppose here) can be accomplished. For example, I think explicitly: 'The square above the hypotenuse, and so on,' and then on the question 'What do you say?' I 'mechanically' repeat the sentence. It is still for me not an empty play on words, for I still believe, and perhaps I stand for what is said with interior 'lively conviction'; yes, exteriorly it may also be noticeable in tone, as when I assume that the other would like to be of a different opinion here. In this repetition I 'perform' the general belief, but I do not articulately perform individual acts of subject-positing, predicate-positing, and so on. An even deeper level is even possible, according to which I take up reading what I have read in a 'confused' way purely receptively. The 'meant' stands there as being, as things stand there in the perception, if I pass over them with the look without any positing activity (action)...."

[109] Hua XX/2, p. 37. This is, let me note, an early indication of inquiring back, though not with the methodological sense it will take on later in his work.

Chapter 3
Toward the Source and Horizon of Acts of Inquiry

Abstract This chapter follows how inquiry appears in the earlier expressions of Husserl's transcendental project. So, if the previous chapter shows how he investigates the logical problematic of meaningful sentences and expressions, showing their foundation to be in intentional acts of consciousness, this chapter shows how he discovers the pure ego as the source of inquiry and the world as the horizon of it. There emerges a basic distinction between transcendental phenomenological inquiry and natural inquiry. Where natural inquiry leaves the source and horizon unquestioned, transcendental phenomenological inquiry proceeds under suspension of any positing—an ἐποχή—in order to understand how any position taking appears at all. I also consider his analysis of practical inquiry from his new transcendental approach, which begins to call into question the limitations of the early formulations of transcendental phenomenological inquiry.

Keywords Pure phenomenology · Transcendental · Source · Horizon · Natural inquiry · ἐποχή

> We must constantly keep in mind our principle, which is prefigured by the nature of the problematic of cognitional critique. All natural cognition, all natural science is radically put into question and must therefore be treated as problematic. What is problematic we must not treat as unproblematic.[1]
>
> The questions put to nature and to nature overall are to be distinguished from the questions put to the possibility of cognition of nature; and again, the questions of the possibility of a nature are to be distinguished from the theoretical-meaning questions – questions which are put and have to be put to the sentences and sentential connections as the meaning content of the scientific theories – and the corresponding questions of cognition, the questions about the relation between cognition and meaning. If cognition is the riddle, if it becomes the problem, then there is no other way than to study it itself, and it then becomes self-evident, especially after our detailed considerations, that this study is a study of essence and must be carried out on the ground of pure consciousness, in the sphere of pure and absolute self-givenness.[2]

---

[1] Hua Mat VII, p. 38.
[2] Hua Mat VII, p. 97.

3.1 Preliminary Remarks—The Radicalization of the Transcendental Question

The appearance of the *Logical Investigations* brought Husserl some renown. Although he did not achieve the position of *professor ordinarius* until 1906 in Göttingen, after being there since 1901, he nevertheless had already gained the notice of sympathetic colleagues and a group of students there, throughout Germany, and, to some extent, the world.[3] That recognition did not mean that he himself was settled in his positions, however. Indeed, Husserl himself remained fixed upon living up to the principles of the phenomenological method. After his early breakthroughs, there came important developments, especially through to his move to Freiburg in 1917, as he continued to inquire into the origins of sense and meaning.[4] With this inquiry, phenomenology opens what Husserl calls a "new world" of the "most interior life," yielding—as I bring to the fore here, in this chapter—new dimensions both *for* and *of* inquiry in co-operation with others.[5]

Through this chapter, I trace some lines of that way of thinking that comes to be known as the "transcendental turn" of Husserl's phenomenology, especially insofar as it provides more radical answers to those original, ancient questions. For, if the earlier work first asks about the logical problematic of meaningful *sentences*, describing their foundation in intentional *acts* of consciousness, it nevertheless does not inquire into the *source* and *horizon* of these acts. Indeed, Husserl finds his own phenomenological inquiry as operating within a world it takes for granted, leaving, moreover, the source of its acts, the pure ego, hidden, covered over. He finds, in other words, that the rich work around the cognitional critique of the *Investigations* was, at least in a certain manner, *naïve*.

To clarify the sense of such a naïveté, I expound, in the second main section of this chapter, Husserl's differentiation of *natural inquiry* from *transcendental-phenomenological inquiry*. Here, I discuss how he puts "natural belief"– a sort of primordial *doxa*, in which natural inquiry proceeds—in suspension with a methodological ἐποχή. This suspension allows the phenomenologist to inquire into how matters appear, including the world itself, without participating in them, without taking for granted their being such and so. Indeed, rather than crossing-out previous

---

[3] The slow path to recognition was not without frustration, for Husserl. As he reflects, in a 1931 letter to Ernst Harms, at Hua Brief VII, p. 109: "Unfortunately, I only happen to belong to those workers and thinkers who have been deprived of the actual spiritual community of the official academia at any time, and I can enjoy as confreres of this fate so completely, beside Socrates and Nietzsche, a whole series of not insignificant spirits of the human history; so this fate makes the actual prod of the *Zeitgeist's* creative output so difficult, because one always confronts such an unfortunate resistance during this prodding. You will understand what I mean by this. –Even my doctoral thesis was rejected many years ago, by the editor of the relevant journal, as 'insufficient,' to then have experienced in his journal itself and further over 30 reviews and processing in the 3 following years."

[4] Husserl's inaugural lecture at Freiburg was given on May 3rd, 1917, though he was appointed in January of 1916.

[5] Husserl (2011), p. 281.

phenomenological insights, this methodological operation brings them back into question, though now within a more concrete account of the subject-world correlation. A prime example of this is his understanding of the distinction between transcendental-phenomenological and natural inquiry itself. This distinction, inadequately understood, though indicated, in the early formulation of the "unnaturalness" of interior investigation, now appears in relation to the transcendental question about any inquiry at all. In other words, the "nature of" the unnaturalness is disclosed by bringing to question natural belief itself, thereby overcoming previous phenomenological naïveté.

The problematic may be provisionally presented by returning, with Husserl, to Plato. For it is Plato, he finds, who sets naïve belief and evidential knowledge—δόξα and ἐπιστήμη—into relation with a demand for insightfully self-justified knowledge. In other words, it is Plato who sets the task of a rigorous philosophy through self-knowledge—γνῶθι σεαυτόν! From a sketch of these points, I turn to Husserl's understanding of the shift from first philosophy as metaphysics to cognitional critique. This shift puts into questions the unquestioned foundations of metaphysics by taking up the old transcendental question about the possibility of any cognition at all. With all that in mind, let me turn briefly to some aspects of Husserl's use of the terms δόξα and ἐπιστήμη, then set them into relation with his reading of Plato.

3.1.1 An Elucidation of δόξα and ἐπιστήμη vis-à-vis Inquiry

Husserl himself does not straightaway take *doxa* in the broad sense of a "belief in being." His delineation of this sense, for which I reserve the Latin transliteration, emerges with his discovery of the intentional correlation of subject and world, where the being of the latter may be taken for granted by the former, in a sort of presupposed, unquestioned or "naïve" belief. At this same time, he also comes to distinguish, on the subject's side, the relation of *noetic* and *noematic* poles of an intention, where the former has to do with modalities of *belief* and the latter of *being*.[6] Before he comes to these positions, however, the term appears in the context of a presentation and its meaning.

At the end of the "Fifth Investigation," for example, Husserl employs the Greek δόξα to illustrate an unclarified ambiguity in the term *Meinung*, namely, between "opinion" and "meaning."[7] Understood from the perspective of his intentionality

---

[6] These are of the possibile, impossible, probable, necessary, doubtful, questionable and so on. See Husserl (1983), §102–107. With respect to the previous chapter's theme, that is, how logic relates to cognitional critique, see also, Hua XXXV, pp. 470–71.

[7] This also recurs in lectures and manuscripts, for example, in a manuscript from 1904, at Hua XXXVIII, p. 73: "The word 'opinion' ['*Meinung*'] is ambiguous. Sometimes it is a synonym for 'belief,' especially for un-insightful belief (δόξα); sometimes it is called – and we do not avoid this expression either—the objective, which appears by interpretative conception or otherwise becomes intentional, meant. The expression intention, intentional object, seems to say 'meaning' ['*Meinung*'] 'object in the sense of meaning' and the like. Again, the sense of the speech of meaning seems to

analysis, an *opinion* follows from an "un-insightful belief" (*un-einsichtiges Glauben*, as he writes), which lacks the sort of *insightful meaning* in accord with fulfilled justification or "grounding" (*Begründung*) that yields a belief in being. So, it is not that an opinion, in this sense, is completely lacking reason. Rather, such a position is "taken on" (*annehmen*) uncritically, that is, without asking about the truth of the position "in itself," without attending to and accepting evidence that would ground the position.[8] By contrast, then, an *insightful* meaning takes a position on the ground of an evidentially filled judgment. The opinion is meaningful, then, but is not of the same class as insightful belief, the prime instance of which is scientific knowledge or ἐπιστήμη.

Nearer to the broad sense of a "belief in being," the term δόξα also appears in the context of Husserl's investigations of unified belief and the "building up" (*aufbauen*) of meaning in experience.[9] For example, in order to make a judgment, one must not only hold a prospective judgment, as a "possible belief," but also do so in relation to other already held positions, that is, in a context of *actual belief*. For example, when I consider making the judgment, S is P, say, via the question "Is S p?" it is in relation to the possible judgment "S is P" as well as to other judgments, about "Ss" and "Ps." When the judgment is made, when S is posited as P, it accrues as an achievement synthesized within already determinate, unified belief, just as further judgments would build upon this, and so on.[10] So, the judgment about whether S *is* P sits in an already given context of belief in *being* or a *doxa*, in a broader sense.

Indeed, at base, there is a sort of "*protodoxa*," as Husserl comes to put it. By this, he means that, in experience, being may be accepted *without question*. Although presentations may be called into question, this calls for further acts, as we saw previously, unto a reflective judgment that would determine their being or being so; since neither these operations nor the unity of meaning needs to be made thematic, meaning may "build up," without further ado, setting a horizon of unified belief that is more or less taken for granted. In fact, with these points, we are on our way to understanding the *world* as the "collective horizon of possible investigation" and the

---

have reference to attention or even to say something identical with it. The observed is specifically meant in contrast to the unobserved."

[8] In Husserl (2001b), §7, Husserl not only uses the language of an uncritical "taking up" but puts it into relation to "mere opinion" (*bloßes Meinen*) and insightful knowledge (*einsichtiges Wissen*), adding in the later addition to the text, it as *pure essential intuition* (*als reine Wesensintuition*).

[9] As an example of this in relation to hypothetical judgments, see a writing from 1909 at Hua XXXVIII, pp. 263–264: "We speak of judicative-opinion, judging in the special sense is opinion, δόξα. And the "to think" is to constitute the 'act'....Going back to our considerations above, the whole hypothetical judgment content, when I just perform the hypothetical judgment, is the object of the δόξα, meantnesses of the judgment, and in this respect there is no preference for the antecedent opinion and consequent opinion. And both of them belong to the one judgment opinion building them up, to the one judgment act. Against it: If I turn to a new judgment content and see (mean, assert) it, and the old one still remains in view, this can be understood in two ways. Either I keep the old one still in my view as a propositional assertion, be it also collectively, S is P! and in addition, this is still there (what I still have to look at more closely and so on), or I keep it in the way of a stirring, a mere factual appearance, without asserting that still now (the act is therein)."

[10] See, for example, Husserl (1983), §104.

radical suspension of *doxa* necessary for its investigation.[11] Now, however, let me continue to motivate the problematic by taking up the relation of belief and inquiry in historical terms.[12]

Regarding inquiry, Plato's *Meno* is the *locus classicus*. Beyond Parmenides' vision, which relates something like the mythico-religious quest of an elect individual and excises opinion as a way of knowing, Plato here reenacts the process as it might occur for anyone seeking to understand from the basis of their beliefs. Indeed, in the *Meno,* he elucidates how there is a broader *belief* from within which the *a priori* is grasped.[13] In other words, he shows how the subject might be led to attend to the data, to ask questions, and to have an insight or "to get the idea."[14] Still more, he means to guide others to have *insight into their own operations*. Husserl takes notice that, in this process, *inquiry pairs with insight* as establishing philosophical science over-against un-insightful opinion and does so *by nevertheless relating to doxa*.

Consider a passage from Husserl's manuscripts, worth quoting at some length:

> For each thinkable judgment...it holds that it is true or false, that it is correlatively spoken fulfilled insightable or not (negatively insightable). This is not the same as saying I had to insight it, could insight it at all, the insight requires its determinate motivation and this need not be given. The young one in the *Meno* does not always have his Socrates at hand, guiding his motivation. But *a pr<iori>* such an evidential formation is possible with the corresponding thought content and if that so an ego that passed from the commitment, or from the blind belief to evidence.[15]

---

[11] Husserl (1983), §1.

[12] Husserl's understanding of meaning and opinion intertwines with his reading and teaching schedule. He himself notes the increased number of introductory courses in the history of philosophy that came alongside his directly phenomenological lectures. This sort of zig-zagging seems to yield a wider vista of interpretation, as he begins to more clearly relate his phenomenological analysis to the tradition. In the later reedition of the "Sixth Investigation," from 1920, where he stresses first the progress on "theoretical difficulties," presumably through the Göttingen period, then his need to focus on "general philosophical reflections" during the Great War, followed by teaching in Freiburg and a tendency toward system.

[13] It is not lost on Husserl that Plato presents the problem in the *Theaetetus*, albeit in its own way and in its own context. See the remark at Hua Mat IX, p. 30: "It is true that the question of the nature of genuine knowledge (ἐπιστήμη as opposed to mere and δόξα) has been much discussed by him [Plato]—I recall in particular the *Theaetetus*—it is indeed a fundamental question for him; but he does not get beyond formal determinations, such as are necessary and valuable in logical-methodological intent. This behavior of Plato's is well understandable in the developmental situation which his life's work marked out for him. It corresponds exactly to the behavior of the reformatory practitioner Socrates...." I highlight this final sentence, too, as the *relation* of theory and practice are put directly into question by him, in a way that they were apparently not by Socrates.

[14] For more on the grasp of the idea in relation to insight, see Hua XXIV, pp. 155-156. Indeed, here, where he asks about the meaning of insight, "What is *Einsicht*?" he comes to ask about the *lumen naturale*, that is, about the way in which one can understand at all as well as do so *with more clarity*. This, in a sense, is our basic point here: one can have insight in an analogous sense, a higher one of which, for Husserl, is in self-understanding, that is, in *becoming increasingly aware* of oneself.

[15] K II 4/ 20: "Für jedes erdenkliche Urteil...gilt das es wahr oder falsch, das es korrelativ gesprochen erfüllt einsehbar ist der nicht (negativ einsehbar). Das sagt nicht, dass dasselbe Ich es einsehen musste, überhaupt einsehen konnte, das Einsehen fordert seine bestimmte Motivation und die

Here, Husserl provides some important clues to understanding the appearance and operation of inquiry. To follow them, let us begin with the phrase, "insight requires its determinate motivation and this need not be given," as it indicates the role of inquiry in moving from blind belief to insightful belief. First, let us recall first that, for Husserl, *motivation* indicates the relation of conscious acts. An investigation of motivation thus considers how acts relate to other acts, how acts set conditions for other acts, how certain acts fulfill complex operations, how accomplishments build up over time, and even how normativity becomes constituted over time.[16] Sensibility, for example, gives a foundation for asking, for asking *about*, but it does not "cause" the asking, as we do not *need* to ask, do not *need* to have the insight, do not *need* to make the judgment.[17] But if *determinate* inquiry and insight appear, their indeterminate *possibility* must be somehow "prior" to the actual operation of the acts. Of course, the phenomenologist does not impose such possibilities upon data, but rather grasps them as given constitutive conditions. So, the phenomenologist can say that the "questionable" experience motivates questions essentially, since this is "part" of the *a priori* structure of questioning, and can say so without claiming that one *must* ask a question if the experience is able to be questioned. Such determinate motivation may actually occur, but it also may not, after all.

We can illustrate and further elucidate the point with respect to inquiry by turning, with Husserl's help, to the *Meno*. Early in the dialogue, there is an attempt to define virtue, arising with the issue of whether one can teach another to be virtuous. Socrates, characteristically bemused, asks his interlocutor to tell him what is meant by "virtue" at all or in general, for, "if one does not know what it is, how would one know of what type it is?"[18] To be sure, Meno has opinions about them. At first, in fact, responds by listing some virtues, which accord, he says, with each person's activity and age.[19] These are presuppositions, taken up from everyday experience in his culture. Socrates, of course, is not satisfied with Meno's list, since he is merely pointing at many virtues, ready-made opinions, rather than making an insightful judgment of what virtue is. So, he asks again for *what* virtue *is*, that is, he asks for the one "look" (the εἶδος, a word which comes from οἶδα which means to "see" or "know") through which they are all known as virtues.[20] After failing to get an answer to the question, Socrates suggests that they continue "to inquire together"

---

brauch nicht gegeben zu sein. Der Jünger im Meno hat nicht immer seinen Sokrates zur Hand, der seine Motivation leitet. Aber apr <iori> ist ein solches Evidenzgebilde mit dem entsprechenden gedanklichen Inhalt möglich und wenn das so ein Ich das vom Einsatz, oder vom blinden Glauben zur Evidenz überging." This manuscript is perhaps from the later teens, according to editors.

[16] For an extended analysis, see Sokolowski (1970).

[17] That is not to say that there is not a *demand* for asking. Again, this will be further differentiated in the third and fourth chapter, where broach how "motivation" may mean something like a "spiritual causality" in the *relation* of "Why" and "Because." See Hua XXXVII, pp. 109–110.

[18] Plato, *Meno*, 71b: "...ὃ δὲ μὴ οἶδα τί ἐστιν, πῶς ἂν ὁποῖόν γέ τι εἰδείην;" Here, Plato seems to be playing on the etymological connection between οἶδα and εἰδείην, both of which are connected to ἰδέα, as I note below.

[19] Plato, *Meno*, 71b-c "...καθ' ἑκάστην... τῶν πράξεων καὶ τῶν ἡλικιῶν."

[20] Plato, *Meno*, 72c: "...ἕν γέ τι εἶδος ταὐτὸν ἅπασαι ἔχουσιν δι' ὃ εἰσὶν ἀρεταί."

3.1 Preliminary Remarks—The Radicalization of the Transcendental Question

(συζητῆσαι). From this point, we come to the situation around Husserl's point about Socrates "guiding motivation."

However, the inquiring together results in a skepticism about the possibility to inquire at all. Indeed, there comes the famous "paradox," succinctly formulated for Meno by Socrates at 80e: "…Can one inquire about what he knows or about what he does not know? For one does not inquire about what is known—for it is known, and there is in no need of inquiry into it; nor would one inquire about what is unknown—for one does not know that about which he inquires."[21] Socrates thinks there is an answer to the problem. And this answer has something to do with, on the one hand, Socrates as a guide and, on the other, the operation of inquiry from blind to insightful belief.

Indeed, throughout the dialogues, Socrates asks questions in order to give the motivation for inquiry and insight. This is part and parcel of the *maieutic* aspect of his dialectic.[22] The example in the *Meno* starts with Socrates calling to the young boy. Upon drawing a figure into the ground, Socrates straightaway asks *whether* the boy knows *that* the figure *is* (ὅτι τοιοῦτόν ἐστιν) a square, to which the youth responds, "I do, in fact."[23] Then, Socrates asks the boy to recognize the definition as a four-sided figure with equal sides, regardless of length—that is, to identify *what* a square is and *why* it is a square—which the boy also does. Having set the figure, he asks him to vary the image by adding length to the sides to double the size of the figure, all of which he seems to do easily enough. But when he asks *if* the figure with doubled sides is double the original, the boy trips up, saying, incorrectly, "Yes." Socrates goes on to show him that it is not double but rather quadruple the original, and then, through a series of questions and answers, how to correctly double the figure. Such is an overview of the event.

The boy's initially incorrect assent is significant, though. For, in the first place, and to reiterate, the boy already knows *that* the figure *is* a square, *what* a square is and *why*, and can imagine the figure with varied lengths. The exercise thus neither focuses upon the initial grasp of an εἶδος of a square—that is, of the necessity and universality of relations that constitute a square—nor does it spend much time on the formulation of a concept as a definition of "square." All this the boy had beforehand. The pressing issue is, at present, how the blind beliefs, the "commitments," as Husserl put it, became *mis*-leading presuppositions *rather than* leading clues to the insightful judgment of its *being so*. The beliefs had the motivating force rather than the inquiry

---

[21] Plato, *Meno*, 80e: "…ὡς οὐκ ἄρα ἔστιν ζητεῖν ἀνθρώπῳ οὔτε ὃ οἶδε οὔτε ὃ μὴ οἶδε; οὔτε γὰρ ἂν ὅ γε οἶδεν ζητοῖ – οἶδεν γάρ, καὶ οὐδὲν δεῖ τῷ γε τοιούτῳ ζητήσεως – οὔτε ὃ μὴ οἶδεν – οὐδὲ γὰρ οἶδεν ὅτι ζητήσει."

[22] See, Hua Mat IX, p. 34. Also, for Plato's Socrates or, as Husserl says, "the Platonic dialectic, the child of the Socratic reaction against skepticism," overcomes the sophistic skepticism of the day by setting the ideal of a self-justified rational method, as he says, again, at Ms. A IV 5/116b.

[23] Plato, Meno, 82b. This appears a translation of F I 40/56–57: "The scientific surveyor may draw his characters in the sand or on the blackboard, but when he speaks of lines, places, circles, and so on…. he understands an 'exact,' a 'pure' presentation in any experience and therefore cannot be seen in it."

toward truth. If it is to be possible to have insight, there must be a way to it, a way of weighing the evidence—*a way of inquiry*.

So, in the second place, the boy is in fact led by Socrates, first into a difficulty, then back out. For that, Socrates again *seeks with* the boy, guiding his motivation.[24] Here, Plato has Socrates tell Meno to watch out for the fact that he does not give the boy anything but only guides him back through what he already had, what he already "knew," that is his *belief*.[25] Through the inquiring-together, the boy becomes interested and begins *to ask for himself*, on the basis of his opinions, that is his previous judgments. In other words, he seeks an answer to that which has become questionable to him in order to overcome the limits of the impasse. When this occurs, he begins to play with the presented, wherein the type of figure itself sets limits of its *variation*: if sides are not equally lengthened, for example, the square ceases to be a square, but becomes otherwise, say, an oblong rectangle; likewise, if an angle is taken away and a new line drawn, it is a triangle. He comes to a correct assent, in fact, through his own inquiry—guided, to be sure—which moves upon the foundational conditions of *doxa*. The "paradox" of Meno is thus performatively refuted by the operation of inquiry.

Of course, as Husserl notes, one does not always have a Socrates at hand. But recall that the discussion of the *Meno* occurs within the context of the question of virtue and knowledge. Plato presents, in this context, the beginnings of a habitual turn of mind, a μετάνοια, to *theory*. As Husserl again brings to the fore, that the entire example hinges on the *possibility* of determinate seeking or inquiring after them. His clue about Socrates "guiding the motivation" of the young boy elucidates the constitutive conditions for inquiry, namely, a concrete doxic horizon correlated to a yet indeterminate questioning spirit. What Socrates is doing is bringing others to experience and to have insight into their own ability to ask and answer questions. This represents, in short, a methodological break from blind belief to self-justified insightful belief, from δόξα to ἐπιστήμη.

These historical considerations do not only provide a glimpse into Husserl's understanding of the role of inquiry the break from δόξα to ἐπιστήμη, however. They also give us an image for his own role as guiding inquiry in the breakthrough to the transcendental-phenomenological inquiry. Saving for later chapters further explication of the generative motivations for this breakthrough, let me first turn to Husserl's radicalization of the ancient transcendental question in the differentiation of *natural* and *transcendental-phenomenological inquiry*.

---

[24] See 84c-d, for example: "…οἴει οὖν ἂν αὐτὸν πρότερον ἐπιχειρῆσαι ζητεῖν ἢ μανθάνειν τοῦτο ὃ ᾤετο εἰδέναι οὐκ εἰδώς, πρὶν εἰς ἀπορίαν κατέπεσεν ἡγησάμενος μὴ εἰδέναι, καὶ ἐπόθησεν τὸ εἰδέναι." I stress the sense of πόθος, the root of ἐπόθησεν, as a "request." It can also mean a yearning, or even a sort of prayer, in religious context.

[25] See 84c-d: "σκέψαι δὴ ἐκ ταύτης τῆς ἀπορίας ὅτι καὶ ἀνευρήσει ζητῶν μετ' ἐμοῦ, οὐδὲν ἀλλ' ἢ ἐρωτῶντος ἐμοῦ καὶ οὐ διδάσκοντος· φύλαττε δὲ ἄν που εὕρῃς με διδάσκοντα καὶ διεξιόντα αὐτῷ, ἀλλὰ μὴ τὰς τούτου δόξας ἀνερωτῶντα."

3.2 Natural and Transcendental Questions

> [With] the question about the transcendental possibility of knowledge....Is pre-given nature not a problem? We put it in question....The radical criticism of all presuppositions of natural cognition. To "put them into question" altogether, and thus the whole natural knowledge at all (which is not the same as to put into doubt)....[26]

Husserl's transcendental project appears with his continued attempt to answer the transcendental question about the possibility of cognition at all. The extension of the problematic back to his early lectures does not work against but rather only qualifies the widely accepted position that Husserl's so called "transcendental turn" occurred in work between 1905 and 1907. During this time, he explicates those operations essential to transcendental phenomenology, namely, the *ἐποχή* and the *phenomenological reduction*.[27] In the following three subsections, I elucidate the path of the question, the appearance and operation of inquiry in the early formulations of transcendental phenomenological method:

A. first, I sketch further of how Husserl understands classical *metaphysics* in relation to his distinction between *natural* from *transcendental* inquiry;
B. second, I turn to the *method* of transcendental philosophy, distinguishing the method of *critical transcendental-phenomenological inquiry* from Cartesian *universal doubt*;
C. third subsection, I trace the *pairing of inquiry and intuition* as they proceed *under an ἐποχή that suspends all positing*, as inquiry proceeds with a *phenomenological reduction* and *eidetic reduction*.

Through these, I clarify Husserl's *progressive-intuitive procedure* within a *Cartesian approach*.[28] This approach is progressive insofar as it proceeds to the egoic sphere, intuiting the pure ego as "absolute." Indeed, this way of transcendental inquiry tends toward *intuiting the transcendental ego as the source of acts*, allowing the world to fall away. Although he later emends the shortcomings of this approach, especially with the regressive-inquisitive method, it is a breakthrough in his understanding of the reordering of *first* and *second philosophy*. For, with the Cartesian approach, transcendental phenomenology becomes taken as first philosophy.[29] To say more about how that is so, let us return to his understanding of metaphysics.

---

[26] Hua Mat VII, pp. 3–4 fn. 1: "Frage nach der transzendentalen Möglichkeit der Erkenntnis....Ist die Vorgegebenheit der Natur kein Problem? Wir stellen sie in Frage....Radikale Kritik aller Vorgegebenheiten der natürlichen Erkenntnis. Sie insgesamt, und damit die ganze natürliche Erkenntnis überhaupt "in Frage stellen" (nicht dasselbe wie bezweifeln)....".

[27] For an in-depth account of some of these conversations (especially with the Neo-Kantian school), see Staiti (2014).

[28] Again, I follow Steinbock's formulation here.

[29] See Luft's "Introduction to the Translation" in Husserl (2019), pp. xlii–xliii.

3.2.1 Metaphysics: The Transcendental Question and a Demand for Absolute Cognition

As we have already glimpsed, Husserl recognizes that, from the transcendental question raised in antiquity, there emerges the science of metaphysics. In Aristotle's formulation, this is a "theory with insightful knowledge of being as being."[30] As Husserl puts it, this asks and answers the questions, "What is the absolute? What is actuality in the ultimate sense?"[31] Metaphysics, in its original sense, is thus a continuation of a natural orientation toward *actuality*, though now taken up in an *absolute* sense.

Once again, the early orientation to actuality is, for Husserl, understandable. It is, he says, that which "stands before one as a given fact" in everyday living, for "natural knowing" takes it for granted, in other words, as a sort of *doxa*.[32] It make sense, once again, that ancient philosophy appears with "natural" philosophers—the *physicists*—trying to find basic elements of nature, of φύσις in the sense of "actual nature," presupposed as "being there" for investigation. Although they break from practical living to a significant degree, they do not seem to question this in relation to their own pursuit. Even with their novel investigations of "causes," which mean to go to the "roots of all things" or πάντων ῥιζώματα, their questions are about, not so much to the belief in the being of nature *per se*, but about the fundamental elements of its composition. If Plato, in contrast, sets the task of insightful understanding, differentiating practice from theory, Aristotle, as we said, establishes a science of "insightful knowledge of being as being"—*metaphysics*.

Husserl is aware, of course, that the name of Aristotle's work, *Metaphysics*, not unlike "Organon," comes from later catalogs.[33] In this context, it most probably meant that it sequentially "came after the physics," μετὰ τὰ φυσικά. But it is also suggestive, as he also points out, that it goes beyond, in a certain sense, *physics*. In this respect, Aristotle breaks from earlier, naturalistic conceptions of being: he seeks to understand being *as* being. He investigates being as *absolute*—in the sense of "set

---

[30] See Aristotle, *Metaphysics*, 1003a21, "ἔστιν ἐπιστήμη τις ἣ θεωρεῖ τὸ ὂν ᾗ ὂν καὶ τὰ τούτῳ ὑπάρχοντα καθ' αὑτό." See Hua IV, pp. 95–96, quoted at length in a footnote below.

[31] Hua XXXVI, pp. 22: "The metaphysician asks: What is the Absolute? He asks about "actuality in the ultimate sense." He seeks certain "interpretations of empirical actuality." What are his motives? Natural comprehension takes the actuality of experience as an ultimate. But now one becomes attentive to the difficulties of the relation between experiential actuality and cognition."

[32] See Hua Mat III, 81. Consider also, Hua Mat VII, p. 4 fn 1, from 1909: "Knowledge of Nature. Boundaries of the natural spiritual bearing. The question about the transcendental possibility of cognition....Natural cognition does not begin with setting as problematic whether there is an actuality at all, in order to decide only then, but it begins with the thesis of actuality. What is that which is already law? What is its nature? Is that here? Is that actual? Also in natural science: the actuality of nature is a given: a unique spatio-temporal world, which is assumed by all (also presupposed) cognizers as the one and same, even if it is to be determined only after its being. To orientate oneself scientifically in it, to master it cognitively, that is the task. Is the pre-givenness of nature not a problem? We put it in question."

[33] See Hua Mat III, pp. 233–234.

away from" other conditions (as a analysis of the Latin, *ab-se-luo*, suggests)—and so to be understood *in itself*. As such, in this "first philosophy," Aristotle treats that which is common to all sciences without determining that which is being investigated in specific, or "second" sciences. Metaphysics unifies other sciences by *critically* understanding that which they all study "in general," namely, *real* or *actual being*.[34]

So, though Aristotle goes beyond earlier natural philosophers, his first philosophy retains something of the impulse of his predecessors. There is an attempt to understand actuality. In fact, metaphysics deals, as Luft summarizes, repeating Husserl's point, "[W]ith the first causes (αἴτιαι) and the principles (ἀρχαί) of things."[35] To that end, Aristotle differentiates the four causes in his *Physics*—which, we hardly need to note, is the science of φύσις, of actual nature—namely, material, efficient, formal, and final. In his analysis of movement and change over time, each being has a particular relation to its ultimate final cause, its ultimate principle in the actual divine prime mover.[36] The latter's act is understood as the cause of being, which becomes known, *mutatis mutandis*, as the *causa essendi*. So, the original designation of "metaphysics" as *first philosophy* is instructive insofar as it points to this priority of *actual being*.[37]

Husserl understands such a metaphysical approach as "objectivistic." That is not to say that he understands it to divorce the subject from the object nor that he understands its positions simply as false. Not at all. Rather, it is that he understands how they take the *objective* pole of the correlation of *subject-object* relation as taking priority or, indeed, as *critically* naïve of the correlation at all. The result is that, in a certain sense, Aristotle's first philosophy presupposes second philosophy: this is true in the way metaphysics emerges historically from the second philosophies, but also insofar as second philosophies, as sciences of nature (the *Naturwissenschaften*) proceed, in a manner likewise to their foundation in antiquity, namely, without a critical, theoretical foundation of their own knowing.[38] Of great import, for understanding the theme at hand, is the fact that a belief in being is left unquestioned. In other words, the actual "What" of the investigation—actual, real being—takes priority over the critique of the "How" of its coming to be known.[39] Notice, for example, that Aristotle begins

---

[34] See Hua XXIV, pp. 99; also, Hua Mat II, p. 11.

[35] Hua Mat II, p. 11, quoting Aristotle, *Metaphysics*, 981b28.

[36] Husserl is, of course, aware of this comprehension. See, for example, the remark at Hua XXIV, p. 115 ff.

[37] See Hua XXVIII, pp. 181–82.

[38] Mat Hua IV, pp. 95–96: "The empirical sciences are not creations of a purely theoretical mind: built on an absolutely critical basis in strictly logical methodology. Emerging from the pre-scientific conception and wisdom, even the most highly developed, most exact natural sciences carried with them uncritical concepts and presuppositions originating from that pre-scientific conception of the world."

[39] The issue may be put, in intentional terms, between focus upon the achievement on the noematic side and the achieving on the noetic side. Consider Hua Mat IX, pp. 100–01: "This is, I say, quite conceivable, because whoever considers the possibility of an achievement at all and, for instance, in a general way the possibility of a certain kind of achievement, has not directed his gaze to his psychic interiority of achieving, to his representations, evaluations, willings, but to the typical forms of the

the *Metaphysics* itself with the claim, "All humans, by nature, desire to know."[40] He recognizes human, rational nature in relation to its *absolute objective*, namely, being. The question, for him, "What is the absolute?" means "What is the objective of the actual desire to know?" This objectivistic starting point thus takes for granted the natural world as "the sum total of objects of possible experience and experiential knowledge...."[41]

In contrast, through transcendental phenomenological inquiry, the world appears as *horizon*.[42] The metaphor as horizon that emerges in this period is apt, as it brings to mind the range *in* which and *from* which matters appear, rather than the sum of objects. Indeed, in order to bring the world to question, Husserl "switch off nature," attending directly to the *riddle of transcendence*.[43] With this, questions about nature are distinguished from questions of how nature is known at all—that is, *natural* from *transcendental* questions.[44] In doing so, though, *Erkenntniskritik* is taken as "first philosophy" and metaphysics as the investigation of facticity, actual being, becomes "second." As Husserl knows, this echoes that Cartesian impulse that puts a sort of

---

goal and of the way, to the possibilities of the particular forms of goals to be set and of the means appropriate for them. So, the view is directed noematically, to the *what* of the achievement....In noetic respect the classification of the cognitive processes in the psychology of man disturbed, while a purely noetic science doctrine is able to assert itself only on a higher stage of development of philosophy."

[40] I discuss the issue of the critiques of the subjective and objective poles further in the next chapter, as Husserl directly addresses it in terms of socio-historical development, for example at Hua Mat. IX, pp. 7–8: "So much does the pure love of knowledge take possession of the Greek mankind that already Aristotle begins his immortal metaphysics with the famous words, which he puts down as self-evident: 'All men strive by nature for knowledge.' The purely theoretical activity, the pure striving for knowledge is here already considered as the original endowment of man, as belonging to the specific of human nature. This is correct in the Aristotelian sense of entelechy, but not in the ordinary, real sense. For in truth man, like the animal, is originally completely filled with practical interests, interests of usefulness, of self-demands and communal demands, and it was a new thing, the beginning of a new epoch of mankind, since the theoretical interest awoke and became independent, at first in individual, excellent personalities, to the dominant one." Here, Husserl understands Aristotle as speakign to the striving to know as "pure" or a priori. This seems to puts Aristotle nearer to his own understanding, where the phrase "by *nature*" shifts to an answer to the transcendental question, is a condition for the possibility for knowing at all. Nevertheless, Aristotle still does not give a critique of this striving to know in transcendentally purified terms.

[41] Husserl (1983), §1.

[42] Husserl (1983), §27.

[43] Hua Mat, VII, pp. 77: "We switched off nature, the own I as well as the foreign I, and we switched them off for the sake of the riddle of transcendence. But don't we have to be consistent and pursue this riddle everywhere in all its analogous forms? Is it of any use to question so called nature according to its existence and to leave equal questionings untouched? Never and nowhere nature is absolutely given...." There is a similar sentiment at Hua Mat VII, p. 97: "If cognition is the riddle, if it becomes the problem, then there is no other way than to study it itself..."

[44] Husserl says, at Hua Mat VII, p. 97: "The questions posed to nature and also to nature in general are to be separated from the questions posed to the possibility of cognition of nature; and again, to be separated from the representational questions of the possibility of a nature are the meaning-theoretical questions, questions *posed* and to be posed to the propositions and propositional contexts as the meaning content of scientific theories, and the corresponding cognitive questions, the questions about the relation between cognition and meaning."

3.2 Natural and Transcendental Questions   53

priority upon cognitional critique. So, he spends considerable time distinguishing his method from that of Descartes.

That Descartes seeks to find an indubitable or "unquestionable" foundation for science is well-known. That certain foundation would allow for a building up of scientific knowledge impervious to skeptical erosion. According to Husserl, however, Descartes does not *merely* doubt, but also puts to question, at least at first.[45] Nevertheless, the phenomenologist must resist confusion of the two operations, in order to avoid falling back into objectivist which stands upon a naïve belief in the being of the world. Hence, Husserl emphasizes the role of inquiry in phenomenology: "What he [Descartes] doubts, we put into question."[46] Let me turn to the significance of this difference now.

3.2.2 Doubt Compared to Inquiry

Husserl says, in the context of presenting his new transcendental-phenomenological method, "To put into question, properly understood, in no way means the same as to doubt."[47] In short, this is because there is a difference between bringing a matter into question in order to determine it and doubting a matter in the sense of modalizing belief, that is, taking it as possibly being "otherwise" without seeking to determine it. Likewise, transcendental inquiry, unlike methodical universal doubt, brings matters to critical awareness without either presupposing or participating in them through modalization. Allow me some clarificatory remarks.

To begin, the Cartesian approach seeks an "indubitable" or "unquestionable" foundation. There is an ambiguity in these words, however. For example, "unquestionable" can be taken to mean an essential *impossibility for being called into question* or it can be taken to mean a matter is *insightfully known*, that is, wherein the validity is patent, without further question, and so "without a doubt," as it were. The former is,

---

[45] Hua Mat VII, pp. 43-44: "The reflection we have begun there will have long reminded you of the first and second *Meditations* of Descartes. In fact, he was the first to put the demand of absolute knowledge at the peak of philosophy and to try to satisfy it. Unfortunately, it remained without perfect satisfaction in his *modus procedendi*. For while he eliminated all pre-givens by putting them in question, he very soon operated again with pre-givennesses himself and finally missed the right sense of his original intentions, which had not become completely clear to him."

[46] Hua Mat VII, p. 47: "Descartes stands on the ground of skepticism. He doubts being-in-itself, and he does not allow the possibility of a knowledge of being-in-itself. For our part, we do not do that, not seriously. What he seriously doubts, we put in question, and if we think ourselves into the situation of skepticism and highlight what we ourselves as skeptics could not doubt, then we actually only highlight what is not in question or what is not affected by the putting in question, because the reasonable possibility of inquiring already presupposes it."

[47] Hua Mat VII, p. 43: "So, if we want to subject the operation with pregivennesses in natural cognition to a radical critique, we must try to question them altogether, and although putting into question, rightly understood, does not at all mean the same thing as doubting, we can at first quite well follow the method of trying it with universal doubt."

in certain manner, a countersense: such a position works against the law of any thinkable judgments as true or false or, as Husserl succinctly puts it later, *"each possible judgment is thinkable as a content of a question."*[48] I could, for example, transpose the judgment, "This is unquestionable" to "Is this questionable?" or, more, "How do you know it as unquestionable?" Of course, this transposition may be done merely formally and not as an actual, authentic question. In any case, that some matter is, in fact, insightfully known as self-evident does not make it *unquestionable*, strictly speaking. Indeed, there are essentially no restrictions on that which is questionable.[49] In fact, one can ask a question about something known as well as something not yet known, Moreover, one may also put a position into question in order to determine it critically. This critical inquiry does not mean, forthwith, "abandoning" a position, believing it to be "otherwise," or even negating it.[50] In this respect, critical inquiry may instead *raise a matter to an awareness wherein further insightful judgment is sought about the matter*.

Doubting, on the other hand, is more restricted in scope. As a modalization in belief, it does not, by itself, seek determinative fulfillment: it neither aims to affirm nor to negate that which is placed in doubt, but rather takes it as possibly being "otherwise."[51] To be sure, it "opens" dimensions of experience, inasmuch as it brings some matter to a specific, thematic awareness. When I doubt, for example, that it is a classmate in the hallway, I do not yet *ask if* it is or not; rather, I take up the doubtful, constitute it as that which is "in doubt." Although I could take this doubt and bring it to question, that is, try to determine that which is doubtful to be this way and not that way, try to determine the disjunction, "either it *is or* it *is not*," the doubt itself does not seek this determination. Rather, *doubt puts that which is thematic into the mode of possibly being otherwise*. So, to a more foundational point, for Descartes, I cannot doubt the "I" as it is doubting without being involved in the following counter-sense: *I* cannot doubt that *I* am doubting, since I would need to take up an "otherwise" directly related to the belief in its being.[52] *Nevertheless*, I can *question* both my doubting and inquiring, and I can do so without any counter-sense.

---

[48] Emphasis my own. See Hua XI, p. 60: "Jedes mögliche Urteil ist denkbar als Inhalt einer Frage."

[49] This does not mean that there are no other restrictions, however contingent or accidental, as one may experience in the horizons of the material, intellectual, mental, psychological, and so on.

[50] Hua Mat VII, p. 37: "To put to question manifestly does not mean as much as to negate or to doubt also with respect to the validity. Rather, according to the literal sense, it want it to be said that we want to put into question all natural cognition, all natural science, yes, to all science in general; we want to make them objects of research, namely, in the direction that interests us here: We want to bring to the final clarity the essence of the cognition that is active in them, the possibility of the cognitive achievements that are carried out in them, the final sense of the cognized objectivity that is to be brought out through relation to the cognition, and what still more inquiry like that."

[51] See for example, Hua III/1, §31.

[52] Hua Mat VII, p. 43: "I can put it in question, I can try to doubt it, but immediately it is completely clear, the question, whether it is, is, as posed, so already answered, and absolutely answered. On the being of the seen of the reflection as an absolute given, all doubt cancels itself, every attempt of the settlement, 'it is not,' <cancels itself.> The being of the *cogitationes* is absolute and in the reflection absolutely given."

3.2 Natural and Transcendental Questions

So, to reiterate, inquiry may arise from or alongside doubt, seeking to determine that which appears as doubtful, *but it need not*. Inquiry is free to ask both *within a doubt* and, as it were, *without a doubt*. Husserl thus sometimes uses the phrase "pure question," for a question without a relation to another modalization like a doubt or a wish, since it is "unmixed" with other intentional qualities.[53] A significant result of this analysis is that he finds how it is possible to put the spheres of immanence and transcendence into question, without counter-sensically doubting their being.[54] This is the crux of the present issue. Let us consider it, first with the Cartesian *modus procedendi*, as Husserl finds it.

Once again, Descartes, as Husserl recognizes, seeks a foundation for the building up of all knowledge.[55] Taking up the ancient transcendental question, he seeks absolute cognition, but he does so by turning inward *to* and *for himself*. Without rehearsing here the step-by-step process of his universal doubt, let me bring to the fore how he falls back into the *actual* conditions that ground this universal doubt. According to Husserl, he takes the sphere of immanence as "real immanence" and, without putting *that* into question, imagines it as over against "real transcendence." In other words, he does not critically inquire into intentionality as it is *given* but instead posits opposed substances—"things," in his dualist position of the *res cogitans et res extensa*. From a failure to question their relation, there comes an imagined split between the thinking and extended things.

For Husserl, in contrast, phenomenology asks about the *questionability* of cognition. So, even if he allows Cartesian doubt as a guide for opening a sphere of questionability, he does not mean to leave the *how* of the opening unquestioned.[56] In this respect, Husserl recognizes that there is given some belief, some horizon on which to begin and to which to put questions.[57] But one need not participate in it naively,

---

[53] For a discussion about this within the context of wishing, which we discuss in later chapters, see, Hua XXVIII, pp. 118–120: "And above all, we do not need to draw the wish (however great the temptation is) into the concept of the question (though this usually happens). Doubt and the wish for certainty regarding one of the disjunctive possibilities do not raise a question of whether A or B. There is a peculiar intentional tendency which we must separate and call the peculiar essence of the question. Therewith alone constitutes for the consciousness the questionable as such, which we must regard as a modalization of simple being, as well as questioning as a modalization of belief. If the peculiarity of the question is given, then further acts can intertwine-with it, and so we grasp, for example, the wish-question is already a complication compared to the pure question."

[54] Importantly, later, Husserl directly references the fact that the being of the doubting and inquiring is not doubted—however, *we* recognize herein that it is to be put into *question*. See Hua Mat, VII, p. 43.

[55] See again, Hua Mat VII, pp. 42–43. This way of speaking recurs in the later lectures on Descartes, from the 1920's, for example, at Hua I, pp. 6–9.

[56] Witold Plotka, in his work, indicates the presence of inquiry in transcendental phenomenology, in this respect. However, he does not explicate its operation, and so misses the distinctions of procedures and approaches. See Plotka (2012).

[57] Hua II, p. 33: "What a science calls into question cannot be used as a predetermined foundation. However, since the critique of knowledge places the possibility of knowledge in general, and that is as a problem in terms of its ability, all knowledge is called into question. If it begins, no knowledge can be considered given.... It must therefore not take anything from any pre-scientific sphere of knowledge, every knowledge bears the index of questionability. / Without a given knowledge as a

without bringing it to question. So, Husserl *does not* mean to search out absolutely certain foundations in the manner of Descartes.[58] He means instead to bring foundations to question, to purify them from presuppositions, in order to understand their source. Taken in this respect, one can better understand the formulation of his *principle of principles*, namely, that "*that every originary giving intuition is a legitimizing source of cognition, that everything originarily* (so to speak, in its "personal" actuality) *offered to us in "intuition" is to be accepted simply as what it is given*, but also *only within the limits in which it is given there.*"[59] The science of phenomenology seeks foundations upon originary sources: bringing these sources to critical awareness and, indeed, essential self-awareness, is not a matter of doubting them but rather raising them into a question to find the font of questions.

Still, in the Cartesian approach, Husserl does tend to understand the "pure ego" as *indubitable*, as Steinbock shows.[60] I find that this is exacerbated as the intuition of the ego becomes emphasized over the operation of inquiry.[61] To elucidate this lapse as well as to show its corrective, I turn to a review of *how* transcendental-phenomenology *puts into question* via an ἐποχή, under which further operation of inquiry proceeds, paying special attention to where this inquiry gives way to intuition.

---

beginning, there is no knowledge as progress. So criticism of knowledge cannot begin at all. There can be no such science at all."

[58] Hua Mat II, p. 90: "Unlike Descartes, we do not seek absolutely secure foundations on which we could build the overall edifice of human knowledge according to absolutely secure principles, by which this knowledge itself should gain the character of absolute certainty in all its parts….. But like Descartes, we first put in question everything, we allow nothing to be valid from the outset—not God and world and I—not the convictions on which our possibility of practical living is based, not the highest and strictest sciences, we allow, I say, nothing to be valid, because for the time being we do not even know what is valid and what is in the sense of some assertion and alleged knowledge."

[59] Hua III/1, p. 51.

[60] Thus, the above quote continues: "Now, following Descartes, we first of all make clear to ourselves that even if we stretch our doubt so far, one thing is nevertheless indubitable and cannot be impacted by doubt, that even if we want to put in question everything, one thing is out of the question, unquestionable…." The move to that which is "unquestionable" here seems to follow more closely the first sense sketched above, namely, the sense that it is grasped sufficiently, without demand for further question. As Steinbock elucidates, this is evidence of the *static* approach –the limits of which Husserl will overcome later.

[61] Consider the following from Hua Mat VII, pp. 78–79: "Before all such questions and problems, doubts, there is first of all only one position: What is questionable for us, in our direction of thinking here, we must treat as questionable and only hold on to what is the basis of our questioning and considering as meaningful questioning. So, we must not give away the Cartesian evidence, but on the other hand we must understand it correctly, grasp it correctly and limit it; but not limit it too narrowly. It appeals to the absolute self-givenness of doubting in doubting, of perceiving in perceiving, and so on. Thereby it reminds us of the principally non-problematic and designates in advance the field in which problem solving must take place."

3.2.3 Inquiry in the Intuitive Method of Transcendental Phenomenology

Now with Descartes as a methodological guide, Husserl presses the question of the possibility of knowledge at all. The danger—one to which Descartes fell and to which Husserl means to overcome—is taking for granted being. Upon closer examination, Husserl distinguishes between a real immanence, which is still questionable, and the self-given, "unquestionable" givenness of the pure ego. But what is the status of this "unquestionability"—and is it confused with the Cartesian standard of *indubitability*? The answer is not so easily won. To show how so, let me fill out, in terms of inquiry, Husserl's early formulation of the intuitive phenomenological procedure.[62]

In order to put cognition into question, Husserl formulates the notion of an ἐποχή.[63] The Greek, ἐποχή, is fitting of Husserl's sense. It is a compound of ἐπι-ἔχω, means to with-hold, to hold-back or to suspend. In the history of philosophy, it is present most

---

[62] The following is an outline of four moments in the first stage of phenomenological reflection, following Husserl's sketch at Hua II, pp. 4–7:

- "(1) In the first moment one becomes questionable whether such a science is possible at all. If it puts all cognition into question, how can it begin, since every cognition chosen as an exit is also put into question as cognition?...."
- Then, the question: "(2)...What makes these cases unquestionable and other cases of pretended cognition questionable? Why in certain cases the inclination to skepticism and the question of doubt how can a being be met in cognition, and why, in the *cogitations*, not this doubt and this difficulty?".
- From this, there comes the question about how cognition gets beyond itself. However, this question "falls away" [*fällt bei*], if the question about real immanence is resisted in preference for the transcendental question. And so, Husserl continues: "(3) at first, one is inclined and takes this for granted to interpret immanence as real immanence and probably even psychologically as *real immanence*," but it is the transcendental sphere which is taken as indubitable.
- So: "(4)...to bring cognition to evident self-givenness and to see in it the essence of its achievement, that is not to deduce, induce, calculate, and so on, it is not to derive new things with reason from things already given or taken as given." We thus ask again about transcendence in immanence.
- "From all this, the phenomenologist begins to "win back" the world by understanding achievements of cognition, understanding the how of transcendence from understanding the immanent operations."

[63] Consider Hus Mat. VII, p. 18 fn.1: "Now, we have to ask, what about this presupposition of natural cognition? Is it not a problem? Can we not ask about its right? It does not matter to be really skeptical and to seriously doubt whether we are actually there and our environment is actual, whether a nature encompassing us is actually, which we treat everywhere as a given, therefore never considered fact. It may be a fact, but that does not prevent the possibility of asking the question whether it finally stands up to criticism, or of asking the question whether and how it requires justified justification, and thus also what then, if the whole of nature and all naive givenness is called into question at all, remains as an undoubted given, whether and how a cognition can be established that is absolute cognition, namely free from all givenness assumed on credit, so to speak." Also, Hua II, p. 19: "Cognition is a fact of nature, it is experience of any cognizing organic beings, it is a psychological fact."

notably in the ancient Skeptics, who included the withholding of position taking as the desired *outcome* of their investigations, their seeking or their "inquiry," (ζητέειν).[64] For them, as we have already seen, such suspension of position taking was a key moment in their effort to achieve a state of ἀταραξία. As Sextus Empricus summarizes in "Chapter III" of his *Outlines of Pyrrhonism*, "The ἐποχή is a state of mental rest owing to which we neither deny nor affirm anything," which means "…an untroubled and tranquil condition of soul."[65] Note that, for the skeptic, a seeking of a determinate end in an answer is to be suspended, as it implies a *zeal* for judgment that was at root "troubling," since no knowledge seems to be certain.[66] Transposing such positions into questions, which are not declarative, is the method for showing that to be so. For Husserl, in contrast, the suspension is a *new beginning of inquiry* that seeks answers.

Indeed, Husserl's ἐποχή does not lead to mere skepticism. It is not a matter of doubting the possibility of knowing, not taking it *as-if* it were impossible or, for that matter, even as-if it were possible.[67] No, for him, the ἐποχή puts the presupposition of the *being* and *possible being* into question.[68] Thus, like the presuppositionless of the *Logical Investigations*, the ἐποχή calls into question previously won knowledge, including customs or learned positions. From this, the inquiry of the phenomenologist may seek *how* cognition occurs. In other words, the phenomenologist "puts in question" *any* position taking and *all* possible positing of being as they proceed under the ἐποχή.[69] Such inquiry is no longer directed to the *what* and *that* of transcendence but rather to the *how*.

---

[64] Husserl notes, in Ms. B IV 9/3a-b, that, for Sextus, the effort is to show that "…die gedachten Sachen sind aber nicht seiende…" ["… but matters of thought are not beings…"] In other words, such skepticism tried to show that thinking and being did not meet, that there was no identity between the two, and so that the seeking could be detached from seeking being without being disturbed by something immanent to it. To repeat, this is not the case for Husserl.

[65] Sextus Empiricus, *Outlines of Pyrrhonism*.

[66] "Zeal" itself has its roots in ζητέειν. Thus, for the skeptic, being *zealous* indicates a sort of rivalry that is disruptive of tranquility.

[67] In line with what he says at Hua II, p. 43 and, later, at Hua VII, p. 50, Husserl notes that the givenness of the being of the *cogito* is unquestionable, though, we note, *with respect to its own being*: "The being of the *cogitatio* is absolute given: That against skepticism. But for us it comes into consideration that it is unquestionable being given, namely not afflicted with the riddle of transcendence. Basically, the unquestionability of the *cogitatio* with respect to its own being given was already anticipated in the formulation of the riddle. Whoever asks: 'How is it to be understood that cognition should grasp something transcendent to it?,' or even, whoever asks: 'How should cognition reach beyond consciousness?,' is likely thinking: 'If cognition would merely look at what is given to consciousness, then there would be no occasion for a question.'"

[68] The operation keeps *in question* that which is problematic in order to bring to a "first" cognition. See Hua II, p. 31: "The ἐποχή, which the critique of cognition must practice, cannot have the sense that it not only begins with it, but also remains with it, to question every cognition, thus also its own, and not to allow any given fact to be valid, thus also not that which it itself establishes…." Husserl will even say that all that is objective being, all of that which is questionable is bracketed, see Hua XXIII, p. 201: "All being of objective, 'bracketed,' that is, I have put it out of all question, every terminating statement, every 'decision' 'once and for all.'"

[69] Consider Hua II, p. 29: "The ἐποχή, which the critique of cognition must exercise, cannot have the sense that it not only begins with it, but also remains with it, to question every cognition, that is, also its own, and not to allow any given to be valid, that is also not that which it itself establishes." Also

3.2 Natural and Transcendental Questions

So, the phenomenological suspension of position-taking puts in question the world as the "universal situation for questions," putting it "out of play," as Husserl says later.[70] By his "out of play," I mean that the phenomenologist does not allow any position-taking to support or give a ground for further inquiry. Still, the world is not *annihilated* by the phenomenological suspension. Once more, transcendental-phenomenology brings this *doxa*, the belief in the being of the world to question in order to bring it to awareness and to understand it. Upon bracketing the world and attending to the sphere of immanence, the phenomenologist discovers the *general thesis of the natural attitude*: a general "belief" in the world, what Husserl calls a "primal form" (*Urform*) of *unmodalized being* of the world as "there."[71] The thesis is that the world *is*, rather than "may be" or "may not be," as any knowing activity, any *cogitans*, naturally operates. This horizon is *pre*-given, that is, already posited beforehand, as a *presupposition*. By putting this into question, transcendental inquiry operates within "pure" consciousness.[72]

---

consider a similar passage, from Hua XXV, §31, p. 182: "…Necessity of the radical questioning on phenomenological ground to avoid mistaken questions….That all these are mistaken questions is already excluded by the radical way in which I carried out the consideration before (a radicalism to which, however, only the breakthrough <of> phenomenology educated me)…..What astonishes me there, this wondrous involvement of every 'being' in consciousness, and what is and can be questionable in it, that concerned: the all-nature and the all of transcendences of every sense. Either I have transcendental questions, then I must not treat as transcendentally unquestionable anything that is transcendentally questionable; or I have no transcendental questions at all. But it lies in the sense of such questions to affix the index of this questionability to every transcendental being, that is, to accept none as transcendentally given. But the transcendental givenness is present in any case wherever we place ourselves on the ground of a naturally naive cognition, instead of making it the subject of a transcendental questionable one. If I go more deeply, I recognize that the transcendental questioning lies in principle in a totally different dimension than every natural, every transcendentally directed inquiry."

[70] Hua XXXIV, p. 249: "In this respect, the phenomenological ἐποχή has the effect to put this kind of 'occasional' judgment and thus all world-judgments 'out of' play or to deny me this basic validity, offering as ground of being for judgments to be formed. But with this, the being of the world for me, just the me- (and in further consequence us-) -as-being-being is not cancelled. The ἐποχή only means: the world only does not serve in phenomenology as universal situation for inquiry, and with it all special situations and special situation judgments are left out of play."

[71] Hua III/1, p. 240. For Husserl, it is necessary that a *foundation* of science is not *questionable*, since there cannot be a sense of "progress" without a beginning point that is unquestionable. We will need to question this further in the next chapters. For the position, see Hua II, p. 33: "What a science questions, it cannot use as a given foundation. However, since the critique of cognition sets the possibility of cognition as a problem, all cognition is questioned. If it starts, then no cognition can be considered as given. Thus, it may not take over anything from any pre-scientific sphere of cognition; every cognition carries the index of questionability. Without a given cognition as beginning, there is also no cognition as progress. Therefore, critique of cognition cannot begin at all. Such a science cannot exist at all"; to do so, as he says at Hua Mat VII, p. 22: "We gain this level precisely by freeing ourselves from all presuppositions of natural cognition, putting into question all its presuppositions, leaving them entirely *in suspenso*."

[72] Again, see Hua XXV, pp. 160 and 182 (§21): " <Pure consciousness as the sought area of origin of the transcendental questions> In the natural attitude, nature is constantly there for us, and any particular natural objects are given and set in it, originally given by natural perceptions. This is the

So, phenomenology yields an attitude that is "purified" of positing. From this attitude, it is possible to attend to that which appears as it appears. However, though the ἐποχή puts in question positing and opens the phenomenologist to givenness, this newly opened sphere, by it itself, Husserl finds, is one of flux. In other words, there is a demand for a further methodological step necessary to bring the appearances to attention and to determination. There is a need, in short, to *reduce* or "to go back" to how matters appear herein via a *phenomenological reduction*.[73]

I differentiate between a *general* and *strict* use of the phrase "phenomenological reduction" in Husserl's work. In a general sense, this reduction operates under the overarching inquiry initiated by the phenomenologist. On the other hand, it may be understood, in a strict sense, as further determining the general inquiry by attending to *this* matter in relation to *this* or *that* one, and so on, while remaining open to however matters are given.[74] Now, Husserl also finds "*no need to assign any motives* as to why phenomenology disengages the positing of experience," because, under the phenomenological suspension, the "only question…is whether there is something to research, whether there remains space for a science."[75] Matters are given, and are given under the phenomenological interest.[76] As such, phenomenological inquiry seeks only to grasp essential relations in the data of consciousness. However, to determine these essential relations, a further reduction is necessary, namely, an *eidetic reduction*. For, if the phenomenological reduction provides phenomena to which the phenomenologist might attend, it does not straightaway yield necessary or universal structures and relations of the phenomena. To clarify, it is helpful to draw an analogy from natural cognition.

In *natural cognition*, ideation may be first distinguished from a sort of empirical induction. By this is meant a repetition of empirical intuition that may constitute an empirically generalized type. One may encounter a tree, indeed, walk-by it each

---

attitude in which the pure consciousness and subject of consciousness is 'hidden.'" And, I suggest, following Husserl, transcendental inquiry *mediates* this "hidden" dimension, bringing to awareness.

[73] See, for example, Hua II, pp. 29, 23, 43, and 45.

[74] Thus in the later work of the *Cartesian Meditations*, Husserl will all but equate the ἐποχή and the reduction, while calling the former a "universal condition under which to pursue constitutional research"; see Husserl (1960), pp. 22, 149, and especially 83: "Manifestly the conscious execution of phenomenological reduction is needed, in order to attain that Ego and conscious life by which transcendental questions, as questions about the possibility of transcendent knowledge, can be asked." See also, from Husserl (2019), p. 57: "I perform the phenomenological reduction; the existence of the events, like all of nature, is put into brackets. And just as the existence of what is perceived is put into brackets, so are the recollected natural events. What is the result of this for the phenomenological data?" He goes on to note different types of data that appears, to be determined by the phenomenologist. The differentiation of these comes clear, for example, in Husserl (2006), pp. 318–322 and 331. Later, he speaks of a many sorts of suspensions, including of traditions and beliefs (see, for example Hua XXIX, 374–380).

[75] Husserl (2006), p. 50.

[76] Again, the motivation for phenomenology itself, I find, with Husserl, must be understood in an historical-teleological inquiry. The "Why" of phenomenology emerges in the exigence of the questioning spirit, unfolding in history. Thus, we find, in subsequent chapters, that the phenomenological *philosopher* does take up into his life that which is discovered in *phenomenology*.

morning; this accumulation of experiences of the individual "this" gives the possibility to distinguish another tree *as* another, similar tree, that is, as a tree of the same type. Of course, this occurs *within the limits* of that type, of "What" it is, as it has been constituted, for example, having the same leaves, fruit, and so on; also, the more often, the more probable the judgment and clearer the type becomes. Nevertheless, this is to be distinguished from an *ideation* that is the grasping of *what* is necessary for that to be a tree of that type: the latter is not merely empirical, as Husserl stresses, but is presentive of a novel object of cognition.[77]

For such a grasp, ideation goes back—again, *reduces*—to the *a priori* structures universal to each of that species. This is so on account of the complex ideative activity that "transmutes" (*umgewandelt*) the perceptually given to an *eidos*.[78] I return to this complex point below, but let me note here only that essential to it is the process *of free-phantasy* where a variation of limits of the given that may or may not adequately yield the essence in or the essential seeing (*Wesenschau*). We have, in a way, already an example of *eidetic variation* and *seeing* already in the example of the *Meno*: Socrates varies the image for the boy until he understands that his original answer transgressed the limits of the question, the doubling of the square, even though the square as such remained intact. In this eidetic reduction, there is a *weighing* of evidence. Indeed, the varying itself provides the data to be weighed, as it "plays" with the given figure in a way that puts in tension the givenness: where the square is given, the sides can be imagined otherwise, for example, taken away, extended, and so on. These limits are set in a relation of *what* the square is and *that which is put in question.* That is to say, there is also a sort of setting of relevance to data that is characteristic of inquiry, as the intention directed to the *eidos* itself sets aside, as Husserl notes above, that which is irrelevant, that which does not meet the criteria of "must" having to be given to be *what* it is.

For these reasons, one experience is sufficient for an eidetic intuition, unlike the aforementioned empirical induction. It is possible to grasp the essence of, say, a square with only one experience of a square. The perceptual figure can be varied in imagination such that the necessity of the four-sides and the sum of their angles as three-hundred and sixty is grasped: if I take the square, add one-side, take another away, and it ceases being a square; but I can change the color, expand or contract the angles without changing what it is. The act that grasps this "gets the idea" of that which is necessary and universal to all presentations of squares. And this idea, as I previously noted, is *abstracted* from the perceptual data as what Husserl calls now a "novel object," not yet related back to the *real.* One has the *ideal* as *possibly* or "hypothetically" true of that which is given perceptually; there is a need to relate the ideal back to the real, in order to verify it as really true. I have also already noted how one can only judge an instance *to be what it is* on the basis of grasping *what*

---

[77] Hua III/1, p. 14: "The essence (*eidos*) is a new kind of object. Just as the given of individual or experiential intuition is an individual object, so the given of the essential seeing is a pure being."

[78] Hua III/1, p. 13: "Every such What, however, can be 'put into idea.' Experiential or individual *Anschauung* can be transformed into *essential seeing* (Ideation)—a possibility, which itself is not to be understood as empirical, but as a possibility of being." See also Hua Mat II, p. 254.

it is.⁷⁹ Moreover, ideations and concepts can build upon each other, in as much as one's understanding of what something is can build upon previous understandings and formulations, just as the doubling of the square can build upon knowing what a square is and what it means to be doubled, and so on.⁸⁰ In any event, all this is considered as occurring in the *natural attitude* that naively posits the horizon of being. Transcendental phenomenology, for its part, does not seek the *what* of the real, actual world but rather the essential structures of the *how*, after the suspension of any positing.

Indeed, the operations of transcendental phenomenology are set in an order such that, at the beginning of Husserl's transcendental project, his approach is decidedly and purposively Cartesian. This means that the transcendental question occurs under an ἐποχή of all judgments of the real, of any positing, in order to attend to the immanent sphere of egoic being. The Cartesian variation of the empirical ego shows that it is not able to be doubted, that it is *given* in an "absolute" manner. Indeed, the ego is given along with any variation, at all. As such, in this immanent reflection, the ego is found as that "upon which every question about it must find its immediate answer."⁸¹ Further, through a *phenomenological reduction*, the ego is given to itself in self-presence as immediate such that an *eidetic reduction* of it can provide a "pure" intuition of an ego, that is, an intuitin of the ego as purified from any content whatsoever. Thus, following Steinbock, the Cartesian approach may be identified as "progressive" and "intuitive." Again this is because of its order of procedure: it *progresses from* the factual world *to* the realm of egoic being in which one is given to oneself *immediately* and so, finally, it is possible to raise *self-presence to the level of an eidetic intuition*.

With the progressive-intuitive procedure, Husserl recognizes that the *ego* as the *a priori source* of acts, as a "transcendence in immanence."⁸² So, after grasping the source of acts, he finds, it is possible to "win back" the world. For the pure ego is that which is founding for *being* and, as such, the world appears as *founded* on the *founding* absolute region of egoic being. However, because of this apparent one-sidedness, Husserl will even say that the world can fall away as *relative* to the

---

⁷⁹ There is also a distinction between the grasp of an idea, the formulation of an idea in a concept, and the judgment which relates these, which I do not need to address at present. Consider Hua III/1, p. 33: "All this naturally transfers from the essences to "concepts" as significations."; also, Hua III/1, 48: "Certainly, essences are "concepts"—if, by concepts, one understands, what the ambiguous word allows, just essences. Only make clear that the talk of physical products is then a nonsense, and likewise the talk of concept formation, if it is to be understood as strict and authentic."

⁸⁰ See Hua XXIV, pp. 388–390, and at Beilage XV: "…as the first stage of a thinking consciousness builds itself up directly on simple intuition. An ideating consciousness, however, can also build up on a consciousness which already brings a species to view."

⁸¹ Hua II, pp. 30 and 34. Also see, Hua XXIV, pp. 208 and 213.

⁸² Husserl (1983), §57, especially, p. 133. Elisabeth Ströker notes that this position moves beyond what Husserl calls an "act phenomenology" of the Investigations, insofar as the objective and subjective pole, the noesis and noema, was "largely undifferentiated." For more on these points, see, Ströker (1997), p. 85.

absolute egoic region.[83] In fact, as Steinbock goes to great lengths to show, here the criteria of indubitability in the Cartesian approach "usurps the principle of presuppositionless for [the] maxim of indubitability."[84] For, as the ego is taken as indubitably given in *immediate* self-presence, the phenomenologist also abstracts from its temporal dimensions, as I address further below. At present, let me underscore how it is significant that the intuitive becomes emphasized here over the inquisitive: as the temporal dimension is reintroduced, *inquiry is methodologically necessary for the meditation of becoming aware of the becoming of the subject and the world*. In any case, at the beginning of the transcendental project, this Cartesian presupposition occurs alongside what Husserl identifies later as a *static* method.

In a static method, immanent intuition seems to yield adequate givenness because it limits consciousness to what Steinbock identifies as a "now-phase." Since it abstracts from temporal dimensions, the ego may be given "at once." Husserl later sees this as an artificial limit, restricting the questionability of subjectivity, setting artificial limits on consciousness to become critically aware of itself: as he himself notes, censoring the progressive-intuitive procedure, it "in one leap" the transcendental ego by emptying it of content.[85] Indeed, he will later also confide in Eugen Fink that taking the path to the pure ego in order to found science is a "sheer muddle."[86] Still, this approach also gives important leading clues and his analysis in it itself gives a demand for overcoming its limitations, as can be seen in his treatment of practical inquiry, to which I turn now.

3.3 Natural Inquiry Within the World

> This originality of becoming in the stream of consciousness is quite a peculiar one. The thesis and synthesis comes by the pure I doing the step and every new actual step; the Ego lives itself in the step and "appears" with it. The positing, positing on, positing before, positing after, and so on, is its *free spontaneity and activity*; it does not live in the theses as a passive being therein, but they are radiations from it as an original source of production.[87]

---

[83] Using the language captured by Steinbock (1995), p. 10. Also, Steinbock (1995), p. 14. Such a "winning back" is not so much a rebuilding of all achievements in the world-horizon but rather coming to understand that they all have the same source, namely, in immanently generated knowledge. Later, in the regressive and regressive-inquisitive approach, achievements are in play, and so there is no need to "win them back."

[84] Steinbock (1995), p. 25.

[85] At Hua VI, p. 43. Also, Husserl (1970), p. 155: "…[T]he 'Cartesian way'…has a great shortcoming: while it leads to the transcendental ego in one leap, as it were, it brings this ego into view as apparently empty of content, since there can be no preparatory explication; so one is at a loss, at first, to know what has been gained by it, much less how, starting with this, a completely new sort of fundamental science, decisive for philosophy, has been attained."

[86] See the editor's note at Fink (1988), p. xxxvii, also see p. 155 fn. 111.

[87] Husserl (1983), p. 291 and Hua III/1, p. 281.

From the distinction of natural from transcendental inquiry, Husserl considers the appearance and operation of natural inquiry *in* the world. In the following three subsections, I address some aspects of this, shedding light on its difference from the earlier analysis:

A. I first show how he expounds the *pure ego as source* and *radiating center of inquiry* operating in the world;
B. from this, I expound some points of his investigation of *practical* inquiry, including the matters of ideation, now in the context of the natural and transcendental attitude.

3.3.1 The Pure Ego as Source of Inquiry

After the "naïve" work surrounding the *Logical Investigations*, Husserl goes back into transcendental sources and origins. There, he finds the primordial source in the pure ego, the *initiation* of which means a *radiation* of egoic acts which becomes determinate in the horizon of the world. Inquiry thus operates in the horizon of that world, insofar as questionable being appears.

In other words, in the natural attitude, questionability appears with modalization of belief, *not* of the *being of* the world, but of *beings in* the world.[88] As such, answering is the fulfillment of inquiry as founded in the world as horizon, and the fulfillment of its operations "builds upon" the meaningful world. Here, in natural, "naïve" inquiry, the being of the world is still a sort of *doxa*, insofar as there is a positing of its being that goes unquestioned. Transcendental phenomenological inquiry, for its part, puts all that into question and goes back to its source.

Transcendental phenomenological inquiry discovers the "pure ego" as the source of egoic acts. These egoic acts appear in mundane thinking, directed toward an object in the world. As Husserl puts it, "In every actional *cogito* a radiating 'regard' is directed from the pure ego to the 'object' of the consciousness-correlate in question, to the physical thing, to the affair-complex, and so on, and effects the very different kinds of consciousness of it."[89] Such a "radiating 'regard,'" of course, is already specific, already determinate intention, even as it refers back to the pure ego. Thus,

---

[88] I call this, following Eugen Fink, "world-captivation" and, by extension, "world-captivated inquiry." By this is meant a sort of inquiry that does not ask about the world per se but rather operates under a naive acceptance of it within a *natural attitude*. To express in one stroke the manifold problematic in Husserl's work on this point, I adopt this rendering of Eugen Fink's term, *Weltbefangenheit*, or "world-captivation. Without proper reflective inquiry by a subject upon its own operation, there is a captivation *to* the subject's horizons; moreover, without discovering the *pre*-intentional world-horizon *from which* objects appear, that is, the *transcendental world-horizon*, it is captive *in* the domain of that which is given. Thus, we say, world-captivated inquiry remains "caught up" (in the sense of *accepting* as *ad-capere* or *be-fangen*—as being "toward capture") with beings in the world. For further discussion on the concept and its history, see Bruzina, (2004), pp. 187–188.

[89] Husserl (1983), p. 200.

Husserl will call the pure ego the "positional origin" (*Ursprungssetzung*).[90] The next chapter shows how Husserl further differentiates origins between passivity and activity, let me bring to the fore here what he has to say about the "initiation" of egoic activity.

The *initiation* of the pure ego "sets-into" (*ein-setzen*) the world egoic activity.[91] This setting-into of the pure ego is *spontaneous*. As such, it is something to which subjects find themselves present rather than something it constructs for itself. Indeed, Husserl notes, subjects naturally live in the "so to speak, *dominating* spontaneity."[92] A primordial example of this is the general thesis of the world into which the ego is spontaneously set. Upon this primordial position, further egoic activity appears. So, as Husserl says, "While we 'live in' the deeming likely, inquiring…[and so on], we do not effect any primordial positing."[93] Indeed, natural inquiry, neither the belief in being upon which it proceeds nor the source of that belief is thrown into question.

Phenomenological inquiry puts the possibility of position-taking at all into question, however. Of course, this is not given in straightforward perception: I cannot simply look-outward or point-inward to the pure ego, even if I can hear or see the outward effects of its initiation and radiation; nor can I point outward to the world, though it everywhere surrounds me. To understand the initiation and radiation of the pure ego in the world, *transcendental phenomenological inquiry is required*. Through this inquiry, the dominating spontaneity and the world as such is brought to question. Now, the appearance and operation of natural inquiry itself indicates the pure ego as a condition of its possibility. Thus, in Husserl's transcendental phenomenological inquiry, there is a sort of zig-zag through which the interior depths of natural inquiry are illuminated in light of the transcendental dimension.

---

[90] Husserl (1983), p. 291 and Hua III/1, p. 281: "…[the Ego] does not live in the positings as passively being therein; the positings are instead radiations from the pure Ego as from a primordial source of productions. Each thesis begins with a starting point, with a punctual positional origin; so too the first thesis, like every further one in the context of synthesis." It is worth noting that sense intuition, in a qualified sense, is the "ultimate source" of position taking in the natural attitude, see Husserl (1983), p. 82. The qualification, of course, is that this intuitive foundation supports further building up of sense—this is a point to which we return in the next chapters, under the rubrics of "passive and active synthesis" and "lifeworld."

[91] Hua III/1, pp. 281–282 and Husserl (1983), pp. 291–292: "Every positing begins with a *point of initiation*, with a *positional point of origin*; so it is with the first positing, as with every further one in the concatenation pertaining to the synthesis. This 'initiation' belongs precisely to the positing as positing qua distinctive mode of original actionality….But every act of no matter what species can begin in the mode of spontaneity pertaining, so to speak, to its creative beginning in which the pure Ego makes its appearance as the subject of the spontaneity….This mode of initiating is immediately, and according to an eidetic necessity, converted into another mode. For example, perceptual seizing upon, taking hold of, are immediately and without a break changed into the 'having in one's grip.'"

[92] Husserl (1989), p. 13–15.

[93] Husserl (1983), pp. 267–268 and Hua III/1, p. 257.

3.3.2 Inquiry in the Natural Practical Attitude

There are, to be sure, many parallels in Husserl's early analysis of the intentional essence of inquiry and his somewhat later of practical inquiry in the natural attitude. At both times, he finds, for example, inquiry as a seeking to determine conflicting or, more exactly, questionable presentations.[94] Now, though, he further differentiates that which is *questionable*, as on the side of the *noema*, from a corresponding noetic seeking to determine.[95] He also speaks to the world and the subject as conditions of the possibility of inquiry and action. The world, once again, becomes the questionable horizon and the subject as that which questions and whose answers build a meaningful and valuable world. An important aspect of this analysis appears in what Husserl calls "question of the will." By attending to this question, he brings to the fore the dimension of "wanting" in a *striving for decision*, the "doing" as *carrying out* the choice one makes, and the overarching concordance of one's "*willing*" that is *constitutive* of who one is and the world in which one lives.[96]

To explain further, in practical activity, Husserl finds given an intention of an end, something *wanted* as a goal that would fulfill the intention. Herein, there is given an end that is "achievable" as something "reachable" (*Erreichbar*) or not.[97] If that end does not appear as achievable, a practical person would dismiss as "*impractical*," that is, as not-possibly-achievable. That does not mean a person never wants apparently unachievable ends, of course. It means that, in the question of the will, there is a *consideration* (*Überlegung*) of the matter one aims to realize and a specific *deliberation* (*Erwägung*) or "weighing" of possibilities.[98] A mark of practical inquiry,

---

[94] Husserl also still understands the *question* as an expression, as the speech-form, of such a modalization of consciousness. See, for example, Hua XL, p. 137: "It is rather its own modified consciousness, which finds its expression in its own form of speech: question. But the asking consciousness refers to the same state of affairs as the judgment or conception in question. If I express what is asked, I bring the state of affairs to a self-conception." Again, the question is not an *original* position taking, but a position taking upon this starting point; nevertheless, the question is indeed a novel sense, realizing a possibility in the data.

[95] See, for example, Hua III/1, p. 245: "That something is possible, probable, questionable and so on, can itself be conscious again in the mode of possibility, probability, questionability, correspond to the noetic formations, the noematic formations of being: It is possible that it is possible, that it is probable, questionable; it is probable that it is possible, that it is probable; and so in all complications."

[96] He will also call this sense, the broad or "universal essence" of action "volitionality" (*Willentlichkeit*); see Hua XLIII/III, pp. 273–74 et al.

[97] Hua XLIII/III, p. 228. See also, Hua XXVIII, p. 52. Husserl will even talk about the "existing" or "present" world of practicality. Consider B I 16 / 2a: "Vorhandenes und praktische Welt. 'Ich habe Vorhandendnes,' zu einer Gegebenheitsweise der einen Welt, der Welt der wirklichen und möglichen Vorhandenheit für mich und für jedermann…" ["Present and practical world. 'I have presence,' to a mode of givenness of the one world, the world of actual and possible presence for me and for everyone…"].

[98] On the relation of these terms, consider, for example, Hua XXVIII, pp. 232: "There is a disjunction of willing in the choice, that is its basic character, and the correlate is the disjunctive question of being. Choice is initially a kind of questioning, just not theoretical questioning (or doubting). But that is not the full *choosing*. We understand thereunder a deciding on the basis of such a

3.3 Natural Inquiry Within the World

questions of the will is this considering and weighing. As practical, it aims *to realize the desired end* by carrying out the decision.

Practical inquiry intends a *choice* and *decision to act*. The question of will, which transposes the form of the question. This is, as Husserl puts it, "[S]hould I choose A or B or…as a possible course of action"?[99] In this, there is a weighing of possibilities within the context of action. It aims toward a *choice*. This aiming as a process of choosing can be distinguished from the conclusion of the process, as Husserl himself notes in the ambiguity of the word "choice:":

> The word is, of course, ambiguous. It means sometimes the conclusion of the process, that is, the practical answer to the disjunctive practical question; as when, when buying, it is said: I choose this dress, my choice has fallen on it. 'Choice' also means the whole process of deliberation, possibly with the conclusion in the actual choice decision.[100]

To clarify, Husserl continues, at the conclusion of the process of choosing, there is "the practical Yes, and in case of disjunctive inquiring, the choice."[101] At this moment, one makes a judgment, choosing that which appears as the *best* possible choice for fulfilling the aim. That it is "best" means, in this context, that the choice is achievable, that it can be carried out through action. In the fourth chapter, I take up further the question of the "ought" or the "should," in terms and what is *truly valuable* and truly good to do. Here, it suffices to say that the "should" means the givenness with that possibility which best fulfills the intended aim (accepting, for the time being, that it may be that this is not something truly worthwhile). In other words, "if I want this, then I should do this." The choice carries over, however, in the *performance* or *carrying out* the choice.[102]

Where there is an answer of the will, there comes the demand to act. To express this, Husserl virtually transposes the *Meno* paradox: "I have decided for Yes or No

---

doubting, closer to such a going-back and -forth consideration and deliberation [*Überlegens und Erwägens*]….[C]onsideration already designates the direction towards a solution of the doubt by a decision and with the "weighing" that "weights" are involved, similar to the presumption of doubt and the presumption decision, which terminates in the decision, the following 'greatest weight' [*Übergewicht*]." See also Hua XXXVII, pp. 5–6 and 252–53, and 342.

[99] Husserl lists at least four stages of this inquiring, for example, at Hua XXVIII, pp. 230–31, from 1911: "Analysis of a choice between two possibilities…. / 2) I question, now choosing: Should I A or B? If I question so, then I have not only thought of A and B as a possible willing goal, the actions are also meant as distinct: The A-goal lies not on the way to goal B and vice versa./ 3) It also means: I think to myself A as done, but nothing else (not B and nothing otherwise), and I think to myself B as done. I think of each as done alone…/ 4) We make the following consideration: In every activity there lies a practical having-for-value. The deed appears as a realized value, whereby the action is already thought of as a possible action. 'I should do A' does not mean merely that willing-goal A is aware in this sense as a value." I take up the fourth point about evaluation, deliberation, and action more directly in the fourth chapter.

[100] See Hua XXVIII, pp. 119–20.

[101] See Hua XXVIII, pp. 119–20.

[102] See Hua XXVIII, pp. 119–20: "A practical consideration is nothing else than the performance of a question of willing, but not only that, but also the performance of those modifications and additions of the inquiring acts, which lie on the way to the decision of the question, thus of processes of the fulfillment of the inquiring intention: these led favorably to the *terminus ad quem* of the fulfilling process, thus to the performance of the answer of the will."

simpliciter, then the questionable thing is no longer a questionable thing for me, and I can no longer reasonably ask wherever I have so decided. Where I already know, I cannot ask."[103] Of course, Husserl does not mean here that it is "unquestionable," in the sense that one cannot call transpose the judgment into a question: where one is wrong, where there has been a false choice, the demand for the question, the questionability may reemerge.[104] Rather, he means that the judicative decision has the stamp of an absolute. The decision is illuminated, he says, "by the clarity in which the contexts of grounds and justifications are perfectly given and the answer proves to be the reasonable answer."[105] There are, in other words, *reasons* for the choice. And those reasons includes the answer to the willing question of whether this "should" be done, about which I discuss further in subsequent chapters.[106] If one makes the judicative decision, one puts one stamp on it, and therewith comes the demand to act, to *do something* in response to the knowledge.

With the preceding, we come nearer to the traditional understanding of the will as a rational appetite that tends toward a choice in accord with reason. A choice is made under the broader rubric of the process of choice, which has its aim, its end. Thus, we might say, reason operates under its "reasons," that is, under its ends. The initiation of the ego occurs, in other others, within an attitude—if I may, the pure ego "sets into" action within "a stance," an *Ein-stellung*. For, as I already noted, by the word "attitude," is meant, first, Husserl's broad sense, clearly stated later, as "habitually fixed style of willing life."[107] Setting aside the issue of "habitually fixed style," which is an issue I clarify in the next chapters, let me focus on the words "willing life." As the will has an end in mind, so an attitude has an overarching end that sets into relation, even sets in order, its other subordinate ends.

So, in the natural attitude, generally speaking, "Human beings who are living naturally, objectivating, judging, feeling, willing,"[108] navigating objects as *actually in the world*. As an attitude, it is a willing life that takes for granted the *world* in its aiming to further determine the world. Of course, the "natural" attitude may also be theoretical. Where practical living is toward *doing* something in the relative world, theoretical will to *knowing* the world "in itself," where this "in itself" means understanding matters as in relation to each other rather than in relation to the subject's

---

[103] See Hua XXVIII, pp. 119–20.

[104] Hua XXVIII, pp. 132–133: "The choice is a false choice, or, as we can also express it, since every choosing consideration is an inquiring: The question of will has found a false answer of will...."

[105] Hua XXVIII, p. 118.

[106] Hua XXVIII, p. 49. Hua XXVIII, p. 153: "The goal of will fully and wholly lies in what we indicate as the objective ought."

[107] At Husserl (1970), p. 280. These points are nearer to the final sense of will, mentioned above. The phrase goes on to mark "directions of the will or interests that are prescribed by this style, comprising the ultimate ends, the cultural accomplishments whose total style is thereby determined. The individual life determined by it runs its course with this persisting style as its norm." These interests, the historical situation of the operation of this style, this norm and ideal we discuss further in the next chapters. Here, we sketch only the intentional structures, prior to accounting for the genesis and generation.

[108] Husserl (1983), p. 51.

3.3 Natural Inquiry Within the World

willing and doing. This distinction is significant, for these ways of willing—these *attitudes*—set the *conditions of what counts* or the *criteria* for a fulfilled question. This may be clarified further with respect to the question about "What" something is.

In the natural attitude, in general, the questions "What is this?" and "Is this actual?" do not put into question actuality itself but rather accepts it as, so to speak, "there" as within the horizon.[109] Again, for Husserl, ideation is an active seeking to determine an object in a *special interest in the universal*.[110] Saving close discussion of the sense of "interest" for the next chapter, where I present how it is a matter of being "amongst being" (*inter-esse*), let me here introduce how interest in the universal directs intention to the end of an essential grasp. This process is a matter of constituting a novel object, the "*eidos*."[111] Neither this object nor this process is empirical, though it relates to perception; again, the novel objects are not given perceptually but rather given as constituted from an activity of the ego. Indeed, the ego transmutation of an individual "this" into an *essence* or an *eidos* grasps the necessary structures of the presentation such that it refers to each instantiation of its type. This *novel* grasp of the ideal object, as Husserl will say, is a grasp of "What it is."[112] Still more, this grasp is an "essential judgment" (*Wesenurteil*).[113] Since *all judgments are thinkable as the*

---

[109] So, the *problematic* of actuality is put into question by this transposition of the *transcendental question*. See Hua Mat VII, p. 16: "Natural cognition does not start with the problematic beginning, whether there is an actuality at all, in order to decide only then, but it starts with the thesis of actuality. No matter how far back we go, there is always already 'actually there.' Every natural question is: 'What is this?,' namely, in view of what is already posited as actual. Or it is: 'Is that here, namely, in this actual environment of mine, among these real things giving itself as actual indeed also a real?' So too the question 'Is this actual?' is never and nowhere the question about the being of actuality at all. This is obviously also true for the beginnings, I mean for the very first steps of natural science. It admittedly wants nothing less than to accept the opinions of ordinary life about nature as given."

[110] Hua XLI, p. 274: "If an interest is exclusively determined by such a concrete species-moment [*Artmoment*], then a sphere of relevance and irrelevance has been distinguished with it. And this is true whether the interest is a practical one in the ordinary sense or a so-called theoretical interest, a mere interest in "what it is," but already that but already before all refraining from theory, already beginning in pure experience, for instance in a kind of mere looking"; on more about the interest in the universal, see Hua XXXI, 78 and 80.

[111] Hua III/1, pp. 13–14: "The essence (eidos) is a new kind of object. Just as the given of individual or experiential contemplation is an individual object, so the given of the essential intuition is a pure essence"; see also Hua III/1, p. 14 and Hua XLI, p. 211.

[112] For example, XLI, p. 117: "In sich selbst ist es, was es ist, von absolutem Wesen" ["In itself it is what it is, of absolute essence."]; also, Hua XLI, p. 119: "Individuum, sein Wesen, seine Beschaffenheiten, innere Beschaffenheiten. Individuum, was es ist, und was es hat" ["Individual, its essence, its natures, inner natures. Individual, what it is, and what it has…"]; and, later, Hua XXIX, pp. 267 and 723.

[113] Hua III/1, p. 18: "…kann jedes Urteil über Wesen äquivalent in ein unbedingt allgemeines Urteil über Einzelheiten dieser Wesen als solche umgewendet Werren" ["…every judgment about beings can equivalently be turned into an absolutely general judgment about particulars of these beings as such."]; also, Hua XLI, p. 38: "…wenn das Urteil ein Wesensurteil ist, das da einen Wesensinhalt meint, der seinem Sinn entspricht" ["…if the judgment is a judgment of essence, which there means a content of essence corresponding to its sense."].

content of a question, let us transpose the essential-judgment, a *Wesensurteil* of "*was es ist*," with its *Wesensinhalt* in the "*Was*," into a question.[114] With that transposition, the question takes the form and content of the transposed judgment, namely, "*Was ist es?*" In other words, the grasp of the "What" in ideation follows from an answer to the question "What is it?" The grasp of the "What" is not, by itself, a judgment of reality. Of course, the "What something *is*" is yet to be determined, for there is no verification of the existence of the *eidos* in the particular instantiation. This is not yet "true," in the sense that is determined as true by a further act of judgment, though it opens the possible verification in a further act.[115] To make this process clearer, let me formulate more exactly the grasp of the "What" through inquiry.

The operation of the What-question must first be set into relation with the aforementioned "transmutation" to the *eidos*. I mark that this grasp of the essence is a fulfillment of conditions, namely, of *necessity* and *universality*. To show how, consider again the process of *free-phantasy variation*: in relation to inquiry, this is an active *weighing* of evidence, as there is a presentation of *possible options*. Such inquiry intends the essence, in order to make an "essential judgment" that is a matter of determining that which the object *must* have to be what it is, what is "relevant" or, put negatively, that which it cannot *not* have. For example, the square scratched in the sand can still be a square with any color, any size or line thickness, but the number of sides *must* be equivalent, *must* have the same angles, for, *without* these, it is no longer a square. When one grasps this, one grasps the essence of the square, which the individual "has."[116] *What* it is becomes set as an "exemplar" that provides further conditions for further questions about other individuals or instantiations of the type.[117]

However, in practical inquiry, the *what* is grasped in the context of *doing*. Indeed, the question "What should I do…?," as I discuss further later, includes acts of understanding the *what*, not *for itself* but only in relation to the *action*. The initiation of the egoic activity itself appears within this attitude. On the other hand, theory, in the natural attitude, appears to understand the *what* without the context of action. However, since it occurs in the natural attitude, it does not put to question the *how*. When that is put to question, in the phenomenological attitude, it is possible to seek the essential relations of how matters are given. The answers to those questions then relate back to the practical activity of the ego in the natural attitude, of course, insofar as they are unified through experience. In this respect, there is also what Husserl often calls the "Idea in the Kantian sense."[118] Broadly, by it, Husserl

---

[114] See again, Hua XI, p. 60: "Jedes mögliche Urteil ist denkbar als Inhalt einer Frage."

[115] See Hua III/1, pp. 17–18; also, again in later lectures, Hua XI, pp. 70–71: "But the juxtaposition [*Die Gegenüberstellung*] of *existence* and *essence*, what does it say but that here two modes of being in two modes of self-givenness manifest themselves and are to be distinguished."

[116] I use the inverted commas here, since the universal is not *in* the individual thing but grasped from its data. See, again, Hua XXIV, p. 300, given above.

[117] Hua XLI, p. 390: "Die Variation des Exempels kann sich beziehen auf die gesamte Eigenschaftlichkeit desselben, auf sein gesamtes 'Was es ist,' <auf> es an sich…" ["The variation of the exemplar can refer to the whole property of it, to its whole 'what it is,' <to> it in itself…"].

[118] For this, see Husserl (1983), pp. 6, 138, 166, 297f., and 311ff.

means an *ideal* according to which limits of perfection and fulfillment are set. In this respect, the Idea of reason sets limits according to what may be determined as being such and so by reason. Transcendental phenomenology, as I show below, not only grasps this Idea but make it manifest as a regulative ideal in knowing itself.

3.4 Concluding Remarks: Correlation Analysis and the Regressive Procedure

> All questions have a question ground, that of being. The usual questions of knowledge of the world, the universal question about the ground of law of a knowledge of the world at all, the being of subjectivity as pure….As soon as I ask the universal question about the possibility of the cognition of what really exists and thus have no world existence as ground, I lose the world as subject and as thematic field, I then have only "the world" as supposed in reality and possibility, and that is subjective. So I stand only, can stand only in the universal thematic field of transcendental pure subjectivity. It is my thematic field, means, I set it in the way of the thesis as being, possible, and so on, also as questionable; but thereby it is already pre-supposed as being in generality and determinability.[119]

Through this chapter, we have further determined Husserl's differentiation of *natural inquiry* from *transcendental-phenomenological inquiry*. To that end, we clarified how "natural belief" in the world, a primordial *doxa*, in which natural inquiry proceeds is suspended with the ἐποχή of phenomenology. Under this suspension, the phenomenologist inquires into how matters appear, without taking for granted their being or the being of the world from and in which they appear. We have also found that the distinctive "Cartesian" approach of *pure phenomenology tends to proceed to an intuition* of the pure ego. This procedure discovers the pure ego as the source of all activities, including inquiry. And so we were able to relate the operation of both natural and transcendental inquiry to their source and term. The next chapter's work goes back into the concrete operation of inquiry in the world, though now from a *regressive* procedure.

With the regressive procedure, Husserl shows the Cartesian progression to the intuition of the pure ego to be *abstract*. The abstraction is from the *genesis* of sense, meaning, and value. This genesis means attending to the temporal dimensions of consciousness in a new, more concrete way.

Now, to be sure, Husserl was aware of these dimensions, even during the *Logical Investigations*. And they become explicitly thematic in his 1905 lectures on internal time consciousness.[120] In these lectures, he discovers, for example, how the ego is

---

[119] Hua XXXIV, p. 20. He goes on, in this text from 1926, to say that the transcendental phenomenologist is able to posit along with the natural attitude, that their themes differ.

[120] Husserl takes note of this abstractness in the *Ideen*. See Hua III/1, p. 182: "The transcendental 'Absolute,' which we have prepared out for ourselves by the reductions, is not in truth the ultimate; it is something which constitutes itself in a certain profound and entirely peculiar sense, and has its original source in a final and truly Absolute. Fortunately, we can leave the riddles of time-consciousness out of play in our preliminary analyses without compromising their rigor." Let me

essentially not given in a "now point," but rather tends beyond immediate givenness and so cannot be adequately intuited as such.[121] To be more exact, Husserl names the temporal dimensions of intentionality the retentional and protentional. It must be emphasized that these are not "mere" past and futural abstractions from the present, but *of the present intention*. As such, a protention is a futural dimension that is not-yet fulfilled or to-be fulfilled, as the "pointing to" of an intention toward its object. A retention, on the other hand, is not itself intentional, at least insofar as it does not indicate an object but rather retains in the present that which has a past. These form the structure of the intention. So, for example, I stand at the front of my home. Within my intention of the frontside that I am intending "there" in the flesh, there is also the protention of the other sides. As I move to the back of the building, the previous, front side is retended, which Husserl calls a "primary remembering" (*primäre Erinnerung*).[122] This allows for the possibility of reawakening the past and bringing to the present in a remembering that places them together—re-membering past experiences, as it were. It is possible to have a fulfillment of the building as "a whole" or an identical unity across time. These already suggest a dynamic temporal density to the *present*, in which the ego appears, once again, as exceeding immediate intuitive grasp.

Indeed, the recognition of time-consciousness seems to complicate the adequacy of a grasp of ego in the progressive-intuitive procedure. Beyond what is claimed in a static method, consciousness cannot be given immediately "now" because it, as Steinbock aptly puts it, "is always *more* than what can be given."[123] The matter thus itself exceeds a concept of a *static* a-temporal, "fixed" ego, thereby challenging the "indubitable" intuition of the Cartesian approach. For, though this essential self-presence is *possible*, insofar as it answers the question about What the pure ego is, it is *abstract*. It abstracts from the *lived-experience*, bringing to focus a now-point. To overcome this, there must be a more adequate, more concrete account.

Yet, the analysis of the time-consciousness lectures also remains abstract. In fact, around 1920, a decade and a half after these lectures were given, Husserl notes, again, that the work was too formal, abstracting, he says, "precisely from content."[124] This means that the analysis grasps the ideal structure of time-consciousness—the form of retention-intention-protention—without attending to those lived-experiences that would fulfill the activity. At the time, such a form was taken as a *structure* of consciousness rather than a *genesis*. It makes some sense, then, that his initial foray into time-constitution does not disrupt the first formulations of transcendental

---

note, in passing, Heidegger's note about the influence of Henri Bergson on Husserl's turn to the temporal dimension of consciousness. See Heidegger (1985), §10a.

[121] For example, Hua X, p. 83.

[122] However, Husserl was not entirely comfortable with calling a retention a "memory," since it is neither a presentation nor a re-presentation. He says, for example, at Hua XXXIII, p. 55: "Retention (the consciousness of post-presentation), strictly speaking, is not memory, so it should not be called primary memory. It is not a presentation." For more on the matter, see Casey (2000), especially, pp. 49–52.

[123] Steinbock (1995), p. 31.

[124] Hua XI, p. 128.

3.4 Concluding Remarks: Correlation Analysis and the Regressive Procedure

phenomenology, for the results of these works were so far compatible: the phenomenologist can prescind from empirical content to the "pure" ego in a static, Cartesian approach because even the work on time-consciousness was still abstracting from content in order to grasp a static structure. Even though he recognizes quite early, in the first volume of the *Ideen*, that there is an entire "concealed dimension" in the Cartesian approach, namely, the temporal, his understanding of it was still too formal to require a methodological change.[125]

At this juncture, let me also emphasize the fact that Husserl never completely jettisons the Cartesian way into phenomenology. For him, it is decisive, even illuminating in its limitations. This is due, in large part, to how it opens the transcendental dimension for phenomenological research, giving the impulse and *leitmotif* for the discovery of the *a priori* correlation of the world and the subject.[126] A static phenomenology can also provide what Husserl calls "leading clues" (*Leitfaden*—a compound of *leiten*, which means "to lead" and *der Faden*, which is a "thread").[127] That means static, a-temporal analysis can provide those structures from which the phenomenologist can inquire-back into its genesis through time.[128] This way proves to be more *concrete*, more completely accounting of the matter in question. In short, then, the Cartesian way can still serve a purpose to further generations.

Nevertheless, Husserl does later censor the progressive-intuitive procedure and Cartesian approach. He says it wins "in one leap" the transcendental ego by emptying it of content, suggesting it abstracts it from the world in which it lives.[129] In order to overcome this, there is a need to readdress methodological procedures. He thus begins to develop a *regressive* and, from this, explicates the *regressive-inquisitive* procedure. The next chapter clarifies how this operates and shows how it discovers the genesis of inquiry, whereas the chapters following further expound its explication and generation.

---

[125] As Steinbock points out, this must be the temporal dimension *and* its recognition shows Husserl to have *already* moved beyond it, that is, *already* recognized a *more concrete* dimension. The need for an abstract or "simple" approach, both essentially and for Husserl, thus becomes a matter of question. See Steinbock (1995), p. 30. Also see Hua III/1, p. 197.

[126] In Husserl's critique of the limits of the *Investigations*, he also implicates the works of others: "In view of the general character of the contemporary literature, I did not believe I could count on any serious attention....[I]t betrayed no sensitivity for the fact that for any truly scientific philosophizing there is still need for the radical beginning sought so passionately by Descartes...,"at Husserl (1975), p. 17.

[127] See the reflections beginning at Hua XIV, p. 41: "Ist die statische Phänomenologie nicht eben die Phänomenologie der Leitfäden...?"

[128] Steinbock (1995).

[129] See Hua VI, p. 43.

Chapter 4
The Genesis of Inquiry

Abstract This chapter takes up how Husserl responds to the limitations of the earlier formulations of transcendental phenomenological method by going back to the origin of inquiry in individual facticity. More exactly, I show his determination of inquiry as an activity that appears within a striving for determination in the intentional life of the individual. In this, I stress Husserl's analysis of how the inquiry seeks to determine and to differentiate meaningful being, even beyond that given in perception. I also bring to the fore an important distinction between interest and disinterest, where the latter detaches from practical interests and concerns in order to strive to determine and to differentiate matters in themselves and in relation to each other. This distinction is essential for understanding science and, indeed, phenomenological science, insofar as these disinterestedly inquire into the "things themselves."

Keywords Genetic phenomenology · Origins · Facticity · Interest · Disinterest

In this intentional life, the ego is not an empty stage of its lived-experiences of consciousness, nor is it an empty point of radiation of its acts. The ego-being is constant ego-becoming. Subjects are by constantly developing. But they develop in *constant correlation with the development of their "environment,"* which is nothing other than the conscious world in the consciousness-life of the ego. Through the ever-new acts of the ego with an ever-new sense, with ever-new layers of meaning, the environment as an environment for the ego is always a new one.[1]

4.1 Preliminary Remarks—Toward a Transcendental Logic of Question and Answer

We have arrived at crossroads on the way to a phenomenological response to those "ancient questions"—the transcendental and the normative. So far, we have followed Husserl through an inquiry into the foundation of logic in intentional acts to the source

---

[1] Hua XXXVII, pp. 104–105.

of these acts in the pure ego. Yet, a pure phenomenology seems to present a path that progresses directly to the source while abstracting from the origins of inquiry. There appears another way of proceeding, however. This way does not require "winning" back the world but instead leaves it in play and "goes back" into *how* it and matters takes on sense, meaning and value. To set out on this path, in this third chapter, I pay special attention to the *genesis* of inquiry.

To do so, I take up Husserl's regressive procedure. By going back into the operations of subjectivity in a correlation analysis, its discovery is twofold. On the one hand, mundane inquiry appears *as a multi-layered striving for determination and differentiation in the intentional life of the individual*. On the other hand, transcendental phenomenological inquiry itself appears as within a movement that *goes-back into the origin and ground of any inquiry at all*. I investigate these aspects through three main sections of this chapter:

1. in the first, I provide a provisional presentation of Husserl's discovery and description of genesis;
2. from this, I give, in the second, a genetic account of mundane inquiry as a multi-layered striving for determination and differentiation;
3. in the third, I address the need for further transcendental inquiry that includes personal and socio-historical phenomena, which also serves as a transition to the problematic of valuation and going-back, not only into the subject, but into the world itself insofar as it carries meaning and value.

Let me begin by setting the stage with a reflection on some of Husserl's remarks on Aristotle's *analyses* of questions in a science causes and origins. This serves to provide a preliminary differentiation of some basic types of questions treated in this chapter, namely, *Whether that, If that, What*, and *Why*, and a clearer sense of the problematic of the "coordination" of question forms to psychological acts described in the first chapter. What is more, by bringing to the fore Husserl's recovery of the operation of *intelligence* in logic—in his *noetics*—we broach the meaning of the *pure question in its originating operation*. This also allows me to highlight the place and role of inquiry in transcendental logic itself, insofar as intelligent inquiry essentially relates to all possible answers. To make more sense of these points, let me return to some of Husserl's comments on Aristotle's analytics, then to his shift away from the Cartesian procedure toward correlation analysis.

4.1.1 Aristotle's "Analysis": Questions in Science as About Causes and Origins

Through the 1910s and 1920s, Husserl's teaching schedule is filled with general introductions to the history of philosophy. Perhaps this, paired with the maturation of his phenomenology, he begins to think about the appearance of phenomenology more historically. He still takes, for example, Plato as *Urvater* of logic, but he now begins to work out how this development exerts a normative authority on culture, unto

4.1 Preliminary Remarks—Toward a Transcendental Logic of Question ...

the emergence of phenomenology.[2] Likewise, he still accepts Aristotle as continuing such a project with his distinction of "first" and "second philosophy" in science, though he begins to penetrate, with ever finer vision, the way in which the original ideal of unified science came to weaken in history.[3]

A disintegration of first and second philosophies was not Aristotle's plan, of course. For him, intelligence plays an essential role in the unity of the sciences as a *principle*, as he says in his *Posterior Analytics*: "If, therefore, we have any other kind of true knowledge, intelligence will be the principle of it. And it would be the *principle of principles* and has the same relation to all things themselves."[4] Despite this recognition of intelligence as a principle of principles, the appearance of intelligence in inquiry, as Husserl makes clear, comes to be explicitly excluded from formal logic, and, as we will see further below, reduced in psychology and presupposed in metaphysics. With this, the stage is set for the fragmentation of science. It is worthwhile to take a few moments to go back into Aristotle's understanding of intelligence in science, however, as it gives a clue to what is in need of recovery.

Now, for Aristotle, it is possible to seek and to have knowledge without understanding the seeking itself. Thus, he says, "Physics is a kind of wisdom, but it is not the primary kind. As for the attempts of some of those who speak about the way it is necessary to demonstrate the truth, they do so through a lack of training in the analysis of this work: for they would go about it with a pre-knowledge [προϋπαρχούσης] but without attending to the seeking."[5] The physicist can quite successfully study objects without studying the work of that study, without understanding their seeking

---

[2] Husserl (2019), p. 58: "However much Plato was at pains to found a logic in this radical spirit, he did not break through to the requisite beginnings and methods, and Aristotle already fell into the quite natural trap of taking for granted a pre-given world, thereby relinquishing every radical grounding of cognition." Also, for the "normative authority" of Plato in European scientific culture, see Husserl (2019), p. 17.

[3] Husserl's lectures on *First philosophy* are replete with this point, as glimpsed in the above footnote. Compare the similar sentiment in the middle ethics lectures, Hua XXXVII, p. 18: "The new philosophy originating from Plato's dialectic – logic, general metaphysics (Aristotle's First Philosophy), mathematics, the sciences of nature and spirit in their various disciplines (such as physics, biology, ethics, and politics) – all of these disciplines were only incomplete realizations of the Platonic idea of philosophy, that is, philosophy as absolutely justifying science. One can say that the radicalism of the Platonic intention aiming at the complete and final rationality of all scientific knowledge became weakened precisely through the fact that [only] subordinate levels of rationality were reached."; Also consider the following from lecture manuscripts on the history of philosophy, Ms. F I 40 1/ 54b: "Die erfüllung deiser aufgabe [viz., of Logic] macht eine eigene Diszipline aus. Aber ihre systematische Aufhlung begann erst mit Platons grosser Schuler Aristotles" ["The fulfillment of this task [viz., of logic] constitutes a discipline of its own. But its systematic approach began only with Plato's great teacher Aristotle."]

[4] Aristotle, *Posterior Analytics* 100b14–17: "εἰ οὖν μηδὲν ἄλλο παρ' ἐπιστήμην γένος ἔχομεν ἀληθές, νοῦς ἂν εἴη ἐπιστήμης ἀρχή. καὶ ἡ μὲν ἀρχὴ τῆς ἀρχῆς εἴη ἄν, ἡ δὲ πᾶσα ὁμοίως ἔχει πρὸς τὸ πᾶν πρᾶγμα." Emphasis my own.

[5] Aristotle, *Metaphysics* 1005b1–5: "...ἔστι δὲ σοφία τις καὶ ἡ φυσική, ἀλλ' οὐ πρώτη. ὅσα δ' ἐγχειροῦσι τῶν λεγόντων τινὲς περὶ τῆς ἀληθείας ὃν τρόπον δεῖ ἀποδέχεσθαι, δι' ἀπαιδευσίαν τῶν ἀναλυτικῶν τοῦτο δρῶσιν· δεῖ γὰρ περὶ τούτων ἥκειν προεπισταμένους ἀλλὰ μὴ ἀκούοντας ζητεῖν." This δρῶσιν is related to our "drama" as an activity, a *doing* of the seeking for knowledge.

or inquiring: Aristotle knew well that a "natural desire to know,"[6] may operate without being made a theme of its operation. In other words, the second philosophies can give reasons for their positions, according to the objects of their inquiry, without justifying their positions by way of an understanding of the principle of these positions.

In contrast, Aristotle's first philosophy does, in its own way, bring to light the activity of seeking in relation to that which is sought. Thus, Husserl recognizes: "…Aristotle begins his immortal metaphysics with the famous words, which he puts down as self-evident: 'All humans strive by nature for knowledge.'"[7] The philosopher, for Aristotle, is not just at work knowing but is also studying the seeking for knowledge itself. So, he continues, in his *Metaphysics*, "…it is clear that it belongs to the philosopher and the one who studies all reality, insofar as it is by nature, to investigate also about the source (ἀρχῶν: 'principle,') of syllogisms."[8] Again, Aristotle says, in the *Analytics*, νοῦς or intelligence is the principle of syllogisms and, indeed, the principle of principles, the source of knowledge. *However*, as Husserl emphasizes, if the *Metaphysics* begins with the desire to know, it *does not make it thematic*, for it is not a topic for first philosophy. And though the *Analytics* itself includes, Husserl says, "good things" about noetics, it too tends to focus upon "the general cognition of being" or *metaphysics*.[9] Instead, it reasserts an objectivist tendency toward that which is *sought*. What is yet needful is a recovery of the operations of the subject of the *seeking*.

But let us take care to recognize the presence of intelligent inquiry in Aristotle's work. For the seeking of knowledge in inquiry does play an essential role in science, for him. In fact, it appears in his science of syllogisms. As I previously noted, with Husserl, scientific knowledge is a matter of *knowing the reason why*, in the sense of identifying the *intelligible relation* or, in an exact sense, the *cause*. For Aristotle, this occurs through question and answer. Thus, in the *Posterior Analytics*, we find four types of questions: τὸ ὅτι (Whether that…); τὸ διότι (Why that…); εἰ ἔστι (If it is…);

---

[6] Aristotle, *Metaphysics*, 980a21: "πάντες ἄνθρωποι τοῦ εἰδέναι ὀρέγονται φύσει."

[7] See, again, Hua Mat. IX, pp. 7–8. There is a further question about the difference between "striving" and "pure striving," which Husserl marks in these pages. Let us understand the distinction, however provisionally, as between a determinate striving, which actually occurs in the world, and the *a priori* ability to strive.

[8] Aristotle, *Metaphysics*, 1005b6–9: "…ὅτι μὲν οὖν τοῦ φιλοσόφου, καὶ τοῦ περὶ πάσης τῆς οὐσίας θεωροῦντος ᾗ πέφυκεν, καὶ περὶ τῶν συλλογιστικῶν ἀρχῶν ἐστὶν ἐπισκέψασθαι, δῆλον."

[9] Consider Hua Mat IX, 87: "He is the creator of 'syllogistics'…. It is called 'analytics' by Aristotle, at least the writings dealing with it bear the titles 'First' and 'Second Analytics.' In addition, good things, although superficial from the present aspect, concerning the noetic logical side. His great achievement is made possible by the discovery of the method of formalization, which is quite inconspicuously present in his method of designating the propositional matter by letters. It is the first discovery of an "algebraic" generalization. Nevertheless, he stopped halfway and did not bring the idea of a formal logic to pure detachment and determination. For in all his logical researches he always thinks of rules for cognition of reality; what interests him is always 'metaphysics,' most general cognition for being, for real in most general generality, and also his logical writings are always referred back to this. This is connected with the little clear position of logic in the context of Aristotelian philosophy."

4.1 Preliminary Remarks—Toward a Transcendental Logic of Question ...

and τι εστίν (What it is…).[10] Of course, this is no mere catalog of questions, for, if it were, it would clearly be insufficient, as there are many more sorts of questions, like those about who, where, how, how many, and so on. Instead, it is a reflection on types of questions necessary for scientific knowledge. Thus, in a sense, the question "*Why?*" is the essential one, as Husserl finds, since it seeks the explanatory *cause* or the *because* that is, more exactly, an *intelligible relation* in the data.[11] Indeed, with it, we should distinguish, from the outset, a *determinate*, particular "Why" and the "teleological Why," as Husserl puts it: by the former is meant a seeking the answer to this or that intelligible relation, this or that *because*, where as the latter indicates the *pure seeking* of all knowledge, all ultimate intelligible relations.[12] Since we return to the transcendental investigation of the teleological "Why" and "Because" at length in the next chapter, let me focus here upon the more determinate one.

Giving a reason means grasping and formulating a cause, a reason why. In this respect, the "What…?" and the "Why…" ask about the cause—they seek a *because*, as it were, of the particular. In Aristotle's analysis, this is a grasp of the *middle term* as an operation of intelligence. So, to take his example, to which we return at length below, when one asks, "What is an eclipse?" one seeks, in transposition, "Why is the moon darkened?" There is a relation here to the experience, the data, and the seeking of the cause: the questions *Whether* that and *If* that ask about the presence of the middle term, in this case, the blocking of the earth, whereas the questions *What* and *Why* ask about its cause, its *reasons*. Another example would be, then, understanding a shape, not unlike in the *Meno*. One might ask another *if* a presented shape *is* square, one has to know *what* a square is and *why*, as well as *whether* there is a shape at all. Now, one could know *what* a square is—a four-sided figure, angles totaling three-hundred and sixty degrees, and so on—and so also know *why* that is a square not a triangle. But one would need to ask, further, *if this* shape met *those* conditions, in order to know *if it is*. That is to say, one would have to intelligently reflect and weigh the given data and the supplied conditions, that is, the "pre-conditions" of the *what* and *why*, such that the judgment that it *is* a square would be an adequate answer to the question of *if* it was a square or not. Aristotle shows, in his analysis, that intelligence is a grasp of these relations. That is, it is a grasp of the "must" or the necessity of

---

[10] Aristotle, *Posterior Analytics*, 89b21–90a34. Perhaps further qualifications, between, for example, το τι εστίν and τὸ τί ἦν εἶναι, but clearly an explicit attempt to determine "we seek four things in order to know."

[11] Husserl sketches this, though in a fragmentary way, at Hua XLII, p. 348: "Science. Judgment, insight as self-possession and insight into necessities and generalities. The Why and the That. Explanatory science. The causal explanation (Why-explanation). The differing Why."

[12] The "pure seeking," for its part, is the condition for the possibility of any seeking whatsoever. It operates, however, in the world. As both are *essentially* in becoming, the subject is not completely transparent in itself. See the important passage at Hua Mat IX, 203: "Further then: Every subject of experience is intelligible in its intelligible operation. But every subject has its factual dispositions, dispositions of character and so on, and develops in its situation factually to just this empirical person. But everything factual stands as in itself unintelligible [*Unverständliches*] under the teleological question of the Why." Also worth noting is that, in this context, Husserl also speaks of a transcendent "pure spirit," which goes beyond the physical and factual nature of human being and is necessary by itself. I return to the point at the end of the final chapter.

the relations such that one understands the reasons for the position. Intelligence is, in other words, the principle or source of knowledge. So, what is lacking from the analysis?

The critical issue, basically, is that Aristotle does not methodologically consider the operation of intelligence as it is given in consciousness and in the world. As Husserl puts it, if science is left without a method to discover *noetic laws* in relation to the *noematic*, there comes a sort of "naïve logic."[13] Since consciousness and the world are not brought to awareness on their own terms, the ideal of a self-justified science is unrealized. Indeed, as formal logic becomes a separate science, psychology becomes one of the second philosophies dominated by empirical concerns, which introduces the dangers of psychologism as well as a sort of anthropologism, since it does not distinguish the data of consciousness as carrying its own exigencies and evidence.[14] From all this, Husserl finds that the transcendental question "falls to the very natural obviousness of a pre-given world."[15]

To be clear, Aristotle himself understood the danger of being uncritical, albeit in his own way. As we quoted above, Aristotle says the physicists proceed under a "pre-knowledge" (προϋπαρχούσης). No single English word seems to fit the range of this term; its sense is something like "arising from sources already present" (πρός "from" ὑπο "under" ἀρχω "sources" or "principles"). Although the inclusion of the word "knowledge" in the translation seems inappropriate at first, since it is not present in Greek, the *Posterior Analytics* gives a clue to its sense, as it begins, "All

---

[13] See Hua XXXV, pp. 373 and 470–71. Also the related points at Hua XXXV, p. 470: "The work that the research of cognition requires of us concerns, on the one hand, the logical relations with respect to thinking, and, on the other hand, the correlative noetic relations; the latter the side of the noesis of consciousness, of thinking as an active and passive life of the ego, which takes place in such and such a way, and on the other hand the correlative noematic relations. The latter can be considered as self-contained, and then we have the work of logic. The others can be considered only in relation to the noematic contents and correlations. Of course, to make this understandable to the beginner is very difficult." And, again, Hua XXXV, 447–448: "And to say it right away: The *a priori* laws of analytics or logic are nothing else than laws of mere consequence, noetically turned, of the consequence of judging, laws of concordance or discordance, of compatibility or of "contradiction" with respect to judging as judging. But they are themselves noematic laws and as such laws of the compossibility of sentences as sentences."

[14] Husserl (2019), pp. 52–55, especially 55: "Thus already in antiquity there arose, in the great spirit of an *Aristotle*, a *first outline of a universal science of subjectivity*, that is, a psychology, which was to concern itself with all mental functions and hence also the functions of human reason. One of the objective sciences in the series of empirical sciences dealing with the cosmos, one science alongside the others, thereby enters into a special relation to logic and ethics, and through these to all the other sciences and their regions. To be sure, the way that psychology comes on the scene makes it a constant cross for philosophers. From the beginning it was not able to master the problematic that we, by taking cognition and unities of cognition as our point of departure and in conjunction with the methodological disciplines of logic and then ethics, have become aware of in these lectures. What was lacking, however much one spoke of the faculties of cognizing and practical reason, was the method that would, in the right way, bring out, systematically and descriptively – thus getting a theoretical grasp on – the spheres of acts to which these faculties are related and hence in general consciousness as consciousness of something."

[15] See Husserl (2019), pp. 57–58.

4.1 Preliminary Remarks—Toward a Transcendental Logic of Question ...

teaching and learning proceeds from knowledge already present."[16] So, the source of knowledge is intelligence but its *achievements* also become a source in its own right. Knowledge appears, in other words, on a previous *belief*, *doxa*. Thus, Aristotle himself begins investigations from ἔνδοξα or "reputable opinions." This is a way of proceeding from sources already present as "pre-given," not as presuppositions but as positions to be put to question. These give, we might say, a *determinate motivation* of intelligence, as previous achievements give *content* for the understanding. Still more, however, science is to seek the "cause" or, better, the *source* of natural movement at all. As human beings by nature seek knowledge, it is included in this natural movement toward an end. Thus, Husserl relates the aforementioned "teleological Why" to a "Where to…" that relates to its final cause.[17] For Aristotle, the science of metaphysics investigates these relationships.

Despite the integration of Aristotelian science, Husserl a subjectivist skepticism adapting itself to objectivist thought.[18] This follows the fact that the source of transcendence in immanent reflection is presented without giving a method adequate to its givenness. Although the philosopher may, in fact, be *aware* of the source of knowledge as well as the fact that it operates in pre-given sources of knowledge, this awareness *does not equal a rigorous science of it*. Without this science, there

---

[16] Aristotle, *Posterior Analytics*, 71a-2: "Πᾶσα διδασκαλία καὶ πᾶσα μάθησις 'διανοητικὴ ἐκ προϋπαρχούσης γίγνεται γνώσεως.''

[17] Consider the following passage from Ms. F I 40/250a-b: "Sie sehen, die Idee der Wissenschaft gewinnt (in der Auswirkung platonischer Impulse) bei Aristoteles einen besonderen Sinn…Das große Thema der Philosophie oder Wissenschaft ist nach ihm das Weltall, die gesamte reale Wirklichkeit. Logik und sonstige eidetische Wissenschaften sind nur Hilfsdisziplinen zur Erkenntnis der Realität. Nur das Reale ist im eigentlichen Sinn seiend. Wissenschaft aber ist, wie vorhin schon gesagt, Erkenntnis aus dem Grund, Wissenschaft geht nicht auf das bloße *oti*, sondern auf das *dioti*, nicht auf das bloße Dass, sondern auf das Warum. Dieses reduziert sich ihm aber allzeit auf ein wozu, nur so gewinnen wir ein wirklich erklärendes Verständnis. Darin liegt dass nach Aristoteles die bloß erzählende Geschichte, auch die klassifikatorisch beschreibende Naturgeschichte keine echten Wissenschaften sind. Sie vollziehen nur eine Vor-Arbeit für die wahrhaft wissenschaftliche Leistung, die in teleologischer Erklärung liegt Zweiflellos würde Aristoteles auch die moderne exacte Naturwissenschaft, wenn…" ["You see, the idea of science gains (in the impact of Platonic impulses) a special meaning in Aristotle…The great subject of philosophy or science, according to him, is the universe, the whole of real actuality. Logic and other eidetic sciences are only auxiliary disciplines for the knowledge of reality. Only the real is being in the actual sense. But science is, as said before, cognition from the reason, science does not go to the mere *oti*, but to the *dioti*, not to the mere That, but to the Why. But this is always reduced to a Why, only in this way we gain a truly explanatory understanding. Therein lies that, according to Aristotle, the merely narrating history, as well as the classificatory describing natural history, are no real sciences. They perform only a preliminary work for the truly scientific achievement, which lies in teleological explanation."]. See also, Hua IX, pp. 210–211, 256, and 368 for its relation to teleology, God, and the final cause.

[18] Indeed, as Husserl so succinctly puts it later, in 1934, at Hua XXVII, p. 195: "The first subjectivism goes through transformations, adapts itself to all developmental heights of scientific objectivist philosophy and to those of argumentative refutations, and thereby takes on new, ever new forms. It asserts, as always in the form of unacceptable paradoxes, its thought-motifs, which are always identical in type. They have their own evidence. They are grouped around the difficulties of the correlation of cognition and the cognized and make palpable the questionability of the meaning of transcendence that arises from it."

emerges an unchecked subjectivist skepticism, for example, in strains of nominalism and psychologism that think of themselves in the lineage of Aristotelian logic and psychology. There is also the other tendency of trying to break from ancient systems, as with Descartes. Indeed, something of this seems to appear in Husserl's own Cartesian approach, which launches a series of expeditions through what he calls a "sheer muddle" or even ending in a "shipwreck." As a result, there comes Husserl's second sailing, so to speak, through the straits of a correlation analysis, under the flag of a regressive procedure, to which I turn now.

4.1.2 The Appearance of the Demand for a Regressive Procedure in Correlation Analysis

We know that, with Husserl's breakthrough to intentionality, following Brentano and his reading of the Aristotelian tradition, he finds consciousness as always "about" or "of" objects. In this, he later differentiates the correlation of *noesis-noema*, where the latter is the subjective pole and the former the objective pole of immanent experience.[19] This also relates to the correlation of *subject* and *world*, which appears as a theme especially with Descartes. Yet, Cartesian doubt operates in a twofold naivete: in the first place, it proceeds without suspending its own position taking, as its doubting still stands on the being of the world; in the second place, it *supposes* the severance of the subject from the world in that doubt, and so mistakenly introduces the need of an account of how to return to the world, how to "win it back," treating each as already constituted "thing." In the regressive procedure, however, Husserl puts these presuppositions into question.

In this respect, Steinbock points out the significance of the shift in procedure within the second volume of the *Ideen*, where Husserl gives an account of mundane constituting consciousness by moving back *from* its mundane, factual being rather than bracketing it straightaway.[20] More exactly, Husserl *begins* with the recognition of a Cartesian ontology, that is, the *res cogitans/res extensa* distinction, and *goes back, ad regressus* to *how* it is constituted. With this, the body is taken beforehand as another extended object (*Köper*), but by attending to it, he finds it to be given not a mere object or "body" but as *also* constituting sense as a *lived-body* (*Leib*). The lived-body is thereby found as not a mere extended thing but constitutive *of* extended things through perception. One can identify, in this way of analysis, attention to how sense and meaning emerge from the becoming of sense over time *in* the process of *self*-constitution.

As Steinbock brings into relief, Husserl uses the example of the body touching itself to elucidate its peculiar character. When I clasp my hands, *I* am *sensing* at the same time *I* am *sensed*. To capture this two-sidedness, that is, that the body is

---

[19] There are various accounts of this development. For a more chronological, see de Boer (1978).
[20] See, for example, Steinbock (1995), pp. 114–115. For more on the work during this period, see Caminada (2018).

subject and object of awareness, Husserl uses the neologism *Empfindisse*, sometimes rendered as "sensatings." This means to show that my lived-body is constituted *as* "here," as that object in a certain place and time but also is constituting the "here."[21] It is given as a zero point of orientation, in the sense that it is that point of reference for spatial sense. Yet, the lived-body is also not given as limited to a present "now"; it is, rather, constitutive of what Husserl now identifies as a "living-present."[22] The ego lives within the streaming present of intentional life-time, taking up past experiences as it extends into the future; with this, Husserl takes the *cogito* in relation to the *pure ego* in self-temporalization and self-constitution, as the pure ego "fixes," as he says, itself in the life of the *cogito* in the constitution of the *concrete* living-present.[23] The ego is not an "empty stage" or "empty point of radiation," as the opening quote of this chapter suggests, in other words, but *at work* in the subjects being-in-the-world.

From this approach, Husserl comes to identify the *monad* as that unity of life under phenomenological investigation. It is neither a singular "now" nor a unity of discrete now-points, however; rather, the monad is a process of *genesis*.[24] As such, it is the bearer of the essential possibility of *practice* in its *situation*, by which we mean here precisely its activity in the environing world.[25] In this regard, the *facticity* of the monad implies the constitution of the world through a unity of lived-experience.

As factical, the monad lives with an abiding *style*. This style, which Husserl sometimes calls the "personal character" of the monad, is based upon a substrate of acquisitions that accrue over time. These may, in turn, develop into ways of acting or *habits* that operate along with the continued development of the monad.[26] That is to say, they are had in such a way that there is no need to reflect upon them to activate them, though, to be sure, they may become so deeply sedimented that they are not re-awakened without reflection. Furthermore, although the monad is a unique

---

[21] See Steinbock (1995), p. 116.

[22] Hua IV, 56. In the second volume of the *Ideen*, Husserl more frequently says that there is a duration (*daurend*) to the present. See Hua IV, pp. 101 and 163.

[23] Hua IV, p. 18.

[24] In the Second Volume of the *Ideen*, this occurs at Hua IV, 108; see also the description of the monad as "continually becoming in time," Hua XIV, p. 35.

[25] Ms. AV 19/5-6: "*Situation als praktische Situation. Das praktische Leben und seine 'Situationswahrheit,' Identität des Seienden, das in Relation zu der praktischen Situation und zum Wechsel der Situationen dasselbe sei, dasselbe aber sich verschieden bestimmend, und in Bestimmungen, die wenn man von der Situationsrelativität absieht, widerstimmig sind, einander widersprechen. Analyse der 'Relativitäten,' der Idee der praktischen 'Situation'*" [„*Situation as practical situation.* The practical life and its 'situational truth,' identity of being, which is the same in relation to the practical situation and to the change of situations, the same, however, determining itself differently, and in determinations, which, if one disregards the situational relativity, are inconsistent, contradict each other. Analysis of the 'relativities,' of the idea of the practical 'situation.'"] This manuscript is especially significant in understanding the distinction of the constitution of *relative* truths from *universal* ones, as well as how the latter transforms from the former, to which I return in the fifth chapter.

[26] Husserl sometimes uses the Latin term *habitus*. This use alludes to the ethical tradition, following Aristotelian sense of ἕξις as an acquired way of acting. He also sometimes uses *Gewohnheit*, "habit" or "usualness," to indicate a normative dimension of practice, which I discuss below.

individual, there are contemporaneous individual monads. In this relationship, there arises an intersubjective *constitution* of sense such that facticity includes meaningful matters that cannot be achieved by a singular monad, as, say, social groups.

Moreover, with respect to this problem of intersubjective constitution, Husserl analyzes what he calls an "affective communication."[27] In this context, this is a sort of empathy wherein the other monad may be constituted by me as another "I can." For present purposes, bodily perception may be taken as exemplary of this "I can."[28] Among Husserl's rich analysis of the lived-body and its "I can" are two essential distinctions: first, the lived-body, as *situated*, lives within free but limited possibilities of movement, it is *kinaesthetic*; second, the lived-body is a willing-body (*Willensleib*), that has a relation to the goal of the ego.[29] My activity has a horizon of possibilities that is situated in the living-present: I *can move* my eyes, tilt my head, and so on; but I *move* within a nexus of possible movements, that is, my movement *can* move according to the situation of my body in its world. So, if my neck has a "crick" in it, it is restricted as compared to previous possibilities, though I can still *want* to move it as I previously could. So, in affective communication, a transference of apperceptive sense may take place between monads. I may, for example, be a spectator at the Boston Marathon, where I can "empathize" with runners: I can "live" in the race as they run down the street by identifying my own "I can" with their experience. As such, I can both become aware of *my own* "I can," insofar as I can or cannot run in the manner they do, and I may also become aware of the "I can" of the other, taking it into my own, as when a runner slips and falls, taking up into my own experience that the lived-body of the other is feeling pain *because my* lived-body can and perhaps has in fact felt pain. In this way, the world is thereby shared and built upon by a community of contemporaneous monads.

---

[27] Still more, affective communication suggests unification of monads; see Hua XI, 175: "Affective communication says: Every addition of affective force of any member of the group connected in distance by homogeneity and detachment increases the force of all comrades." This will take on another sense in the context of feelings and values, as I suggest in the next chapter.

[28] In Steinbock (1995), p. 291, fn 12, there is the following passage from Ms. D 131/125b: "Hierbei ist das Erscheinungssystem, das der freien Möglichkeiten des Durchlaufens, auf mein waches Ich bezogen, das Ich des 'Ich kann das und das tun'" ["Here the appearance system, that of the free possibilities of passing through, is related to my awake I, the I of 'I can do this and that'." That passage continues: "Also wenn sich die Freiheit des Ich-kann ungehemmt verwirklicht, so führt das eine endlose Zukunft mit sich. Aber die Zukunft ist nicht völlig offen" ["so, if the freedom of the I-can is realized uninhibitedly, this leads to an endless future. But the future is not completely open."] Moreover, there is the "I can" of the intellect, of reason, which I, once again, take up below. Consider, here, ist appearance in Ms A V 21/103a: "Doch es bedarf hier einer wesentlichen Scheidung der Sphären der Passivität (der passiven Auffassungsfunktionen, in denen z.B. die Natur für das Subjekt 'entspringt') gegenüber der Vermögen 'freier' Spontaneität, der freien Aktivität der Vernunft. Das sind die eigentlichen Vermögen: ursprüngliches Bewusstsein des 'Ich kann'" ["But an essential distinction is needed here of the spheres of passivity (of the passive functions of apprehension, in which, for example, nature 'arises' for the subject) from the capacities of 'free' spontaneity, of the free activity of reason. These are the actual capacities: original consciousness of 'I can'"]. Husserl will call this "free activity of reason" the "agent intellect."

[29] See, for example, Hua IV, pp. 95, 151, and 285.

Now, let us turn to how Husserl traces the emergence and operation of inquiry for the monad. This will also prepare an elucidation of the very operation of the regressive procedure in phenomenology, the operation of which *eventually* comes explicitly named by Husserl as an *inquiry-back*—a *rückfragen*. With this, the phenomenologist critically inquires-back from either achievements in the world as well as from the world itself. This methodological development also begins to throw into question his monadology, as it shows the socio-historical world horizon as a condition for the sense, meaning, and value. First, though, let us consider more exactly genesis and Husserl's genetic account of inquiry.

4.2 Husserl's Discovery and Description of Genesis from the Regressive Approach

> I am concerned with the phenomenological givennesses as the archaeologist during excavation: they are compiled cleanly, but the actual work is not their description, but the reconstruction. A foundation of what is understood provides a systematic leading-clue to the animation of ever new debris pieces from the junk-room of the ununderstood, and to give a systematic significance: its "function" and its place of origin in the understanding of construction and understanding itself of "origin" also in the genetic sense.[30]

Although nascent analyses of genesis can be found already in the Husserl's Göttingen period, between 1901 and 1916, as is clear in the recent *Studien zur Struktur des Bewusstsein*, a mature employment of the method appears in his "Passive Synthesis Lectures."[31] These lectures, given in Freiburg, in 1920/21, 1923, and 1926, were named "Logic," "Selected Phenomenological Problems," and, finally, "Fundamental Problems of Logic." On the folder containing Husserl's notes, there is the summary title, "Transcendental Logic." Parts of these manuscripts were edited and used for *Formale und Transzendental Logik* and the posthumous *Erfahrung und Urteil*.[32] The *Husserliana* volumes in which these pages have been collected seek to express their content with the title heads *Analysen zur Passiven Synthesis* and *Aktiv Synthesen*.[33]

---

[30] Ms. A V 21/61a: "Ich pflege mich gegen phänomenologische Gegebenheiten so zu verhalten wie der Archäologe bei der Ausgrabung: Sie werden sauber zusammengestellt, aber die eigentliche Arbeit ist nicht ihre Beschreibung, sondern die Rekonstruktion. Ein Grundstock von Verstandenem liefert einen systematischen Leitfaden um nach und nach immer neue Trümmerstücke aus der Rumpelkammer des Unverstandenen zu beseelen und um eine systematische Bedeutung zu geben: seine 'Funktion' und seine Ursprungsstelle im Verstandenen und selbst dabei erst zum Verständnis kommenden Gesamtbau, und Verständnis des 'Ursprungs' auch im genetischen Sinn."

[31] Further description can be found in the working manuscripts in the four *Husserliana* volumes, with the main title, *Verstand,Gemüt und Wille. Studien zur Struktur des Bewusstseins*. See, also, Husserl (2019), p. 465.

[32] Originally published as Edmund Husserl, *Formale und transzendentale Logik: Versuch einer Kritik der logischen Vernunft* (Halle: Niemeyer, 1929), and Edmund Husserl, *Erfahrung und Urteil:Untersuchungen zur Genealogie der Logik*, ed. Ludwig Langrebe (Praha: Academia, 1939). Critical edition of the former in Hua XVII, Husserl (1974).

[33] Hua XI, Husserl (1966); and, Hua XXXI, Husserl (2000).

The English translation, *Analyses Concerning Passive and Active Synthesis: Lectures in Transcendental Logic*, captures the full breadth of this drama.[34] In any case, together, these titles express something essential: they elucidate Husserl's attempt to recover the original sense of logic as a "science of science" through phenomenology.

In the lectures, Husserl notes that the German word '*Logik*' (like the English 'logic') comes from the Greek λέγειν—"to gather together."[35] Its derivatives can mean a 'discourse' or 'expounding upon,' insofar as these gather together meaning into a coherent whole. From this, the noun λόγος can refer to the spiritual act of thinking and speaking itself, as in the historical formulation of *logos* as a "faculty" of *ratio*, *Vernunft*, or *reason*. It can also be used to describe an expressed word or concept; more exactly, a *general* or *universal* word. He thus distinguishes three main senses of *logic* or, as rehearsed previously, namely, speaking, thinking, thought (*Reden, Denken, Gedachtes*).[36] Following upon the *descriptive* work of the *Logical Investigations*, he further develops the *reconstructive* possibilities of his phenomenology. In other words, to recover the genesis of accomplishments of consciousness, rather than merely describing that which is presently given, he begins what he calls a "transcendental aesthetic" that means to build up to a "transcendental logic" or, what amounts to the same, a "transcendental analytic."[37]

Husserl's transcendental analytic is influenced by the Kantian project, though, by it, he means something different than his predecessor. For Kant, there is no synthesis of sense in the sphere of sensibility but only an intuitive reception of relative appearances, of "phenomena." Sense formation instead occurs at the level of the understanding in *a priori* concepts, which are, in turn, not intuitive but only synthetic. For Husserl, on the other hand, an intuition, as a fulfillment of intention occurs in both sensibility and understanding. Thus, a transcendental aesthetic recovers the *origins* of constitution in perception as it provides the content for the activity of understanding. Thus, a transcendental logic attends to the data of consciousness, tracing how matters are given in order to express the lawful regularity of their emergence and operation.

---

[34] For a fuller history, see the translator's preface of Husserl (2001a).

[35] Husserl, (2001a), "Introductory Remarks."

[36] Husserl, (2001a), pp. 1–38, esp. 8.

[37] Consider Husserl's later remarks, from 1919 or so, in Hua IV, p. 198: "I have said earlier that a good piece of a transcendental aesthetics to be called so in the genuine sense reaches into Kant's transcendental analytics, according to our way of talking, the transcendental aesthetics of materiality. But the idea of transcendental analytics or transcendental logic includes still another problem area, which is essentially to be related to the discussed questions of secondary qualities and the sense of physically true nature, for which just this talk of transcendental logic (or analytics, whereby this word is also only the Aristotelian expression for logic) is the characteristically appropriate one. The methodical form of thought processes and reasonings demanded by the peculiarity of transcendental logic....We will try to bring to light the deep sense of this transcendental logic, which has so far not been clearly understood. We will always say 'transcendental-logical' in order to exclude any conflation with the original and never to be abandoned concept of the transcendental, which encompasses the problem area of the clarifications of all essential relations of being and consciousness, and thus to indicate my protest against the popular pretension that the transcendental-logical method is the one and only method for all problems of the theory of reason."

With these points in mind, let us take this as the provisional sense of what Husserl calls the *Ursprungsfrage*—"the question of origins."[38]

To explain further, such allusions to Kant also suggest a further relation to the novel *regressive* procedure. Generally speaking, Kant employed a regressive argument in his transcendental deductions to show the "conditions of possibility," that is, the conditions necessary for the data according to the limits of the data.[39] Husserl proceeds similarly, though with important qualifications: he does so, once again, by going-back *from* the accomplishments of the natural attitude *to* the *pre*-given, constitut*ing* dimension of the subject; here, he may attend to those structures and conditions *of* sense-constitution, then reconstruct their relations of motivation.[40] Moreover, the regressive procedure yields the *normative* sense of constitution; that is to say, it is able to reconstruct how sense, meaning, and value emerge, are fulfilled, develop as well as how they are disrupted, disappointed, or even decline across time, in a *lawful* manner. He does so, to reiterate, by *going back from mundane achievements into those subjective operations necessary for them*. Thus, rather than bracketing the world in order to proceed purely to immanence, he means to give a critical account of how objectivity is constituted in the dynamic, intentional subject in the world. This is, as Husserl sometimes calls it, a "correlation analysis."[41]

---

[38] I would be remiss not to mention how Husserl understands the "question of origins," especially of *ideas*, to emerge as a specific thematic with empiricial psychologists, especially with *Locke*. See, for example, Hua XXVII, (1930), p. 129ff, which is a later explication of that fact. See, also, Hua XXVII, pp. 131–132 and Hua XVII, p. 141: "We must now clarify the meaning of these questions of origin – in the general framework of which the question of the origin of general objects, which is thematic for us here, falls….As is well known, questions of origin are a much discussed part in traditional psychology, especially in cognitive psychology as well as in epistemology, which is either separated from it or united with it…In its first stage, this intentional psychology is related to the modes of consciousness (modes of intentional experiences) that are different in essence and to those of their synthetic unification into new, grounded intentionality, thus descriptively investigating the form-types of intentionality, which <must> belong to every conceivable factual life of consciousness, for everything that is essentially inseparable from it. In its higher stage, however, it is completely dominated by the problems which we call problems of origin."

[39] For more on this, see Ameriks (1978).

[40] In this period, Husserl will, indeed, emphasize the importance of noetics in this process. Consider Husserl (2019), p. 491: "Likewise: I lead noematic logic and formal *mathesis universalis* back to a logical noetics, and likewise everywhere. If I have from the start human sciences, then the cultural formations lead back to the subjective acts constituting them, which constitute cultural objects with their spiritual predicates, and back to the corresponding persons that thereby become thematic as well. If the personalities in turn systematically become a theme, and in addition in the most general manner in the general psychology of personalities, then, naturally, all subjective formations and that means, all objective formations that can be produced in subjectivities, at once with their subjective *noeses*, must be investigated."

[41] Husserl (1988), pp. 176–7: "But the first is the correlation research of consciousness as lived-experience and therein consciousness as such (the *cogitatum*)." For further comparison with the Cartesian procedure, see Steinbock, *Home and Beyond: Generative Phenomenology after Husserl*, (Evanston: Northwestern University Press, 1995), especially pp. 24–28 and 79–85. Again, I will further determine this as *regressive-inquisitive*, in the final chapter, by considering the *operation* of *inquiring-back* where the *world itself* comes into question *from its constitution*.

The correlation analysis of Husserl treats the subjective and objective in relation. Focusing, for the time being, on the side of the subject, he discovers a "fundamental stratification of conscious life," treating them under a *renewed* rubric of *passivity* and *activity*.[42] These are not strict divisions of, say, bodily and intellectual faculties or sensibility and understanding, but rather moments in the concrete life of the monad. In this respect, the passive and active spheres delimit levels of "being aware," of consciousness. At one limit, the passive level is a primordial sphere of constitution that does not include egoic, active awareness. Further, passivity provides the basis for activity and, taken as such, is a *pre*-predicative sphere of *pre*-givenness. Attention to passivity brings it to active awareness, making thematic that which previously was only passive. Phenomenology goes back into subjectivity and brings to light passivity as an origin of sense, meaning, and value.

4.2.1 Passivity and Activity

To determine more exactly passivity, activity, and their relation, it is important to emphasize, from the outset, that the monadic subject is a unity of passive and active spheres. As Husserl puts it, passivity provides essential conditions of the possibility of subjectivity itself.[43] As such, while the passive sphere has its own integrity: the ego is not *null* but rather *latent* therein. Indeed, in the subject, the passive level points beyond itself to the active level—it is, in a sense, "*teleological*."

However, the relation of passivity and activity is not uni-directional. Although the passive sphere pre-gives the content of activity, pointing upward, as it were, active achievements can also flow back into passivity, becoming sedimented in conscious life and so also possibility reawakened by further activity. Indeed, passivity, by itself, achieves only "object-like formations."[44] Though sense perception does posit a sort of objectivity, knowledge of the *transcendent* object *per se* is not achieved there in sense perception; instead, there is a "mere" intuition or *reception*, an immanent constitution or taking-to-be-true (in the sense of *wahr-nehmen*). Thus, passivity provides a substrate of pre-constituted that might be presented to an *active ego* for examination and objectivation. So, Husserl can say, it is the *origin* of truth, though activity is the proper sphere of active truth constitution.

Husserl identifies two key matters in the lawful syntheses of passivity, namely, *association* and *affection*. Association is a synthesis of being-acceptance within the flow of perception. With it, sense is constituted through time as identical and as concordant or harmonious—as "normal." Nevertheless, that which is given appears with an affective charge or, as Husserl says, with differing "propensities to be" in

---

[42] See Husserl (2001a), p. 105; Hua, XI, p. 64.
[43] See Husserl (2001a), pp. 163–164; Hua XI, p. 124.
[44] For more on this, see Husserl (2001a), "Translator's Introduction," §3.

4.2 Husserl's Discovery and Description of Genesis from the Regressive ...

that normality.[45] In other words, there is an *affective* dimension to passivity. In this dimension, he treats a "constitutive duet" between *noesis* and *noema*.[46]

From the noematic side, the given appears with a greater or lesser *affective force* (*Reiz*). By this is meant that the given *itself* appears with a force, without noetic solicitation.[47] A noise, for example, from the subtle arrhythmia of a broken clock or a loud crash of thunder, may give itself in a way that is unsolicited by the subject. From the noetic side, again, there appears a synthesis via association, now taken in relation to the affective force of the noema. Through this, there can be syntheses of homogeneity or heterogeneity, where the former synthesizes *similar* and *uniform* matters and the latter *contrasting* and *discrete* ones. Without delving into all distinctions here, especially insofar as sense perception constitutes space-time, it is possible to note that Husserl finds that there is not a mere flowing of experience but the constitution of sense already in passivity.[48] The crash of thunder is given as unexpected, contrasting to the relative quiet before it as the uniformity of previous passive synthesis is disrupted. There is, in other words, a *synthesis* of data in passivity that gives the ground for further determination and differentiation of sense.

Still more, there comes a unanimity, a *harmony* or *concordance* that is constituted *normal* for the subject. The synthesis of sense yields an overarching concordance, a unity of sense through experience: the ticking of a clock can become "normal" in experience, taken up without further ado. However, my study may also be disturbed by a defect in the second-hand of ticking of the clock, where the previously harmonious synthesis might be interrupted or *modalized*, which occurs with an appearance that is given "otherwise" than anticipated or expected that disrupts the normal concordance of my perception.[49] With this, there arises in experience an attempt to restore the normal, concordant condition.

Such a restoration of concordance may be achieved within the passive sphere itself. Indeed, the fact of further experience itself might resolve the disruption. Without any activity of the ego, not only might a ticking of second-hand might correct itself, but the persistent defect might itself be taken up into experience as normal. If the latter, the subject might constitute a "new normal" by taking up the deviation from the previous normality and refiguring it. *However*, if the concordant synthesis within the

---

[45] Husserl (2001a), p. 82.

[46] On the "constitutive duet" (*Dopplespiel*) between intentional terms, the *noesis* and *noema*, see Husserl (2001a), p. 52 or Hua XI, p. 15.

[47] The demand on the side of the object may be simply *to be*, to be noticed and determined. See: Ms. B III 9/49a: "...das 'Das!,' dieses Seiende in dem lebendigen und ursprünglichen Modus. Genau so verhält sich nun doch mit dem rückblickend auf das Gesetzte des frühen Aktes Gerichtet-sein, z.B. auf das Akterlebnis des soeben abgeschlossenen Aktes...in seinem stehenden Wandel für mich zum 'das!' aber dieses "erfassen" als aktives Perzipieren, in dem ein 'das!' mich beschäftigt..." ["...the 'That!,' this being in the living and original mode. Exactly the same is the case with the being directed retrospectively to the law of the earlier act, for example, to the act-result of the just finished act...in its standing change for me to the "that!" but this "grasping" as active perceiving, in which a 'that!' occupies me...."]. I return to the point in the next chapters.

[48] For a detailed analysis of Husserl's analysis of time, including this point, see Warren (2009).

[49] See Husserl (2001a), pp. 66 and 68–70; Hua XI, pp. 27–28, 30, and 36.

passive sphere is disrupted in a way that cannot be resolved in passivity, a *determinate motivation* appears for the ego to turn toward it and strive to restore concordance. This turning Husserl identifies as the first moments of activity.

To clarify the turning, let us underscore how Husserl understands *motivation*. For him, it is a general expression for spiritual "causality." The genetic method can reconstruct the motivational relations such that we understand how it is possible for the acts to relate while attending to the content of those acts; thus, we may say that the ego does not turn because of an affective allure but instead is "moved by" the force of the given to attend to it. In this way, the question of origin—the question about "Why," and especially of the question, "Why the act of the ego or of each act has been performed"—acquires a special meaning that is especially important to us.[50] Taken thusly, phenomenology seeks "Why" the *whole* subject acts, performs, that is to say, the phenomenologist seeks the understandable relation of acts within subject as a whole in the world.

When the phenomenology inquires-back into motivations, they do so especially with regard to *how* acts relate to contents. Taken in this respect, passive motivation is the "mother ground of reason," as it is that upon which and from which intellgence operates—a sort of *nihil est in intellectu quod non prius fuerit in sensu*.[51] In other words, it is not only that passive perception provides content to intelligence, but that intelligence operates on passive synthesis. Indeed, Husserl uses the Aristotelian term *intellectus agens* or *active intellect* to delineate the spontaneous activity of "setting into play accomplishments of the ego."[52] Thus, he says, "What I had in mind under the title of 'active intellect'…was the categorial act of the understanding, the mind, and the will."[53] It is *categorial* as it is constitutive of objectivity, which, it must be

---

[50] Hua XXXVII, p. 110.

[51] As summarized, for example, by St. Thomas Aquinas, *Quaestiones disputatae de veritate*, q.2, art.3, Arg.19. See Hua XXXVII, supplement 5: "We can now also say: *Passive motivation is the mother-ground of reason* and has as such receptivity for the *intellectus agens* and the subject of active reason in its rational reign. And therewith is *potential reason*, because what *intellectus agens* brings forth [*herauszeugt*[is already moored in the mother-ground [*das ist in dem Mutterboden schon angelegt*"]. The terms Husserl uses to describe the matter of egoic activity characteristically varies with his perspective. He uses, for example, *Verstand* and *Intellekt* as virtually exchangeable: *Verstand* most usually is paired with *Sinnlichkeit* to allude to Kant, whereas the use of *Intellekt* seems to have a psychological reference to Brentano as well as the tradition so influenced by reactions to Aristotle. In any case, both are used in the *Passive Synthesis* lectures and surrounding manuscripts.

[52] See Husserl (2001a), pp. 104–105; Hua XI, p. 63. See also, Hua XXXVII, p. 112: "*The realm of reason* are the *acts* performed by the ego, and this especially according to the sides of the positions in these acts performed by the ego as positions of and of sense contents. The novel occurrences, which in the act-sphere, the sphere of the *intellectus agens*, have specifically their own motivations in the act of thought, which are the *motivations of reason*. That says, these motivations stand even under questions of rationality and irrationality, of lawfulness or unlawfulness, and this in the differentiating, through the basic kind of prefigured sense pertaining acts and act-positions; in other words, according to the <sense> of *beauty* as the aesthetic lawfulness, the *theoretical truth* as the logical lawfulness and also the *ethical lawfulness*." I present some aspects of these latter points in the next chapter.

[53] Hua XXXIX, pp. 34–38: "But what I had in mind under the title "active intellect" was the categorial action of the understanding, the spirit, and the will. Objects of a representational sense,

stressed, the ego did not have prior to activity. Yet, there is the intellect itself, of which he speaks in manuscripts as the *intellectus ipse*, likely from the Leibnitizian addition to the Aristotelian, *nihil est in intellectu quod non prius fuerit in sensu, nisi intellectus ipse*.[54] This, Husserl says, is the "epitome of a pure possibility, as the original *a priori*...the possibility of 'reason' of 'understanding.'"[55] These points relate, of course, to Kant's understanding of the intellect in terms of an *ectypus* and *archetypes* ("an image and in itself"). However, unlike Kant, Husserl is not *deducing* an *a priori* form or *faculty* but rather is *describing and reconstructing* the relation of acts of sensibility and understanding, perception and intelligence as appearing in the subject as a whole.

Passive perception and active intelligence thus appear as different though related operations. Where passivity is found by the phenomenologist as a sphere of *pre-constituted sense*, that is, of received sense constituted in perception, egoic activity *gives itself* sense.[56] Of course, the intellect is not fashioning sense from nothing. It is acting upon and within sense from passivity, at once undergoing and acting from the concrete conditions of givenness. So, again, Husserl finds that the ego is not merely absent as null in the passive sphere but is an essential possibility of the subject, that is, it belongs to the structure of the ego to *be active* and so *activated*, as it were. Thus, in the latter respect, as James Hart aptly puts the matter, "The I is 'awakened' to a proper agency in response to itself at the passive synthetic level."[57] Something in passivity may be given with such an affective force that it "I wake up," as it were, as the thunder abruptly moves my active awareness. In the former respect, the active intellect constitutes sense which the ego was not given in passive perception. Thus, Husserl will more specifically name the *intellectus agens* or active ego as the "wakeful radiating center" of subjectivity. Here, as *agens*, the intellect *spontaneously* seeks to determine.

The wakefulness of the active intellect includes a radiation toward determination. Indeed, the essential point to understand here, for Husserl, is that it appears as "constantly in the process of determining more closely," always striving to know more, and so also differentiating sense.[58] The active ego or intellect is not satisfied, we might say, with pre-constituted sense from passivity. Rather, it is *agens* or, perhaps more illustratively, ποιητικός—it is "poetic" in the sense of *creative or productive of sense and meaning*. In this respect, Husserl treats three moments of the process

---

which can be brought to original experience only in ego-actions, which are not merely receptive, but produce objectivity according to their special nature for the very first time, are called 'categorial objects' or 'objects of the active intellect.' We call all forms 'purely categorial' that are pure correlates of activity, which is therefore its own source of originally objectifying genesis."

[54] See, for example, G.W. Leibniz, New Essays Concerning Human Understanding, trans. A.G. Langley (London: Macmillan: 1896), p. 111.

[55] Hua LXII, p. 169.

[56] See Hua XVII, p. 131 and Hua XXXI, pp. 40–41. Husserl includes here the will, further evidencing the interpretation in the previous semester of the sense of a "rational appetite" in relation to action.

[57] See, for example, Hua IV, pp. 112–113 and 119–120. Also, for further explication of the points, see Hart (1996), 112.

[58] See Husserl (2001a), pp. 127–128; *Hua* XI, pp. 84–85.

of determination in the active ego: the first moment is a matter of identification of sense; the second produces the universal as a novel object; the third is the determination of an "as such" judgment. Perhaps a brief review of these three steps will serve to clarify this difficult issue. From a sketch of this framework, let me trace Husserl's genetic analyses of the emergence of inquiry, as he recovers inquiry *as a multi-layered striving for determination and differentiation of true being.*[59]

In the first place, there is the process of identification in the *attentive regard* in the *examination* of the active ego. Such an examination does not yield new objects but constitutes themes from passive pre-givenness by bringing them together, actively synthesizing them. I turn my head to see, for example, that the ticking noise is from the clock, thereby identifying these in my consciousness. In the second place, an active relating and determining can produce a novel object as a universal. As we have already noted, that object is not a matter of *perceptual* induction but intellectual seeing it produces a novel object in the *idea*, as I ask, "What is making that noise?" or, to transpose this into the *reason* that the question seeks, "Why is there a noise?" These questions cannot be fulfilled simply by *seeing* the clock; there must instead be an *understanding* of *what* it is in relation to *why*, the reason. In the third place, then, the universal judgment becomes the *basis* for the judgment "in general." This *conceptualizing* judgment operates by association of similarity and categorial interest in the universal, making it possible to apply this "whatsoever" to particular instantiations, if they fulfill the required conditions. It associates, to continue with the example, the universal grasp of what a clock is with other clocks, including this one that seems to be broken.

Again, each of the above levels of achievement may flow back into passivity. Achievements of the active ego can be *sedimented*, contributing to the pattern or structure of the normality of the passive sphere. For example, the grasp of a universal sets a possibility for future experiences to be associated, determined *as* subsumed under its sense: once I grasp *what* a triangle *is*, all three-sided figures may be determined *as* triangles without having to re-formulate and the original judgment *per se*. Moreover, the following back into the living fabric of subjectivity plays an essential role in an aspect at which we have so far only gestured, namely, the *genetic sense of normality and normativity*. I turn to this, in the next subsection, in order to prepare for investigation of inquiry, especially in order to make sense of how there emerges in experience modes and methods of inquiry.

4.2.2 Normativity as a Theme of Genetic Phenomenology

Husserl's phenomenology does not pre-suppose notions of development and normativity, then drape them upon experience. Instead, these are grasped from a reflective analysis of *the operations of subjectivity* itself. In other words, *transcendental* phenomenological inquiry seeks to understand the lawfulness of immanent norms "at

---

[59] The following threefold distinction can be found in the general outline of the lectures.

work" or *operative* within experience, and so, too, within the world. With this, transcendental logic responds to that other ancient question about *normativity*, insofar as it gives the laws according to which genuine and authentic thinking may operate.

To begin with a clarification by contrast, Husserl's constitutive analysis carries an implicit critique of a naturalistic concept of normativity. As Steinbock explains, a naturalistic conception takes it to be "according to nature," that is, as something set according to an abstract and static "ideal."[60] One might say, for example, that the right hand is dominant in "accord with nature," such that, if one is not right-handed, one varies from the norm, from what one "ought" to do. Any such variation is then taken as *ab*-normal, or even *sinister* as a "deviant," as if there is something *wrong* with being otherwise. In contrast to this, a genetic constitutive analysis discovers that which is *normal* in relation to a sense constituted *within* experience. Considering again the issue of "handedness," when approached thusly, is in reference to the meaning in operation, namely, in how one handles the world. Moreover, the *abnormal* is not a mere deviation from a preset norm, but as a constitutive break, as a rupture in the normal. The normal, in short, neither comes simply from the outside or the inside, but rather is understood as it emerges from one handling one's world. Since this may be easily misconstrued, especially if one does not consider how it relates to Husserl's *eidetics*, let me clarify further.

Again, Steinbock recognizes how the *Logical Investigations* tended to use a sense of "normal" experience as distinct from normativity in the sciences.[61] Where the latter tends to mean those that either study regulative laws or proceed according to those laws, the former tends to speak to a "coinciding" of sense such that a conflict of meaning is "not normal." Thus, as we saw, the question appears within such a conflict of meaning, within a modalized intention that is not "normal," in the sense of a coinciding or fulfillment. Although this construal forms a basis for his latter work, he moves beyond it as he investigates how it unfolds through time. So, in the genetic program, he uses the term to describe the unification of sense lived-experience or, as Steinbock makes clear, how differences interact in formation of identical sense through time.[62] The aforementioned analysis of concordance and discordance speaks to this, as does the *anomaly* that is an interruption or a *break* in concordance. In this break, an experience is *given* such that a discord is constituted, for which Husserl uses terms with the root *-bruch*, like *einbruch, unterbruch, durchbruch*.[63] So, put negatively, if something is functioning "normally," it means that it is proceeding as unified, without break.

---

[60] For the detailed analysis, see Steinbock (1995), pp. 129–169.

[61] See Steinbock (1995), p. 130.

[62] Steinbock (1995), p. 130.

[63] See, for example, Hua Mat VIII, pp. 77, 245, and 288. Also, Ms. D 13 I/123a: "*Anomalität....das Problem der Erfahrungsunterbrechung...*" ["Anomality....the problem of the disruption of experience..."]; also at 232a: "Aber 'normal' heißt das erst durch Kontrast mit Anomalität, die von diesem ersten, notwendig zuerst konstituierten System der Einstimmigkeit abweichen" ["But 'normal' is called that only by contrast with anomality, which deviate from this first, necessarily first constituted system of unanimity."].

From a genetic perspective, Husserl comes to understand normality as it functions in reference to *optimality*. Regarding this, Steinbock finds Husserl making two main distinctions of the optimal: in the first place, within intentional experience, *the optimal is differentiation in unity*; and, in the second place, the optimal is a matter of being *"in itself."*[64] Consider briefly how the normality of sight is constituted *through* seeing, where the optimality of seeing implies seeing more and seeing more differentiation in the seen. I might, for the first time, put on eye-glasses (to borrow a recurrent example from Steinbock): I have my normal way of seeing, constituted before wearing glasses; upon trying them on, however, my sight becomes suddenly *clearer, more differentiated*, and a new optimality breaks through. The previous norm, that is, my previously "normal" seeing, along with its sense of the optimal, is retended *as* "crossed out." In this, I still retain the crossed-out but do so precisely as "abnormal," insofar as it now relates to that which is the "new normal." Indeed, I can remember previous experience now as non-optimal, in reference to the new norm: the clarity of sight is associated as "better" than the fuzzy way of seeing before; my sight prior is now taken as against this optimal or as abnormal. In this way, any *normative notion* of "worse" and "better" obtains in relation to this optimal. This, however, also relates to that which is *essential*, that is, that which is a lawful regularity graspable in experience, as an "in itself."

To reiterate, the above constitutive analysis is not reducible to mere accidental events. This is for a few reasons. In the first place, the analysis grasps an *ideal* of what the operation is to be, "in itself." The seeing is still a seeing, clarified as an act within a certain set of relationships, and so on. Furthermore, in the second place, the activity of seeing relates to its actual occurrence in accordance with the ideal will be *optimal*. In other words, if the seeing actually occurs, and occurs as determining and differentiating being, then it is optimally a seeing. There are *limits* to what counts as sight, according to *what sight is*, but this is grasped in relation to the relations of operations. So, in the third place, the analysis can also make clear that discord with the ideal to be the criteria of *decline*. Sight can decline, can become worse, and blindness, though its harboring its own sense, relates to sight as being unsighted, without sight. Inquiry likewise has its ideal sense which relates to optimal operation. By grasping *the essence of inquiry*, the phenomenologist understands what it is in intending answers and its optimality in striving for more answers, for increased differentiation, such that, if it does not meet this ideal, it fails to be what it is. In short, through regressive approach of the genetic method, the phenomenologists can understand the immanent and operative norms of subjectivity.

A significant further point is that a genetic account of *development allows* for the possibility of a *new norm* from out of operation. On the one hand, there is a development—or, to play on the German word, *ent-wickeln*, "un-folding"—of possibilities from conditions set from previously realized possibilities. In this respect, the phenomenologist does not impose abstract constraints, like one *ought* to be right-handed to handle the world. Rather, through regressive inquiry, can show how, in *handling* the world, there emerges an ought such that there are better or worse ways

---

[64] Steinbock (1995), p. 139. See also Hua XI, p. 23.

to do so. This helps us understand that concordant experience is normal, not merely in the sense of recurring or repeating, but in relation *to the fulfillment of the teleological sense of an operation and sets of operations*. On the other hand, new and novel ideals from previous conditions may develop. For example the phenomenologist may inquiry-back into the conditions from which handedness came at all, as, say, infants develop or even, as I take up in the fifth chapter, through the development of various species.

Now, however, let us trace the complex genesis of inquiry in the "history" of the monadic individual subject. Doing so, we discover inquiry as a multi-layered striving for determination and differentiation. This "multi-layer" is a *set* of operations within the monadic subject. In it, we find the origins of inquiry in passivity, first, as awakening the active ego and, second, as the substrate for it to ask what it will. From this genetic perspective, the proper sense of questioning is unveiled in the *process of responding* to evidence, without which one remains frustrated or disturbed. But since the monadic subject is essentially in a process of becoming within a becoming world, there is always the open possibility of ever more questions and responses. In sum, Husserl recovers inquiry as a striving for fulfillment within the process of becoming for the monadic individual, within *facticity*, such that responses can pattern future experience and methods can accrue in a process of optimization. So, let me begin, finally, with the analysis of the genesis of inquiry.

4.3 Inquiry as a Multi-layered Striving for Determination and Differentiation

In the lectures on passive synthesis, Husserl construes inquiry as "multi-layered striving toward overcoming modalization through a judicative decision."[65] I reconstruct his analysis of this through the following four subsections:

A. the first goes back into the passive sphere, where otherwise unified perception may become "questionable";
B. then, the second, considers the turning of attention which relates the passive and active spheres, where I identify a distinction between "Whether that" and "If that" as they relate to various modes of the "What" and "Why" questions;
C. in the third section, I emphasize a distinction between *interest* and *dis-*interest and introduce how these ways of inquiry can set into attitudes in experience.

First, let me note, with C.S. Broudier and John Bruin, that Husserl's genetic project represents a renewed approach to inquiry, distinguished from the first theory of the *Logical Investigations*.[66] Broudier, for his part, claims that "[Husserl's] attention

---

[65] See Hua XI, pp. 58–59.

[66] Broudier (1983), pp. 387-410. John Bruin also purports a twofold differentiation of Husserl's "theory of questioning" in his, *Homo Interrogans* (2001). I find the matter to be more complex, especially in how these developments relate to each other, as I present throughout these chapters.

switches from the analysis of the meaning of expressions and expressed acts to the description of degrees of being-certain and the genesis of knowledge: it is, in a way, a switch from a phenomenological logic to a phenomenological psychology."[67] While I agree that there is a switch of attention in the genetic analysis, I would qualify the shift from being one phenomenological logic to a phenomenological psychology. For the genesis of knowledge, for Husserl, *is* a logical matter, properly understood. Phenomenological psychology, for Husserl, is a way into the *a priori* method of *thinking, thought,* and *said*—of λόγος. As such, it relates to, even if it does not directly consider, the more "logical" analysis of meaning of expressions. Perhaps this is what Broudier means when he says that it is "in a way" a switch. With all that in mind, let us consider the genesis inquiry.

4.3.1 The Origin of Inquiry in Passivity

Again, passive perception, taken broadly, may be construed as the sphere in which being is accepted by the subject. Perception is *immediate*, in the sense of positing being without active verification or reflective mediation. Insofar as it takes the given simply to be, "without question," it may be understood as a sort of "judgment," though not in the sense of an active verification of true being. Rather, there is here a normal unification of sense—a *passive synthesis*.

Indeed, Husserl sometimes calls this perceptual harmony of sense a sort of "believing."[68] He even identifies it as a *doxa* and, more strictly, an *Urdoxa* or primordial belief.[69] It is possible for concordant perception to be modalized, of course. Indeed, it is essentially possible for something to be given as "otherwise," that is, given in a "variable mode of being or a variable mode of validity," of possibly-being rather than certainly-being.[70] In this respect, otherwise unified perception may become "questionable." This being-questionable appears when there is a presentation of multiple possibilities with a contesting or conflicting propensity to be such that a belief in being is "called into question." In other words, such a disruption motivates a striving for unity within the living-present. That means that, if concordance cannot be reestablished in passivity through confirmation of one of the possibilities, it might demand attention of the active ego in a "primitive inquiry."[71]

To be clear, such "primitive inquiry" is yet within the passive sphere. To elucidate the emergence of this and place it into relation to active inquiry, consider two groups of "possibilities" that Husserl identifies: first, there are *enticing* possibilities, which appear as problematic or questionable, and, second, there are those that are *not enticing*, which appear as open or closed possibilities. Those of the latter type appear

---

[67] Broudier (1983), p. 399.
[68] Husserl (2001a), pp. 74–78; Hua XI, pp. 36–38.
[69] See, for example, Hua III/1, §117.
[70] Husserl (2001a), p. 75.
[71] Husserl (2001), p. 103.

4.3 Inquiry as a Multi-layered Striving for Determination and Differentiation

where a possibility is given without enticement, where it has no demand speaking either for or against it. So, an *open* possibility is one that bears no affective force and so may be determined through the given of any object within a range. For this Husserl gives the example of an intention of "speckled color," wherein any color will fulfill the intention, since there is no demand for blue, red, and so on, nor any enticement for any specific color but simply *color*. On the other hand, a *closed* possibility is where the affective force is so strong that it virtually excludes opposing possibilities. Here, there is given, as he says, "an apodictic exclusion of opposing possibilities, of a conceivable being-otherwise."[72] There are also those of the former type, namely, *enticing* possibilities. Foregoing an exhaustive list of these, germane are problematic or *questionable* possibilities. These are those experiences in which one possibility is, as he says, "contested by another givenness, a givenness of another in the flesh, givenness of another <apprehension> permeating it and in conflict with it."[73] Here, conflicting matters are united as *in conflict* or related as enticing. A conflicting relation creates a disjunction: it is *either* this *or* that. For example, if the figure in the window appears as both "woman" and "mannequin," where each has a demand speaking in their favor, the experience is "questionable." The essential point is that those apprehensions "contending with one another have the same mode of validity, 'questionable'...," that is, in their vying for confirmation they are related as both being *possibly* so.[74] And all this emerges in passivity.

So, prior to turning to the determination of the possibility in confirmation, it is important to make note of Husserl's use of inverted commas around "questionable" here. In a sense, questionability is taken *analogically* in passivity. For the modalization in passivity, the "primitive inquiry" is given "without inquiring in the strict sense."[75] Still, there does arise a questionable experience, both from the noetic and noematic poles. Thus, Husserl will say, "straightforward 'being' of the objective sense is transformed into 'doubtful being' or what amounts here to the same thing, 'questionable being.'"[76] To make more sense of this, further consideration of problematic, doubtful and questionable possibilities are in order. With this, we find that, though these three are basically the same in passivity, *questionable* possibilities differ insofar as they are brought to active question.

To begin broadly, a "problem" appears in an affective relief, that is, into even further into prominence *as* problem. Indeed, the affective prominence of a problem depends on already concordant experience, for where there is a problematic possibility, there must be a previous synthesis from which it appears and to which it refers. If there is not, the problem does not stand out, for there is no background

---

[72] Husserl (2001), p. 88. To be sure, the sense of "apodictic" must become the theme for future investigations, insofar as it is not a "metaphysical" but phenomenological principle based upon conditions for fulfillment.

[73] Husserl (2001), p. 74.

[74] Husserl (2001a), p. 36.

[75] Husserl (2001a), p. 49.

[76] Husserl (2001a), p. 38. Again, "being" is placed into quotes, as it is a matter of passive and not yet active objectification.

from which to appear in relief. What is more, there must be a continual striving for further synthesis. If there were not, there would not be a *problem* as a modalization but just a flow of events. In other words, there must be normal, concordant experience for a problem to emerge. To illustrate the point, we might turn to the Greeks, who sometimes used the term προβλήματᾰ in the sense of a *hindrance* or obstacle. It signifies, literally, something "thrown-forward" or "thrown-before" from πρό-βάλλω (similar, at least etymologically, to the Latin *ob-iectum*). The sea-faring Greeks thus sometimes employed the term, προβλήματᾰ, to name promontories appearing from the horizon. Moreover, these obstructions appear as a hindrance *on the way* to somewhere, as προβλήματᾰ were conflicting with navigation. A problem, in short, is something with which one must reckon to fulfill an aim, whether a shield or wall is a problem to an advancing fleet or, as Aristotle explicates, as other's positions in an argument, or, in our case, belief in being.[77]

From this description of the problem as something standing out, we may further distinguish that which is *doubtful*. Again, as Husserl notes, in doubt, both possibilities are held in a "mode of acceptance (*Geltungsmodus*)."[78] In this acceptance of both as *possible*, the possibilities are held as being-doubtful. In this, there is not yet an attempt to determine which possibility is so, as there will be in inquiry, though it is opened as a possibility.[79] This possibility is opened insofar as the possibilities themselves are presented, that is to say, there emerges a disjunctive wherein one possibility does not yet speak in favor over the other. The doubt thus present possible courses of passing judgment, without passing judgment, that is, without deciding one way or the other. It is understandable that Husserl brings these together in passivity, for, like the problem, doubt brings out something from concordant experience and presents problematic possibilities in relation to each other. However, doubt, unlike a mere problem, does not decide on one possibility or the other in terms of their being.

For example, I go for a walk in the park on a windy day. Although I do not pay attention to the flitting of leaves in the trees, they are passively constituted, as I do not take notice of them, but they are given in perception. Without me turning or actively attending, a squirrel may run across the branch. This may present a problematic possibility in passivity, say, insofar as the presentation disrupts a concordant perception. In passivity, the squirrel conflicts with a leaf such that it does not associate these as the same. In other words, the squirrel and the leaf *conflict*, *permeate* each other in a way that holds both possibilities "up in the air." A problem comes to the fore in perception, an obstruction to concordant belief, such that it leads straightaway to a doubting about which is which. In such doubt, there is not an attempt to determine which possibility is so, though this is opened as a possibility—it is "questionable," in quotes. This implies that the given is taken as exhibiting possible courses of judgment, but also that the ego does not yet awaken to strive to pass judgment on the

---

[77] See Aristotle, *Topics*, β, 108b34–110a34.

[78] See Hua XI, p. 36: "Im Zweifel haben die beiden miteinander streitenden Leibhaftigkeiten den gleichen Geltungsmodus 'fraglich,' und jedes Fragliche eben ein Strittiges und Bestrittenes durch ein anderes."

[79] Husserl (2001a), p. 76; Hua XI, pp. 36–37.

4.3 Inquiry as a Multi-layered Striving for Determination and Differentiation

doubt. That is to say, the ego does not yet awaken to strive to decide one way or the other, but the possibilities are simply held as doubtful.

Again, such a "questionable" presentation in passivity may be fulfilled even prior to any activity. This occurs through what Husserl identifies as a "confirmation," which is "the most original form of decision."[80] Simply put, it takes up one of the possibilities into concordance, as being thus and so. This can happen from the simple fact of further experience; the continued movement of the squirrel might allow differentiation of it from the leaves. If so, it is constituted in passivity as "different" from the leaves. In this regard, one possibility in perception "weighs" more than the other. The possibility is confirmed: it is a squirrel and not leaves—A and not B. So, on the noematic side, there is a propensity to be, whereas, on the noematic side, there is a propensity to confirm the possibility. But now let us relate the "primitive inquiry" with the sphere of activity, without going right away to activity inquiring.

For Husserl goes on to differentiate the question from the doubt as it is in *genesis*.[81] Where active inquiry, properly speaking, emerges to determine the doubtful or questionable possibility, as the subject actively *striving for decision*, there is already a propensity to confirm the possibility in passivity. And so, Husserl asks, "[I]s not the propensity itself such a striving…?"[82] That is to say, does not the disruption within the affective field itself *already elucidate* a striving to determine true being? Indeed, the propensity (*Neigung*: meaning a "tilt" or "leaning") suggests that perception is always already affectively charged: the world is not inert and the subject is not neutral, even in its passivity. What is more, Husserl will thus say that "inquiring already gives rise to this striving."[83] This phrase suggests, at once, that the passive disruption *gives rise* or *yields* (*ergeben*) a striving for concordance, but also that a *prior* striving yields *primitive inquiry*.[84] In other words, "questionability" appears for the subject that has the possibility *to* question toward a horizon that is essentially able-to-be-questioned.[85] So, while we may distinguish active inquiry or inquiry strictly speaking from the passive sphere which does not include activity, there is still a sense in which "primitive inquiry" is an inquiry. Taken as such, the radiation of the active intellect is not restricted to a field directly in front of our eyes. Rather, it radiates through experience, illuminating dark horizons, ever-readied to bring a matter to question. To that, let us turn now.

---

[80] Hua XI, p. 76. Husserl uses the term *Bewahrheitung*, which may also be rendered as "verification." Here, I reserve that for confirmation in the sphere of activity.

[81] Husserl (2001a), pp. 77–78.

[82] See Husserl (2001a), p. 50.

[83] Husserl (2001a), p. 100.

[84] Hua XI, p. 59: "What is now the peculiarity of inquiring as an obviously peculiar act comportment of the ego? The passive disjunctive tension of the problematic possibilities…motivates an active doubting, a comportment that puts the ego into act splitting. This leads to an uneasiness and an original drive to get beyond it, to come back to the normal state of unity. A striving for solidity arises, which is ultimately an uninhibited, pure decision. That already yields an inquiring [*Das ergibt schon ein Fragen*]."

[85] Also, from a horizon that is *essentially questionable* but not necessarily *called into question* See Husserl (2019), p. 523.

4.3.2 Intellectus Agens: *The Noetic Activity of Inquiry*

In the above, I followed Husserl's analyses of modalized belief in the passive sphere of perception. Discovered here is a striving to determine which already yields an inquiring. This does not mean the subject is always *actively* inquiring. It means, rather, there is a striving to determine in relation to a data that harbors the possibility of modalization that is constitutive of the subject. To shed more light on this, in this section, I follow how Husserl treats the awakening and operation of the active ego as *intellectus agens*. This occurs, on the one hand, with a turning of attention that Husserl calls a "bridge" from passivity to activity.[86] This brings questionability into awareness through inquiry. On the other hand, there is also inquiry that, rather than being motivated from perceptual disruptions, freely fashions its own questionable possibilities as it seeks to differentiate and to determine being.

To begin, however, let me emphasize that all activity takes place in a field of attention. *Attention (Aufmerksam,* in German) itself is a matter of making patent a theme in conscious experience, as is apparent in the term "marking out" (as the German elucidates, *Auf-merken*) matters which are the "same" (*–sam*). It is thus *not merely a matter of taking a closer look* but rather *a matter of a bringing to the fore something in conscious awareness*. Of course, there may be an increase in perceptual attention, of taking a look, of listening closer. Yet, there may also be an increased awareness of questionability, of heightening one's awareness of responsibility, and so on, which are not merely perceptual. So, by *theme* Husserl means a matter of intentional experience where there is a *specific interest, attention,* and *special* activity of bringing to order—in short, a *synthesis* of being in being-aware.

To explain further, at one limit of thematization, there is a "general" interest within lived-experience of the natural attitude. In this respect, interest *is not* "in addition" to lived-experience but essential to it—by interest here is meant the broadest sense of *inter-esse*, that is, being among-being or being in the world.[87] Although objects within such a general interest are not given straightaway as thematic, in the strict sense, they are given in a "thematic field."[88] This field is unified already within those regulative laws of *passive* synthesis, even prior to the *active* heightening of interest by the ego in attentive regard. It may be understood, then, as the *horizon* of possible investigation—*the world*—from and in which objects of specific interest emerge. Thus, thematic intending, at least in the natural attitude, appears from this pre-given, passive thematic field. On one's walk, to continue the example from above, the squirrel amid the leaves might motivate one's attention, and this *sforzando* is founded upon already being *inter-esse*, already being in the world, as that from and in which themes emerge. But, once again, even this moves too quickly. For there is a further distinction between *specific* and *special* interest.

---

[86] See Husserl (2001a), p. 168 and Hua XXXI, p. 4.
[87] See, for example, *Hua* XVII, p. 369 and Hua XXXI, pp. 16–19.
[88] Husserl uses the notion of "field" (*Feld*) variously. For this broad sense, see, for example, Hua XVII, 364, and *Hua* XXXIX, pp. 332–334.

4.3 Inquiry as a Multi-layered Striving for Determination and Differentiation

In a specific interest, egoic attention arises as directed to an object or "group" of objects. This is "specific" insofar as it is an open *specification (Besonderung)* of an otherwise unthematic or "unspecified" field.[89] In the first moments of this, that is, upon the awakening of attentive regard, a given is made *patent*, or "opened" in the possibility of being constituted directly as a theme, rather than being left *latent* in the field of passivity. For example, I turn toward the unthematic "questionable" appearance: I do not have in mind "squirrel and leaves" as a determinate *what* but only an open possibility of x and y (more exactly, x or y held in relation) as "*doubtful and questionable being*" as constituted in passivity. The specific interest that arises in the turning of attention thus begins to call matters together in the initial moments of thematization.

However, strictly speaking, turning of attention is only a moment in thematization. Although egoic activity "begins" in the turning, it is only initial moments in the process of bringing the experience to order. If there is to be *an intentional theme*—and so, too, an active questioning taken strictly as an intention directed toward determining a specific content—givenness *must be synthesized as interconnected in an act*. More exactly, a theme must be set in experience by a mediating thematizing act of *identification*. This occurs through a relating and determining within a *special interest of the intellect*.[90] For example, a questionable possibility in passivity can be constituted by the active intellect as a special theme as it identifies *this* content *as* "questionable." This means that the active intellect *gives itself* the questionable as its theme for consideration, striving to determine one or the other possibility. Again, to be careful, the active intellect does not ask willy-nilly, but "undergoes" the question, insofar as inquiring *gives rise to* or *yields* the striving. Through this identification, an inquiring-intention in the active ego turns to the modalization and seeks an active verification as a determination of being so. Since this appears in the complex that strives toward the end of determination, Husserl will say, such intentions are a *practical striving* for judicative decision that intends the determination of the *being* and *being so* of some given.[91]

In the striving to determine, then, there is the "Whether that" question which seeks to determine a modalization.[92] The question has a special, determinate content following the motivation from passivity, "whether x is...." The question of *whether* the square is a square appears upon the pre-given shape as well as in the horizon of doxa, after all. *However*, this decision is not merely a matter of apperceptive synthesis, for further passive perceptual experience is insufficient for confirmation. Instead, the decision is a matter of an active determination that has the character of "not otherwise," treated in terms of a *response to evidence*.

Thus, Husserl finds, in a sense similar but beyond his earlier analysis, "The proper sense of inquiring is manifest in and through the process of responding or in the

---

[89] Husserl (2001a), p. 84; Hua XI, p. 44.
[90] See Husserl (2001a), pp. 106–107 and 505–506.
[91] Husserl (2001a), pp. 102–3.
[92] See Husserl (2001a), 99.

response."[93] We should take note, however, that he now puts this in genetic terms, as the proper sense is "manifest *in and through* the process...."[94] The reason for this is at least twofold: in the first place, a response fulfills the intention, if it genuinely a questioning and not rhetorical or "empty," that is, if it *means* to be fulfilled; and, in the second place, the response at once pre-figures and is pre-figured by the *sense* of the question. This is so insofar as the response guides the questioning intention toward it, so to speak, insofar as an answer must "fit" the question and it seeks such fulfillment, through the process of inquiry. It is also the case that the response relates essentially to the question such that there must be fulfilling conditions in order for there to be a question at all.

Indeed, in inquiry, in relation to the response, the question has the *form* of judgment. As Husserl says, "[F]orms of judgment that in a parallel manner fit the sense-content of the questions, implies that the questioner already consciously anticipates these possible forms of response, and that they already occur in the articulation of the questions themselves as the contents of the question."[95] The inquiry operates as a transposed judgment, anticipating its fulfilment in a judgment. With this in mind, the specific question does not come from "nowhere," but already takes up some noematic content that it has transformed by taking as theme: the question *whether or not*, to continue the simple example, provides a possible form of judgment with the sense-contents borrowed from perception. Thus, the specific question will "breakdown," if the possibilities do not fit its sense, if they are *irrelevant*. In questions of verification, for example, it is not just that the possibility that speaks in favor of its own being is the adequate possibility but also that it is decided that it fits the question: if the given speaks in favor of *whether that* something is, the response to the question is the assertive judgment: "It is" or "It is not"—as the Greek, πότερος, which means "which of the two," suggests. It is not possible to answer "blue" or "speckled" to such a question because that declaration does not fit its form.

So, the fulfillment of the inquiring intention is itself a matter of *identification*. This may also be put in a twofold manner: in the first place, the *process* of responding identifies which possibility has adequate evidence; in the second place, the *intellectus agens* that *gives itself* this identification. As I have already explained some points in the process of identification, let me mark that the fulfillment of this identification occurs upon the "decision" of the *active* ego, in the verification of true being. I use decisions in quotes here only to emphasize that Husserl differentiates a decision to act and a choice between options in an inquiry. With the latter, when the intention is fulfilled, there is an identification of intending and intended, meaning with meant such that experience returns to concordance. Thus, in the decision, Husserl will say, the problematic disjunction is transformed into a conjunction, into a harmony of sense that releases the tension of questioning.[96] The fulfillment, he says, is satisfying. It

---

[93] Husserl (2001a), p. 101.

[94] Husserl (2001a), p. 101.

[95] Husserl (2001a), p. 101.

[96] Hua XI, pp. 357 and 360, where he says the following: "The answer always means: transforming the respective problematic disjunction of problematic possibilities speaking against each other into

4.3 Inquiry as a Multi-layered Striving for Determination and Differentiation 103

is an achievement of its activity. With it, knowledge grows and provides a basis for action.

Of course, Husserl does not mean that one is causally forced or determined to make such a decision. Not only is one free to make incorrect choices but the possibility for false judgments is a matter of fact. Rather, the *evidence* is such that one "ought," in order to be reasonable, make the decision. Of course, I still do not yet speak of the *value* or "rightness" of the question and response (which would be a question of *legitimacy*, which I address in the next chapter), but instead a sense of "correctness" such that, upon deciding incorrectly it is "inconsistent," "unfitting" and inadequate to the intention. Where this happens, the intention remains unfulfilled, without an adequate response, and so there remains a demand for continued inquiry, for further relevant and pertinent questions. That the subject may, as a matter of fact, not attend to this demand, does not change the phenomenological fact that inquiry intends a fulfilling response.

In any case, inquiry bears an ideal in its operation. Indeed, the *intellectus agens* is hardly satisfied with determining a singular, specific answer: its ideal meets with how the *ego* is constantly in the process of *determining more* closely, always striving to know more, radiating outward, so to speak, as well as *differentiating further being*. We must be careful of course, the subject may operate in accord with the ideal or not and, as we see in the fifth chapter, it take some time before it is made methodological in history.[97] In any event, to begin to clarify the active intellect, it is helpful to return to the issue of how inquiry relates to questions of actuality.

For example, I may ask whether something is really thus and so, *if that is so*. In this respect, I can turn to the pre-constituted sphere of perception and ask if that which has been determined there is truly and really so. Husserl calls this a *Wahrheits oder Wirklichkeitsfrage*, a "truth- or actuality-question."[98] This *Wirklichkeitsfrage* is activated, Husserl says, without "that which for us is a doubt."[99] In other words, it is not merely motivated from a conflict in the perceptual sphere but is the intellect "putting perception freely into action according to prefigured possibilities."[100] So, the *Wahrheitsfrage* operates along with Husserl's essential recognition that *any possible judgment is thinkable as the content of a question*.[101] This is so as the sort of immediate "judgment" that occurs in passive perception may be brought to question, may be actively "made" or taken as questionable. This is why he says that such

---

an unproblematic conjunction of realities agreeing with each other and speaking for each other…for with it comes relaxing fulfillment of striving, comes satisfaction."

[97] Again, the *cogito* is a matter of situated lived-experience, whereas the Ich, the *ego* is the pole of lived-experience (*erlebnis*) that accrues with lived-experience as the "point of acts radiating outward" (*Ausstrahlungspunkt*). For this, see Hua XI, p. 360.

[98] Hua XI, p. 63: "Dann in der Bestätigung ist das schon als seiend Geurteilte mit dem neuen Charakter ausgestatten "wahrhaft und wirklich so," so dass wir diese Frage auf als Wahrheits- oder Wirklichkeitsfrage bezeichnen konnten."

[99] Hua XI, p. 63: "Das aber ohne, dass für uns ein Zweifel ist."

[100] Hua XI, p. 63: "…frei tätig das Wahrnehmen nach vorgezeichneten Möglichkeiten zu verwirklichen und zu sehen…".

[101] Hua XI, p. 60: "Jedes mögliche Urteil ist denkbar als Inhalt einer Frage."

a questioning puts perception into action according to *pre*-figured possibilities: the pre-figuration occurs precisely within perception, from which I can ask *whether* it is true categorially. That is to say, the inquiring turns to that already synthesized sense in passive perception in order to bring it to question, seeking to make patent being "really and truly so." This process is a matter of the active ego, as Husserl puts it, seeking to ratify (*rechtfertigen*) perception, which is possible regardless of previous modalization. As such, let me mark, the affirmation of the *really* and *truly* so is further a categorial act of reason that follows from inquiry. When there is a fulfillment of such a question intention, it strengthens perceptual belief by taking it up into activity: it determines a state of affairs to *be* so.

Of course, the answer to the question that seeks to verify previous experience may be "No," if, for example, the perception turns out to be wrong or mistaken.[102] From a mistaken decision there arises a demand for further inquiry, if that "No" yields a new disjunction, a new "if *not this*, then...?" It is not only that perception can be verified or mistaken, however, as that sort of recalling of previous accomplishments can also be mistaken. In this respect, consider how, in the *Meno*, the boy already knew the square and, mistakenly, used that recall to determine that it was doubled by Socrates. From this mistake, Plato has Socrates slow the conversation down by asking the boy to verify if the judgment he made was *really* true, *if* it was double size. After the boy returned to say, "No," a determinate inquiry also rose in him. Operative in this example, though, is further dimensions of inquiry, in which the inquiry is setting into explicit relation the *what* and *why*, which transforms the *whether* and *if* questions about actuality. Let me explain.

To begin, the free "play" of the active intellect means that it can bring to question both previously ratified experience and that it seeks to determine ever-new possibilities given in the horizons of experience.[103] Moreover, it differentiates new and novel egoic objects. For that, there arises a sort of interest directed toward essential structures, which may then be brought back into relation to actuality. Building upon what was previously said about this process, I aim here to show how there is a *differentiation* and *determination* of being by the active intellect through inquiry. For that, consider, rather rapidly, three points, the mainlines of which we have already prepared in the above:

---

[102] Husserl, in a note taken while reading Cassirer, writes that the animal always says "yes" to actual being...[whereas] man is the "one-who-can-say-no," in Ms. A V 24/6b: "also Das Tier sagt immer ja zum wirklichen Sein, auch da noch wo es verabscheut, flieht, der Mensch ist der 'Nein-sagen-Könner,' der Asket des Lebens, der ewige Protestant gegenüber der bloßen Wirklichkeit." This follows from the fact that the animal *per se* does not have an intellect but instead naïvely posits being through the lived body. Thus, animals, as Husserl also says, have "no questions and therewith no answers," in Hua MAT VIII, p. 211: "Das Tier hat keine Fragen und somit keine Antworten." The animal (understood in a *constitutive sense*) does not *raise* the question, that is, does not bring the questionable to consciousness such that it can say, "No"; or, Again, there is no "questionable being" brought to judicative decision through intelligence. Where a question arises, there is also given some level of subjectivity that is beyond the "animal."

[103] Hua XI, p. 60: "Natürlich kann sich das Spiel hier wiederholen, das Wirklich und Wahre ist ja nicht ein ernstlich Endgültiges, da sich neue Horizonte eröffnen" ["Naturally, the play can repeat itself here, the real and true is not, after all, a seriously final, as new horizons open up."].

4.3 Inquiry as a Multi-layered Striving for Determination and Differentiation   105

1. Ideation is an active seeking to determine an object in a *special interest to the universal*.[104] It is not empirical and so is not, in that sense, perceptual.[105] Indeed, it *transmutes*, as he says in the first *Ideen*, an experience of an individual into an essence (*Wesen*) or an *eidos*. These are *novel* objects that are, again, not given perceptually but rather given from an activity of the ego.[106]
2. An essence is given in an essential sighting (*Wesenschau*). It is neither an empirical generalization nor typification that arises from unified perceptual experience but is given to the ego through a different mode of essential interest.[107] In other words, a grasp of the essence goes beyond the constitution of either differing objects as "similar" or a singular object as "same" through time, which perception can do. It is a grasp, as Husserl will often say, of "what it is and what it has."[108]
3. The grasp of the essence is a fulfillment of conditions, namely, of necessity and universality.[109] Before describing these conditions any further, let me underscore that such a grasp, as Husserl finds, is a matter of essential judgment (*Wesenurteil*).[110] This is not, of itself, a judgment of actual reality, to which I return below.[111] It is strictly a judgment of the essence. Now, once again recall that all judgments may be thinkable as the content of a question. If so, it is possible to transpose this particular judgment with its particular content—namely, the *Wesensurteil* of "*was es ist*" with its *Wesensinhalt* in the "*Was*"—into the form of a question. This would be the question, "*Was ist es?*" In fact, the question

---

[104] Hua XXXV, p. 274: "If an interest is exclusively determined by such a concrete species-moment, then a sphere of relevance and irrelevance has been distinguished with it. And this is true whether the interest is a practical one in the ordinary sense or a so-called theoretical interest, a mere interest in 'what it is,' which, however, is already. But that already before all refraining from theory, already in the pure experience, for instance beginning in a kind of mere inspecting."

[105] Hua III/1, p. 13: "Erfahrende oder individuelle Anschauung kann in Wesensschauung (Ideation) umgewandelt werden - eine Möglichkeit, die selbst nicht als empirische, sondern als Wesensmöglichkeit zu verstehen ist." See also, for example, XLI, 211.

[106] See Hua III/1, p. 14: "Das Wesen (Eidos) ist ein neuartiger Gegenstand. So wie das Gegebene der individuellen oder erfahrenden Anschauung ein individueller Gegenstand ist, so das Gegebene der Wesensanschauung ein reines Wesen." For intuition in terms of activity, see, for example, Hua XI, p. 363.

[107] In terms of the interest in the universal, see, for example, Hua XXXI, p. 80: "Vollziehen wir bestimmende Einstellung, so ergibt sich nach Konstitution des Allgemeinen eine von Grund aus neue Bestimmungsweise." See also, Hua XXXI, p. 78.

[108] For example, Hua XXXI, p. 117: "In sich selbst ist es, was es ist, von absolutem Wesen." See also, Hua XLI, p. 119: "Individuum, sein Wesen, seine Beschaffenheiten, innere Beschaffenheiten. Individuum, was es ist, und was es hat." Also, Hua XLI, p. 207 and Hua XXIX, pp. 267 723, et al.

[109] See Hua III/1, p. 12: "…sondern den Charakter der *Wesens-Notwendigkeit* und damit Beziehung auf *Wesens – Allgemeinheit* hat."

[110] Hua III/I, p. 18: "…kann jedes Urteil über Wesen äquivalent in ein unbedingt allgemeines Urteil über Einzelheiten dieser Wesen als solche umgewendet Werren." Cf also, XLI, p. 38: "…wenn das Urteil ein Wesensurteil ist, das da einen Wesensinhalt meint, der seinem Sinn entspricht."

[111] See Hua III/I, pp. 117–118; also Hua XI, pp. 79 and 81: "Das als wirklich dastehende und als wirklich Gesetzte ist dann bestimmt als wirkliche Vereinzelung des Eidos, das Mögliche eine mögliche Vereinzelung." The judgment of an essence in an individual is a matter taken up below.

"*Was ist...?*" is especially pervasive throughout Husserl's work *as operative*, that is to say, it is present *as Husserl is asking his own questions concerning essential structures.*[112]

As said above, an inquiry that intends the essence strives to determine that which is *necessary* to the matter in question. This is a matter of determining that which the matter must have or, put negatively, that which it cannot *not* have to be *what it is*. In order to determine these limits, there is a weighing of possibilities toward the judgment "in question." *However*, since these limits are not pre-given from perception, they must be produced "freely" by activity. It is that which Husserl identifies as *free-phantasy* that can take an object and vary it "as-if" it is something different.[113] The object in question, in other words, may be freely varied in phantasy in a way that does not posit being, without positing it *as-such* but, again imagining it "as-if." For example, the triangle on the chalkboard can still be a triangle with any color, any size or line thickness, but it *must* have three-sides, for *without* them, it is no longer a triangle. In this respect, Husserl says that phantasy has a "double sight."[114] As imaginative, it operates from the perceptual sphere, taking up the perceptual object up and imagining it, but it also does so without regard to actuality. This allows the setting of possible limits of the object into which the essential grasp might occur. So, again, I can imaginatively vary the color, size, line-thickness of the triangle without disruption of the shape; but as soon as I remove an angle, it is no longer *what* it *was*. The intuition of the essence is the response to "seeing" this necessity, the "must" in the data. This essential seeing is a sort of essential judgment which does not yet pronounce anything on the actual, real being of the object as being *what it is*. Rather, the *essential judgment* grasps What it means to be a triangle or Why it is a triangle. In other words, the grasp of *what* it is clarifies the reasons *why* it is, that is, its formal cause.

In line with this more traditional terminology, Husserl will also say that the essential judgment sets the stage for the problematic of the "One in the many."[115] This is so because, through it, the active ego gives itself a meaning that can apply to any instantiation of that type whatsoever (*beliebigkeit*).[116] This emphasizes the significance of reiterability in the differentiation and determination of being. However, this is *not* a matter of repetition where encounter of the many might constitute a sense of the "similar," insofar as this object may be identified as similar to that one. Rather, it is a grasp of the structure of what makes it possible to be taken as similar. The

---

[112] For examples see the following: Hua XXXI, p. 89: "Was ist syntaktische Formung?"; Hua XXVII, p. 143: "Fragen wir: Was ist Erkennen....? Fragen wir zunächst allgemeiner: Was ist Vermeinen von etwas....?;" Hua VI, p. 66: "Was ist nun die universal Wissenschaft der neuen Idee anderes....als Allwissenheit?"; Hua VI, p. 99: "Was ist das nun, personale Einstellung?"; an Hua VI, p. 319: "Die geistige Gestalt Europas" – was ist das?".

[113] See, for example, Hua XXXI, pp. 74-6. See also Hua XXXV, p. 455: "Die allgemeine Frage...".

[114] Hua XI, p. 75: "Indessen hat die Phantasie sozusagen ein doppeltes Gesicht."

[115] Hua XI, p. 78.

[116] Hua XI, p. 81: "Das Allgemeine konstituiert sich, sagten wir, mit Beziehung auf einen offenen Umfang, und damit haben wir schon die Funktion der Beliebigkeit entfesselt."

essential judgment is a grasp of the *universal*, a *novel* object formed "from the original well-spring of activity" of the *intellectus agens*,[117] which gives the conditions for the judgment of the many in relation to this one. Indeed, the active intellect not only determines but differentiates a dimension of being not given to perception.

From the above, let me further differentiate essential judgment from judgment of actuality. For the grasp of the *what* is distinct from the determination of *whether that* something is and from *if it is* some *what*. For, in the first place, as we have seen, I may grasp and determine whether something is without any idea, however clear or vague, of what it is. In this case, I may have an open specification of an object, the broadest possible range of "is" or "is not": when a shadow, for example, in the trees motivates me to turn and I ask, Is that...? This is essentially distinct from asking "What is that? Is that a squirrel or a leaf?" So, in the second place, it is possible to ask whether something is What it is *only on account of having understood that What*.[118] In this respect, I cannot ask *if* what that is is a triangle without first having grasped *what* a triangle *is*. If I have answered that question, though, I can determine *what this* given *is* and *that is what I think it is*.[119] This sort of judgment comes to term, in short, in grasping the conditions that *must* be for the particular given to be determined *as what it is*, that is, *if it is* some *what*. The determination of actuality here thus occurs upon a differentiation of being.

However, the intellect can also seek to determine and to differentiate in either an *interested* or *disinterested* manner. Given the importance of this distinction, let us take a moment to consider it.

4.3.3 Interested and Disinterested Inquiry and the Constitution of Inquiring Attitudes

Let me underscore, from the outset, that there are various senses of *interest* in Husserl's thought. Broadly, as we have seen above, interest may be taken as *inter-esse*, in the sense of lived-experience as "amongst being," as the Latin suggests. In this sort of interest, the ego "is absorbed in each act," while operating upon the presupposed foundation of the being of the world.[120] In a sense, this interest not only has specific themes but also has the world as a general thematic horizon. Indeed, at the base of such interest is the affectivity of passive perception, wherein a given may appear with an affective force that awakens my specific interest, with a demand to

---

[117] Hua XI, p. 79: "Das Allgemeine tritt uns als eine neuartige Gegenständlichkeit entgegen, als eine Verstandesgegenständlichkeit, eine Gegenständlichkeit aus ursprünglichen Quellen der Aktivität...".

[118] Hua XI, p. 42.

[119] See, for example, Hua XXXI, p. 81: "Das neue Urteil, das erwächst, ist 'Dies ist ein a,' das sagt, ist Einzelheit der Spezies a."

[120] Hua XVII, p. 369.

make a specific theme, even to "come into question" where it is made a special theme for the active ego.[121]

Beyond the sphere that is beholden to origins in passivity, Husserl identifies a *disinterest*. Before turning to these directly, however, let us recall the difference between *theoretical* interest and *practical interest* in the *natural attitude*. Practical interest sets its goal in action, in achieving and attaining some good, whereas theoretical interest seeks to determine what is true in-itself, without having practical end of acting or doing. Theory, on the other hand, detaches from any pre-figuration or presuppositions in relation to the subject's practical striving. In other words, as Husserl notes, theory is a being interested in the truth regardless of whether one "likes it or not," according to the "matter itself."[122] Although theoretical interest itself can become a "practical habit," even setting into what Husserl calls an "inquiring attitude," as I address below, it nevertheless differs essentially from practical interest and a practical attitude, insofar as it detaches from the goal of doing something.[123] What is more, all this occurs in a natural attitude, in which the world, the subject, and their correlation remain unquestioned. Indeed, theory in the natural attitude may be called an *interest*, as the ego is absorbed in its acts and is so captivated within the horizon of the world. Yet, there is possible a sort of *disinterest* even in the natural attitude. It is just not yet raised to the level of transcendental disinterest.

Now, though there is in German the equivalent adjective "*desinteressiert*," Husserl seems to prefer the use of "uninteressiert" and, in fact, it within quotes.[124] These quotation marks characteristically indicate that Husserl is aware of the ambiguity of the term. For this is not an *absence* of interest, as if the subject is no longer "amid being." Thus by *dis*-interest Husserl does not mean a lack of interest—an *Interesselosigkeit*—but rather that ego no longer "takes part" or "detaches" (*unbeteiligt*) from aspects which reduce to its relativity in the determination and differentation of being. Put otherwise, it does not take itself as the "center" and "sole" condition for

---

[121] Hua XI, p. 426: "Das Gegenwärtige, das als Weckendes fungieren soll, hat, konnte man sagen, ein besonderes Interesse, und nicht alles Ähnliche, sondern solches, das ähnlich ist in der Beziehung, der ein ähnliches Interesse entsprechen wurde, kommt in Frage."

[122] Hua XVII, p. 78: "Das Urteil muss wahr, das ist sachgerecht sein (durch Anmessung an die 'Sache selbst' als originaliter zu erschauende), gleichgültig, ob es mir und meinen Genossen lieb oder unlieb ist, ob es mich und uns alle "bis an die Wurzel" trifft..." Also, at Hua XLII, p. 527: "[die theoretisch eingestellten] klammert sein Lebensinteresse, sein praktisch als schicksalsbedingter Mensch für Sein und Nichtsein "Interessiert"-Sein, aus; er interessiert sich für das Sein und Nichtsein im Sinn der Wahrheit." It is worth noting the use of *schicksal* here in relation to perceptual, practical life-interests. Husserl begins using this in a sense related to the pre-constituted lifeworld, that is, the world which one receives, from which one is not aware and so to which one at the mercy, so to speak.

[123] Ms. A V 22/1: "[Theoretische interesse:].... practical habitus rein bestimmt als seine ins Unendliche fortgehende Vorhabe in Hinsicht auf eine unendliche Totalität von Erzeugnisse, als ein ideell unendliches Erzeugnis systematisch zu verwirklichen" ["[Theoretical interest:].... practical habitus is defined as its infinitely ongoing intention regarding an infinite totality of products, systematically realizing an ideally infinite product"] For the "inquiring attitude," see Husserl (2019), p. 522. Luft and Naberhaus render this, understandably, "interrogative," a term which I reserve for communicative issues, preferring here instead the more general "inquiring,".

[124] See Hua VI, p. 332, Hua XXIX, p. 217, Hua XLII, p. 503, and Hua MAT, VIII, p. 354.

4.3 Inquiry as a Multi-layered Striving for Determination and Differentiation 109

being and being so. In disinterest, one does not separate or sever oneself from being but rather takes being in itself as that which is to be determined and differentiated. Another way of putting all this, in terms of the will, for, as we have found above, the good of the question is in the answer, in the sense that the question aims toward a response that would fulfill it as an intention. There is thus a basic difference between following motivations: in the first place, "Why do I want this? Well, merely because I want it" and, in the second place, "Why do I want this? Because I want to know the truth in itself for its own sake, even if this speak against my relative wants, even if it pains me." The latter suggest a disinterested motivation and the former an interested motivation.

To explain further, Husserl identifies at least three main modes of "uninterest" or disinterest: practical, theoretical, and phenomenological. At one limit, what we will name practical *uninterest* is the background of indeterminacy where there has yet to be any attention or specific interest nor any special demand or propensity to be on the side of the object.[125] In conscious experience, this may be identified either as the outer "fringes" of interest or the "obvious," which is also in line with the more common use of "uninteresting," as something does not motivate me to attend to it or is simply not in my purview. There is, further, a *theoretical disinterest*, which operates within the being of the world but does so freely. In it, the positing of being neither ceases nor is suspended, but is taken up and transposed to a seeking to determine and differentiate being.[126] In disinterested theoretical inquiry, for example, the intellect disengages from passive motivations, and "plays" within that which is pre-given in the world. Indeed, in one manuscript, Husserl calls disinterest a sort of "playing while at rest."[127] Let me here make a distinction between that practico-theoretical and that theoretical operation that tends toward "pure" theory. Intelligence plays in practical thinking as well, as it seeks to navigate problems. Theory, in contrast, may be characterized as a "detached looking around" that seeks further determination of the given "in itself," without practical aim.[128] A standard example is in the geometer who takes up shapes and figures in order to understand ideals and laws of geometry that are not given in those material shapes. Finally, at the other limit, there is the *phenomenological* disinterest, which is a radical disinterest insofar as suspends all

---

[125] For example, Hua XV, p. 55: "Für uns als entwickelte Menschen hat alles schon seine Bedeutsamkeiten, ist alles von Interesse, auch die 'völlig uninteressanten' Hintergründe sind nur relative uninteressant, sie stehen nur außerhalb des besonderen, herrschenden und vielleicht beruflichen Interesses, sie gehören keinerlei positivem "Lebensinteresse" zu...." Husserl seems to suggest here that one could turn and make it interesting and that, indeed, someone who is "developed" is able to find meaning in it.

[126] For example, Hua VI, pp. 78 and 332.

[127] Hua XXIX. p. 217. Also, A V 22/ 4: "Dieses Uninteressiertseins besagt etwa im Status der Erholung spielend sich betätigen..." See also Ms. A V 22/1, cited above.

[128] Hua VIII, p. 98: "Die Uninteressiertheit, von der hier die Rede ist und durch die ich zum "unbeteiligten Zuschauer" und dann theoretischen Betrachter und ev. Erforscher meiner selbst werde...".

positing of being in order to differentiate and determine *how* being appears.[129] Indeed, phenomenology brings to awareness the conditions of interestedness *per se*, without somehow abstracting from these conditions, and, in this way, may also be called a "transcendental interest."[130] This brings to awareness the fact that, as Husserl points out, "each answer leaves a question open or opens to a new question," with each hanging-together in a way that creates an endless horizon of possible questions.[131] As such, phenomenology also serves to illuminate asking the further question in order to come to an answer as an optimal way of intelligently determining and differentiating being. Indeed, it shows and participates in how intelligence aims to determine and to differentiate true being in itself, namely, by detaching from egoic interests. Thus, Husserl identifies the "love" of the truth as radically non egoist.[132] Disinterest is thus needful for a genuine phenomenological philosophy.

To come closer to these issues, let us briefly return to how Husserl thinks these ways of inquiry may become habitual, set into "habitual ways of willing life" or *attitudes*.[133] As we know, passive synthesis occurs without egoic activity but nevertheless points to activity. It is *teleological* insofar as it might motivate activity, providing the substrate for it in *pre*-given objectlike-formations. Husserl also discovers how active achievements also flow back into the field of perception, *in habitus*, from above downward. In this movement, the *ego* informs the *cogito*, the *intellectus agens* informs, as it were, the intelligent subject. Wakeful accomplishments of the *ego cogito* can sediment themselves, that is, they can flow back into passivity as "acquired" achievements.[134] Yet, the *ego* as the source of acts—the pure ego, the analogue of the *intellectus ipse*—is free to question both these achievements again and again and ever-new givenness.[135] With this, the ego has acquired the *possibility*, the *potential intelligence* that may be reawakened.

Following these distinctions, Husserl speaks of different modes of "habit." There is, at one limit, the habitual life of passivity in lived-experience, brought up into the normal concordance of the *cogito*.[136] The lived-body, to qualify the point, has habitual ways of movement that are both constituted and lived-out without any egoic activity: I might come to blink rapidly when I lie, for example, or tap my foot when I am nervous—I do not attend to these, I do not actively choose it, but they express a meaning and do so with some habitual regularity. While everything habitual belongs

---

[129] For example, Hua XXXIV, p. 31: "Bei der transzendentalen Epoche setze ich außer Geltung, bin aber uninteressiert. Daher uninteressierter Zuschauer…nicht aus Erkenntnisinteresse an der Welt and so on, sondern aus Interesse am Bewusstsein und seiner Erkenntnis, and so on."

[130] For example, Hua VI, p. 176. See also Hua LXII, p. 518.

[131] Hua XVII, p. 78.

[132] See, for example, Hua XXXVII, pp. 321–325.

[133] Hua VI, p. 326: "Einstellung, allgemein gesprochen, besagt einen habituell festen Stil des Willenslebens in damit vorgezeichneten Willensrichtungen oder Interessen, in den Endzwecken, den Kulturleistungen, deren gesamter Stil also damit bestimmt ist."

[134] Hua XXXI, p. 23.

[135] See, for example, Hua XI, p. 366.

[136] See, for example, Hua XI, p. 296.

4.3 Inquiry as a Multi-layered Striving for Determination and Differentiation

to passivity, the habitual may nevertheless become active and come from activity.[137] Active achievements can flow back into passivity, to return to the example above, with the problem of the "one and many," as not only can continued perception constitute types in induction but the grasp of an essence also patterns future experience of the particular instance.

Furthermore, ways of acting or constellations of acts can become habitual. For example, as Husserl says, inquiry may become a "habitual practical attitude."[138] Again, by *attitude* Husserl means a way or style of willing life.[139] This means that inquiry may thus become effective as a way of willing life as concordant—that is, it may set into an *attitude*—in a horizon from which ever-new questionability is given. Of course, there are limits to the need for inquiry in specific situations; in other words, there is operative a principle *sufficient* reason, which means there is a point where no further questions are demanded, where all conditions have been fulfilled.[140] A practical person will not have the demand to keep asking questions where some answer "gets the job done." But *theorists*—as any student with experience of a professor possessed by a question could attest—might reawaken questions, not only to test, to confirm, to challenge, but just to understand the answers in increasing measure, with increasingly clarity and distinctness. In any case, the fact of ever-new givenness is in relation to the radiating and striving of the active intellect, for which, as Husserl says, "everything questionable for cognition must allow itself to be reduced to something unquestioned."[141] Intelligence seeks to determine and differentiate harbors within itself the ability to optimize its operation into a habit and attitude.

All this begins to uncover the exigency for going-back or inquiring-back into the motivations of these attitudes themselves. Indeed, a genetic account already begins to show how different *styles* of inquiry for the individual emerge and how they build upon previous achievements. Here, there also arises the question about how these attitudes emerge and develop, establishing themselves across generations. Before that, however, there is the question about why these ways should be taken at all. For though one *can* one *need not*, and so that it is worthwhile must be pursued.

---

[137] Hua XI, p. 360: "In der Ichaktivität aber besagt es [Habitualität] nicht dasselbe." Also, Hua XI, p. 432: "Alles Habituelle gehört zur Passivität. Also auch das habituell gewordene Aktive."

[138] Hua XI, p. 62: "Wir haben dann das primitive Fragen als praktisches Streben gegen Urteilsentscheidung hin und dann weiter als eine habituelle praktische Einstellung, die eventuell für längere Zeit wirksam ist, immer auf dem Sprung in entsprechende Wollungen, Bemühungen, Handlungen überzugehen, Wege der Lösung zu probieren, usw."

[139] Hua VI, 326; also, Hua XI, pp. 5–6.

[140] See, for example, Husserl (2019), pp. 519–527.

[141] Husserl (2019), pp. 519–527.

4.4 Concluding Remarks: The Need for Further Genetic Analysis

> And like any other scientist, he [the philosopher] is motivated by the love of wisdom, after which he is named and which at first is nothing but a scientific love of truth in the manner of a habitual devotion to the value-realm of truth, which is contained in the essence of the sphere of judgment. Through this love of truth, he too, therefore, allows himself to be defined by an abiding life decision aimed at what is greatest and best in this realm of truth, within the limits of what is practically possible.[142]

In this chapter, we have been following Husserl's correlation analysis under a genetic method and regressive approach. By going-back from mundane accomplishments, the process of their constitution appear as questionable. Indeed, a genetic account discovers how inquiry is a multi-layered striving to determine and differentiate being. What is more, this way discovers how different *styles* of questioning for the individual can emerge over time, building upon previous achievements, as new data and problems come into view. These modes and methods of inquiry are not always available to the individual, then, but rather emerge genetically through experience and in accordance with *a priori* possibilities of reason.

I have so far focused upon the cognitive dimension of reason, however. In Husserl's work, there are further questions about the relationship between cognition and valuing, about how values appear and are determined as true in experience. In this, I find, inquiry again appears as essential.

---

[142] Husserl (2019), p. 214.

Chapter 5
Knowing, Valuing, and Further Reflections on Inquiry and Method

Abstract This chapter turns to Husserl's understanding of the relationship of cognizing and valuing, investigating especially how inquiry appears therein. Along with raising the question of the judgment of value, I pay special attention to Husserl's analysis of the question of the will, in which there is a deliberation about the best possible choice and what should be done. I also bring to the fore the intelligible relation of motives, in what Husserl identifies as the "Why" and "Because." By inquiring into these relations, the phenomenologist can understand the lawfulness to reasons why. Finally, I make clear a few senses of method and normativity in Husserl's thought, especially as these illuminate how methods relate to each other. Indeed, from these points, an understanding of phenomenological ethics as a practical science emerges, insofar as it makes clear which actions should be done and why.

Keywords Ethics · Values · Motivation · Normativity · Inquiring-back

> In "knowledge" that is rational, without the "living," though secondary rationality of insight. The indispensability of the "mechanical," the practiced technique, indispensability of self-training. But <is> the human being a trained animal? Behind it stands one who trained and knows "Why." In such training, one has trained oneself. The human being in responsibility, in the relative. He has his purpose: …Physical ability, training of the same for certain bodily procedures, hand movements, and so on…. But also intellectual training. Self-responsibility: He is ready to speak and to put an answer to himself at any time. He justifies—he can justify the Why, also the Why of the training. But also this: that he wants to be ready for self-responsibility, that he can justify the Why at any time, is a purpose; he also considers this according to his practical possibility, also for this he finds self-training necessary. Relating back of the ego to itself.[1]

---

[1] Hua XLII, p. 451.

5.1 Preliminary Remarks—Ethics as a Practical Science

We have found, thus far, how the multi-layered striving of inquiry comes to term in a judgment, mediating the subject's determination and differentiation of being. In this chapter, I venture further into Husserl's treatment of how inquiry appears and operates in valuing, willing, and acting subjects. Doing so elucidates the essential role of inquiry in knowing what ought to be done and in carrying out this knowledge in action.

Moreover, this chapter goes further into what Husserl understands as *self-responsibility*. For, with this phrase, he means not only "owning up," as it were, to what one actually does, but also acting in accord with phenomenologically elucidated norms and ideals subjectivity. Such an elucidation is possible, I find, on the basis of answering reflective questions about "Why" acts relate and "Why" one *should* act in such and such a way. Phenomenological inquiry thus serves to clarify how human being may fully realize itself and its world in full self-responsibility. The work of this chapter thus expands the sense of inquiry into the reasonable and responsible life of the human being, for as Husserl summarizes: "inquiry belongs to the sphere of judgment and cognition; indeed, it belongs to them inseparably."[2] I expound these points through three main sections of this chapter:

1. In the first section, I consider inquiry appears in knowing and valuing. I do so first by readdressing Husserl's earlier analysis of the *objectivation of values,* now with respect to assessing, evaluating, deliberating, and willing intentions. I then follow his analysis of these operations in a genetic register, in which he treats the relation of motivation in terms of a "Why" in relation to a "Because," including the question of a legitimate motivation and whether something should be so which can be justified through reflective inquiry at any time. From this, I go back, albeit briefly, to ways of becoming aware of the socio-historical conditions of these motivations, that is, of socio-historical *sentiments* (*Gesinnungen*), via a sense-reflection on both the *self* (*Selbstbesinnung*) and on the *world* (*Weltbesinnung*).
2. In the second section, I explicate some senses of *method* in Husserl's thought, especially in order to further determine how inquiry appears and operates in methods. Here, I distinguish a *spontaneous* or straightforward and a *reflective way* of proceeding, the latter of which explicitly establishes an intelligent check on conscious operations, whereas the former does not. Although both are intelligible, that is, both have understandable relations of motivations, a reflective method has *insight into* the optimal way of proceeding, setting it as an ideal according to which operations should proceed. In other words, a reflective method grasps the *Why and Because* of operations and explicitly formulates it as a regulative ideal to be taken up and carried out. From this, I show how Husserl takes the transcendental method of phenomenological philosophy as inquiring-back into, grasping, formulating, and appropriating the normative operation of the cognizing, valuing, and acting in order to achieve a radical *self-responsibility*.

---

[2] Hua, XI, p. 62.

3. In the third, concluding section, I relate insight and inquiry in various procedures, approaches, *leading clues* and *motifs*. With the concept of leitmotif, I introduce a peculiar relation appearing in and obtaining between methods in which appears the problematic of how the *socio-historical world-horizon* carries achievements and gives a range of possibilities. This brings to the fore the demand for the phenomenological philosopher to become increasingly aware of *how* this world carries conditions for its possibility, just as Husserl becomes increasingly aware of the methodological demand to *inquire-back* into the world-horizon. In this respect, this section also prepares the next chapter's investigation of that generativity.

In order to prepare the chapter's investigation of the relationship of knowing, valuing, and acting, let me first provide some background on Husserl's understanding of the practical science of ethics.

5.1.1 The Unity of the Sciences and Their Unifying Principle

In Vienna, between 1884 and 1886, Husserl attended two lectures on practical philosophy from Brentano. These had a lasting impact on Husserl's thought, in general, and his ethical thought, in particular.[3] In them, Brentano retains a classical distinction between practice and theory, in which the latter is knowing the reason *why* for its own sake and the former is action-oriented, that is, toward *doing something*. Logic, to return to that example, may thus be taken up either as knowing the relations of propositions for its own sake or as a tool, for the application of knowledge about the correctness of thinking to thinking itself. Ethics, for its part, is a *practical science* that aims to understand while also guiding action—in other words, ethics seeks reasons why actions should be taken.

Alongside these classical distinctions, Brentano holds that each scientific discipline contains a *unity* and an *order of cognitional acts*. Husserl, in his positive assessment of his teacher, gives the following summary of that position: "Scientific disciplines of every kind, whether theoretical sciences or a practical discipline, are not arbitrary compilations of cognitions. Unity and orderly contexts prevail in all."[4] So, in order to understand and to guide scientific disciplines, it is necessary to understand these unified and ordered contexts. In this respect, Brentano finds the following, again according to Husserl: "In the theoretical sciences, the unifying principle is *the unity of a theoretical interest*, but in practical disciplines it is the *unity of*

---

[3] See Hua Dok I, pp. 13. Husserl says, in his early ethics lectures (Hua XXVIII, p. 90) that Brentano was the "impetus for all my attempts at formal axiology"; in the middle ethics (Hua XXXVII, pp. 14–15), he says about the "highly significant and influential Viennese university lectures on practical philosophy," that thinks back "upon with great gratitude even after forty years." Indeed, to these Husserl often refers, especially to the volume, *Grundlegung und Aufbau der Ethik*, which is on practical philosophy.

[4] Hua XXXVII, p. 15.

practical interest, the relation to realizing a practical end."[5] So, to reiterate, though theoretical sciences have their techniques—their goals, ends, and means according to which they operate—they are not unified by a practical interest. A confusion or, at least, an unclarity about theory and science arises when one totalizes, so to speak, the unity of practical interest, as if it also dominates the sense of the theoretical sciences. On this point, some initial clarity is brought to this distinction by underscoring that the German word *Kunstlehre*—again, "technique," "technical discipline," or, here, "practical discipline"—is the word often used for the Aristotelian term τέχνη. This term is not meant in the modern sense of technological "machination," then, but more like a "know-how." This know-how appears, once again, as a certain *order* and *unity* of conscious operations, set especially in relation to a *practical end*. A theoretical science may include such know-how but its aim is to understand, not for the sake of a unifying practical end, but rather for its own sake.

The idea of science as an interest in truth "for its own sake" is, of course, an ancient dictum.[6] Husserl knew well the usual question put to it: "But, one might ask, is this interest not in the true sense practical, is it not a purposeful striving directed to a kind of realizable end, just as any extra-theoretical interest, only directed to other ends?"[7] He responds to this question by acceding that the theorist is indeed directed to an end, namely, to "the realization of truths," and that, in the practice of the theorist, there are techniques for realizing this end. However, in the *unity of theoretical interest*, the ideal of knowing truth "for its own sake" prevails in the striving of the scientist. In this respect, as we saw above, in theoretical "interest"—or, perhaps better, *disinterest*—the scientist *detaches* from accomplishing any *deed*. In the context of theory, the practical technique of the theorist is thus taken as a means relative to the higher end of knowing for its own sake. Of course, further deliberation and action can occur while taking heed of theoretical knowledge. If so, though, a new practical interest arises, with an end not given in unity of theoretical interest itself. In short, then, the unity and order of the context is given differently in each case.

Which interest prevails in ethics, then—theoretical or practical? Once again, ethics, as a practical science, is a science of *right living*, of living as one *should*. As such, it is not merely *descriptive*, saying "what is" the case, but rather *normative*, saying what ought to be the case and why. In other words, it is ordered toward action, though action now informed by insight into the right ordering of reasons and of means and ends.[8] Because ethics means to grasp and to apply the right ordering of means and ends in all contexts, it becomes, for Husserl, an ultimate practical discipline. Indeed, as he puts it, "every *science must subordinate to the comprehensive*

---

[5] Hua XXXVII, p. 15.

[6] As Husserl puts the issue, while noting that Brentano did not sufficiently clarify it: "Under theoretical interest one understands here obviously that 'interest,' which impacts sciences like mathematics, natural science, psychology – an interest, as they say, *in truth for the sake of truth,*" at Hua XXXVII, p. 16.

[7] Hua XXXVII, p. 16.

[8] Thus, as the Ullrich Melle notes, "Husserl began his early ethical lectures, like Brentano, with the Aristotelian determination of ethics as the practical science of the highest ends and the question of the knowledge of the right final ends," at Hua XXVIII, p. xvi.

philosophy of ethics, the queen of practical disciplines."[9] So, we might answer the question about the prevailing principle of ethics with the following twofold response: with respect to understanding unity and order of contexts, ethics is a science that has its unifying principle in theoretical interest; with respect to applying insights into the unity and order such that it guides action to the best possible end, its has a practical interest, though raised to an *insightful* action of knowing *reasons why*. Because ethics itself contains both interests, it is a "practical science." This position also gives a foundation for understanding of what Husserl later clarifies as the "philosopher in the precise sense," namely, "the one loving universal world knowledge and practically striving for it."[10]

Now, with these provisional points in mind, let us take up more directly Husserl's treatment of the relationship between knowing and valuing and the place of inquiry therein.

5.2 The Relationships of Knowing and Valuing

"If we speak objectively or <axiologically>, we speak of objects and values; if we speak phenomenologically, we speak of the organization, so to speak, of reason. Reason is a title for the teleological *a priori* governing the relevant act spheres; I call it teleological here because it goes to relations of rightness and wrongness and the direction to object and value is that direction in the sense of rightness."[11]

The section takes up the question of relationships of knowing and valuing through two subjections:

A. To begin, I return to the problematic of *objectivation*, now considered in terms of the *relationship of cognition and valuing*, then to the axiological issue of the *relations between values,* especially as these appear in Husserl's earlier ethical writings, before 1917;
B. From these points, I turn to his middle and later ethical writings, from about 1917 to 1937, which further explicate how *feelings emerge in the subject*, and ways of increasing awareness of one's feelings that is rational or "reasonable," that is, as being able to answer "Why" one feels and does something and why one *should* do so.

Through these points, the section introduces how inquiry plays an essential role in Husserl's ethics as a reflective and critical check in the making of oneself and one's world.[12]

---

[9] Hua XXXVII, p. 18.

[10] A V 26: "4b/5a Der 'Philosoph' ist hier gedacht als der universale Welterkennnis Liebende und praktisch Erstrebende" ["4b/5a The 'philosopher' is thought here as the one loving universal world knowledge and practically striving for it."].

[11] Hua XXVIII, p. 343.

[12] For an overview of Husserl's ethical thought, see the editor's "Introduction" in Husserl (2024), v-xxxviii.

5.2.1 Objectivation and Values

Husserl finds that the development of a strictly scientific ethics was weighed down by practical motives, unlike the development of *logic*.[13] Since logic has been developed further than ethics, at least in the sense of a strict science, he also finds useful a method of analogy, about which he says: "Once you have sensed analogies between logical and ethical objectivation and seen parallelism of problems in some stretches, it must be of great value to look for motifs, for questions in the more rigorously researched logical regions which at first could not be presented in the confusion of the less explored axiological."[14] He will thus take laws of logic as a clue to understanding laws of the *objectivation* of values and in the relation of values to each other, that is, in *axiology*.

Indeed, in Husserl's early writings on ethics, he persistently presses the phenomenological question of the relationship between cognizing and valuing alongside questions of axiology. To understand why this is so, while bringing to the fore some analogies he uses, it is important to understand that values are contents of intentions of a particular class, namely, *feelings*. As Melle expounds, it is through feelings that values appear and are able to be clarified as felt.[15] Feelings, put provisionally, move us toward that which moves us—in other words, values give, as I clarify below, a reason why we are moved, as we aim at some good, the value of which is moving. Of course, it is another question if we *should* be moved, if it is really or merely apparently a value, if it is not just something I want but something really worthwhile. So, while feelings present values as objects, it is through further cognitive acts that values are determined to be merely apparent or really true. Thus, the need to address the question about the relationship between these intentions—the feeling-intention and the cognitive-intention—in the whole rational subject is evident. For that, logical investigations can serve to guide the question about whether feelings objectivating or non-objectivating. Of course, we will also need to ask here about the role of inquiry, if any, in the objectivation of values.[16]

---

[13] Husserl laments, in fact, that there are schools of logic but not schools of valuing and willing. See Hua XXVIII, p. 347: "In ethical terms, we are, as it were, our whole lives as if children; we naively valuate and act without any higher systematic schooling. How completely different in an intellectual relationship, how do our intellectual activities rise above the level of naivety and of course practical wisdom through scientific training! The school we all go through is a school of science. But we do not go through a school of valuation and willing in a somewhat analogous sense. Accordingly, the ethicist is inclined to tie all of his considerations to what is given at the lower level, and this also depresses the level of ethics as a science."

[14] Hua XXVIII, p. 348. This has its historical roots, according to Husserl, in Aristotle, though he carries it out in a different way, without a "pure" ethics. See also Hua XXXVII, p. 30.

[15] See Melle (2002), p. 233.

[16] See Hua XXVIII, p. 337. What Husserl calls here a "laborious discussion" seems to imply questions, given the list is similar to the usual "wishes, questions, volitions…," about which he was also dissatisfied in his earlier treatment, though he here does not expressly include "questions."

5.2 The Relationships of Knowing and Valuing

The question about the objectivation of values appears, Husserl says, within a "jungle of difficulties."[17] In order to clear away some of the thickets, let me underscore his point about how objectivating acts are oriented toward a determination of the being of objects, whereas non-objectivating acts, of themselves, are not so oriented. With this in mind, it makes sense that Husserl says that "value is not being, but is something related to being or non-being, belonging to another dimension."[18] If the content of a feelings-intention is a value, a feeling nevertheless does not intend the *being* of the object. Still, value *relates* to being and non-being such they may be determined to be *truly so* by way of objectivating acts.[19] In this sense, valuing acts are non-objectivating, though they have their own integrity as presenting values as objects.

Taken as such, the phenomenologist understands several complex relations between the spheres of valuing and cognition in the whole subject. Firstly, a cognitive presentation founds valuing, as I have a feeling *about* something that is presented to me. From this presentation of the value in relation to the cognitive object, there relates a determination of the being-true of the value, for which a further act of intellect or reason is needed, about which I say more below.[20] As there is a relating of valuing and cognizing, so can feelings as well as values be founding for further acts of valuing and cognizing. In other words, upon feelings or values, as Husserl puts it, "new objectivations are built, which pull the valuative ones into a higher context of objectivation."[21] I can, for example, have a feeling *about* a previous feeling, as when I am upset with myself that I was previously angry (note that this does not say that my feeling intends that which I was angry *about* but rather the feeling itself). Likewise, I can ask about that previous feeling, make it an object for inquiry, in order to determine whether it was present, what it was, if it was, if it *should* have been, and so on. In short, just as the determined values can become foundations for further feelings, so the acts of feeling can be objectivated and become the foundation for further feelings in relation to previous ones. This complex makes it especially difficult to describe the experiences and to determine their lawful relations.

To clarify matters, Husserl, in these early writings, treats a process of objectivation of values in parallel to his logical investigation, drawing analogies from the latter

---

[17] Hua XXVIII, p. 253.

[18] See Hua XXVIII, pp. 205 and 339–340: "*Objectivating acts are, if not in the proper sense, then in a teleological (normative) sense 'directed' towards objects. Object is being.* Object and states of affairs, being and non-being and truth and untruth, these belong to the objectifying acts, however we clarify the concepts belonging to the used words. *On the other hand, valuating acts are not "directed" to objects, but to values.* Value is not being, but is something related to being or non-being, belonging to another dimension. Value relations as such are not mere states of affairs, so, if we use on both sides the really analogous and parallel speech of being judged, which can really be carried out. Also here the being judged is a teleological-normative one, and so on. Above all, it is to be said that the directing-oneself, which belongs to the peculiar essence of the non-objectifying <acts>, is not a directing-oneself towards the objects of the presentations, perceptions, judgments, and so on, on which they are based."

[19] Hua XXVIII, p. 338.

[20] Hua XXVIII, pp. 340 and 205.

[21] Hua XXVIII, p. 324.

for the former. He finds, again, a basic relation of foundation, wherein a cognitive presentation founds a feeling. A feeling of joy, for example, is *feeling joyful about* something. Taken as such, Husserl says, "The joy is not a concrete act in its own right …without some such foundation, there could be no joy at all."[22] Joy thus appears as a quality, in the strict sense of a non-objectivating act, upon the objectivating act of presentation. That means, once more, the feeling does not direct itself to the truth or true being of the *object* it is about. *However*, the value as an object and its correlated feeling-intention remains in the evaluation and assessment of the object. For, that which I am joyful about may be verified as truly being *worthy* of joy, even as I remain joyful about it or, perhaps, even as I become doubtful about it or put it to question.[23] Indeed, the instance may be verified by reason as *truly* or *apparently* valuable, with or without disrupting the integrity of the feelings and the value. In order to elucidate the process of determining the value and being valuable or not, it is necessary to turn to the intertwined issues of evaluation that terminates in the judgment of the value.

Let me stress, from the outset, that the value judgment is a rational process which also includes feelings. This is so, not only as I am "holding onto" the value that is to be judged, but also insofar as feelings play a role in moving the subject toward the judgment of the value and, as we will see below, toward the action which would realize something valuable. For these reasons, let me first speak more broadly about the question of the will in the context of action, which includes the judgment of value. I will then turn back to the value as motivating the judgment. In both, inquiry also appears as an essential moment of determination and differentiation.

In the context of action, the will relates to an end, to some *good*. Where there appears possible means of reaching that end, of achieving that good appear, so does there appear the question of which possibility to choose. As Husserl finds, "Choice is initially a kind of inquiring," and a kind of inquiring that occurs in deliberation.[24] To clarify this sort of inquiry, Husserl speaks of an analogy between *questions of will* and *questions of being*.[25] For while questions of will come to term in an action, in a *deed*, rather than the "Yes" or "No" of a judgment of questions of *being*, they share the deliberative features. To reiterate some of these features, recall that multiple possibilities are presented in deliberative choice—the inquiry includes the sort of weighing of possibilities, intending which would fulfill the intention. So, like a question of being, which holds possibilities for consideration in assessment, there is, in evaluation, a sort of holding-for-value [*Werthalten*].[26] This *holding* of value

---

[22] Hua XIX, p. 419. To reiterate, from the first chapter, he will also call this an "act-quality," further distinguishing it from an act-content or matter.

[23] Again, as Husserl puts it at Hua XXVIII, pp. 332–333: "Judgment thereby points us back to the total class of objectifying acts, which, after all, are all "objectifying" by virtue of their ability to enter into contexts of identity and thus into contexts of judgment. One also says in general that the object is something that is identical with itself, being and as being so or so being …."

[24] Hua XXVII, p. 232.

[25] For example, at Hua XXVIII, pp. 115–119.

[26] Hua XXVIII, p. 231: "The will is based on a holding of value: If I think of myself in a will, then I see that which is wanted as value-held and that at which the 'opinion of the will' is directed. It is not to value-supposing, but to wanting-supposing. Now one can say: The same thing says in

is not yet a *having* of value [*Werthaben*], strictly speaking, as the value has neither been determined to be truly valuable. Instead, in holding of value, an inquiry takes the value content given by the feeling and assesses it in relation to the intended end, even as the feeling evaluates its value. Indeed, deliberation in the question of the will is about the relations between whether the means will achieve the end and, further, whether the means and end are that which *should* truly be wanted at all.[27] Within this process, Husserl finds that there arise questions such as, "Do I want A or B or what else should I do? If I now see that A is inferior to B, it is already evident that I should not."[28] The inquiry itself gives rise to the seeking of this should, which is to be determined in judgment as being the case or not.

For now, however, let us understand this "should" simply as appearing in the context of the *relative* end, rather than in the sense of that which ought to be achieved in relation to an *absolute* end. After all, one may take the path that one "should" take in order to realize what one wants, but that does not mean one *should* want that at all. The thief, for example, might grasp that the "best" course of action for realizing her aim is to bind the homeowner, and, indeed, that she "should" do so to be successful in getting what she wants. The decision of will makes the judgment that this possibility is the best choice, "Yes" or "No," and then carries it out in a deed. To get to the sense of "best" and "should," in an absolute sense, it is necessary to follow Husserl further into the issue of the *consistency* of preferring and the preferrable.

To begin, Husserl distinguishes, with Brentano, *noetic* and *ontic* laws. As he says, "one can say noetically…:'It is reasonable to prefer what is considered good to what is considered bad.'"[29] The good is preferable, in one respect, for it fulfills the intention as such. So, from this noetic law, Husserl further distinguishes the ontic law of Bretano, namely, "A good and known as a good is preferable to a bad and known as a bad."[30] This preferability appears on the basis of the objectivation of the held value as *truly good* or not, where the truly good is, so to speak, *preferable in itself*, according to its being or "ontically." Not only does this point back to the question of reasonableness, to which I return shortly, but also to what Husserl calls the "fundamental piece of all future pure ethics," namely: "'The better is the enemy

---

the wanting there is the wanted as that which should be, and the should or ought-to-be, that says a position correlates that is analogous with being…."

[27] Hua XXVII, p. 231: "Because in every willing (deciding and doing) there is a should-position that can be correct and incorrect, and it implies as a fundament a valuing position (a holding-for-good) that in turn and < in > in its manner can be correct and incorrect. So what says the 'Should I A or should I B?' I can also say: Do I want A or do I want B? Sometimes we express ourselves that way. But we notice that this (expression) is ambiguous and therefore choose to avoid it."

[28] See Hua XXVII, p. 233. Also, Hua XXVII, p. 231: "Because in every willing (deciding and doing) there is a should-position that can be correct and incorrect, and it implies as a fundament a valuing position (a holding-for-good) that in turn and <in> in its manner can be correct and incorrect. So what says the 'Should I A or should I B?' I can also say: Do I want A or do I want B? Sometimes we express ourselves that way. But we notice that this (expression) is ambiguous and therefore choose to avoid it."

[29] Hua XXVII, p. 91.

[30] Hua XXVII, p. 91.

of the good'....It says: 'Do the best among the achievable!'"[31] Now, the *better* is the enemy of the good, insofar as the "better" sets itself against that which is *among the achievable*, that is, the *good*. In other words, the "better" here is something "projected," so to speak, as better than the achievable choices. The best choice is not something that you cannot achieve. The best among the achievable is to be preferred, not only to the inferior choices among the achievable, but to that which is imagined as possibly better. Thus, Husserl extends this so-called fundamental piece, in another manuscript, written around the same time as the previous lines: "Do at any time the best among the achievable in the entire sphere subjected to your reasonable influence! It is Brentano's formula, which is somewhat overfilled, but in which, in our opinion, there is nothing essential to improve."[32] This, he names a "formal categorical imperative," the material of which is filled out in various situations in which the imperative is given.[33]

It is important to note that Husserl formulates the categorical imperative here in its *subjective* aspect. He transposes it within the context of objective, axiological laws with the following: "The best among the achievable in the whole practical sphere is not only comparatively the best, but the only practically good."[34] Again, "the better" is not the *practical good*, is not the "comparative best"; rather, the "best among the achievable" is the good to be judged as such in the practical judgment. Thus, Husserl stresses that there is not a *categorical imperative* if it is construed as hypothetical: as he puts it, the imperative "does not yet say 'Do the best among the achievable!,' wherein no 'if' ['*wenn*'] is spoken of."[35] In other words, there is no *proviso*, no tag to the categorical imperative that would say, "Do the best among the achievable…if you feel like it" or "…if you would." The imperative is *absolute* and *unconditional*, even while given within subjective experience.[36] There is thus given a demand to judge that *this* is the best achievable, insofar as these values relate to that which I seek.

So, values appear in a field of *preference*, wherein a value appears as *preferable* to a disvalue. In a choice, for example, I decide that *one choice is preferable to the other*, that is to say, I have made a judgment of value within that weight, following upon inquiry in the choice.[37] Even where I decide that I will choose the disvalue, perhaps to show it is possible, it means I have made that choice because I *prefer* that. So, the preference and preferable do not yet say anything about the value in itself, that is, that values that *appear as* preferable *should* be preferred. To say something about this, it is important to make distinctions in the *reasons* for the choice which emerge from the preference. To further clarify this, let me identify two basic standards that

---

[31] Hua XVIII, pp. 220–221.
[32] Hua XVIII, pp. 350–351.
[33] Hua XVIII, p. 351.
[34] Hua XVIII, p. 220.
[35] Hua XVIII, p. 352.
[36] Hua XVIII, p. 345.
[37] Hua XXVIII, pp. 232–233.

should be underscored throughout Husserl's work, namely, between the *egoist* and the *true and genuine* subject.[38]

Basically, the egoist takes the *relative* good as a standard of choice, whereas the true and genuine subject takes the *absolute* as the standard. As such, the egoist prefers that which "should be" and "should be done" to get what she wants, but the true and genuine person prefers that which "should be" and "should be done" in order to realize what is truly valuable in itself. There is a *consistency* in the latter, insofar as the feeling and cognitive intention of the truly good is actually achieved, unlike the egoist who fails to fulfill even his ego, properly speaking—insofar as the ego essentially strives to transend itself to the absolute. To get clearer on these points, recall that, in judgment, the prospective judgment becomes the actual, posited one. Again, in the judgment, there is a position-taking of being and being such and so. Now, that judgment can be made based on what I want to be true or based on that which is true in itself—*absolutely.* That "absolute" does not mean that I have nothing to do with it; it means rather that I have detached my *relative* wants and instead want only that which is "in itself." So, when I bring a choice into question, intending the "Yes" or "No" in the question of being, I intend the fulfillment of that question. Of course, my desires and feelings can distort that intention, but, in so doing, they skew the intention, as it were, away from that which it intends, namely, the truth. Likewise, when a judgment of value is made, the position-taken is that "this is truly valuable, truly worthwhile." Thus, where I bring the choice in question question of the will, I raise the question in relation to a "should," not only in *relative* but *absolute* terms, as I intend the *absolute* which is worthy of being reached and being achieved. Where egoism prevails, I take the position that only *I* am truly valuable, truly worthwhile. *However*, and once again, this fails to realize fully the ego itself, as it restricts the ego to its own sphere, even as the ego radiates outward to the absolute. Thus, where this occurs, the tension of inquiry remains: the subject is at odds with itself, is *inconsistent* with its orientation to true being and value.

So, *reasonableness*, in this context, means a *consistency* of the rational subject. To clarify this further, Husserl turns to an analogy between the logical law of convenience or consistency (*Konvenienz*). In logic, this law describes the *relationship* between sentences, as the relationships are "suitable" or "fitting"—following the Latin *convenientia*—to the argument. This can mean, of course, both that the form of the argument as well as the material is consistent with itself. Likewise, in ethics, it can mean that the relationships between values (which is lower, higher, absolute, relative, and so on) are consistent; it can also mean that the subject is consistent with itself in its striving to realize values in the right order, that is, in its reasonableness. Together, that means that which is valued, judged, and done is consistent with that which is the case.[39] An *unreasonableness* is thus an inconsistency. In this respect, Husserl says, if the values motivating the choice are wrong, then the choice is unreasonable, and

---

[38] For example, Hua, XXVIII, pp. 42–44; also, clearly at Hua XXXVII, p. 190: "…Egoism falsifies moral judgment, suppresses, for example, the true motives which are not effective moral ones (this is one of the great themes of phenomenological enlightenment)."

[39] See, for example, Hua XVII, pp. 148–149: [P]ure joy of cognition is worthy in itself, a volition directed to this joy, is in itself convenient, an intention following it is in itself suitable, just as an

the one who makes and carries out that choice acts unreasonably.[40] Once this latter failure occurs, Husserl says, there arises in the subject a "shame" in the fact that the real value does not exist.[41] In other words, the feeling of shame appears where that which should have been done was not.

So, there is a building up of the subject and the world, for better or for worse. Indeed, already in these early lectures, Husserl also recognizes the socio-cultural context in which judgments of value appear and are built-up. Thus, he says, "….We are often at odds (*uneinig*) with ourselves, disapprove of what we previously approved of, or approve of what we previously disapproved of, or find ourselves in embarrassing conflict (*Widerstreit*) with others, or are called upon as judges to settle other people's disputes [*Streit*]…."[42] There are not only internal but external pressures, wherein a "being at odds" or "disunity" appears in relation to others such that *we become a question to ourselves*:

> Thus, the question becomes burning for every aspirant: How can I reasonably order my life and striving, how can I escape the agonizing discord with myself, how can I escape the justified reproach of my fellow men? How can I make my whole life a beautiful and good one and, as the traditional expression goes, how to attain genuine eudaimonia, true bliss?[43]

With these "burning questions of the heart," as Husserl puts it, human persons first develop in "wisdom" traditions. This means, again, at first, a sort of "empirical-anthropological" ethics and, as such, it appears upon a recognition of the *empirical person and persons*. The person, in this sense, is the unity and identity of the subject as accruing acts, constituting habits whcih influence further acts and actions in their developing personality.[44] In this respect, Husserl often stresses the *concrete* inter-weaving or intertwining of all these acts in the person and the personal environing

---

intention that is directed towards an ignoble joy, for instance as joy in animal cruelty, is in itself inconvenient and in further consequence, axiologically considered, an disvalue, regardless of the subject that so wills.

[40] Hua XXVII, p. 92: "We can also say: the preference of held-for-better is in itself a value, but this value is abolished if the values of the motivating acts are wrong. Only when we abstract from the question of value on the part of the motives do we give preference to value par excellence; for example, in the practical sphere: purchase of a fake Madonna picture <by> Raphael—a genuine picture of a third-rank painter."

[41] See Hua XXVII, §14, and pp. 90–91.

[42] Hua XXVII, p. 11. Indeed, he continues, "Our own actions as well as those of our neighbors are accompanied by constant judgments about "right" and "wrong," "purposeful" and "not purposeful," "reasonable" and "unreasonable," "moral" and "immoral.""

[43] Hua XXVII, p. 11.

[44] As Melle summarizes, there are three levels of person, for Husserl, consisting of both the individual and of the collective person. In the first place, persons make themselves through spontaneous, free, and chosen acts. In this respect, they are responsible for their being as well as the being of the community. The person is not pure spontaneity and freedom, however. For, in the second place, the person is situated in an environing world beyond their control and responsibility. In the third place, there is the sense of person which expresses most profoundly who one is. With these three in mind, it is possible to indicate the parameters to what is meant by "achievable." For the person, while influenced by the socio-cultural horizon, is not restricted to it. There is a more profound demand and calling within one's living. See Melle (2020), p. 243.

world.⁴⁵ It is important to note that the values appear to the person *relative* to this situation and, again, considered concretely, the person will relate to this value and be a value themselves in relation to other persons in their environing worlds.⁴⁶ From this situation, the "wise" person appears as the one who is able to assess and evaluate well. In other words, there appears the *exemplary* person—the φρόνιμος who is able to answer best *in situ*. This wise person appears within the spiritual formations of his culture and its morality, that is to say, within a certain "worldview." By this is meant a sort of "understanding" or agreement between persons in what Husserl calls a "personalistic attitude."⁴⁷ This attitude reproduces its ideals in the form of education, as bringing up persons to act in such and such a way, such that there is an "interpersonal communication."⁴⁸ This communication bears the sense of the rightness or wrongness of actions, *answers* to the burning questions of the heart, to a degree. I say "to a degree," since Husserl will claim that there is a deeper sense of rightness or wrongness that will meet the *transcendental* demands, such that it is possible to put to question the rightness or wrongness of particular positions in the worldview as well as of the worldview overall. In this sense, there appears the "impersonal" aspect of philosophical life: there is a demand to be detached and disinterested from the self and group, from environment and customs, in order to seek truth *in itself*.

With the appearance of theoretical interest, as a matter of fact, there emerges a search for the *idea* of what Husserl calls a "perfect life."⁴⁹ Within the practical science of ethics, this means a search for a *guiding idea*, that is, an idea that would guide action and give an answer to that burning question about how to live life. Thus, the philosophical life seeks answers to the following questions, in Husserl's words:

> What should <I> do, what is for me or what is in general a way to describe the practical best, the highest practical good for humans? This then leads back to the question of what is good

---

⁴⁵ Hua XXVIII, p. 183. Also see Hua XVII, p. 348) and Hua XIII, p. 235. On unity of the ego, see Hua XIII, p. 244. And on personality as *habitus* influencing other acts, Hua XXVI, pp. 170, 174, as well as Hua XXV, p. 48. A similar sentiment repeats at Hua XXV, p. 107.

⁴⁶ See Hua XXVIII, p. 8.

⁴⁷ For example, Hua XXV, p. 49: "Wisdom or *Weltanschauung* in this specific sense, although it includes a variety of types and gradations of value, is, as need not be explained further, not a mere achievement of the isolated personality, which would in any case be an abstraction; it belongs to the cultural community and to the time, and in relation to its most pronounced forms it makes good sense to speak not only of the education and world view of a particular individual, but of that of the time. This applies in particular to the forms to be dealt with now." See also Hua XIII, pp. 109 and 134.

⁴⁸ See Hua XXV, pp. 51 and 331–332. Also, Hua XIII, p. 24: "The form of the spiritual world is the *commercium* of personalities by means of the lived-body....[Fn. 1:] Personality = real I-subject." Persons can "understand" or come to an "agreement" (*Einverständnis*) about our action. Such an understanding or agreement is not the same as empathy, though it may occur with it. In empathy, recall, there is, Husserl says, "putting into the place" (*Hineinversetzen*). This putting into place can be deeper if one "lives into" (*Sich-einleben*) or "feels-into" (*Einfühlen*) the other. See, for example, Hua XIV, 186–187, et al.

⁴⁹ Hua XVIII, p. 227.

in a broader sense, of being valuable in general, how it is to be determined according to its value gradations, what value laws it is based on, and so on.[50]

These questions seek, in short, insight into that which places a demand upon our living as one should. To find answers to these questions, Husserl, in the early ethics, stresses the relationship between the phenomenological and axiological. Here, we have highlighted only a few points of his analysis in order to bring to the fore the role of inquiry in ethics as a practical science. Now, let me turn to his middle ethical writings, where the focus comes to be upon the phenomenological understanding of the motivations between acts of cognizing and valuing. This shows how phenomenological ethics seeks to know *Why* one should live in such and such a way and, indeed, to know the ultimate *teleological Why*, that is, the ultimate reason for living in such a way.

5.2.2 The "Why and Because" in Philosophical Ethics

The Why, the *causa*, can be a *ratio* in a precise sense. We could call, at first, "rational motivation" each that has such a *ratio*.[51]

Husserl, in his middle ethical lectures, given between 1920 and 1924, restates a basic point from the earlier lectures: "Feeling is subjective, value is objective."[52] A critical illustration of this distinction appears in his treatment of hedonism, which, he finds, bases itself on the subjective feeling rather than the objective value. Hedonism is a sort of *egoism*, in other words, as it sets itself to the norm, "One ought to pursue pleasure," and thereby reduces that which is valuable to *one's own pleasure or agreeable satisfaction*.[53] Even here, however, hedonism relies on the fundamental correlation of subjective and objective—the hedonist's pleasure falls away, after all, without that which is really and truly valuable, even if they do not take it as such. In any case, the hedonist's *reason why* is their own pleasure, their own satisfaction and enjoyment, which, taken as a norm, overlooks the objective value, again, both of themselves and of the good for which they strive.[54]

The example of the hedonist also shows how, for Husserl, human striving is intelligible, as it has its *reasons, chains of reasons*, and, indeed, *ultimate reason why*. Indeed, the subject lives according to a "Why," which may or may not be explicitly known by the subject. Before going into how these reasons why may be brought to awareness through inquiry, it is important to underscore how there are not

---

[50] Hua XVIII, p. 227.
[51] Hua XXXVII, pp. 80–82.
[52] Hua XXXVII, pp. 68–69.
[53] Hua XXXVII, pp. 40–41.
[54] Hua XXXVII, p. 79.

5.2 The Relationships of Knowing and Valuing

only relations of motivating *acts* but also *contents* of motivation.[55] That means the relation of Why and Because is *concrete*, discoverable in the relations of acts, with their general laws of motivation. So, again, if the "Why" is the reason, the "causa" or the "ratio," as Husserl puts it, the "Because" is the "the general expression for the way spiritual matters of fact occur 'on the ground of' other matter of facts or 'because' these occurred."[56] Now, these reasons may or may not be explicitly conscious in a human being's everyday activity. I may, for example, begin thinking about the seaside because of a warm breeze, but I may not consciously ask and answer why this was so motivated. However, *I can ask why*, that is, I can *inquire into* these motivations and chains of motivations. Thus, Husserl says, in an important passage of the middle ethical lectures:

> To inquire into the 'origin' of spiritual facts and to carry out here 'explanations,' to speak of Why and Because in the viewpoint of spirituality, that gives a totally other sense than in the viewpoint of natural scientific putting questions to nature that then carries out natural scientific explanations and talking of Why and Because.[57]

In fact, Husserl continues, such a scientific explanation requires the phenomenologist to *ask about* spiritual achievements.[58] So, I suggest that here he begins to formulate how the phenomenologist *inquires-back* from spiritual achievements in order to find an answer to the question "Why?"

The point is of utmost importance, methodologically. After all, the phenomenologist must *mediate* these intelligible relations by taking up the achievements, and *inquiring-back* into the subjective operations and motivations necessary for them. Indeed, phenomenological inquiry plays an essential role in making understandable, intelligible, for it tends to a grasp of the motivational connections and relations that are not otherwise evident, between both acts and contents. Such a mediation *must be an inquiry*, I suggest, for mere perceptual attention is insufficient to the task. One cannot *perceive* the *essential* connections of motivations, nor can they *mediate* the "Why and Because" structure, they must instead be *understood*.[59]

Now, though motivational connections are *intelligible*, it is not the case that all motivational connections are *actively intelligent.* There are instead both passive

---

[55] Hua XXXVII, pp. 82–83: "On this side, if we have sufficiently clarified the sense of the question of Why, which played the role in the hedonic argument, it should now be pointed out that according to the normal and correct sense of word 'motive' does not mean 'motivating act,' but rather concerns the content that comes to position in it."

[56] Hua XXXVII, p. 82: "The Why, the *causa*, can be a *ratio* in a precise sense. We could call, at first, 'rational motivation' each that has such a *ratio*."

[57] Hua XXXVII, pp. 106–107.

[58] Hua XXXVII, pp. 106–107: "To ask why an ego behaves as it behaves [*sich so verhalt, wie es sich verhalt*], whence it has its spiritual habitus, how a character trait developed, or to ask whence a spiritual formation of the human environing world has its spiritual meaning, which explanatory ground has a literary appearance, an artistic direction and so on." Also consider. Hua XXXVII, p. 107: "To trace a spiritual matter in this way back to its 'origin,' explaining it in the context of motivation by disassembling the actually decisive motivations; that means, making the spiritual become 'understandable,' and, finally also, the becoming itself with the spiritual content constituting it."

[59] Hua XXXVII, p. 107.

and active "reasons why."⁶⁰ To elucidate the difference between the active and passive connections, Husserl gives the example of asking himself "Why" he thinks of Engadin, a region of Switzerland; in response, he finds that a name of a person was mentioned that is associated with memories of the place, which *motivates*, through a passive association, an active identification.⁶¹ We may say that one recalls the place *because* the person is mentioned, and this relation is intelligible, even if not intelligent.

There may also be unintelligible, "irrational" givenness, which does not have a direct chain of motivations. Husserl gives the example of a "bang" that disrupts any chain of motivation: though this might become a ground for further motivation, by itself, it does not appear within any concordance.⁶² Now, insofar as the bang has no genesis, its motivation is unintelligible. Of course, it is the case that this noise appears in an already given perceptual field and so is not wholly without relation to other acts. Indeed, as we know from above, both passivity and activity appear in the *horizon of belief*. Perhaps this explains why Husserl has "reservations" about this terminology of *rational and irrational*,⁶³ preferring instead the language of "active and passive," and, further, *primary* and *secondary passivity* because there is already a patterning of experience such that both the perceptual and intelligent have their horizons.⁶⁴ In any case, this is important, for one can take up beliefs passively, without actively grasping the reasons for Why and Because.

Beyond the intelligible but unintelligent, ir-rational or passive motivations, there is that which is "unintelligible." Unlike the disruptive "bang" mentioned above, which does not have a determinate motivation, there is the sheer lack of motivation, as with acting *unreasonably* or *failing* to act according to "right reason." There may be intermediate intelligible connections, but *no ultimate reason "Why."* For, there is, in the end, no rational ground for acting unreasonably. There is, rather, a *failure* to be reasonable, to grasp and to carry out the reasonable option. If one seeks for an ultimate reason *why* one fails, one finds no ultimate reason but rather a null-point. In this connection, Husserl will suggest that standing in opposition to truth is falsity, whereas failure to will a value is "sin."⁶⁵ That sin itself is simply a failure, a lack of ultimate reason and goodness, however real its consequences. From these points, we may reconsider the genesis of the *legitimation* of reasons through intelligent *insight*.

---

⁶⁰ Hua XXXVII, p. 108: "The question of origin, the question 'Why' has a second possible sense in the realm of the spiritual. Overall, in the spiritual spheres two motivations intertwine, namely, the rational and the irrational; the motivation of the higher, the active spirituality and the motivation of the lower, the passive or the affective spirituality."

⁶¹ Hua XXXVII, p. 108.

⁶² Hua XXXVII, p. 110.

⁶³ Hua XXXVII, p. 109.

⁶⁴ Hua XXXVII, pp. 107–108: "The difference between rational and irrational motivation. The question of origin, the question 'Why?' has a second possible sense in the realm of the spiritual."

⁶⁵ Hua XXXVII, p. 134: "Denial of mathematical sentences is counter-sense; whoever offends against the mathematical laws falls into *error*. But whoever offends against an ethical law falls into *sin*."

5.2 The Relationships of Knowing and Valuing

By making known the "reason why," reflective, intelligent insight into reason gives a new grounding or justification for the *legitimately* "right" action.[66] While such a reflection might arise spontaneously, especially where it is motivated by a failure of reason, a methodological reflection arises to determine the ordering of operations in the context of decision and action. Thus, in phenomenological reflection, attention is now upon both cognizing and valuing in the whole striving subject in relation to the true and truly valuable. With respect to the origins of reasons, then, there is Husserl's parallel between value-apperception (*wertnehmen or "value-ception"*) and truth-apperception or, simply, *perception* (again, *wahr-nehmen*), where the latter has the sense of "truth-taking," the former has the sense of "value-taking." Again, drawing from previous analyses of the logical sphere, Husserl finds that a *presentation* in value-apperception may bear the value, but it is *not the value itself*. To determine the true value, there is a process of determining and differentiating value. This process may be more or less insightful, which is meant that the value itself is determined through a reflective understanding of the reason why one is striving and the reason why it is a legitimate striving. So, for such an insight, it is necessary to ask, not only for what one is striving, but also *why* and *why it should be striven for*. Now, each striving will have its reasons why, which may be legitimate according to a relative end. But these relative ends also relate to ultimate ends as means. Thus, Husserl says, "If we ask the one striving: 'Why are you striving for that?', we will usually get answers that make new questions possible, for example, in the case of a means, the question leads to its end, with this to another end for which it is a means."[67] The raising of further questions is only *usual*, as it is possible one refuses anymore quesitons, but also becauase it is possible to reach an answer which gives a final end, a final end-goal of the striving. Indeed, this way of quesitoning oneself reveals the value which gives an *overarching* sense to the whole of one's striving, insofar as it shows the standard according to which one is choosing other possibilities. From this insight into the ultimate end and the question about its worthiness, it is possible to go back through the means to determine whether they are legitimate, whether they are directed to this worthy final end.

For example, consider again the hedonist. They hold, once again, that "overall only pleasure can be the motive and thus the ultimate goal."[68] As an ultimate Why, this sets the standard for the particular reasons; the answer to Why that the hedonist chooses is because their highest value is pleasure—again, it is the *reason why for their other decisions and actions*. To reiterate, however, there is an inconsistency discoverable here, an *unreasonableness as well as an illegitimatcy*. For the hedonist who seeks only the feeling of satisfaction already goes beyond themselves *via the feeling itself*, even while turning away from the value that would fulfill the feeling in preference to their self-satisfaction. In short, the hedonist's reason why overlooks the very reason upon which it operates and is therefore *inconsistent* with itself—is *unreasonable* and *illegitimate*.

---

[66] See Hua XXXVII, pp. 114 and 165.
[67] Hua XXXVII, p. 79.
[68] Hua XXXVII, p. 103.

So, though there are spontaneously good persons, an insightfully good person would legitimize each reason in accord with the very laws of reason. Husserl thus also identifies a difference between the sort of enthusiastic (*Begeisterung*) interiority and a reflective, rational one.[69] Where the blind achievements, so to speak, of the enthusiastic person may in fact be truly good, the reflectively interior subject keeps their life in order with a rational check. That check means the interior person is able to say why they act in such a way, and are able to communicate this to others. The difference of the ways of living makes a difference in their life, how they live, and how their respective world sets in order—or not. For, as achievements "build up," they do so in such a way that motivates, not only further actions, but further feelings. In other words, there can be a building up of sense such that there emerges a *sentiment* or *mindset* (as the word, *Ge-sinnung,* suggests with its root of *sense—Sinn*) in which matters comes "have sense." As the sentiment of enthusiastic spirits rely on "blind" or "instinctive" actions, the sentiment emerging with them precariously relies on their "wisdom." The reflective, rational check on actions, in contrast, invites others to be able to understand themselves and their motivations, to legitimate their actions by "making sense" of it. Indeed, phenomenological philosophy aims for a *Gesinnungethik* that is increasingly insightful, increasingly aware of sense through a sense-reflection or a *Besinnung* (again, as this word suggests, with its root of *sense—Sinn*).[70]

Where a rational being becomes aware of itself through insights into itself, there arises the sentiment to live reasonably. "As I am a rational being, so does this mean I am to set my life toward living reasonably, thus realizing my rationality"—such a statement relates to the question, as Husserl notices: "How must I—such is my question—form for myself my (whole further) life in order to gain a constant life of satisfaction?"[71] Of course, a "life of satisfaction" can be taken to mean the *self-*satisfaction of egoism. But, as we glimpsed above, this is not a reasonable life. Even if I gain some measure of self-satisfaction, I abuse reason in the process, putting it to work for my relative rather than absolute goods and values. On the other hand, there can also be a *true* life of satisfaction which means achieving the best among practically achievable and doing so with increasing insight and awareness of *why*.

---

[69] See, for example, Hua XXXVII, p. 228.

[70] The German words *Gesinnung* and *Besinnung* are notoriously difficult to translate into a single English term. Manfred Frings, in his translation of Scheler (1973), renders it with the phrase "basic moral tenor." The rendering makes good sense. I use "sentiment" for a few reasons, however. In the first place, it captures both the sense of a general state of one's emotional life and a specific feeling in that life, as it is possible to say that one "has the sentiment" or even "shares the sentiment." In the second place, historically, it maintains the way in which he tries to respond to those philosophers for whom we use the term *sentimentalists* (for whom Husserl names the *Gefühlsmoralisten*) by retrieving their insights into the emotions, without sacrificing the valid points of critique by the rationalists; in the third place, the word "sentiment" has the good fortune of deriving from the Latin, sentiō + -mentum—the former of which is related, of course, to *Sinn*, and the latter, like the German prefix *Ge-*, denotes a collective noun. Admittedly, "conviction" works as well, though it tends to have a stronger, more active sense, not necessarily implied in *Gesinnung*, which can be entirely passive as well as active.

[71] Hua XLII, pp. 505- 506.

5.2 The Relationships of Knowing and Valuing

Where this occurs, my life takes on a "rational sense," or as Husserl puts it: "I live in the *Gesinnung* of reason, and my life itself is worth more through this *Gesinnung*. This deliberation is 'ethical,' it shows me the form of rational life. And I am not ethical by mere knowledge, but by free decision."[72]

Indeed, the more insightful the decision, the more free they are. This is so insofar as, through insight, I know the reasons why and bring to awareness all other reasons which may influence a decision. I can, for example, reflectively check my egoism, my relative wants and desires, which may not be in accord with that which is absolutely true. To be free from those is to realize that which is truly good, truly worthwhile, which is that which I most profoundly want. And so my will may come into accord with the true and the good, that is, may be consistent. Now, of course, human beings may never be purely free in this life, as they are given over to the vicissitudes of living in the world. Nevertheless, Husserl continues, "every awakened person (the ethically awakened one) willingly sets in themselves their ideal I as an 'infinite task.'"[73] Such task would mean continually, "infinitely" renewing reason as the ruling sense of one's life—the ἡγεμονικόν, as Husserl later retrieves and reinterprets from the Stoics.[74] Indeed, such a life of reason means *asking questions,* even with a science of highest and last questions. For such an awakening requires reflection on sense, a *Besinnung* which becomes increasingly aware of Why and Because in its life.

For such a task, phenomenological inquiry-back is essential, since it discovers the relations of motives and motivations and has insight into the legitimacy. To further distinguish how so, let me say more about how it is possible to *inquiry-back* either into the *self* or into the *world*. To make more sense of these points, however, it is necessary to say more about the sense of *Besinnung*, then to its qualifying prefixes, namely, a *Selbst-besinnung* which becomes increasingly aware of the activities of the self and a *Welt-besinnung* which becomes increasingly aware of the world in which activities take place.

The word *Besinnung* can mean something like an "awareness," as its verbal root, *besinnen*, in the reflexive, is a sort of "remembering." In this sense, Husserl uses the example:

> …think of the absent-minded professor, who wanted to run errands, but sinks instead into his scientific problems on the way and then suddenly stops with the question: Why did I go here, what did I actually want, whereto, wherefore? Does he find his path because he has forgotten the end, as an end itself? Of course not. That is why he asks the question; he wants to be aware [*besinnen*]. The word *besinnen* is excellent here. For consciousness fits the means with a sense [*Sinn*], and this sense sought in its definiteness is forgotten.[75]

The absent minded professor (perhaps Husserl has in mind himself here) asks a question, seeks a a *reason why* in order to become aware. The question itself is

---

[72] Hua XLII, p. 306.

[73] Hua XLII, pp. 173–174.

[74] Also worth noting, even in passing, is Husserl's later reestablishment of the Stoic term ἡγεμονικόν, which means to suggest a ruling of reason in one's life. See, for example, Husserl (2019), p. 15 and *Einfühlung*.

[75] Hua XXXVII, pp. 114–115.

a movement toward becoming aware, to raising again the sense from something that was forgotten. That sense of "why," that is "why did I go here" is present as indeterminate in the forgetfulness. Without that sense, Husserl continues, "a character of consciousness goes beyond what is given, and without that, every question about Why would lose its motive."[76] What he calls a "going beyond what is given" here is essential to what consciousness is, namely, self-transcending: its "Why" extends beyond that which one has already become aware. As such, one can raise awareness by becoming aware (*besinnen*) through inquiry.

Following this, a *Selbstbesinnung* may be understood as a becoming aware of oneself. In a sense, it is "remembering" the operations required for achievements of the self. By this is meant that it reassembles the why and because in thematic awareness. Thus, in transcendental phenomenological inquiry, the aim is to become aware of the *essential* relation of these operations—the why and because in general. Now, this is true not only in terms of the *self*, as say, the progressive-intuitive procedure proceeds to the ego, albeit without content, but also the relationship of the *self in the world*. In this respect, consider the way Husserl discovers a sense of the self that exceeds even his Brentanian formulation of the categorical imperative:

> This whole ethics of the highest practical good, as derived from Brentano and accepted by me in its essential traits, cannot be the last word. There are more essential limits! Vocation and the interior call do not thereby come to their actual right.[77]

Above, we saw that the *practical ought* speaks to something that should be done by any reasonable subject. But a sense reflection upon the motivations of the ought in the life of the subject reveals that there are *reasonable* demands that only make sense *for me*. Indeed, Husserl says that there is an absolute ought that is "*a priori* only for me, insofar as it arises from myself, in relation to my personal environing world."[78] This, at first, seems paradoxical: Can there be an essential "law only meant for me," almost as Kafka would suggest? To explain, Husserl returns to the example of the mother's love of her child.

This motherly love means, Husserl finds, willing the best for the child for its own sake such that the mother supports and preserves the growth of the child in all circumstances.[79] This love is absolutely unique, that is, it appears within this specific relation between unique persons. Now, everyone *can* experience love for this child, for this child is loveable; and, of course, this unique motivation of the mother is also *understandable* to other persons. Nevertheless, the mother's love is not *given to others* in the same way.[80] So, Husserl notes, "every original absolute

---

[76] Hua XXXVII, pp. 114–115.

[77] Hua XLII, pp. 390–391.

[78] Hua XLII, p. 355.

[79] Hua XLII, p. 356.

[80] Let me note here an important clarification to Husserl's description of the "motherly instinct" as a "blind instinct." By "blind instinct" he does not mean that a mother *cannot* become aware of the conditions in which an instinct operates, but rather that, *where it originally appears*, it is neither something that can be manufactured into existence nor appears from a reflective insightful decision.

ought has something irrational. Does this not have to be sharply emphasized?"[81] Again, this "something irrational" does not mean an original absolute is *unintelligible* or *unreasonable*; it means, rather, that it is absolutely uniquely given in its sense as absolute. Although it is uniquely given, it is precisely because it is given as *reasonable* that we are able to understand each other's absolute oughts in an originary way. That is to say, we can understand the mother's absolute devotion to the child. In this respect, there are values that are *incomparable* but that may nevertheless be taken up into relative comparisons, as, say, the child: as he notes, "Within their absolute ought ("Support your child!"), value comparisons and choices naturally play a legitimate role. But then on the basic ground of the absolutely subjective value form of 'my child'!"[82] Thus, in the absolute "subjective value," there is, he continues, "an unconditional 'you should and must' that is addressed to the person...."[83] This unconditional means that it is binding on the person who is such that "to decide against it is to be untrue, to lose oneself, to sin, to betray one's true self, to act against one's true being (absolute practical contradiction)."[84] This unreasonableness is not of that of the categorical imperative, since that is a universal demand to anyone reasonable, but of the unique call to each person to be themselves which is understandable to all.

To understand these calls more exactly, we must briefly consider some aspects of the complex notion of *vocation* in Husserl's thought. In a particularly striking passage, he plays on its sense as a "calling" and an "occupation": a "Beruf," he says, the "beautiful German word," means a "universality of purpose."[85] Of course, not all "jobs" or "occupations" carry with them a fulfilling sense of purpose, not to mention a universality of purpose: sometimes a job is just a job, as it were. However, even a mere job may be taken in order to fulfill a higher purpose, like supporting oneself or one's family. Also given here, then, is a demand beyond the "job," such that labor itself fits in a higher purpose—a "call" to reasonable responsibility. In this respect, an individual can have various vocations: one may be a brother, a father, a citizen, and a scientist, for example, wherein each has particular demands within their activities. In these, then, there are practical oughts—oughts that one should do or carry out this or that activity, in this or that order. These vocations need not *cancel each other out*, as one can be both a citizen, scientist, and a father.[86] Still, the *relation* of these can be weighed according to their worthiness. And that worthiness will be a matter of their

---

Likewise, the other may not bring the understandable motivation of the mother to understanding, but it is nevertheless *possible*. See Hua XLII, pp. 358–359.

[81] Hua XLII, p. 384.

[82] Hua XLII, p. 357.

[83] See Hua XLII, Appendix XXXIII.

[84] Hua XLII, pp. 392 and 356; he continues, "Whomever unreasonably (incomprehensibly, impractically) decided is unwise, stupid, and, in a certain manner, he damages his value."

[85] Hua XLII, p. 250: "Wherever there is talk of our beautiful German word vocation [*Beruf*], we have in sight a universality of purpose, which is worthy of a unity in itself, of true goals. We do not speak of the vocation of thief or robber, even if a universal will to live as a thief is guiding. In such cases, the goal is an abnormal, an untrue one...."

[86] See, for example, Hua XLII, pp. 390–391.

reasonable order, discoverable through inquiry. Thus, about the reasonable order, Husserl notes a several times in his lectures: "God and ethics do not demand that we, lest we miss church or interrupt a heartfelt prayer, should let a murder happen or that we should let go of a scientific discovery that we have just gotten in our grasp, in order to search the streets and alleys for someone in need whom we could help."[87] We should not let go of something nearly realized in order to seek out something only *potentially* better. Once again, the *better* is the enemy of the good, for the good is achievable and attainable now, whereas the better may not be at all, may only be a fine idea, a manifestation of moral idealism or even a rationalization of lazy reason. Instead, to discover the practically best, inquiry is needed—and to live the best life, a life of inquiry is required.

There is also given herein the aforementioned unique call of each person to be themselves, however. In this respect, it is important to stress that the *subject is not ready-made* but rather strives toward an end that it bears within itself as a guiding idea.[88] The becoming of the subject is a complex play of systems of capacities in the lived-body, as they develop in the world, in the exercise of talents, intelligence, social mores, not only as they are relative to the subject but as they go beyond them to the absolute. Of course, the becoming of the individual human being bears within itself the idea of human being itself; or, put more explicitly in terms of inquiry, there is what Husserl calls a "universal Why" of human being that "answers itself exhaustively in the universality."[89] Further, though, there is the fact that I am *this* person within *this* situation who has a demand on myself which no other person has. From the absolute ought for oneself, then, there thus comes what Husserl calls a "personal question" about who one *absolutely ought to be*.[90] Indeed, Husserl finds that, from this context, there emerges for each person a question about their life: "What is to be made of it?"[91] This question implies a confluence of the universal and the personal such that to be more or less "true" (*treu*, as Husserl himself uses at times) is meant something like when a carpenter says the word, as when things "line up how they should."[92] In this sense, to be "true to oneself" does not mean doing whatever might satisfy

---

[87] Hua Mat IX, pp. 142 and 145.

[88] Thus, Husserl stresses the striving of the egoic subject to be itself, for example, at Hua XLII, p. 338. "An ego has no possible rigid properties. It is not a unity of change in the sense of a physical substance; it does not have a substantial being in this sense. It is rather a unity through a tendency towards self-preservation; it is by striving to be and striving to be itself....And this idea is itself an ideal that the striving life of human beings more or less approach [*nähert*]."

[89] Hua XLII, p. 350: "Universal values and individual values that are worth for the sake of their universality. The rational that has its universal Why—and its Why that answers itself exhaustively in the universality. Yes, because one moves only in the framework of universality or the indefinite possibilities. It is otherwise in the real sphere. The real always remains irrational in a part of its existence."

[90] Hua XLII, p. 519.

[91] Hua XLII, p. 503.

[92] Hua XLII, p. 252: "…to be a human, to be the fullest, the most genuine, the truest human. Clearer: Each of us says: I—I want to live my life, my whole life from now on in all its acts and with its entire content of lived-experience so that it is my best possible life; my best possible, that is, the best I can."

5.2 The Relationships of Knowing and Valuing

oneself, but rather what fulfills *what* and *who* one ought to be. Indeed, in this respect, as Husserl notes, "to 'preserve oneself' means 'to preserve' the true self to which each human ego is 'directed,'" which means, he continues, that the human ego is directed toward the true self.[93] The call to be oneself is, in other words, intertwined with the universal call of reason but as given to *this person* to become who they are through and with reason. Philosophy responds to this universal interior "call" by bringing it to bear in their living, as they resolutely seek to be increasingly aware, increasingly reasonable.[94]

However, if each person has their unique "call," there is also what Husserl calls a *community of love*.[95] Such a community means, not merely the sharing of aims with each other, as insects might, but in willing the good for each other, co-operating in the realization of that good in ever-increasing measure. For, recall, there are unique absolute oughts to each person. As such, there is a demand in self-responsibility to a communal sense of *responsibility*, that is, to *solidarity*.[96] This is not because the group is a larger "self," nor because one is part of the group, but rather human beings are bound together in a way that each individual retains a unique value within the whole which has its own unique value. In this sense, human beings do not only live nearby one another, as Leibnizian monads, but along-with each other.[97] In other words, there is a "co-living" or even "co-operation," in which, Husserl says, "there is an intelligible love that unifies the egos."[98] Here, then, there appears *love*, as Husserl puts it, in the "most excellent sense"—as a very "law of love."[99]

In that law, there is promotion and preservation of the self and the other within the context of the whole. What is more, in the law of love, there can also appear a demand to sacrifice for higher values of society and persons. Thus, Husserl gives the example of washing the child, which is not enjoyable for the child, but is needed for "preservation," as he says: "It can be that no pleasure takes place, but suffering, which

---

[93] Hua XLII, p. 339. See also Hua XXXVII, p. 49. Also, ms. A V II 24, 5/6: "Sprechen wir von der Selbsterhaltung eines Realen, so können wir geleitet sein von einer Erhaltung der Einheit der Realität, wie immer sie sich 'verändern,' wie immer ihre Zeit fuelle sich wandeln mag - wofern nur irgendeine Einheit bleibt" ["When we speak of the self-preservation of a real entity, we can be guided by the preservation of the unity of reality, however it may 'change,' however its time may transform—as long as some unity remains."] And ms. B I 5 II / 5b: "…nennen wir Leben in der 'urnormalen' Form, in der elementaren, primären 'Selbsterhaltung.' Es ist Leben in der Periodizität von Geniessen, nach Sättigung wieder entbehren, nach neuen Werten (zu geniessenden) Suchen bzw. <es> auf sie als handelnd zu gestaltende abgesehen haben" ["…we call life in its 'normal' form, in its elementary, primary 'self-preservation.' It is life in the periodicity of enjoyment, deprivation after satiety, searching for new values (to be enjoyed) or setting them aside as something to be shaped through action."].

[94] Hua XLII, p. 388.

[95] Hua XLII, p. 173.

[96] Hua XLII, p. 173. Also, Hua XXXVII, p. 81.

[97] Hua XLII, p. 505 and again, in Hua XIII, Beilage LIV. For more on these points, see Moran (2018).

[98] Hua XLII, pp. 512–52.

[99] Hua XLII, p. 337: "Of course, the fulfillment of my personal absolute ought is also only an original experience for me and so is preferred. But here rules the law of love…."

is accepted to avoid greater suffering."[100] In other words, the suffering still appears, still presses on the person in love with the child, but the social and personal responsibility for the child overrules the vital discomfort and pain, for a greater suffering it and for all threatens, if it is not endured. Related to this point, there is also a recurring example in Husserl's manuscript of the mother's sacrifice of her son to the nation, if the nation itself really aims to realize higher values, even if that turns out not to be the case, something about which he was personally familiar, as he lost his own son in the battle of Verdun.[101] Also, from this perspective, another's death can be experienced as the death of a *beloved*, as something *meaningful* and, in a sense, *valuable* in relation to a life that can no longer be promoted.[102] The individual can be so overwhelmed about this loss, Husserl notes, that she pushes aside any further questions about other relations and so ends up in despair, in a paralysis of the will.[103] As Augustine puts it, a death can throw one's life and, indeed, all life into darkness—*uo dolore contenebratum est cor meum, et quidquid aspiciebam mors erat.*[104] Yet, Husserl continues, not unlike Augustine, from such an experience, one may also be motivated to look toward a wider context of life and value—"in memory of others who have suffered, who have overcome and withstood…out of instinctive self-preservation."[105] It may seem, at first blush, somewhat crass to say this motivation appears from an egoist's sense of self-preservation; however, in the community of love, such a shift in perspective brings the whole into view such that one has insight into oneself as having a role in one's world, as relating to all the others who make its goodness possible. For a death of a loved one, again as both Husserl and Augustine knew, can *bring oneself and the world to question*, not merely egoistically, but *in relation to other persons*.

Finally, then, with all this in tow, Husserl revises Brentano's formulation of the categorical imperative with the following:

> Do your best, as that which is the best you can do in the sense of the absolute best, towards which the sense of your life should also aim, as is so for all people! So, direct your gaze to the Absolute, that is what discloses to your absolute ought its ultimate meaning! Know that all value of ought – and the demand to help to the realization of all absolute ought of all human beings – has its highest, comprehensible rational sense in a world of God![106]

Along with what we have so far discussed, the reformulation of the imperative introduces the *teleological* sense of "Why" in God and raises the question of the loving,

---

[100] Hua XIV, p. 178.
[101] There may, in fact, be a there may even be a demand of sacrificing an *absolute value* for *another absolute value*. See Hua XLII, p. 346. Husserl (2024), p. 36, 41–47.
[102] Hua XLII, p. 508.
[103] Hua XLII, p. 18, et al.
[104] Augustine, *Confessions*, 4.4.9.
[105] Hua XLII, p. 508.
[106] Hua XLII, p. 390.

5.2 The Relationships of Knowing and Valuing

personal God. To make sense of this, let me reiterate that Husserl finds in intentional life both a *why* and *where to* (*Warum und Wozu*).[107] He means this in multiple senses: on the one hand, the sense of where something is going, to what end, and, on the other hand, for what purpose or why something is. So, while a particular affirmation, for example, says "Yes" or "No" to *this being thus and so*, it also implies an intention to an affirmation of *being* at all which is not exhausted by an affirmation of *this* being. In other words, our intnetion of *this* and *that* implies an intelligible intention to all being, a *teleological orientation* of the subject toward true being and truly good being—indeed, to *all judgments*. This is understandable in the very essence of the intentional life, as the previous chapters have shown, as the ego essentially strives to determine and to differentiate being and that this true being "calls" the ego to it, in its real and true value as being real and true. This oritentation is not reducible to a sort of "relativism," then, as if the intention of being is reducible as the intentional pole of some individual intending and striving ego.[108] Rather, as Husserl puts it, "God is the entelechy and outside him there is 'nothing'....And the world has its being from God and is otherwise 'nothing.' And God is only as a leading and 'animating' principle of perfection, and so on"[109] Again, God, in this sense, is the principle of movement, the ultimate end toward which all strives to realize that which it is. We should note that this is not a *personal* sense of God, as Husserl knows (for more on that, see the end of the next chapters). Instead, it speaks to the ultimate principle of the *where to* and *why*. The personal sense of God, for Husserl, appears the call to be what and who one and who we are in a community of love.

To more fully become aware of these aspects, however, a *Weltbesinnung* is required. Once again, it is possible to inquire-back into the *world* itself, in a *Weltbesinnung,* in order to "remember" the way in which worldly achievements have set the stage for other achievements and, indeed, how certain ideals and goals are demanded by the world itself.[110] That would reveal the world-horizon as that in and from which matters appear and take on sense, not only to this or that subject, but across generations in home/alienworlds. It would also reveal, for Husserl, the teleological sense of the world itself, as indicating the principle of the world, God. Before turning back to this way of sense-reflection, which I do in the last chapter, let me turn to a clarification of the sense of method, which helps us to further differentiate the method of phenomenological philosophy as such and its role in the task of realizing ourselves and our world.

---

[107] Hua XLII, pp. 387–388: "As absolute norm, it is absolute ought. Only the limited ought has irrationality; the total and disclosed is rationality through and through." See also Hua XLII, pp. 335–336.

[108] Hua XLII, pp. 335–336.

[109] Hua XLII, pp. 335–336.

[110] Hua XLII, p. 506.

5.3 Some Senses of Method

> Every action has its way, its manner of achieving the result, its "method."[111]

The task of ethics, as the "the "queen of technical disciplines," is to find how all technical disciplines are unified to one basic end. Husserl, following Brentano, discovers the unity and orderly contexts of these, founded upon the unity and order in the subject's intention of true and truly good being. To make the ordering and organization of these intentions clearer, I further explicate this point in terms of *method*. This also sets the stage for the next chapter, which traces the *generation* of methods, in and for which inquiry plays an essential role.

5.3.1 Methods and Techniques

So, a provisional and general definition of method: *an organized series of acts arising in a movement to some end, the norms of which set together within this context*. This sense of method thus emerges from the operation or in the "execution" of this series of acts.[112] As Husserl says, "A method, after all, is nothing which is, or which can be, brought in from outside."[113]

At one limit, then, there is what Husserl calls an *algorithmic* method. By this is meant a regular, fixed set of "acts," where one plugs-in appropriate variable-contents in order to achieve a fixed set of results. This sense is necessarily closed to novel operations—it is a "blind mechanism." The many tricks of calculation illustrate the point: if one must quickly calculate 15%, simply divide the initial number by 10, then add the quotient to half of its own value. Such a mechanism can be repeated *ad infinitum*, according to the parsimonious nature of its parameters. In any case, this sense is a limit insofar as it is brought "from the outside," though it is itself a result of spiritual or intellectual creation.

Beyond this, there are series of acts in the operations of the spheres of the lived-body and of reason. First, a more general point about how methods might appear within different spheres of acts according to specific matters in those spheres. For the institution of a method depends on the repetition of a similar set of acts which coalesce into a unified way of acting which is directed toward an aim, a goal. So, within its performance or execution, there is a *procedure*, or a series of acts correlated to an aim all of which must be actualized in order to meet the aim. Further, there is the

---

[111] A VII 9/4b: "Jedes Tun hat seinen Weg, seine Weise, das Ergebnis zu gewinnen, seine 'Methode.'".

[112] As such, Husserl says, at Husserl (1983), p. 144: "A determinate method — determined not with respect to its technical particularity but with respect to the universal type of method <to which it belongs>—is a norm which arises from the fundamental regional specificity and the universal structures of the province in question, so that a cognitive seizing upon such a method depends essentially on knowledge of these structures."

[113] Husserl (1983), p. 144.

5.3 Some Senses of Method

approach to the matter which is a mode of actually bringing the method to bear in the performance of the acts on the matters. The approach relates to the *style*, as Husserl will sometimes put it, of performance. Together, these make sense of the *"where"* and "to where" acts are going, and so fill out the multivalent sense of μέθοδος—μετά "in pursuit or quest of" + ὁδός a "way or path."

Having this in mind serves the further elucidation of how habitual ways of acting can emerge from within experience. For there appear normal ways of operation which can be corrected according to an optimality in that very operation. For example, these ways appear in the *perceptual* sphere of the lived-body. Indeed, there are processes in the lived-body that are "blind," though not mechanical, insofar as they emerge through the life of perception. I do not mean here the lower level of the biological organism, like the circulation of blood, where there is not yet any passive or active awareness. I mean, rather, the passive sense of *perceptual normality*, where there is a constitution within an intention to a goal, that is, goal of perception, concordance. For Husserl, the development of the lived-body has to do with *adaptation* within apperception and *selection*.[114] Once again, this does not mean the sort of higher-level selection at the level of activity, but rather the adjustments done within the lived-body itself. Amidst all these possibilities that are given, even at the bodily level, Husserl finds how there is an appeal or favoring, that is, a way in which there is an *inclination* to turn in preference toward one or another possible selection.[115] As an example, consider how subjects adjust themselves when uncomfortable, "without further ado," "without question," as the lived-body finds its way into normal ways of proceeding for it. Indeed, lived-bodies develop according to the possibilities of growth "within" it. There is an organized series of acts arising in a dynamic movement to some end, and these are "striving upward," as Husserl says, toward further determination and differentiation of being.[116]

Beyond the constitution of habitual ways of acting in the lived-body, there are also ways of acting constituted by intelligence. First of all, there is the straightforward operation of intelligence. In this, intelligence builds-up what can be done from the manifold of bodily capacities given as a foundation. For example, the straightforward asking and answering of questions in order to determine disruptions in passivity can be set into a habit, and so yield a sort of *method* of bringing experience back to concordance. Yet there is an essential difference between such straightforward questions and reflection upon questions. There is an analogous difference between an apprentice merely copying what the master is doing and reflectively asking "How do *I* do that?" To be sure, even upon reflection, one follows after the master, clumsily at first, without meeting one's own possibilities as adequate to the masterful movements. Nonetheless, the more one becomes aware, attending to and adjusting to the style of the master, the better one meets his example. The apprentice who masters the method becomes the master by reflectively grasping the steps and the reasons for the steps

---

[114] See Hua XLII, p. xvii and Nr. 11 on adaptation (*anpassen*).

[115] See, for example, Hua XXXVII, Beilagen XIX.

[116] See, for example, Hua XLII, p. xliii.

such that they themselves have the insightful *know-how*. The whole comes into view such that it can be repeated for themselves.

It makes sense, then, that there is an essential distinction between a philosophy and a "mechanical" theoreomatics, for Husserl. The former proceeds, not blindly, but with insight. The latter explicitly establishes an intelligent check on operations, whereas the former does not. Both are intelligible, that is, both have relations of motivations, but a reflective method that has insights into the optimal way of proceeding, setting it as an ideal according to which operations should proceed. In other words, a reflective method grasps the Why and Because of operations and explicitly formulates it as a regulative ideal to be taken up and carried out. Thus, from its institution in Greece, philosophy sets itself to leaving no questions unanswered.[117] And it does so insightfully, with its goal in mind. Thus, Husserl says, "Philosophy has to do with questions that cannot be of indifference…but rather must be a devotion to truth."[118] As such, the question of philosophy is really a "question of conscience" (*Gewissensfrage*), namely, "What do I really and at the base of my heart want?"[119] Philosophy makes these questions scientific, through detached and disinterested inquiry, such that answers, as Husserl continues, "can be brought into the paths of decision by scientific methods."[120]

Phenomenological philosophy, too, means to provide scientific answers for paths of decision. In this respect, the *transcendental method* is the grasping of the normative operation of cognizing, valuing, and acting at all. In its formulation, as I have already noted, it is possible to distinguish three methods of transcendental investigation (static, genetic, and generative); two procedures (progressive-intuitive and regressive-inquisitive) and the various approaches (for example, from Descartes, Kant, Brentano, and so on). Each of these set together the acts in a certain context, revealing matters in a certain manner, though they share, in a philosophical sense, the aim of a scientific understanding of the transcendental sphere which might serve to guide decision and action.

Indeed, as Husserl's reflection on phenomenological method matures, he sees more clearly a genetic relation of motivation between matters and methods that he calls one of *Leitfaden* or "leading clues." Not only does this further illuminate the dynamism emergent in experience that gives rise to methodological norms but it also addresses how new methods are anticipated and demanded as matters themselves exceed the limitations of presently employed methods. I suggest, moreover, a *generative* relation of methods and matters in Husserl's thought, for which I retain the

---

[117] Hua XXXII, pp. 171–172. Also, Husserl (2019), p. 528: "Without an insight into the essence of rational achievement as such, no rational formation, no truth, no theory, no science can have ultimate justification."

[118] Hua XXV, pp. 275–279.

[119] Hua XXV, p. 290: "The question is always: What do I really and at the base of my heart want, and the decision for the standpoint of high mortality means nothing else than to want from now on and exclusively only that and nothing else."

[120] Hua XXXII, p. 4.

term *Leitmotif*.[121] By this, I mean to designate a socio-historical dimension of the relation between matters and approaches, about which I will say more now.

5.3.2 Leitfaden and Leitmotifs: *Clues Appearing In and Obtaining Between Methods*

Taken mundanely, a "clue" is something that indicates other matters other than itself. A clue points beyond itself to something that is sought but not yet determined as such. A detective thus gathers clues, not with the mentality of a collector—as, say, a numismatist whose collecting of individual stamps set into an interest in any stamp at all—but rather in search for a "*lead*" to the culprit. As mentioned above, Husserl's use of the term *Leitfaden* carries this sense as well. For him, a transcendental clue points to further dimensions of sense, leading the phenomenologist to further analysis of matters. In fact, such a clue indicates relations between matters and methods themselves, namely, between (1) material and formal ontologies, (2) ontological and constitutive analyses; (3) and, thirdly, between constitution and ontology itself.[122] In the next section, I give examples of these, so let me point out two general points about relation of matters and methods.

First, matters motivate methods. For example, there is given to the phenomenologist a difference between spiritual and material being. However, givenness from the material sphere can itself serve as a clue to the spiritual sphere of consciousness, as the givenness of the material object leads the phenomenologist back into its constitution through spiritual activity. A method that remains with material being does not adequately account for the difference of these spheres and so does not lead back to the differences of being. Moreover, as matters motivate methods, a matter might exceed the presently operative method. For example, a static analysis clarifies what a structure is, but there is yet a demand to understand how such a structure is constituted through time. The static structure thereby provides "leading clue" to further dimensions of the matter. The phenomenologist may thus begin from a-temporal structure only then to move to problems of genesis, if the phenomena demand it. For example, the static structure of inquiry as a question-intention points beyond itself to the question about its origins. Indeed, where the static method focuses on the simple and moves to complex, matters can demand that it gives way to the relation of abstract and concrete in genesis. What is more, though, the genesis of matters

---

[121] This is an infrequent, though not unimportant term for Husserl; a ἅπαξ λεγόμενον of both the *Logische Untersuchungen* and *Ideen*, it occurs more frequently in manuscripts, especially under a genetic account; see, for example, Hua 18, §46; Hua III/1, §128; Hua VII, pp. 124 and 196. I do not wish to claim that its infrequency frees an interpreter to employ it as one sees fit—to the contrary, the demand for precision is perhaps even stronger. Indeed, the institution of each method will have its *Leitmotifs* that determine "the course of all inquiries into problems of intentionality," as Husserl says in Husserl (1983), 307.

[122] For more on this, see Steinbock (1992), pp. 42–48.

in the individual points beyond itself to more concrete relation of the *generation* of matters. To speak to this point, let me highlight Husserl's use of the term *Leitmotiv*.

Now, Husserl does not, as far as I know, use the term *Leitmotiv* in any systematic way, as he does with *Leitfaden*. Nevertheless, the term does appear in the context of generation matters. For example, Husserl suggests that there are "new impulses" given to science from Cartesian and Kantian or "transcendental motifs."[123] These motifs go beyond the scope of a genetic method, pointing to how matters pass across generations. These serve as clues, passed across generations, which lead the phenomenologist back to the *how* of the institution and re-institution of ideals or norms in history. In this respect, the ambiguity of this word "motif" is illuminating: on the one hand, it can mean a "theme," as in music, where variations or modifications appear within a dynamic range of possibilities in relation to an original institution; on the other hand, it can also mean a "motivation" or an "impulse," as from Latin *motivus*. The givenness of the historical matters, for example, move the phenomenologist to inquire-back from them into the conditions of their possibility, namely, generativity.

Now, it is possible to *abstract* from the generative dimension. It is this fact, I claim, that leads to what Husserl himself calls the "strange circumstantialities" of the *Meditations*, in which the supposedly "radical" investigation is nevertheless led by an historically instituted ideal of science—that is, a *leitmotif*![124] The "strangeness" which Husserl notes arises from this abstraction. In other words, a *generative* relation of instantiation is *at work* or *operative* in his thought, for which only a generative method can account. As Ariadne, though, the phenomenologist may follow the thread to the end, which Husserl aims to do through his attention and inquiry.

5.4 Concluding Remarks: Toward a Generative Analysis of Inquiry

> But now we have to consider that a subject is not alone, already by virtue of its generative origin and its inner development from childhood to maturity, which is familiar and accessible to every ego by memory. From the very beginning, every subject, already as it lives worldly childhood (as a child who has consciously spatiotemporal environment into which it actively lives), finds itself in original community with others.[125]

---

[123] There are also many others, including, for example, Euclidean and Galilean, Socratic and Platonic, and so on; see, for example, Hua VI, pp. 18 and 41 and 78; Hua I, p. 43: "Descartes gave it new impulses through his meditations; their study had a very direct effect on the transformation of phenomenology, which was already in the process of becoming into a new form of transcendental philosophy....precisely through the radical unfolding of Cartesian motifs."

[124] Hua 1, p. 49: "To be sure, we get into what at first seem to be strange circumlocutions – but how were they to be avoided if our radicalism is not to remain an empty gesture but to become a deed?" Later, we claim, he finds a way to deal with these strange circumstances.

[125] Hua XXXIX, pp. 316–317.

5.4 Concluding Remarks: Toward a Generative Analysis of Inquiry

This chapter traced some aspects of Husserl's investigation of the relationship between knowing and valuing, both in acting and reflection upon acting. In so doing, we elucidated his treatment of the essential role of inquiry in knowing what ought to be done and in carrying out this knowledge in action. From this, we further formulated the appearance and operation of phenomenological reflection and inquiry: we went from Husserl's formulation of a methodological inquiry into the meaning of expressive acts, into his radicalization of that inquiry as it proceeds to the source and horizon of intentional acts, then into his genetic inquiry-back into the origins of sense, meaning, and value. Now, finally, let me broach his methodical inquiry-back into the *generativity*.

To prepare that investigation, let me highlight the demand for the generative method by setting it into relation with the genetic. Recall that a regressive method leaves mundane being in play, that is to say, it does not bracket and reduce it straightaway but instead takes it as a clue. This allows the phenomenologist to go back into founding layers of validity, into passive synthesis where *pre*-given conditions for activity. In so doing, a genetic method discovers the monad as unity of becoming which constitutes the living-present. What is more, the monad is taken as the "absolute" constitutive origin of meaning and sense in the lived-present. It is self-temporalizing and self-constituting, even with respect to the world of contemporaneous monads, which are connected through a transference of sense in which their spheres of ownness are nevertheless primary. Indeed, from this perspective, as Husserl says in the lectures in *Passive Synthesis*, the transcendental ego is "immortal"—it is neither born nor dies.[126] By this is *not* meant, as he emphasizes, that the empirical ego is not born or does not die.[127] It means, rather, that there is *no constitutive possibility* for the monad's birth or death—it cannot self-constitute either of these possibilities. However, the givenness of birth and death present a demand for a more concrete method, revealing the *abstractness* of the genetic method.[128]

To clarify the abstractness further, consider how, for the monad, birth is given at the limits of memory. I do not remember my own birth. I can see photos and hear stories of the event, but I cannot evidentially *re*-present it to myself, "there in the flesh," as it were. Nor am I present in this way to my death: not only am I not yet given as present to my death, but there is a question of whether I will be so given in it at all. Although experiencing the possibility realized in others may reveal it as a

---

[126] Hua XI, p. 381: "But every human-ego contains within itself in a certain way its transcendental-ego, and this does not die and does not come into being, it is an eternal being in becoming."

[127] Hua XI, p. 378: "*nota bene* the pure transcendental ego, not the empirical world ego, which can very well die."

[128] Consider, for example, Hua XXXIX, p. 539: Thus, he writes, "In such a history with regard to the historical time it is like within memory of a single man with regard to his time and [to] the time of the individual world taken for him abstractly by itself. If the world spatio-temporally is just a generative one, and if, being itself already undisclosed, [it is] historically constituted, then time without "birth" (= beginning of the generation) and without death (of the generation) is openly beginningless and endless."

possibility of my own, it is not constituted by me *as present*.[129] Thus, such matters appear at the limits of monadic constitution. Nevertheless, the matters are given. My birth is, in a way, apodictically given: I *am* living as *having been* born. My death, to be sure, can only be anticipated, emptily intended, as I have not yet been present for it.[130] But death is given as a possibility intertwined with how I appear in the world as having-been-born. So, birth and death are not, as Steinbock notes from Husserl, merely "incidental facts," but rather *constitutive* of meaning and value.[131] Indeed, to remain at the genetic view of the immortal monad is to remain at an abstract account of constitution, as if the monad creates and destroys the world. The matters are given otherwise. There is a meaningful world *prior* to my birth, a world *into which* I am *born* and which continues after I die. *I* am born and *I* anticipate my death. I am therefore neither *self*-giving nor *self*-grounding in this more concrete sense. Indeed, considered from this perspective, birth and death become a *transcendental problem* or, as Husserl also frequently calls it, a *question*.[132]

I find that Husserl's use of "problem" and a "question" in relation to birth and death is not mere phrasing but following upon the matter itself. Such problems cannot be simply *attended to* for they are *not* present; they must instead be *questioned* or, more appropriately, *inquired-back into* from the prior We of the lifeworld. Indeed, for this inquiring-back, the phenomenologist does not begin from the *psyche* of the monad, but rather from the world wherein these matters carry meaning. So, where the genetic method founds normativity on the lived-experience of the subject, the regressive-inquisitive approach inquires-back from ontology to constitution. For that, it is necessary to have some ontology of the world—that is to say, it is necessary to have some idea of that back-from which the phenomenologist is questioning, in order to undergo a sort of Husserlian second sailing, a second beginning to phenomenology.[133] As a decisive turning point of this new way of reflection, Steinbock points to the importance of the so-called *Kant-rede* of 1924.[134] In it, there is an

---

[129] Hua XV, p. 171: "In building up the performance of empathy as experience of others and mine among others, I first point to alien actual and possible experience as a way of making present that has validity of being, and a modified one vis-à-vis my primordial-original experience."

[130] Steinbock speaks of the "phenomenological precedence of natality." This means both that the evidence of birth is apodictic but also that *newness* or *generation* is as well. See Anthony Steinbock, (2017), especially pp. 31–33.

[131] Steinbock (2017) p. 29. This is from Hua XV, p. 171: "Das wäre ja so, als ob Generativität, mit Geburt und Tod, ein zufälliges Welt-faktum wäre."

[132] See A IV 5/42: "Frage nach Geburt und Tod" and similar in K III 11, 2. Also, Hua XLII, p. 65: "…Frage nach dem Tod," passim; also, Hua Mat VIII, p 434. It is worthwhile to note a parallel issue with the question of the "unconscious," which is not given to one's own consciousness, but can be experienced in generative horizons.

[133] Hua VIII, p. 254: "Now, *before beginning* - <namely, beginning> with reflection on <the> structure of the world of experience – I have necessarily had to carry out *another beginning*: general meditations on the goal of knowledge and science, on norms which I set for myself in natural insight." For more on the "shipwreck" of the first beginning, see the translator's introduction of Husserl (2019).

[134] Steinbock (1995), p. 81.

5.4 Concluding Remarks: Toward a Generative Analysis of Inquiry

attempt to give an account of the world in which the monad lives, for which Husserl introduces the highly influential concept of the *Lebenswelt* or lifeworld.

In the main, Steinbock expounds three senses of an *ontology* of the lifeworld in Husserl's work.[135] In the first, Husserl finds the "intuitiable" world, in which the world is treated as intuitable *simpliciter*, that is, without being considered yet *as* a foundation of sense for a higher, theoretical meaning. In this second, then, this provides the source or foundation for the objective sciences.[136] The differentiation of the first and second sense already occurred with the Greeks in what Husserl calls a "first idealization" of the world.[137] It was the Greeks who established the possibility of investigating the world as an "unending" or "infinite" horizon of beings, striving to intuit true being *in itself* or *ideally*. So, the Greeks established the first "objective world," that is, the world abstracted from subjective conditions. But as these theoretical accomplishments nevertheless "flow back into" the lifeworld, the "merely subject-relative" lifeworld is shown as not being annihilated through the idealization.[138] Thus this third sense of the lifeworld calls into question the first two insofar as it shows that an ontology of the lifeworld demands a *constitutive* analysis, that is to say, it shows it necessary to understand *how* the being of the world is constituted at all, beyond studying *what* it is. Steinbock thus finds Husserl differentiating between the "great task" of a lifeworld ontology that would determine its *essence* and the "greater task" of a transcendental one which would encompass this by accounting for its constitution.[139] The former would be a formal ontology, determining formal and material essences of beings in the world, whereas the latter would be a *transcendental* ontology that would take these matters and, I suggest, *inquire-back* into their constitution. Indeed, to do so the phenomenologist inquires-back from the lifeworld into the problem of the *pre*-given world, revealing a fourth sense of the lifeworld, which Steinbock identifies as the normatively significant home/alienworld.

I turn more directly to these generative matters, especially with respect to inquiry, in the next chapter. Here, let me emphasize how an inquiry-back into the correlative home/alienworld discovers those conditions in and from which matters take on and

---

[135] For a more detailed analysis, see Steinbock (2017), pp. 44–45 and (1995), pp. 88–96.

[136] Hua XXIX, p. 140: "The distinction between the world of actual and possible experience ("intuitive" world) and scientifically true world may be made at times in view of reactivities…but taken concretely and fully, the life world is…".

[137] Hua XXIX, p. 143: "…with a universal abstract structure of the intuitive life-world, the (already by the first idealization) infinite world of the 'one intuition.'"

[138] Hua VI, p. 133. Also, see Carr (1970), p. 335. Carr notes the multiplicity of the notions of the lifeworld at work in the first Crisis volume and, in particular, the difference between the first and third sense here.

[139] Again, he calls the former a "great task" and the latter a "greater task" that would encompass (*mitumspannendend*) the former Hua VI, p. 145: "Thus, here would lie the task of a life-world ontology….Instead of dwelling, we prefer to proceed to what will soon become apparent as a much greater task, and one that embraces it itself." This is emphasized by Steinbock as the clue to the unwritten fourth and fifth part of the Crisis volume, which was to be a phenomenological metaphysics and philosophy. Evidence for it is preserved in manuscripts and from Fink's conversations with Husserl. See, for example, Steinbock (2017), p. 55.

carry sense through history. Here, in other words, appears the matter of generative phenomenology which is *generativity*. By this is meant, again, *both a process of historical and intersubjective becoming and a socio-historical dimension to that process which extends across generations*. As such, a generative phenomenology also reveals the difference between analyzing the lifeworld as an ontological "totality" and "territory" and as transcendental *world-horizon* and *earth-ground*. The world-horizon is an open, pre-thematic, pre-intentional condition from which beings are given, rather than infinite, thematic, intentional "totality" of being-given. Likewise, the earth-ground is a condition from which the lived-body constitutes the sense of motion and space, rather than a zero-point in the lived-body that constitutes its expanding "territories." In other words, where the world-horizon is the condition for the possibility of givenness, receding in favor of the given, the earth-ground is the condition for the possibility of sense-giving of spatiality, that is to say, the ground from which spatiality emerges. In relation to these points, there emerges the possibility to understand the geo-historical lifeworld, as a typically familiar home- and alien. Indeed, there appears a normative significance that is given as "home" in relation to "alien," beyond the monadic constitution of "one's ownness," which are given *as* intersubjective and co-generative conditions.

In short, then, the generative method undergoes both a *Selbst-* and *Weltbesinnung*. Its inquiry-back from the lifeworld brings to awareness the conditions through the subject and the world appear at all. From this awareness, phenomenological philosophy functions as a guide to being reasonable and responsible in the world. To explain further, let me turn now to a fuller explanation of these problematics in the context of the main theme of inquiry.

Chapter 6
The Generative Roots of Inquiry

Abstract This chapter reconstructs Husserl's inquiry-back into the generation of inquiry. In the first steps of this, I expound the emergence of inquiry from childhood curiosity. The original question about why appears within the home, in order to answer why the homeworld has particular meanings and how to navigate it practically. From this, I turn to the transformation of inquiry from within the curiosity of myth to philosophical wonder, as the latter breaks from relative truth and establishes theoretical science, the ideal of which is in determining the universal truth which is true, not just for those in this homeworld, but as true for everyone everywhere. As the instantiations of this ideal following from Greek philosophy tends to the objective pole, the correlation of the subject-world is left unquestioned. So, there arises a demand for the further inquiry of phenomenology, to which I turn next.

Keywords Generative phenomenology · Development · Curiosity · Wonder · Instinct

> Such a manner of the clarification of history by inquiring-back into the original establishment of the goals which bind together the chain of future generations, insofar as these goals live on in sedimented forms, can be reawakened again and again and, in their new vitality, be criticized….An historical sense-reflection back of the sort under discussion is thus actually the deepest kind of sense-reflection on the self, aimed at a self-understanding in terms of what we are truly seeking as the historical beings we are.[1]

6.1 Preliminary Remarks—The Question of History

Through the previous chapters, we have traced Husserl's increasingly concrete analysis of inquiry. After the discovery of the foundation of questions in intentional acts, we went back to the source of inquiry in the pure ego, through its initiation in the world. From this, we went back into the origin of inquiry, into the "history" of the

---

[1] Hua VI, pp. 72–73.

monad. With all this in tow, let me turn now to how inquiry appears, operates, and transforms from its roots in generativity by following Husserl's inquiry-back from generative matters. More exactly, in this chapter:

1. I first sketch some essential matters of Husserl's nascent phenomenology of generativity, namely, the structure of the home/alien world, in which there is a generation of ideals and values;
2. from these points, I reconstruct how inquiry emerges from and participates in the world-horizon, tracing the appearance of the original question of history—the *Why?*—through childhood instincts and practical life-interests;
3. then, I turn to how the original question about generates a mythological world, which transforms into scientific inquiry in the encounter of the Greek homeworld with the neighboring alienworlds;
4. finally, I conclude the work with an overview of the preceding chapters by relating them to the emergence and operation of phenomenological-philosophical inquiry across three stages of history, namely, that of latent, patent, and manifest reason.

Let me again highlight that, through this chapter, we mean to take after the methodological inquiring-back that is peculiar to phenomenology. As I have already intimated, this becomes an explicit operation in phenomenology as Husserl brings to *critical* awareness genetic and generative matters. To carry out this critical reflection on generativity, it is necessary to move back, beyond genesis, into the way meaning appears and develops across generations—that is to say, it is necessary to *inquire*-back into invariant structures in which meaning is constituted and passes through generations, namely, the home/alienworld. As such, the generative method does not only offer a description of historical events. Instead, it inquires-back from historical events in order to become increasingly aware of the conditions from and in which they appear at all. By doing so, the phenomenologist uncovers how an individual's striving for truth appears within a world-horizon that is already mediated by meaning and value, even as it is generative of *new* meaning and value. In other words, inquiry itself appears as transforming and transformative in generativity. Taken as such, our own inquiry is elucidated as participating in generativity. In this respect, Husserl notes, "Transcendental inquiry is itself a world-historical process insofar as it enlarges the history of the constitution of the world, not only by adding a new science to it but also by enlarging the content of the world in every respect."[2]

Indeed, through this chapter, phenomenological philosophy comes to light as a task in *generativity*. To be sure, it is still to be taken up and carried out by individuals. But the individual also takes *after* others, as the task is passed on via an invitation to a community that spans generations. From this perspective, in fact, I suggest, following Husserl, that the *motivation* for phenomenological philosophy is in the *unity of acts through history*. What is more, to describe that motivation is to describe *and* to participate in the historical tension of *reason coming to know itself that is communicated across generations*. In this sense, the task of phenomenological

---

[2] Husserl (1970), p. 264.

philosophy is set in a series of acts which make increasingly manifest reason in order to live in accord with it.

In order to make these points clearer, let me briefly expound some aspects of the development of Husserl's explication of a methodological inquiry-back and sense-reflection on the world, especially in relation to anthropology.

6.1.1 Principles and Givenness

To begin, there is the issue of how to understand the role of history in a rigorous science. A classic illustration of that issue appears in the Kantian distinction between *cognitio ex principis* and *cognitio ex datis*—cognition from principles and cognition from that which is given.[3] Now, the predilection of Kant himself seemed to have been the former, "rational-cognition," rather than the later "historical-cognition," since the ground for a secure science could not be relative and contingent data of history. As such, following the classical ideal of a rigorous science, he pressed the search to secure unconditional *law*—that is, the *universal and necessary*. Indeed, the Kantian search for *a priori* principles of reason meant an attempt to find such a secure basis in the laws governing subjectivity.

From the Kantian foundation, at least some neo-Kantians propounded that the operation of subjective laws in the world would yield *worldviews which had their own lawfulness*. This meant to bring the two spheres of reason and history nearer to each other. Within a broader discussion of the sciences, for example, Husserl notes that neo-Kantians like Wilhelm Windelband and Heinrich Rickert, worked against a philosophical abstraction from concrete events of human history.[4] These thinkers tended to find such an abstraction as a restriction of the meaning of science to the universal or, more exactly, to the sphere of *universal law*. Their response to this restriction is to formulate how historical data or "views" (*Anschauungen* or "intuitions" of empirical data, following a Kantian sense) built up into "worldviews" (*Weltanschauungen*). Again, these worldviews were then found to have their own laws, which were distinct from but related to laws of subjective intuitions. Thus, for them, anthropology as a science of human beings and their worldviews could be treated in the sphere of a rigorous science. The positions of these thinkers could thus hold that two spheres of knowledge—*ex principis* and *ex datis*—as distinct while still lawful and even rational.

The Neo-Kantian position, in other words, holds onto the *a priori* lawfulness of reason, while speaking against prevailing *positivist* positions on science and history. Basically, for the positivist, knowledge and science is to be built upon that which is

---

[3] See Kant, (1998) A836/B864. For more on this point, see Reichl (2021).

[4] Hua XXXII, p. 83: "Already Aristotle restricts the concept of science to the knowledge of the general and does not want to call history science. In this way, an overvaluation of abstraction in relation to intuition is expressed for the sciences."

empirically observable. That means knowledge and science may in fact be "reasonable," but that reasonableness reduces to empirical instances and events in the world. We may already sense, then, the concern a Husserl would have with such a reduction, as it echoes issues from psychologism and other sorts of reductivist skepticism. Somewhat earlier, though, and in a similar vein which influenced Husserl, Wilhelm Dilthey spoke against such positivism and for the need to address an ambiguity latent in the Kantian approach. Indeed, he recognized the need for a critique of the subject that would give a basis for understanding how spiritual achievements lawfully operate in the world, without methodologically abstracting from that operation. For him, in his words, "the conditions for such a solution [of a problem of cognition] would be a demonstration of the objective reality of inner experience and a proof of the existence of an external world from which we can then conclude that this external world contains human facts and spiritual meaning by means of a process of transferring our inner life into this world."[5] Dilthey realized, in short, that a key to a science of spirit was an *interior* understanding of understanding as it was historically operative, in what he called an *explanation* of worldviews.

Of course, there appear important resonances in these positions with Husserl's own views against psychologism and anthropologism in these statements. And, indeed, alongside an engagement and coversation with neo-Kantians, Husserl's exchange with Dilthey between 1910 and 1912 was an important factor in the development of transcendental phenomenology, according to a report from Georg Misch.[6] As I turn to that, let me underscore how Husserl understands that, in phenomenology, principles are formulated via intelligent inquiry into givenness. Indeed, Husserl formulates phenomenology's *principle of principles* itself is given, namely, as a demand to accept that which is *given* simply as what it is given as being and within the limits in which it is given there. Phenomenological science can be self-justifying, not only because it resists any presupposition, but also because it methodologically accepts givenness *as* it is given in intuition. With this method, Husserl is thus able to say about positivism, in the first volume of his *Ideas*, "If 'positivism' is tantamount to an absolutely unprejudiced grounding of all sciences on the 'positive,' that is to say, on what can be seized upon *originaliter*, then *we* are the genuine positivists."[7] With this principle of principles, in fact, he is able to include, as he says, in the letters to Dilthey, "certain sorts of relativity,"[8] for matters are given *to this* subject, from a sphere of its "ownness." Nevertheless, Husserl also says in this letter, "All objective validity – religion, art, and so on – refers to ideal and thus absolute ('absolute' in a certain sense) principles, to an *a priori* which, as such, is thus in no way limited by anthropological-historical facticities."[9] In other words, objective validity *refers* to a

---

[5] Dilthey (1989), pp. 71–72 and 253, for remarks on consciousness and presuppositionlessness.

[6] From Misch (1967), p. 328. Also, as appears in Hua Dok I, pp. 87–88: "H<usserl> reports that few conversations in 1905 with Dilthey in Berlin (not his writings) meant an impulse that led from the H. of *Logical Investigations* to that of *Ideas*."

[7] Husserl (1983), p. 39.

[8] Husserl (1981), p. 205.

[9] Husserl (1981), p. 205.

6.1 Preliminary Remarks—The Question of History

priori principles which are grasped *in* but not reducible to the historical facticities. As we may put it now (though Husserl does not in this letter), the principles are explanatory of the facticities insofar as they give an answer to their "Why" and "Because." This gives a science of spirit that can give an explanatory account of the *how* of history, in a way that, Husserl apparently thought, brings Dilthey's thought so near that there were "no serious difficulties no serious differences whatsoever" between them.[10]

Despite the confidently expressed agreement, Husserl's position on the relationship between phenomenology and anthropology was not yet fully developed. He had not yet made clear a method of explaining, as Dilthey put it, how the inner life of subjectivity related to the world. Indeed, he would need to work out the method of correlation analysis of the subject-world that included an inquiry-back into the world itself. In these letters, though, Husserl does point in this direction by suggesting that the researcher must "relive" that which he is studying.[11] Of course, by this Husserl does not mean an impossible recreation of the situation, as an historicist might suggest, and about which both he and Dilthey had serious reservations; he means, rather, that the researcher must bring those conscious operations to the fore that are necessary for the meaningful expression in order to grasp the ideal and then to relate it back to the data. This methodological point of view goes beyond, he suggests, worldview philosophy by understanding the essential laws in the *constitution of the world* as such. However, for this understanding, that aforementioned second sailing is indicated—a new way of inquiry, namely, a regressive-inquisitive inquiry.

A regressive-inquisitive inquiry, as we have seen, leaves achievements in play as a *clue* for phenomenological reflection. The inquiry may go back into the operations and conditions necessary for them, undertaking a sort of "un-building" or "de-layering" excavation, in order to then reconstruct the relations of motivation necessary for sense-constitution.[12] As such, this regressive procedure yields a normative sense of constitution, that is to say, it is able to *critically* reconstruct how sense, meaning, and value emerge and develop as well as how they are disrupted, disappointed, or even decline across time, and how they do so in a lawful manner. What is more, in so doing, there is a sort of "reliving" of the experience, insofar as it is taken up into the phenomenological researcher as well, referring back to the possibilities within herself. Through this, then, there is also a *becoming aware* of how matters take on sense at all. Yet, as we have also seen, this can occur by way of a sense-reflection on the self or on the world. The question becomes how to investigate these, as already glimpsed in the exchange between Dilthey and Husserl, without collapsing the world itself into a subjective relative "interiority."

---

[10] Husserl (1981), p. 205.
[11] See Husserl (1981), pp. 205–206.
[12] Hua XXXVII, p. 307.

So, following these methodological developments, both psychology and anthropology take on a special importance for phenomenological investigation.[13] In themselves, these sciences observe, interpret, and report facts regarding human activities and achievements in the world. In relation to transcendental phenomenology, they provide content from which to inquiry-back. However, and once again, the issue for the phenomenologist becomes accounting for how the world itself appears as carrying sense and meaning. This issue comes to head in a lecture to the *Kantgesellshaft* from 1930: "Phenomenology and Anthropology."[14] In it, he lays out—as he claims, *contra* his "antipodes" Heidegger and Scheler—how transcendental, constitutive phenomenology might relate to anthropology.[15] For this, he explicitly proffers his method of inquiring-back as *supplement* to (rather than striking-out of) the Cartesian approach.

To explain further, the lecture begins by setting out a "crisis" of modernity, a fork in the road, as it were, between anthropologism and transcendental philosophy. Husserl aims, of course, to continue to champion the choice of the latter, avoiding reducing the laws of meaning and value to mere contingency, to relativism. So, after recounting how a Cartesian approach to transcendental phenomenology opens a new region of being, he turns back to the "transcendental puzzle of the world" by way of a methodological inquiring-back into its sense.[16] That means taking up the world itself, which is, recall, the "horizon of horizons."[17] To get nearer to this point, however, let me give an overview of a few senses of *horizon*, as Husserl means the term.

In a maximally broad sense, "horizon" describes the correlation of subjective and objective poles of experience. These poles may be further characterized as "attitude" and "world," where an attitude is understood as an "habitually fixed style of willing life" and the world is intended as the unified "horizon of horizons." Now, there are various horizons of experience in which meaning and knowledge develop. Indeed, Husserl will treat the latter in at least three ways, for which we are especially referring to the work of Steinbock and Klaus Held[18]:

1. In a perceptual/psychological construal, a horizon is a "halo of indeterminate determination" attendant to the intention of objects.[19] In this sense, objects in the world carry their own "inner" and "outer" horizons that are implicated in an intention. An inner horizon refers to other determinations possible within the object; an outer refers to the other objects possibly implied by that object. The house has its inner horizons as its various exterior sides, its dimensions, its interior, the type of flooring, and so on. Its outer horizon refers to its environment,

---

[13] For further investigation of this relation, see Breyer (2015).

[14] Husserl (1997), pp. 485–500.

[15] Husserl (1997), pp. 485–486. He says in slightly later letter to Mahnke that the work is "against" Scheler and Heidegger and, again he says again, to Ingarden, that he must read more of his "antipodes" Scheler and Heidegger, which is also recorded in Hua Dok I, p. 365.

[16] Husserl (1997), 496.

[17] See Hua VI, p. 326 and Hua XI, pp. 5–6.

[18] See Steinbock (1995), p. 106.

[19] Hua III/1, p. 145.

the residents, and any other references to it. Through the fulfillment of intentions, these horizons can expand, that is, indeterminacy can be filled out through determination. Moreover, the *world per se* is implied as that in which all referential implications are set. But this "background" referent can be made thematic as well, which leads to the second and third sense of horizon.
2. All referential implications can be brought into a universal horizon, into a *totality*, an *infinite* (*Unendlich*) horizon. This construal brings into relief the world as a horizon for investigation. In this sense, knowledge of the world develops through fulfilled intentions. In this respect, we may also distinguish what Husserl calls from *near* and *far* horizons,[20] by which is meant how an apperceptual inclination to matters that stand in relation to apperception. This may also be used analogously for a horizon that is present, nearer insofar as those referential implications are to the foreground or to a "near world." In any case, the attention here is upon that which is *given* in the horizon, however, not the horizon as giv*ing* or as the *condition* for the given.
3. Lastly, then, Husserl has a *transcendental* or, what Steinbock identifies, with Klaus Held, as a "modal," notion that treats the world-horizon (*Welthorizont*) as that *from which* objects emerge.[21] In this sense, it is fundamentally *open* rather than *unending*. Further, as the condition for givenness, it at once delimits possibilities by referring to those horizons of givenness already present but also gives the possibility of *new* and *novel* possibilities.[22] This is a "generative" dimension, in the sense that it generates new possibilities, not arbitrarily, but within a range or horizon. This range is set according with previous accomplishments, that is, in history.

With this threefold distinction, there appears fundamental ways of orienting to the world: first, by making thematic or thematizing objects *in* the world; second, by taking the world *as* an object; third and finally, taking the world as the horizon *from which* objects appear. Of course, a difficulty in attending to this last, transcendental or modal aspect to horizon is that any attention to it naturally begins to *objectify* it. As Husserl will say about this issue: "The sea itself changes to land wherever it is pursued."[23]

In order to become aware of the transcendental sense of horizon, a phenomenological *Besinnung* is required. As Steinbock explains, "*Besinnung* intimates a mediating reflection, a thoughtful or mindful inquiry that takes the criteria of clarity and distinctness as a goal rather than starting point."[24] Taken as such, *Besinnung* is a thoughtful

---

[20] The terms "near" and "far" or "proximate" and "remote" become ubiquitous in Husserl's middle and later work, so much so that Fink considers them among the basic phenomenological points; for a characteristic appearance, see Hua XLII, p. 4.

[21] Steinbock (1995), p. 107.

[22] See Hua VI, 360.

[23] Hua XXXIX, 139.

[24] Ibid. See also, Dodd (2004), pp. 1–11, but esp. p. 8, where he sketches the way *Besinnung* means to awaken to meaning of the world, not indifferently, but through coming to terms *with* its meaning, by keeping "open the possibility of its functioning in the mode of critique."

sense-reflection within and upon the world-horizon. As it is a raising of awareness to and on development of the sense, meaning, and value in the history in which one *participates*, one does not grasp everything "at once." A *Besinnung* must instead be critically and continually practiced. What is more, by it is meant neither an immanent reflection, in the sense that it would take the world as simply relative to an absolute ego, nor does a reflection which takes the world statically, as if constituted as once and for all; instead, in a critical sense-reflection, the world itself is taken as carrying meaning and sense *as* it is in process of being-constituted. Thus, such a critical sense-reflection becomes aware of the world-horizon, not merely in the facts of its socio-historical process of becoming, but in the very laws of that becoming itself. I suggest that *it is precisely the inquiring-back that mediates this becoming aware*, as it seeks to grasp the intelligible relations of matters of fact and spiritual laws.

As we saw above, an inquiry-back into the world requires clarification of the senses of the *lifeworld*. What is more, phenomenological inquiry-back relies on the matters presented from investigations into human being and living—that is to say, of *anthropology*. So, though Husserl ends his lecture on "Phenomenology and Anthropology" on the hopeful note that phenomenology can overcome the modern crisis, he does not go into the "large topic" of the "intrinsic affinity" of phenomenology and anthropology.[25] He does take this up elsewhere, however.

In this respect, Husserl later engaged with the French anthropologist, Lucien Lévy-Bruhl. For example, in an important letter from 1935, Husserl says to Lévy-Bruhl that he has set his own work aside in order to focus "for several weeks" on a series of works "on the mentality of the primitives."[26] Bruhl held that "primitive man" was "pre-logical," that is to say, he held that these humans participated in the world through sense-impressions, without a logically ordered way of proceeding. Husserl's appreciation of Lévy-Bruhl not only does not take up this position, but also works directly against it. In fact, Husserl's expanded sense of logic comes to include the way in which anthropology eventually means to discover the ideals and values which move them in their own home/alienworld, but does so by recognizing the lawfulness of these motivations. This position is more in accord, for example, with the early ethnographer of North American peoples, Paul Radin, who censured Lévy-Bruhl for going back *from* the western worldview to attempt to find it in something alien.[27] Husserl, for his part, comes to be especially interested in how the world itself appears and takes on sense across generations for people.

---

[25] Husserl (1997), p. 501.

[26] See Hua Dok III, p. 161.The amount of time is significant, since he was, at the time, working as quickly as possible to organize his own manuscripts and to prepare the newest introduction to his phenomenology in the *Crisis* writings. There are some important studies on Husserl's letter to Lévy-Bruhl. Moran and Steinacher (2008), San Martin, (1997), and Bernasconi (2005).

[27] See, for example, Radin, (1927), pp. 18 and 28. The Jesuit Pierre Charles also critiques these issues in Charles (1930).

6.1 Preliminary Remarks—The Question of History

With these points in mind, in the letter to Lévy-Bruhl, as well as in the working draft not yet published, Husserl emphasizes how to understand the problem of *historical development* from anthropologically gathered facts.[28] From the anthropological point of view, Husserl says here, historical relativism is justified, legitimate, since these are historical matters of fact.[29] Yet, that relativity is not the final word of knowledge. Husserl here marks there is a demand to understand how humanity has the world which actually exists for it *in and through a generative unity*.[30] And to understand humanity in such a way, it is necessary to inquire-back from its lifeworld, into *how* that world generates, into the concrete world-horizon, into, as he says, *generativity*. In this way, Husserl takes all persons as participating in generativity, as generating sense, meaning, and value that is yet understandable.

Indeed, Husserl says to Lévy-Bruhl that his work made him sensitive to something "overwhelmingly new" in the way to understand the actual existing world.[31] To understand his excitement, it is important to understand that, at the time, his methodology was finding its way beyond the "worldview philosophies."[32] What I meant to bring to the fore in this, to repeat a by now recognizable refrain, is that the *inquiry-back is essential to the entire enterprise*. Not only does Husserl say in the letter that the philosopher inquires-back, but, he continues, in his unpublished notes in preparation for that letter, how the phenomenologist must "Start from *my* humanity, my historicity. And inquire-back...But *inquiring-back* for a *universal*, the collective-humanity with <their> special human comprehensive '*development*.'"[33] These clarifications are important because they show how the phenomenologist himself is moving into a *communication* with spirit across generations on the basis of a *Weltbesinnung*, as he puts it in the notes.[34] This movement would not impute anything upon those living in the world, but would precisely learn from their already constituted worlds *how* they were constituted in a *mediating inquiry* on this sense. It seeks, to put it otherwise, the intelligibility of their "Why and Because."

To make this method clearer in relation to its matter, let me sketch further the parameters of the nascent generative method in Husserl's thought, paying special attention to the operation of inquiring-back.

---

[28] This is found in the folder K III 7, from which I cite below.

[29] See Hua Dok III, p. 164.

[30] See Husserl, Moran, Steinacher (2008).

[31] See Husserl, Moran, Steinacher (2008).

[32] For more on this point, see Sato (2014).

[33] K III 7: "Ausgang von *meiner* Menschheit, Meiner Historizität. Und Rückfrage nach Aufstieg und Abstieg? Aber Rückfrage nach einer universalen, die Gesamtemenschheit mit <ihren den> sonder menschheiten umfassenden 'Entwicklung.'" Emphasis my own.

[34] K III 7: "Von der Geschichtlichkeit aus – in die Philosopher? In die objektive Wissenschaft? Besinnung – individuelle Besinnung. Mein Leben verlauft in der Welt, wie in meinen Interessen, lebend in meiner Lebenswelt, mit all dem was für mich an Sozialität, an Kultur lebendig ist?" ["From historicity - into the philosopher? Into objective science? *Besinnung* - individual *Besinnung*. My life is going on in the world, as in my interests, living in my life world, with all that is alive for me in sociality, in culture?"].

6.2 Preliminary Sketch of Some Generative Themes

> Also appearing thereby, in different steps, first in respect to human beings and then universally, are the problems of generativity [*Generativität*], the problems of transcendental historicity, the problems of the transcendental inquiring-back [*Rückfragen*] which starts from the essential forms of human existence in society, in personalities of a higher order, and proceeds back to their transcendental and thus absolute signification....Accordingly, within the absolutely universal epoché, in respect to beings having this or any other kind of meaning, the appropriate constitutional questions have to be posed. ...This includes the problems that phenomenology itself poses, at a higher level of reflection, to the phenomenologist....[35]

Husserl did not expressly announce a generative method, at least not in the same manner as he did for the static and genetic. He does, however, attend to matters that seem to exceed the limits of the static and genetic method, for example, the home/alienworld. By attending to how he treats these, it is possible to expound what is *demanded* of a generative method. Steinbock's work on generative phenomenology "after" Husserl demonstrates and develops these basic points. In the following two subsections, I provide an overview of some of these matters, in order to bring them into a phenomenology of inquiry:

A. first, I present some senses of the lifeworld in relation to an analysis of home/alienworld;
B. second, I show Husserl's treatment of instinct and reason in a generative context.

Together, these set the stage for the investigation of the origin of the question and its subsequent transformation through history.

6.2.1 The Home/alien Problematic in the Question of Generativity

For Husserl, the homeworld (*Heimwelt*) is the familiar world, in which subjects are "at home." He thus sometimes refers to life in it as life the *opinion communis*.[36] Taken as such, the home is not merely an achievement of an individual. It is, rather, a horizon of belief, passed across generations, enduring through a "generative unity."[37] Also, given along with the home is the sense of *alienworld* (*Fremdwelt*), which is

---

[35] Husserl (1970), pp. 187–188. I note that Carr renders *Generativität* as "genesis" and *Rückfragen* simply as "inquiry," thereby missing some of its sense. See, for example, Hua VI, §55, pp. 191–192.

[36] See Hua XV, pp. 142 and 155. A VII 31. "Leben in der *opinio communis*, in der heimatlichen Umwelt."

[37] For example, put from the perspective of historical constitution, Hua XV, p. 393: "Therein lies also, he reveals the endless generative past in which he and his unitary co-humanly presence have become...." At its lowest level, this is given as a condition of his living, for example, Hua XXIX, pp. 154–155: "The lowest level is man in his home in the narrowest sense, however primitive or 'cultivated' it may be. What does 'home' mean there? His 'house' (it may be a cave or his tent as a nomad, and so on), his land (his desert, his jungle area), his field and garden and so on, but also -

constituted, as the unfamiliar, as not-being-home. Of course, both the home- and alienworld as well as their relation can be more or less explicit to a subject or group of subjects, as I address below. In any case, the home is that from and in which meaning is constituted and accrues in the socio-historical or generative life of these subjects.

As introduced above, the generative perspective calls into question the genetic "absolute" of the monad. Indeed, rather than taking the monad as self-grounding or as constitutive of space through the lived-body as a "zero point" of orientation, a generative perspective treats the home in terms of geo-historical territories. What this means is that the earth itself has a significance for the grounding of meaning; the earth becomes a *ground* (the "earth-ground" or *Erdboden*) upon which meaning and value develops.[38] From that, the location and landscape in which people are "at home" become constitutive of their determinate sense. To the Greeks, for example, Mount Olympus was not some abstract place but *that* mountain upon which the gods dwell. And that mountain orients their space, their directionality, for example, whether they are going away from it or toward it. Even when leaving home, these other, alien places appear in relation to the homeland. This having of a homeland is not an individual achievement, of course, but *"pre*-given," to be "taken" up by the individual, both in its meaning and value.

Moreover, a generative perspective moves beyond a conception of the monad as self-temporalizing. Meaning and value "stem" from a tradition, have their roots in a tradition, even while an original or primordial generation of *new* meaning and values are possible. This occurs as the *world-horizon* carries meaning and value across generations in a way that is open to the generation of new meaning and value. The mountain can remain a place of dwelling for the gods, but it can also become a place wherein people once believed it was a dwelling place of gods—not only in a negative sense, but in a sense of a "heritage" to which one relates, as a present Greek may sense.

In short, then, a *home* is a certain place at a certain time but extends through times and across places. To explain further, let me sketch two main ways the relation of home/alien is constituted is through *appropriation* and *transgression*.

Appropriation, for Husserl, is a process through which one both constitutes the meaning of the homeworld for oneself and participates in its becoming.[39] This need not occur through an active, critical reflective understanding, of course, but also occurs through a straightforward, "passive" participation in the homeworld. One belongs to one's home regardless of reflective awareness of "home." It makes sense, then, that Husserl sometimes says that the homeworld is something "pre-had" (*Vorhaben*): the ambiguity here of *Vorhaben* as a "project" or plan is intentional, for

---

since home is already something of 'world' - his 'relatives,' his family, his tribe. This homeworld is correlate of his own existence; he is personal subject for this world and is subject of his 'life....'".

[38] See Hua XXIX, p. 215. See also, Husserl (1940), pp. 307–25 and Husserl, (2002), pp. 117–131.

[39] Steinbock succinctly formulates this as "the process of co-constituting the homeworld." See Steinbock (1995), p. 220.

it indicates how one takes up such sense as already meaningful beforehand, through appropriation.

Moreover, along with this appropriation of the home, the alien itself takes on a sense. To be sure, this occurs with a sort of asymmetry, as Steinbock shows, insofar as the home is the position from which the sense of the "alien" emerges. This may occur more or less indeterminately, as the alien, prior to an encounter with the alien, is only a vague, indeterminate sense. Indeed, the alien may initially be given as the constitutive limits of the home, that is, as that which goes beyond the home's borders, so to speak. In any case, the alien *as* alien appears, without appropriating it into the sense of home as such.[40] Nevertheless is a process of making sense of the alien from the home in what Husserl calls *transgression*.[41]

There are also various possibilities of a transgressive experience, according to Husserl. The alien may appear as *incomprehensible*, for example, as completely other than the familiar home. Indeed, he says that such an experience is constituted as a *rupture* in sense, albeit one in which the validity of the homeworld remains intact in the face of the contrasting alienworld.[42] Through the further determination of the alien, it may be destroyed or conquered. In these sorts of transgression, the borders of the home are expanded to encompass the alienworld. In a way, this, too, constitutes the alienworld, though it does not lead to any meaningful development of its sense, but rather retends as that which was destroyed and conquered. Beyond this destruction of the alienworld, Husserl also finds that an encounter with the alien world may motivate meaningful development of worlds. For example, he says, through encounters there may come an "actual understanding" and appreciation of the abilities of the other, alien-nation.[43] In this, it is possible to appropriate meaning from the alienworld into the home or to give meaning from the home to the alien. It is possible to learn, for example, how to cultivate and to cook with certain plants in certain conditions. In fact, not only might a normal activity in the alienworld be understood as working for them, but it might be taken as an optimal way of working, that is to say, the way might be taken as a "better" way than that in the home, motivating its adoption, its appropriation into the home.[44] Worth noting, too, is that such learning and "actual" understanding does not preclude the possibility of colonization, of a conquering destruction of the alien in a reassertion of the home, as a surfeit of unfortunate and often horrible history shows. In contrast to this, however, there would be a communication of homeworlds, giving rise to what Husserl calls a

---

[40] See Hua, XXIX, pp. 13 and 374.

[41] See Hua XV, pp. 139, 232, 429, where the term "*Überschreitung*"—"transgression"—appears.

[42] Hua XV, p. 431: "The concrete analogy is broken - humanity enters into connection with an "alien" humanity. To be sure, the contrast of home or familiar and alien is part of the constant structure of every world, and in a constant relativity."

[43] Hua XXIX, p. 42.

[44] Ms. K III 7/16: "Handel. Erzeugung von Nutzobjekten, nicht zur Befriedigung der eigenen unmittelbaren Bedürfnisse im eigenen Stammesleben, sondern mittelbar: für die Fremde, um von ihnen her begehrte Kulturobjekte ihrer Sphäre zu gewinnen und so die neuen Bedürfnisse zu befriedigen, die aus dem Heraustreten aus der eigenen Lebensnormalität entspringen."

"second home."⁴⁵ Even here, however, one does not lose the *first home*, but instead, grows as the "tree that adds rings," as he says, so long as meaning does not diminish or is not forgotten.⁴⁶ Perhaps here is where the idea of Europe appears for Husserl, as Germans remain German but do so in relation to other Europeans.⁴⁷ In any case, the issue of development here is key, as it underlies the unity in generativity.

Husserl tends, in fact, to focus upon "questions of development (*Entwicklungfragen*)," especially in terms of guiding *ideal goals*.⁴⁸ To explain, let me reiterate Steinbock's succinct formulation of generativity (*Generativität*): generativity is at once a process of becoming and a socio-historical dimension to that process which extends across generations.⁴⁹ This means that the world is generative of *new and novel* meaning and value *and* that this occurs across generations in a basic structure, namely, of home/alienworld. Generativity covers the entire becoming of the natural and spiritual world, for Husserl. Indeed, the socio-historical appears upon and within the natural world: the building-up of meaning and value includes it but goes beyond the natural world, somewhat like how homes are built from the materials of the land, in relation to the demands of the land, while also having their own sense as artifice.

To clarify these points, it is necessary to sketch how Husserl uses this manifold notion of "institutions" or "establishments" (*-Stiftungen*).⁵⁰ To begin, there may be an *original* or *primordial-institution* (*Ur-stiftung*). This establishes an ideal to which further activity operates and refers. This is also *teleological*, implying its ultimate fulfillment or final institution (*End-stiftung*). In this respect, what Husserl sometimes calls the ἐντελέχεια or that end toward which it tends, refers at once to the ideal and the open process of its realization through history.⁵¹ Through this process, the ideal can be a *re*-instituted *"after"* (*Nach-stiftung*) the primordial-institution. However, as novel issues are encountered, such a re-institution may be *renewed* or *transformed* (*Um-stiftung*) rather than being *merely repeated*. There may thus be a *new* or *novel* institution (*Neu-stiftung*) emergent from the original institution which may itself have been a new- or re-institution. There is, in short, Husserl finds how there is the

---

⁴⁵ Hua XXXIX, p. 177: "The living environment world is the present with a past that is in a certain way ordered to it and a future that is marked out from it. In the closest living environing world – home – there is nothing alien for the mature one (not for the child). Alien is here opposite to home. It has the character of the continuous normality, in nature as in humanity, according to things, according to animals, according to people, according to culture-typical things and so on. Here there is only the abnormality of earthquakes, of other natural disasters, of popular epidemics, of madmen, but taken up as rare, as unusual occurrences of their own type. One can get to know the alienness and thereby become completely familiar with it, and it becomes the extended second home...."

⁴⁶ Hua XV, p. 429: "Building up of environments....Every relative environment is constituted as a normality, which has its normal horizon-sense for everything that belongs to it, experienced or able to be experienced, known and unknown."

⁴⁷ See Miettinen (2020).

⁴⁸ Hua XLII, p. 337: "The main thing is: To ask for the reason of a development, the only reasonable question, and to describe the development according to its deepest meaning, and to describe its leading ideal goal and structure."

⁴⁹ See Steinbock (1995), p. 3.

⁵⁰ For a clear exposition of this concept within Husserl's *Crisis* works, see Dodd (2004), pp. 72–78.

⁵¹ See Husserl (1970), p. 15.

possibility of new ideals *from within* the operation of an ideal. There thus becomes the question of the relation of these ideals and the overarching sense of them. The answer to that question comes through an inquiry into which "overrules," so to speak, the process of development.

With respect to human being, for Husserl, the development of reason is essential, in which I wish to emphasive here two significant aspects.[52] On the one hand, there is a development reason in the determination and differentiation of being, as horizons are filled-out with true and good being. On the other hand, there is the development of the *ideal* of knowledge, of what "counts" as reasonable, that is, as legitimate *reasons why*. With this second sense, reason establishes itself as an ideal in history. In fact, there is a history to the way reason discovers and grasps its own possibilities—the way it "comes to itself."[53] At the confluence of these two points, inquiry operates within established possibilities of knowledge that accord with essential possibilities of reason. In this respect, Husserl treats three stages of reason. First, there is a stage of *latent* reason—*latens* or "hidden," insofar as there is neither attention to nor account of its performance or achievements *per se*—in which inquiry operates naively within the world-horizon, striving to determine *relatively true being*. Second, there is a stage of *patent* reason—*patens* or "open," analogous to what we found in the third chapter, now insofar as it opens to everything given in the world-horizon, including itself—in which inquiry opens to *universally true being* but nevertheless does not inquire back into the constitutive source of it. Finally, there is a stage of *manifest* reason—manifest (*offenbarer*, as we will find Husserl puts it) to itself as constitutive within the world-horizon—in which inquiry here turns to reason itself—operating according to those norms it discovered and made manifest in it. In a word, this tendency of reason is a tendency to *interiority*.[54]

---

[52] Husserl (1970), p. 15: "To be human at all is essentially to be a human being in a socially and generatively united civilization; and if man is a rational being (*animal rationale*), it is only insofar as his whole civilization is a rational civilization, that is, one with a latent orientation toward reason or one openly oriented toward the entelechy which has come to itself, become manifest to itself, and which now of necessity consciously directs human becoming."

[53] For example, Hua VI, p. 273: "But seen from within, it is a struggle of the generations of philosophers living and surviving in spiritual community of the bearers of this development of spirit – in the constant struggle of the, 'awakened' reason, to come to itself, to its self-understanding, to a concrete itself...."

[54] Consider Hua XXIX, p. 225: "...as it is and becomes before the philosophy of life conviction, its right and, insofar as it nevertheless carries a content of absolute truths <in itself> in the change of relative validities, here a content of absolute truth, which, however, would have to be evaluated only in a universal scientific philosophy according to its substrata, presuppositions and mythical prefigurations...." Also consider Hua VI, p. 176: "In all this, however, there prevails-and this makes scientificity, description, phenomenological-transcendental truth possible - a fixed typology, which, as already said, is a typology of essence to be embraced methodically as a pure a priori." Again, on the way in which reason makes itself manifest by coming to its own essential possibilities, consider Hua VI, p. 53: "Is it not a problem that sets into line with the problem of instincts in the ordinary sense? Is it not the problem of the hidden reason, which knows itself as reason only when it has become manifest?".

6.2.2 Instinct and Reason

To understand the development of reason in history, it is necessary to clarify the concept of *instinct*. Nam-in Lee's seminal study has already argued for the novelty and import of a *transcendental* theory of instinct in Husserl's work.[55] In his work, he indicates some of the difficulties of such an expression, especially as the concept of instinct became more *biological–mechanical*.[56] In a biological–mechanical construal, instincts are generally presented as factual and causal, as, for example, an instinct of "fight or flight," in this construal, means that the instinct triggers behavior in situations, as a causal response. Then, to explain that response, such a construal searches for chemical reactions, neural stimuli, and so on. In a similar way, the instinct of "self-preservation" may be given as the "reason" why people behave in a certain manner. Since such mechanisms are everywhere operative, they are taken to have an explanatory power for behavior: one wants to live, above all, so sometimes one must take from others, one *must* overcome, overpower others, and so on. Indeed, in this sentiment, even friendliness appears as a mechanism for such self-preservation—what other "choice" would one have?

In contrast, as Lee makes clear, the phenomenologist understands instinct as constitutive of sense and meaning. Thus Husserl, as we may now put it, inquires-back into how instincts appear and are constitutive of sense, without positing a totalizing explanatory viewpoint based on reductive, naturalistic methods. Doing so, he finds instincts given as sources of all ability and ability systems, that is, of all "I can."[57] Since these operate in a world that is essentially a system of possibilities, they may generate new instincts, new possibilities for the "I can" in its various situational exigencies.[58] With regard to the former, their appearance, for Husserl, is a matter of "transcendental birth," in the sense that they constitute the primordial-beginning

---

[55] Lee (1993).

[56] Lee (1993), p. 4.

[57] Hua XLII, p. 102: "Original drives, [original or] primal instincts are not mechanical forces. They are the sources of all ability, of all systems of ability. The world has its correlate in the developed ego in a system of capabilities, which is a systematic unity of capabilities."

[58] For example, Hua XLII, p. 102.: "…that always new instincts, founded in the original instincts, which generally come into function immediately at every birth, spring up"; also, with regards to development of instincts through 'needs' or 'exigencies,'" Also, consider K III 7/ Bl. IV: "Was ist das 'Erfindung'? Neue Instinkte? Instinkte der Notlagen? Instinkte aus der Wandlung der Notlagen…" ["What is 'invention'? New instincts? Instincts of exigencies? Instincts from the transformation of exigencies…"].

(*Uranfang*) of subjectivity.⁵⁹ This does not occur *ex nihilo*, of course, but generatively, proceeding from the previous generation. Thus, Husserl speaks of instinct as both "inborn" and "innate" (*angeboren* and *eingeboren*, respectively): they are inborn precisely as not being actively constituted by the subject, by the child, and they are innate insofar as they are *teleological* of that constitution.⁶⁰ For these reasons, we may identify instincts as *generative matters*. Let me clarify further.

An instinct, prior to its operation, may be called a original or primordial-instinct (*Urinstinkt*).⁶¹ These "in born" instincts point toward their fulfillment. They are purposive but nevertheless indeterminate, having, as Husserl says, a "dark horizon."⁶² By this is meant that they neither have a determinate end nor an active guidance (for example, some overarching process of "choice") toward that end. Instead, they develop along with their *interest* in the end. In other words, it is *through* their operation and fulfillment they "sketch out" or "pre-figure" their goals.⁶³ Thus, once the primordial, innate instinct is enacted in the world, further instincts develop through the various fulfillments and disappointments of their activity. The development of what Husserl calls "always new" instincts neither destroys nor annihilates the previous instincts, however. Instead, these operate as new possibilities founded upon the primordial instinct, as there is an increasing differentiation within the unity of the developing ego.

In fact, Husserl later understands *reason itself as developing from instinctual life*, especially from basic "self-preservation."⁶⁴ The development of reason, in other words, emerges upon the increasingly conscious life of the living organism. The emergence of "lower" abilities of biological awareness from the bodily organism are then unified in the lived-experience of the subject. Indeed, the constant instinctual striving desires the new as well as the fulfilling, "preserving" satisfaction, which, as it radiates ever-more, builds upon the previous ever-new kinds of meaning and value. In this respect, I emphasize here the sense of German *Neugier* as a *greediness for the new*—as the compound of *neu-* ("new") and *gierig* ("greedy")—in relation to Husserl's use of *Begier* ("desire" or to *be-greedy*, as it were) to describe a dimension of self-preservation that gives the momentum toward some good, that is, the relationship of motivation between some good and the subjective striving. Below, I present this in terms of child development in relation to the appearance of inquiry.

---

⁵⁹ Hua XXXIX, p. 477: "The ego in the original beginning (the original birth) is already the ego of directed instincts"]. Also Hua XLII, p. 42: "My transcendental birth. The innate instincts...."

⁶⁰ See Hua XLII, p. 121: "Every transcendental ego has its native - innately it carries the 'teleological reason' for its streaming constituent transcendental life." Also, Hua XLII, p. 176. Also see Hua XLII, 104: "The instinctive ('innate') enters into all apperceptions and objectivations afterwards and assumes the new form of 'activity' perfecting itself through practice."

⁶¹ Hua XLII, p. 120: "that ever new instincts, founded in the [original or] primal instincts, which generally come into function immediately at each birth, spring forth...."

⁶² Hua XLII, p. 85. See also Hua XLII, p. 96.

⁶³ Hua XLII, pp. 246–247: "Or does it behave here just as in all instincts, that while they are fulfilled and by fulfillment they pre-figure their goals...."

⁶⁴ See Hua XLII, p. 134: "Reason itself <is> transformed instinct, through all rational life <passes> the instinctive affection and intention."

6.2 Preliminary Sketch of Some Generative Themes

Let me further prepare that analysis by first turning to the *generative* development of children through the passing of instincts.

To begin, from this perspective, birth becomes a *transcendental* event, as there is an entrance or beginning of subjectivity in birth which implies a *prior generation* as well as a *new generation*.[65] Now, for Husserl, there is a sense in which the child has "no sense of generative existence of humanity."[66] That does not mean the child is not *in* this generative existence, of course, for the child is born as *human* into its *home*.[67] Rather, the child is not yet aware of that generative existence in which it participates. Instead, the child's instinct is "blindly" directed to a goal, even as it participates in the home/alienworld, however simply and dimly. Husserl will even call this binding together in instincts a way of making sense of "conservation of species," which is another manifestation of self-preservation, generatively understood.[68] In this respect, those entrusted with the child are entrusted with the species, as the next generation. That means there is a responsibility for the instincts that are passed on and, still more, generated in their operation.

Consider the relationship between parent and child, in this respect. Here, Husserl finds that the child's instincts intertwine with the instincts of the parent, especially engaged with the mother.[69] This is so as the child takes up, from conception, the mother as a source of fulfillment and satisfaction. Of course, the situation is different for the mother herself, as Husserl points out: to her, the child is not an "objective" matter but a person whose worth relates to the mother in the original "We."[70] In relation to the mother, the newborn appears as a new generation but also as a unique individual and, in this sense, an *absolute value*. Indeed, the mother seeks to preserve the self of the child which is at once its own self and uniquely hers. Thus, as the child's world develops *along with* this sense of generation, so does its self-preservation intertwine with its constitution as beloved. That is to say, in the child's activity as a subject, there is a demand to live up to this sense—*to self-preserve*, as it were, in relation to the other. Given within this is, of course, to preserve in an orderly and organized way, that is to say, in *rational* or *reasonable* way. As such, Husserl

---

[65] E III 9/4: "My transcendental birth. The innate instincts – the awakening instincts in the flow of the "passive," the "ego-less," the primordial ground constituting time."

[66] Hua XV, p. 140: "In my childhood, the sense of the generative existence of mankind and of a history was still closed to me, I was yet unaware of anything about tradition, for me there was no tradition."

[67] See, for example, Hua XV, p. 233 fn 2: "Natural development of human being to the human being of his homeworld by childhood; the homeworld as the correlate asserted to him. Then, however, problems of history, the development of the homeworlds and humanities in correlation and in the togetherness." See also Hua VI, p. 162 and Hua Mat VIII, p. 75.

[68] See Hua XLII, p. 384.

[69] Hua XLII, p. 465: "The maternal instinct, intertwined with the nourishing instinct and the objectifying instinct, works itself out in empathy and in the most original human love, as love for the mother." It is possible to consider the role of the *caregiver*, in this respect, though Husserl does not spend time on such a relation.

[70] Hua XLII, p. 465: "The children are children of this mother not as objective facts, but <they are> values for her in their individuality and related back to the individuality of the mother."

will even say that, from practical life-interests there is an appearance of a "true self-preservation" in rational tasks.[71]

Before the higher operations of reason, however, through the operation of instincts, Husserl traces an "unveiling" of human existence from lower levels of instinctual life interests up to higher levels of rational-life.[72] At the "lowest" level of this development, there is the operation of instinctual life in the family and national context. Instinct operating, in other words, in a world that is already meaningful but that only takes on meaning through those initial instincts. Through the building up of these instincts, within the generative home/alien, the instincts also modify themselves in order to better navigate the world. In that way, for example, practical reason emerges and refines itself in order to make decisions, choices for reaching certain ends. And, eventually, there is the emergence of the detached disinterestedness of theory, which is also a fulfillment, a satisfaction of reason, of that "inborn" ideal. When it appears in history, it sets a new possibility for self-preservation in self-responsibility, as it means to realize reason everywhere as an ideal according to which it lives. Thus, the "highest level," phenomenology *makes manifest* the ideal of reason and, in this way, it "stands above" rationalism, as an *Überrationalismus*, as it invites others to understand *for themselves* how reason operates at all.[73] Thus, Husserl envisions a "beautiful new age" ushered by phenomenological awakening, where insight into true being, into truly rather than apparently good being, can be achieved and, indeed, realized.[74] All this refers back to the development of "instinctual" life.

Let us fill out further that development by inquiring-back into the establishment of the world and appropriation of the home in early childhood. It shows how the original question of history emerges and operates, establishing the original goal to know *why* that is so.

6.3 The Generation of World-Inquiry as Participating in the World-Horizon

---

[71] See, for example, Hua XLII, p. 449. Also, Hua XLII, p. 488: "The very meaning of self-preservation is 'true self-preservation.' I have chosen my being as what I want apodictically; I have recognized and set myself as something that should be absolutely necessary." Hua XLII, p. 487: "The ego, subjectivity in general in its striving for 'self-preservation.' Self-preservation practices subjectivity, in it every individual ego, insofar as it is aimed at goals with which they remain, with which they can stop 'forever.'".

[72] Hua XLII., p. 445: "The uncovering of the necessities of life, of the human existence of the lower stages, a revelation which the rational life of the highest stage accomplishes as science (or already pre-scientific, but as raw rational consideration).".

[73] The notion of an "over-rationalism" is present in the *Krisis* texts and used explicitly in the important letter to Lucien Lévy-Bruhl in 1935. Husserl uses this to indicate a higher state of fulfillment. See Husserl, *Briefwechsel VII*, pp. 161–64.

[74] As he puts it in a letter to Gustav Albrecht, including as an appendix to this book.

> ...[L]iving in this world, one could put all his practical and theoretical questions only to *it*—could refer in one's theories only to it, in its open, endless horizons of things unknown.[75]

> All natural questions, all theoretical and practical goals taken as themes...have to do with something or other within the world-horizon.[76]

> But the phenomenologist and phenomenology itself stand in this historicity.[77]

In the following two subsections, I reconstruct Husserl's recovery of the roots inquiry in the home/alienworld:

A. first, I expound the notion of childhood, presenting how instincts and practical life-interests operate within an environment that at once carries the meaning of the homeworld and is open to new meaning generation;
B. second, I show how a child's curiosity and various modes of imitation within a world of purposes motivates the attempt to understand *why that is so*.

Through all this, once again, Husserl traces an "unveiling" of human existence from lower levels of instinctual life interests to higher levels of rational-life. Let me stress that most of Husserl's reflections on the matters investigated here were not meant for publication. As such, they are often incomplete and unorganized, incipient or even inchoate. Nevertheless, they are characteristically careful and incisive, presented as research to be tested against the phenomenological evidence. With this in mind, let us inquiry-back into childhood and the emergence of inquiry.

6.3.1 Birth, Childhood, and the Development of Instinct Toward Inquiry

For Husserl, childhood is not merely the objective age of an individual. Once again, he understands it constitutively, using the term to delineate *how* matters take on sense and meaning. In this way, "childhood" is a straightforward way of living in the world, in which meaning is constituted primarily by the lived-body.[78] He distinguishes, further, a "first" and "second" childhood. The achievement of the first

---

[75] Hua VI, p. 50.

[76] Hua VI, p. 148. See also Hua VI, p. 382: "Every inquiring and demonstrating which is in the usual sense historical presupposes events as the universal question-horizon…".

[77] Hua XV, p. 393: "Aber der Phänomenologe und die Phänomenologie stehen in dieser Geschichtlichkeit." A phrase so emphasized by Steinbock.

[78] Husserl analogically uses the phrase "philosophical children" as well as "spiritual children," for example, at Hua VI §9b and §17. Hua XXXIX, pp. 4–5, and 69. I do not think that this conflicts with Merleau-Ponty's admonishment of the idea of an "archaic state" in common between child and primitive. Rather, the matter must be understood as constitutively analogous. See Maurice Merleau-Ponty (2010), p. 137.

childhood is the formation of "world-representation" (*Weltvorstellung*).[79] In the first, the validity of the world is formed as *pre*-given, pre-constituted as "already being and becoming," and so he sometimes refers to this as the constitution of nature, of the natural world.[80] The achievement of the first childhood is lasting: indeed, Husserl identifies it as an *Urkind* insofar as it is a primordial-institution or establishment of the "living in the world."[81] It is in this world that the "second childhood" lives and develops, while also reshaping the primordially established world.[82] Now, to be sure, most achievements of childhood are not "remembered," though they are nevertheless carried throughout life. Indeed, these are carried through generations, as meaningful events in the homeworld.

As such, Husserl inquires-back into the beginning of "primordial subjectivity" that happens in generative conditions. In this respect, the constitution of home occurs straightaway. For example, Husserl says, the child's "streaming, concrete present is, so to speak, the womb, in which, from an embryonic germ through its embryonic stages, the infantile world is formed and comes to birth."[83] There is, in other words, not only a matter of factual birth, but a moment of *transcendental birth*, upon which the spring of the concrete present begins to rush forth. From the moment of this birth, he finds that the very development of the lived-body, into the emergence of the kinaesthetic "I can" itself gives a foundation for modes of imitative subjectivity, upon which I expand below.[84] At present, let me emphasize how there is a *teleological* sense of becoming that appears already in the embryo—there is already given here an indeterminate sense of what the being is to become, again, what Husserl calls an *entelechy*. All this occurs in a *generative* universe in which *generativity is already present*.

For childhood is given as immersed in a world *with others*. This occurs already at birth, that is, with the *newborn*: as Husserl stresses, the sense of the "newborn"

---

[79] Hua Mat VIII, p. 74: "Of the 'first' childhood we say that in it and for it the 'world-representation' must first be formed...."

[80] Hua Mat VIII, p. 75: "The achievement of the first childhood, however, is: the given universe of being as the universe of all that already is and in all time as the horizon of being, the universe of all entities of interest that already are and will be, the universe of all natural interests of the ego." Also, ms. B III 9. 67a, quoted below.

[81] Hua XLII, p. 221: "How do I understand the primordial-child – as 'living in the world' from the 'primordial foundation' of its existence, instinctively directed toward the world? The whole development from the beginning and so on <is> 'instinctively' governed...".

[82] Hua Mat, VIII 43: "...and world conception here means the world already valid for the child of the second childhood as the already existing one, the environing world into which it lives, towards which it lives, values, strives, considers, etc....."

[83] Hua Mat VIII, p. 73: "...his flowing, concrete presence is, so to speak, the womb in which, from an embryonic primordial germ through embryonic stages, the world of the first child finally develops and birth takes place." Also, Hua XV, p. 178: "The generative context includes newborns, or 'early-stage children' in general, embryos, so to speak, which are understood as preliminary stages for actual children."

[84] On these matters, Meltzoff and Moore's work finds neonatal development essential to the formation of the world and, indeed, through "imitative" means. See Meltzoff and Moore (1977), pp. 75–78. Also, see Zhok (2013), pp. 29–40.

is in the arrival of a child in a world already being constituted, where life is already happening, where it is already in development.[85] So, to reiterate the earlier point, Husserl explains, "the world constitution is not the responsibility of this single growing human being but the intersubjectivity of adult and already adult human beings—analogically speaking, repeated."[86] The child takes up the world into which it emerges and becomes a part of it, in a complex of original institutions, new institutions, and re-institutions.[87] Of course, Husserl notes, the child is not straightaway aware of her participation in generativity.[88] Indeed, the generative sense of human existence is closed to the child and she is unaware of tradition in any wakeful, egoic sense, though her apperception does constitute a "primordial tradition."[89] By this is meant that the child develops habits and norms through the regulative associative constitution of perception *within the world*. The environing world becomes meaningful for the child through continued experience, in a play between an already meaningful world and an individual in that world who is building up themselves and their world. Although this is done "blindly" or "instinctually," it nevertheless gives a foundation for further development.

So, the child, from the beginning, appropriates the home. Indeed, her developing habits and norms take on characteristics of the homeworld into which she is born. Taken in the broadest, most pregnant sense, we may express this in Husserl's phrase: "Education is the basis of development."[90] This sense of education is not yet that of a deliberate and elaborate pedagogy, but rather the way in which being in the world "*forms*" human beings as children. In this respect, with the development of the bodily environment, the child takes up in its "primordial tradition" the sights and sounds, so to speak, of its home/alienworld. A child, for example, that grows "accustomed" to a monochromatic world of her nursery may easily be disrupted by polychromatic wallpaper of the kitchen, precisely because it is not identifiably familiar as her familiar home. Likewise, though she is agape at first, she quickly

---

[85] On the "newborn," see Hua XV, 178, 605, as well as Hua XXXI, p. 529 and Hua XXXIX, p. 263.

[86] Hua Mat VIII, 73: "… but of course the constitution of the world is not a matter for this individual adult human being, but for the intersubjectivity of adult and already adult human beings - whereby the game, analogically speaking, repeats itself."

[87] Hua XXXIX, pp. 28–29: "But human beings stand in the chain of generations, in which each one grows up as a child and grows into the communal world, as a world, which it must first of all constitute itself in its first single-subjective and then through empathy progressing genesis. This world has comprehensible cultural determinations, which have sprung from the mental activity of the ancestors. These for their part are likewise children and children's children and living into a world of just such tradition."

[88] Hua XV, p. 140: "In my childhood, the sense of the generative existence of mankind and history was still closed to me, I knew nothing about tradition, for me there was no tradition. Only others knew that even my games, my fairy tales, and so on, were transmitted to me from an ancient tradition - through the others who stood in it." See also, Hua XV, p. 519.

[89] Hua XV, p. 519: "Apperzeption: *primordiale patente Tradition…*".

[90] Hua XLII, p. 441: "Human development repeats itself in every generative individual ego, in its individual development as education to become a human being as a human being in the historical present."

takes up the way of moving and speaking, the patterns of meaning and values that make up the fabric of her homelife.

To expound further, however, let us go back into the beginning of affectivity or primordial affectivity *as* instinctive from which the original question stems. Considered genetically, the instincts operate throughout the individual's life, building upon primordial instincts, differentiating new possibilities throughout her development. Generatively considered, the child, as bearer of instinctive operations passed across generations, may generate new instincts through its development in the home/ alienworld. In this respect, there are what Husserl calls *primordial instinctual drives.* These are not, he notes, "mechanical forces," but instead "sources of all ability and systems of ability [*Könnenssysteme*]."[91] As mentioned above, these systems of ability are a system of various "I cans," so to speak, such that, once they are activated and set together in normal ways of operating, the ego has the capacity to recall as within its *system of capacities* (*Vermögenssystem*). Genetically, these systems are centered within the individual lived-body that lives within the sociality of a "We." From this perspective, there is a "preferred primordiality" in the individual's lived-body, though there is also given an identification with other bodies in the world. This sort of undifferentiated "We" of sociality is not at a high level of awareness, of course, but is rather a basic condition of givenness. Generatively, however, this condition is understood as exceeding the genesis of the individual and its constitution within the sociality. This is so, insofar as the world-horizon gives the conditions for which such a constitution is possible at all. Indeed, it is in these conditions, in fact, that "self"- preservation appears.[92] I use the inverted commas here in order not to confuse this self-preservation with that of the Hobbesian sort of egoistic self-interest; for, unlike the Hobbesian abstraction, the *conditions* for Husserl's sense of self-preservation as self-constitution, that is, the "building of the world through instincts," appear *within* the generative conditions of a primordial "We."[93]

---

[91] To extend the above quote, consider Hua XLII, pp. 102–103: "So, *we need to presuppose for the early childhood to already a system of drives*, which includes all the *intentional original-passivity*, which is presupposed for any development and is always at work in it. The primordial-ego with its drive system in primordial form and primordial content [*Urgestalt und Urgehalt*] affects passivity and then activity: *in the drive system there lies already the soil* [*Anlage*] *for the entire world constitution as entelechy*....Primordial drives, primordial instincts are not mechanical forces. They are the sources of all ability, all systems of ability [*Könnenssysteme*]. In the developed ego, the world has its correlate in a *system of capacities* [*Vermögenssystem*] that is a systematic unity of capacities: every possible experience is a line of abilities. Every empirical thinking of mine is empirical thinking of my capacities; and my capacities are in constant development and have their source in primordial capacities."

[92] Consider the generativity of self-preservation at Hua XLII, p. 429: "My existence in self-preservation (in perfect form: my life satisfaction) encompasses, implies self-preservation, and so on, of my family (in marriage), then also siblings, and so on. Not on the same level, in the graduality of this implication of care. Order of preference and deferral: first my own 'generation,' then comrades and theirs, and so on."

[93] The conditions also include the generation of the "instinct of love." See Hua XLII, Supplement XII: "The building up of the object world from instinct.... Instinct of love. Generative love."

Consider, for example, eating or nourishment as a special instance of the specific *instinct of self-preservation*. For the human being, self-preservation, at a lower level, is a life-interest foundational to the lived-body. Within this, there is the instinct to eat, to fulfill the organism through nourishment.[94] As such, this instinct has its correlate in the hunger drive, which appears as "blind," pointing indeterminately to nourishment. This means that, when a child is hungry, there is not immediately an intention to some specific food but rather given a specification of "needing fulfillment" toward which she is driven. As hunger increases, there is an increased interest in fulfillment, in satisfying the drive for food. The interest becomes specified as possible food options are presented. However, the hunger itself, which appears alongside the instinct, is not completely annihilated upon eating. Instead, it is a sort of "habituality" of the ego that is built-up upon instincts.[95] Indeed, Husserl uses the term *Sehnsucht* for the hunger-drive, which implies a deep yearning that cannot be fulfilled, as this drive is always present: I am "always yet hungry," he says.[96] That is not to say that it is not more or less satisfying, only that the drive is always present. To clarify further, let us consider his explication of two moments to the drive, one positive and the other negative.

Positively, hunger appears with the drive to eat. In it the ego becomes the *hungering* ego—the "I am aware of my having hunger" (as one would say in German, "*Ich habe hunger*.") Again, though initially indeterminate, it becomes intentionally determinate through experience. The child instinctually presses its lips together, suckling in order to eat. The bottle stands in as a source of food, and that instinct builds upon that source. So, upon seeing the bottle, she reaches out, her eyes grow big, focused upon the specific source of food—she desires *that* bottle, not just *any* food *whatsoever*. In this way, instinct is "sketched out" or pre-figured constitutively. On the one hand, it is "positive" in relation to its fulfillment. On the other hand, it is "negative," or even a "negative drive" in relation to the satisfaction of a drive for food, that is, in the fulfillment of the drive.[97] That this fulfillment is a "negative drive" may be counter-intuitive, at first blush. However, it is negative insofar as it fills the original

---

[94] Along with the instinct and life-interest of eating, let me note that Husserl finds the values of nutrition and nourishment. At this level, the constitution of the optimal food—the quality of its nutritive *value*—depends on how it fulfills the life-interests of nutrition and nourishment. The importance of the hunger drive appears in the child's self-preservation but also in the development of society and culture, as with agriculture, the grouping of people, and, in fact, its fulfillment is essential to the appearance of curiosity and wonder, insofar as its fulfillment is necessary to give sufficient foundations for leisure and play. Consider Hua XLII, p. 461, Hua XLII, p. 420 and Hua XV, p. 599.

[95] Hua XLII, p. 93: "Hunger is a habituality of the ego, continuous during the conscious drive, inactive during the interruption of consciousness, and yet in a certain way continuous, namely, in the manner of 'yet still,' of 'hungering,' also 'meanwhile,' though not being 'aware' of this."

[96] He will also say that one is always "called upon" to be hungry, see Hua XLII, 460: "Enjoyment of food. - I am regularly hungry, but in my 'personal being' I am not 'called' to eat, though even when I am hungry I am 'called' again and again to look for food, which of course is already prepared."

[97] Hua XLII, p. 94: "Relaxing the drive (as "hunger") in fulfilling approaching action, with the negative drive in removing action, and that is pleasure, drive fulfillment itself and not an accompanying datum, feeling of pleasure."

drive, abating the positive movement, but does so *without annihilating the original drive*. The original drive is still present but now only in the "mode of fullness."[98] It is not simply that this mode is temporary but rather that it is the fulfillment of the instinct that is "permanent" or always present in life.

The eating process described above is largely a kinaesthetic example of generative development. In one sense, it is "automatic," inasmuch as the child *can* move, has the ability, *instinctually*, though this has its developmental basis even from the embryonic stage. To clarify further, take the example Husserl suggests in chewing.[99] The suckling movement of the newborn is innate, as it were: it is, generally speaking, within the sphere of her "I can." It emerges in a world in which it meets given sources of nourishment, say, the lived-body of the mother herself. As such, the system of capacities comes to form itself around the mother and her body. There are instances where the newborn's instinct does not operate, of course. However, where this is the case, she is not scolded; it is, rather, a cause for concern precisely as concern for her preservation and development, for her *capacity to be*. In contrast, it is through the development of the "personality" of the child that she may constitute the "proper" and improper way of eating.[100] For example, in this household, it is unacceptable to chew "with one's mouth open," whereas, in this other house, it is acceptable. When at home, the latter child will not inhibit that which has become "instinctual," that is, what has become normal, familiar. However, the encounter with the other's home may bring such a habit into relief, especially upon hearing the correction of the habit. There thusly appears a play of appropriation and transgression at work in the development of first and second childhood.

From this foundation, let us, finally, turn to how the original question emerges from the fulfillment of life-interests and development of instincts within generativity, then to how this curiosity varies into questions of philosophical wonder.

6.3.2 Instinct, Imitation, and the Original Question of History—Why?

To readdress the issue as a whole, let us begin with the fact that Husserl identifies curiosity as an instinct within reason.[101] As such, it is inborn but develops as it is

---

[98] Hua XLII, p. 94: "er ist noch Trieb, aber im Modus der Fülle" ["it is still a drive, but in the mode of fullness"].

[99] Hua XLII, pp. 94 and 135.

[100] The propriety or impropriaty is a matter of the development of the so-called "actual child," that is, the child operating in the world; on this, consider, for example, Hua XLII, p. 130: "Mundane acts, mundane instincts. The development of the child, the 'actual child' (as that in the world of constituted being), his instincts directed towards food, towards the mother's help, and so on. Abstention - normality of fulfillment overcoming inhibitions."

[101] Hua Mat VIII, pp. 194 and 210: "but it must also be said that as soon as the distant horizon stirs curiosity, the apperceptive transference will begin." See also Hua XLII, pp. 4–6 and Appendix XVII.

6.3 The Generation of World-Inquiry as Participating in the World-Horizon 171

enacted in the world. I find that Husserl treats two levels of curiosity. There is a "lower" level of perceptual curiosity, from which a second, "higher" intellectual curiosity emerges. This lower level remains within the passive dimension of *affectivity*, appearing along with other instinctual life-interests. It is a matter of kinesthetic interest as a "following" of new data in the perceptual sphere.[102] In it, the subject at once synthesizes this newness and takes pleasure in this process of becoming.[103] The higher level is the active level of a "playful looking around" that appears once lower level life-interests are fulfilled.[104] It is this mode of attention in which questioning first appears. But let us determine more exactly these conditions.

From the lower level, the subject lives in an original affective *curiosity*. Indeed, as Bower points out, this curiosity is an "affective presence," ever-ready and ever-interested to constitute the new in experience.[105] From this perspective, I wish to emphasize, once again, the sense of *Neugier* as a *greediness for the new* paired with the *desire* or *Begier* for satisfaction. By the *new* is meant a specific synthesis or constitution in lived-experience; Husserl even sometimes dashes the *syn*-thesis (as is possible with the Latinate equivalent *con*-stitution) to emphasize the "setting-together" of a given that was not a part of the previous unity.[106] With this, he elucidates

---

[102] Hua Mat VIII, p. 323: "The instinct of 'curiosity' says original affection....Interest in this change, in the 'I follow' the kinesthesia and training of the will to rule over this kinesthesia and its consequences, whereby intentional unities, the change as a change in appearance from the one that appears and from a field of unities, in which these one among others is constitute." Also, Hua Mat VIII, p. 324: "But one cannot say: Before the attention is the hyletic datum and has a pleasure character, which it is, by virtue of which it arouses my curiosity, as if the pleasure were once again a datum that affects. The datum is already there before me for me, just as affecting, we certainly have the difference of the datum and its graduality of the affection, the graduality of addressing me."

[103] B III 9/67a: "Das erste der Weltkonstitution in der Primordialität ist die Konstitution der 'Natur' aus der hyletischen Urnatur, oder vielmehr aus dem dreifachen Urmaterial; sinnlicher Kern, sinnliches Gefühl sinnliche Kinaesthese. Dem entspricht der 'Urinstinkt.' Zum ständigen, staendig wandelbaren, in den Sinnesfeldern staendig einheilichen und im Miteinander der urspruenlichen Zeit und durch die zeitlich Form der lebendigen Urgegenwart ständig sich hindurchziehenden Kern gehört die ständig allgemeine 'Freude oder Unlust an der Sinneswahrnehmung,' ein allgemeines 'Interesse' im Hingezogen-sein, das vermöge der mitgehenden Kinaesthesen instinktiv auf Konstitution von optima,..." ["The first of the world constitution in primordiality is the constitution of 'nature' out of the hyletic original nature, or rather out of the threefold original material; sensuous core, sensuous feeling sensuous kinaesthetic. This corresponds to the 'original instinct.' The constantly general 'joy or displeasure in sensory perception,' a general 'interest' in being attracted, belongs to the constant, constantly changing core that is constantly uniform in the sensory fields and in the togetherness of the original time and through the temporal form of the living original presence, that, by virtue of the accompanying kinaesthetics, instinctively on the constitution of optima,..."].

[104] Play and seriousness is essential in Husserl's analysis. Intelligence emerges within a generative world of play and seriousness, is a mark of humans, unlike animals who "do not ask questions" and "do not live in generativity," for Husserl. See A V 5. 14a and 20b: "Tier weiss nichts von Generation...."

[105] Bower (2014), p. 135.

[106] Ms. B III 9/ 64a: "Ein Neues ist es, wenn ich, kurz gesagt, A setzend und B setzend Einheit der Zusammen-Setzung übe, also nicht eine Thesis übe und dann eine andere, wobei ich die erstere

how there is a unification that appears in the constant stream of experience and a thematization of the "That" that still stands to the fore.[107] In this, the new is taken *as* new, but also as *already* in the field of affective force *as affective*.[108] As such, Husserl's identification of this as the "lowest, all-founding interest" is a deepening of the understanding of the constitutive duet of noesis-noema.[109] It is thus not the case that curiosity arises after new data are given, but rather that these are co-incident, as it were, insofar as curiosity occurs *with* and *in* the horizon of becoming. In other words, within curiosity, each newly given appears with its own force, its own enticements that "play" off the previous synthesis. This means that the announcement of each new object's "That!" occurs from within the horizon within which curiosity plays. This play, as Husserl puts it, "keeps one busy."[110] Curiosity is, in fact, kept busy

---

'noch' in Geltung, sondern synthetisch beides in eins setze..." ["It is something new when I, to put it briefly, bring to unity of setting-together by setting A and setting B, thus not bringing one thesis and then another, while still considering the former as 'valid,' but rather synthetically combining both into one..."].

[107] B III 9/48b: "...ein Erfassen, das selbst kontinuierlich in Behalten übergeht und strömend (erfassend-behaltend) sein einheitliches Akterggebnis konstituiert: das 'Das!,' dieses Seiende in dem lebendigen und ursprünglichen Modus. Genau so verhält sich nun doch mit dem rückblickend auf das Gesetzte des frühe Aktes Gerichtet-sein, z.B. auf das Aktergebnis des soeben abgeschlossenen Aktes...in seinem stehenden Wandel fuer mich zum ‚das!' aber dieses ‚erfassen' als aktives Perzipieren, in dem ein 'das!' mich beschaeftigt, ist doch ein stehendes Identifizierien und selbst wieder Ausgan fuer fortgehende Identifikation der Art der explizierenden...Statt jenes 'Von selbst' haben wir nun das sedimentierende Im-dunkel versinken (in seiner Fraglichkeit)" ["...a grasping that itself continuously transitions into retention and flowing (grasping-retaining) constitutes its unified act-result: the 'That!,' this being in the living and original mode. Exactly the same is the case with looking back at what was dictated by the earlier act, for example, at the result of the act that was just completed...in its constant change for me to 'that!' but this 'grasp' as active perception, in which a 'that!' what occupies me is a standing identification and itself again the starting point for ongoing identification of the kind of explanatory... Instead of that 'by itself' we now have the sedimenting sinking in the dark (in its questionability)." Also B III 9/49b: "Das-Setzung und damit in dieser Ständigkeit auf das strömende ‚Neue' gerichtet (darin liegt die Zukünftigkeit und von da eo ipso fortbehaltend und das behalten also mithabend...." ["That-positing and thus in this constantness directed towards the flowing 'new' (therein lies the future and from there e*o ipso* retaining and retaining that with oneself...."].

[108] See Hua Mat VIII, p. 324: "But one cannot say: Before the attention is the hyletic datum and has a pleasure character, which it is, by virtue of which it arouses my curiosity, as if the pleasure were once again a datum that affects. The data is already there before the for me, just as affecting, we certainly have the difference of the data and its graduality of the affection, the graduality of addressing me."

[109] See Hua Mat VIII, p. 325: "The lowest, all-founding interest is therefore that of the original and ever further functioning curiosity, or we should say better, the experiencing and, actually taken at the bottom, the experiencing interest of sensation."

[110] Hua Mat VIII, p. 73: "...and in which it is, in which the others already exist as objects and upon which the other subjects of living, influencing, of being busy are as subjects who, with one another, including the child, always constitute new beings, the world always new design." See also Ms. B III 9/48b-49a: "...das urimpressionale Selbst in seinen stehenden Wandel für mich zum ‚Das!' aber dieses 'Erfassen' als aktives Perzipieren, in den ein 'Das!' mich beschäftigt..." ["...the original impressional self in its standing changed for me to 'That!' but this 'grasping' as active perception, in which a 'That!' occupies me...."].

6.3 The Generation of World-Inquiry as Participating in the World-Horizon

"following" the new—it is interested, so to speak, in seeking to take newness up into concordance. With sight, for example, seeing is a matter following that which is given to sight, the ever-new flow of appearances. After a while, of course, many matters become familiar, set into a field of sight that is "mundane." But even that harmony can be disrupted if a new "That!" appears otherwise than expected, or with a greater affective force than other objects in the field. *Nonetheless,* this would occur within the already operating horizons of the all-founding curiosity that is ever-ready for the new. The satisfaction of curiosity may thus be said to in the fulfillment of the new that runs off into infinity.

The satisfaction of curiosity gives a twofold pleasure. On the one hand, the fulfillment of intention arising with the instinct is pleasing. On the other hand, the very seeking for fulfillment itself is pleasing. An instance of the first occurs in sight, as when I look to see that which appears, the fulfillment of seeing *that* is pleasing. Husserl notes that this point is in accord with Aristotle's recognition that "all humans by nature take joy in *aisthesis*."[111] But the continual affective interest and this itself is pleasing.[112] In this respect, as James Mensch points out, Husserl finds a certain "pleasurable affection" in this instinctual drive itself, as it is in a constant state of *receptive* fulfillment.[113] This is not somehow completed in one instance of perception but operates in the dynamism of *apperception.*

Lower curiosity, in the above sense, provides a foundation for the emergence and operation of a higher curiosity. Where original affective curiosity is present immediately with the lived-body, a higher sense of curiosity is what Husserl calls the "outcome of originally formed life-interests."[114] Husserl speaks of this as arising where there is a break in "serious living," that is, when primary life-interests, like hunger, are satisfied. If demands of lower levels are left unfulfilled, they are apt to pull development down into their needs. In fact, even where reason is developed and refined, it might be reasonably put to pressing practical needs of living. In any case, the higher curiosity is analogous to the lower, insofar as it follows newness, taking pleasure in this as well as in taking it up into concordance. However, for Husserl, this higher level operation appears in the life of a more highly developed subjectivity, with sufficiently developed instincts and capacities. It is necessary, for example, to be physically able to look around at all, which the newborn cannot do; further, a higher curiosity requires greater spiritual resources, as it requires drawing, not only physical capacities, but on the ability to "drop" practical concerns, disrupting their

---

[111] See Hua Mat VIII, p. 32. Also, from Ms. C 16 IV/30b: "Da gewinnt das aristotelische 'Alle Menschen haben von Natur aus Freude an der Sinneswahrnehmung' seine Wahrheit."

[112] Hua Mat, p. 324: "If we call 'curiosity' a feeling of pleasure, then this pleasure in being there is, so to speak, in the state of enjoyment, but here in itself the ongoing affection."

[113] For more, see Mensch (1997).

[114] Hua VI, p. 332: "…curiosity, which has its original place in natural life, as an intrusion into the course of 'serious life,' as an effect of originally developed life interests…"; also, Hua VI, 332: "Curiosity (here not as a habitual 'vice') is also a modification, an interest that has detached itself from the interests of life, has dropped them"; and, moreover, Hua XLII, p. 461: "As a second original instinct (opposite that of 'curiosity'). But that should not be an order. Both are there in one, and actually hunger is the first thing."

affective charge, in order to enter actively into a world of play.[115] The newness of the play-world is creative, in other words, as an artist is creative, Husserl says, within the painted world.[116]

To differentiate these levels further, consider Husserl's point about the development of the will between lower and higher curiosity. At a lower level, Husserl finds a "compulsive" action, that is, one that is based on drives (which he captures with the term *Triebhaft*, a "having of drives," as it were). The suckling of the child, again, is instinctually compulsive, directed toward the good of nourishment. Within the newborn's curiosity, this rather quickly develops into a determinately directed will, say, toward the good of the nourishment provided by the mother. It does not end there, though. For where practical needs are fulfilled and so able to be dropped, there emerges a play world between the child and the mother, in which the wills of the two continue to "intertwine."[117] In this emergent world of play, the child is able to put into play her kinesthetic "I can," while relating to the mother. In it, therefore, there is not a sort of "coercion," as would occur where the mother would move the child, but rather *communication*.[118] In this communication, there is a mutual effect, beyond but also upon the physical contact.[119] Take, for example, a game of peek-a-boo. The child's tireless excitement of the "new" disclosure of the face occurs. In this, there is also a communication here which occurs within the conditions of a "We," even as there is a playfully differentiation of "I" and "thou." If the "thou" of the adult becomes too distant to the child, however, the game will no longer be satisfying to the child. In fact, the game will abruptly end, as there is a breakdown in the world of play that sustained it. The result is the child, not only receding back to its "I," but crying out to communicate that it desires to return to a comfortable, satisfying safety of the "We." Indeed, through communicative contact, the child comes into intimate relation with the movements of the mother, her physical, emotional, and willing movements. In this respect, we broach the issue of *imitation*.

At a lower level, imitation is a copying of movement, an intertwining of ability and capacity with empathy at the level of the lived-body. It is a copying of an exterior movement by bringing it into the interior by "making after" (*nach-machen*) another.[120] This appears, in our example, when the young child, following the adult, blinks and tenses her face muscles or squeezes and releases her hand. This is close to, but not the same as, "aping after" (*nach-äffen*), in which there is neither an active understanding of the meaning of movements nor is there a foundation being given for such an understanding. Likewise, though at a higher level of communication, the

---

[115] Hua Mat VIII, p. 315: "Stimuli of the heart, possibly curiosity [*Gemüts-reize, eventuell Neugier*], doing something playfully, the result does not become permanent acquisition; the values are forgotten in a special way. The playful values, goods (value structures) are devalued in a special way, 'thrown away,' dropped - not like failure as crossing out within an interest, not as irrelevant, as sectional, and so on, 'dropped,' pushed aside."

[116] See Hua XXXIX, p. 376.

[117] See Hua XIV, pp. 169–170.

[118] A similar point by Husserl is indicated at Hua XIV, pp. 169–170.

[119] See Hua XIV, pp. 165–167.

[120] See Hua XLII, p. 525.

child as well as the parent learns to imitate vocal expressions in a way that expresses meaning.[121] There is a need here for a creativity that expresses itself beyond mere aping imitation, toward a expression of an inner life which understands what is recognized by the other. From the point about imitation in vocal expressions, in fact, Husserl asks, "What role could this play?"[122] He responds that imitation can lead to the child learning to *hear sounds spoken as a reference, as indications* that "point out" differences. More exactly, he says that the child learns to say names, "Momma" and "Poppa" and that these indicate momma and poppa: this sound *means* momma, this one poppa, and so on.[123] There also emerges, then, the child differentiating the "I" of herself in relation to others. What is more, this differentiation appears alongside the differentiation of objects, for the child is surrounded by a world of practical objects, the purposes of which she learns through imitation.[124] While being fed, for example, the child might take up and grasp the spoon herself, waving it around, perhaps eventually putting it in her mouth. This is clumsy, at first, of course, but through repetition and imitation, there comes some mastery in its use. Indeed, the purpose of the utensil as a "use object" (*Gebrauchsobjekte*) is taken up into the meaning of the child's world by way of the already meaningful home. In other words, imitation is a way of constituting and appropriating meaning in the world.

Such appropriation may be further clarified through two points. In the first place, the purposes of objects in the world are given as "pre-constituted" with respect to the child. There is a sense in which their "Why and Because" are given as already having been answered. In the second place, the child *participates* in their meaning and value, when she takes up ways of acting within her own sphere of possibilities through imitation. *Nevertheless*, such imitation does not expressly give an answer to the *why*,

---

[121] The point is drawn, from the perspective of the mother at Hua XV, p. 606: "Perhaps note: the child utters involuntary sounds in involuntary kinesthesia, it repeats them, produces the same ones voluntarily, learns to want to repeat and voluntarily produces all of its sounds (used at all in general). His sounds include possible kinesthesia. But the mother, for her part, utters similar sounds, initially imitations of the child's. The child hears it, has it, but without its associated kinesthesia, which is aroused associatively but is not there, instead the zero kinesthesia from which generation begins."

[122] Hua XI, p. 606: "Das Kind wiederholt selbst - die Mutter ebenso - welche Rolle könnte das spielen?" Husserl answers the question elsewhere, for example, at Hua XV, p. 630: "In the communion that constitutes human life in its very original form and in everyone from childhood onwards, imitation plays a major, constant role."

[123] Hua XV, p. 606: "The child first learns 'Mother,' 'Dad,' and so on. The mother does not say to the child 'I'll come right away,' 'I'll bring that,' but 'Mama is coming,' 'Momma is bringing.' How does the child come to say 'I'...?".

[124] See Hua XV, p. 611: "A simultaneous and successive tradition. On the human level: 'understand tradition as foreign experience, accept validity' –as experience; in addition, tradition through communication, through habitual practical apperception, habitual participation according to the 'model' of others (custom). The 'you do it like this.' In this way there is also tradition from generation to generation. The adults are already in the habit, the children 'grow into it' through imitation and instruction." Also, Hua XV, p. 420: "The child is primarily surrounded by functional objects; in everyday use it learns to understand them in their purposefulness, and so the child, surrounded by purposeful neighbors, learns to understand their purposeful activity as such and understand purposeful objects not only as objects of use, but as objects that have become teleological (prehistory)." See also Hua XXIX, p. 378.

but rather only takes up and takes after the reasons why. So, the meaning and value are presented as something new, something affectively charged in the horizons of the child. Thus, the child becomes curious about *"Why that is so."* Indeed, where this curiosity arises, the child seeks to determine *why* there is this purpose, this "end" or "telos," and *why* that which she participates in is so—she wants to know the *because*, as it were. Indeed, all this gives rise to an original question of "history"—Why?[125]

Husserl's inverted commas around "history" suggests that we consider the phrase more closely. The child's question is *about* history, as it seeks to understand the reasons *why* in the homeworld. Furthermore, this manifestation of the *why* question is an original institution of inquiry—it is the original question *of* history. As such, it is upon this manifestation which subsequent inquiry builds. To be sure, refers back to the "pure question," that is, the very possibility of reason to question at all, but it does so as the first radiation of that question into the world. There is a determinate motivation to this question. As such, the manifestation of the why-question seeks to understand meaning in the home: the question "Why?" appears as the child wakes up to generativity, that is, to the becoming that stretches across generations and is generative of new meaning. More precisely, however, it first seeks to know *why is that so*: in other words, what meaning does *this* have here, what is its *purpose*, and so the question is *specific,* focusing upon the *That* which appears with a certain demand.

As curiosity takes over this first determination the why-question, with its seeking of motivations, it appears as an incessant "Why?" As is familiar to those who have spent time around children, the child's inquiry rather quickly puts to question, not just this or that questionable object, but also the questionable *world* itself. Indeed, the initial question, at first, presses the reasons within the home/alienworld—"Why do I and we do this or that and them otherwise?" All this points forward, in fact, to the way to the a sense of the questionability of being of the world as such, as the instinct of reason presses on toward that long path of knowing *why*. First, however, let us notice how the child gains certain answers about history, that is to say, about its world.

In relation to these answers, there arises distinction between a passive and active "education" or "formation." In the former respect, a subject can act according to customs, mimicking others, following after them or "taking after" (*nach-ahmen*) ways or styles of being in the world.[126] From this, one can ask from a passive appropriation of customs—as Husserl notes about this, "What would they think about my actions, how would they judge them?"[127] However, this question does not necessarily appear on the basis of actively appropriated reasons why. For that, there is a need for further reflective inquiry into *why* these actions are done. An active

---

[125] Hua XV, p. 420: "Nachahmend ist es tätig und spielt es Tätigkeit; es erwächst Neugier, Interesse für das Gewordene, Interesse für das 'warum das so ist.' Die Frage des Warum ist ursprünglich Frage nach der 'Geschichte'" ["Imitatively it is active and plays activity; Curiosity grows, interest in what has become, interest in 'why is that so.' The question of why is originally a question about 'history.'" Indeed, the manuscript from which this comes more generally concerns the life that is "communal from the very beginning" as a "purposive life."

[126] Hua XLII, p. 525.

[127] Hua XLII, p. 432.

6.3 The Generation of World-Inquiry as Participating in the World-Horizon

education and formation would mean developing a reflective, habitually insightful way of acting. As we have already glimpsed, that means there taking up reflectively and insightfully taking up ideals and values. Where this occurs, there arises a "second nature," as Husserl puts it, echoing the tradition following Aristotle.[128] Now, that occurs, too, in relation to an imitation of those who live out those ideals and values, but an imitation in the sense that one has appropriated the ideals within oneself.[129] One must be *true* to oneself, not alone, but *with* others.

So, there is a sort of communication of the ideal of reason such that there is also a communalization. That is to say, a community arises that means to make it the explicit ideal of the community. And the genuine community aims for those to come to be alike, akin thenselves, but also for those to come to be themselves, in a way that exceeds the previous generations by building upon them. Thus, in a letter, Husserl speaks of the emergence of philosophy:

> Already Anaximander has distanced himself from Thales and Aristotle from Plato. And I can no longer believe that Plato resented him for this. The true teacher is like a father. And what does Hector wish to his Astyanax?- The people may say: "he still rises far before the father."[130]

In short, the original question why presses the community to understand itself, not only in the face of each other, but before an ideal. Indeed, the call of the question of "Who am I?" and "Who are we?" presses upon us from an ideal end not yet realized in the world. It is especially through these that human beings express their journey mythologically, a point to which I turn now.[131]

---

[128] Hua XLII, pp. 340–341.

[129] Consider Husserl's points, to which I return below, at Hua XLII, p. 525: "The ideal in me as my model, I as the role model of myself. Other, adoringly beloved people as my models; living after them, I want to become more perfect. What is here the first in itself? Are there wholly easy problems here if a deeper interpretation is sought? Is exemplary 'imitation' ('imitatio Christi')? Great, excellent people have those who ape them. Does it not in addition to the imitation? Yes, because it focuses only on the exteriority, one will say, while such aping ones are not able to understand the spiritual greatness, the properly worthy of reverence." See also Hua XXVII, pp. 100–103.

[130] Husserl, *Briefwechsel,* Brentanoschule, p. 23. Husserl includes here, philosophers, as with this passage about Aristotle; Hua XIV, p. 200, "If I empathize with Aristotle, it is the past Aristotle. I can no longer have an effect on him, but his earlier thoughts are now having an effect on me, the ones he generated earlier are the same ones I am now re-creating and which now continue to have a motivating effect on me...."

[131] For example, Hua, p. 39, "Appendix XI: ⟨Content:⟩ Environing world, Homeworld: Human being as that of his environing world. Fate. Myth. Struggle for existence. Self-formation. Fate.... Human being as a designer of his environment so that it could satisfy him. Mission in life, self-determination, struggle for existence, destiny, mythicization of the powers of destiny... The mythical, the unknown, but personally apperceived as resistance: the 'dark destiny,' demons, gods, and so on."

6.4 From Myth to Philosophy: A Transformation of the "Why" Question

In the previous section, we traced the appearance of the question, "Why is that so?" We found that the confluence of lower and higher instincts through lived-experience in the world-horizon gives rise to a striving to determine and to differentiate being—the first *why question*. As the child develops, her curiosity seeks to know the world in which she develops, seeking to understand the practical purposes of things in relation to herself, bringing to question the teleological sense of her homeworld itself. In this section, I turn to how Husserl discovers this way of inquiry to constitute the world of *myth* and how this mythical world gives a foundation for the emergence and differentiation of *theory*. I do so through three subsections:

A. first, I present how the mythical world emerges from answers to questions about obscure and alien matters which appear in the homeworld;
B. then, I show how theoretical inquiry emerges from this background, as the *opening* of theoretical inquiry to the reasons why of matters in themselves and between each other, "irrelative" of the home, a first appearance of which occurs in the encounter of the Greek homeworld to the alienworld;
C. finally, I address how, concurrent with the development of science, there is a *demythologizing* of the world.

Through these seconds, there is a transformation of the *Why* question, from the *why is that so* of curiosity to the *why is that what it is really* or *ideally* of theory. This gives a foundation for understanding the appearance of phenomenological science, which seeks to make manifest reason in its seeking to know *why*.

6.4.1 Myth: Meaning and Value Relative to the Homeworld

Husserl finds that the historical world of human beings is also initially constituted as the mythical world.[132] By this he does not simply mean that the world first appears full of fantastical forces, beasts, monsters, and deities. More basically, this means that the homeworld is at first constituted within an attempt to make sense *why that is so* within a relationship of proximate- and remote-horizons.[133] After all, there appear matters and forces which sometimes work in favor, sometimes against human practical living. *Why is that so*? The attempt to explain why matters are so means

---

[132] Hua XV, p. 431 fn. 2: "Yes, this historicity states the constitution of the environing world as a first, mythical world - everything in it is formed mythically."

[133] Consider, for example, the fragments in Hua XLII, p. 4: "The natural development of worldviews. Path to the teleological worldview. / The people in the near horizon. The distance as a limited realm of myth. The widening of the proximate horizon to an infinite horizon, which as it progressed would show itself to be of the same natural structure of being as the near world without ⟨infinity⟩. First expansion of the proximate world to a full world."

6.4 From Myth to Philosophy: A Transformation of the "Why" Question

bringing the alien nearer to the horizon of the home which leads to a sort of myth making. Indeed, as this myth making aims not only makes sense of this or that in the world but also *the world itself*, so there also emerges, Husserl says, there emerge "questions of universal curiosity," in which there is desire to make sense of the constant givenness of "alien" to the ordinary, familiar world.[134] In short, then, myth emerges to determine the *reason why*—to the answer the *why is that so* question—about unknowns in the world-horizon as well as the unknown of the home/alienworld relation itself.

Most originally, the attempt to make sense of alienness appears with answers emergent from the curiosity of the child. Let me be clear, however, that does not mean that the expressed cultural myths are "childish." I mean instead that making sense of the reasons for matters builds alongside the reasons one has appropriated from the home. Thus, the mythical is originally constituted upon that which has been answered, as it brings nearer that which does not yet make sense. So, as the child's questions about the world are yet in relation to themselves and their lived-body, as stemming from the earth-ground, animism tends to be an early expression of myth.[135] Here, the geo-historical earth-ground becomes an extension of the body such that there is an attempt to totalize the world in relation to the body, as the *Allwelt,* the "world-totality." In this, there is a sort of world-question, as it brings a "Because" to the "Why is that so" to the entire world, in terms of the *whole* as a living universe, in relation to the living whole of the subject and the community of subjects. As such, animism does not only offer answers to *why that is so* in terms of the lived-body stemming from the earth-ground, but also in relation to the full range of the whole living subject, including its *intelligence and feelings*. Because the universe is full of

---

[134] Consider Hua XXIX, fn 1: "The mythical powers intervene in the ordinariness of individual human existence and in the temporal course of the historical people's existence. The environing world of man. In the life of the state the human being in all its gifts and its performing cultural creation deals in its actions, each again self-preservation in interpenetration with existence, life and action of the mythical powers. The environing world is thoroughly mythical and at the same time human. The intervention of the mythical and its practice in the everyday practice of self-preservation results in the permanent unity of a two-sided practice." Also, Hua XXIX, p. 389: "In the pre-scientific stage we have also already possible world questions, questions of a universal curiosity, but related precisely to that world of national traditions, in which the mythical is a general and into the most mundane everydayness moving layer. There has always been a curiosity for the world in the universal myth, a curiosity that is not always impractical. As knowledge about being and history of the world of gods, it was the basis of the 'religious' practice and therefore excellently a matter of the priestly cooperatives – of course, this does not lead with <the> Greeks as with the Indians to a world speculation spinning uniformly from generation to generation, which in a certain way can come so close to the later philosophical ones."

[135] Hua XXVII, pp. 188–189. Also, Hua XXIX, p. 38: "Natural, animistic conception of 'nature'– 'nature,' the earthly material, at home in the ground, detaching from it and working on it, earthly 'nature' in connection with air and aerial structures, fog, clouds, rain, continuously mediated with the sky and the heavenly phenomena. This is the realm of myth, on whose favor or disfavor depends on the environing worldly existence, the realm of volcanic eruptions, earthquakes, the voice, thunderstorms, heavenly fire, floods, and so on. The powers of fate, sometimes friendly to human-national existence and sometimes hostile. Human existence in the natural-national historicity, in the horizon homeland and alien, in the homeland the normal existence, the normally self-satisfying forms of self-preservation of a national existence."

life and the whole itself is alive with this life, it is forbidden to harm the Earth and all things on Her—She is living, and to harm a living thing causes pain, restricts the drive of life, and so must be prohibited. Those obscure forces and matters are thus brought nearer by way of this myth.

So, myth functions within a generativity, wherein the earth-ground is taken as the point of orientation in the answer to the question why that is so. It thus grows from that ground, that real place in which people live together. As such, Husserl relates myth as a "first historicity" of a people or *Volk*.[136] A *Volk* is born from a place, together forming a nation—as suggested by the Latin *natio*, from *nascor*: to be born within a nation which Husserl calls a "generative totality [*Allheit*] (*natio*)."[137] As the nation is not constituted by any one individual but by generative unity of the *Volk*, so the people recall their ancestors as given meaning to the homeworld. Indeed, as a *nation* of *Volk*, the homeworld is structured by traditions that remain relative without question, that is to say, the world itself is constituted as a "universal myth" of a *cosmology*.[138] This sense of cosmology—as an "order" or κόσμος—sets together the drives of a community within the horizon of possibilities and actualities.[139] Adn so, myth, Husserl finds, contra Lévy Bruhl, brings an order for the people in their living. Indeed, this cosmology, Husserl notes, "functions for self-preservation," insofar it provides a foundation for answers to *questions about the preservation* of their existence and satisfaction.[140] Again, these questions relate to the attempt to answer questions of

---

[136] I identify it only against the "second historicity" of science. For example, Hua XXIX, p. 41: "The second historicity: the transformation of human existence of first historicity through science, through the theoretical attitude. The vocational occupation with the mythical."

[137] Hua XXIX, p. 269: "Maturation of the conception of the world and at the same time of the historical development of the conception of the world (of the lifeworld) and of the world of life (life-interest) of people as subjects of the respective world conception – the first form of the open endlessness of a world originally of national tradition, a self-contained generative allness (*natio*), then such a nation living among other nations."

[138] Hua XXIX, p. 11: "Ein Volk, eine Nation lebt in ihrer traditionalen Welt…" This recurs at Hua XXIX, p. 44.

[139] Hua XLII, p. 516: "The attitude of cosmology, or of the human beings who drive for it, is decided in the attitude of need for knowledge, the attitude toward the material facts, toward being and being-so and modalities of being, as mediation, without questioning what I value, for my and our well-being and woe coming to question. More exactly: The scientist is in a vocational attitude, a special 'infinite' attitude that spans the endlessness or wholeness of her life and is in 'infinite' living community with her vocational comrades. This is a special practical (and in this sense 'infinite') attitude. There are many 'vocations' in community life, and the same person can have several."

[140] Hua XXXVII, pp. 518–519: "But now we do not have independent vocational research as cosmology, but rather *cosmology functions for self-preservation*, functioning for a further vocationally established universal sense-reflection of the concrete personality directed towards 'true self-preservation.' That indicates, however: we have, first of all, the *science 'cosmology*….'" At the end of this quotation, he indicates that this will develop into a scientific expression of *self-preservation*, to which I turn below. See also, Hua XLII, pp. 261 and 526: "However, in the general experience of the fateful existence of all people, there belongs to life the turn to the universal question: What can we humans do in the face of fate and the on-going possibility of situations of despair or total practical doubt that we all face, putting in question the totality of practical possibilities? In them, the 'possibility of living' becomes questionable, the whole human existence becomes overall in its 'possibility,' that is, questionable in the possibility of a satisfying affirming existence in worldly life

6.4 From Myth to Philosophy: A Transformation of the "Why" Question   181

why that is so, in order to preserve the people in the face of the to-and-fro of fate. *Why is that so? Because* the gods are impetuous, petty, forgetful, *mysterious*. Nevertheless, *be who you are*—a Greek, a Hocąk, and so on. In other words, *destiny* comes into tension with *fate*. For the ideal of existence which emerges with the people also appears within a struggle with various vicissitudes which disrupt its realization. Despite this tension, the people continually strive to make sense of their "situational truth."[141]

Even within myth, then, there is a demand to determine and to differentiate being and good. And where there is a failure to realize the true and the good, further quesitons arise. With that in mind, let me now move now to the emergence of the stage of theory upon the foundations of the mythical stage.[142]

6.4.2 The Meeting of Mythical Worlds and the Appearance of Wonder in Greece

Basically, Husserl finds that theory emerges as individuals from the Greek homeworld encounter alienworlds and as meaning and value in the homeworld begin to come into question.[143] As Timo Miettinen underscores, the early use of θεωρία or *theoria* "stood primarily for the specific civic practice of travelogue. In the practice of *theoria*, a citizen traveled abroad to give an account of events and occurrences in a foreign polis that had usually been hitherto unknown."[144] The word was thus also used to describe the envoy of states to the Olympic games, who were sent to other cities to "have a look around," as the roots of the term θεωρία—θέα and ὁράω, to look and view, the former of which θεάομαι and θαυμάζω, "wonder" comes—suggests. Indeed, in this early stage, "theory" meant a sort of early surveying, prepared, in its practical contours, by the surveying of the land in early geometry.[145]

---

in the form of possible satisfaction." To these questions, at first, come mythico-religious responses, then philosophical and scientific. See also Hua XLII, p. 516.

[141] Hua XXIX, p. 546: "…Wahrheit und Falschheit des vorwissenschaftlichen Lebens. Ich spreche von Situationswahrheit." He will also speak of a "All-situationswahrheit" of generativity that is relates to the world-horizon earth-ground.

[142] Ms. A V 22/48: "das werden der Wissenschaft…Steht der Mensch in der mythologischen Stufe…" ["…the becoming of science…human being stands in the mythological stage…."].

[143] Again, this sense appears early in Husserl's philosophical career. A clear statement is at Hua Mat IX, pp. 6–7. Also, Hua VI, pp. 332–333: "It is therefore necessary in this respect to clarify how from the nature and the life horizon of Greek mankind in the seventh century in its intercourse with the great and already highly cultivated nations of their environment that θαυμάζειν could set in and first become habitual in individuals." Later, it becomes more expressly generative, as at Hua XXIX, 387: "…just as the boundaries of the national community and its uniform tradition are transgressed by national strangers entering into contact with one another"]; see also, Hua XXVII, pp. 78–79.

[144] I learned this first from the dissertation work of Timo Miettinen, a copy of which I am thankful to the author. See Miettinen, (2020). See also, Hua XXXVIII, p. 6, et al.

[145] In truth, geometry is essential to this development, with its origins in the kinaesthetic constitution of space time from the Earth-ground and world-horizon (which includes an account of the "near

These early theorists yet had a practical task which involved encountering the territories of the alienworld as such. At this stage, the home/alienworld is still laden with mythical cosmology. That means the mythical homeworld was still the "metaphysical horizon," as Husserl puts it, from which and in which these theorists viewed the alienworld.[146] In other words, their homeworld was that horizon from which the alien was given as *actual*. Nevertheless, the initial stages of detached observation meant that these Greeks let the alien appear as such in relation to their world. So, in Husserl's example, following Herodotus, during these trips abroad, the Greek travelers would encounter "the same sun, the same moon, the same earth, the same sea, and so on," but would also encounter the difference of sense, meaning, and value of those same objects in the alienworld.[147] As the example goes, a trip to Egypt brought into view Ra, the sun god, but in relation to Helios, their sun god. In this conflict of presentations, there emerges a question—*why is that so?* Indeed, in this, there are the seeks of the theoretical question, *what is it really?* In fact, the conflict about specific object brings with it a conflict between *worlds*.

The encounter of homeworlds is the encounter of what Husserl calls "first objective worlds."[148] These are the worlds in which matters make sense, but they have not yet been objectified as such. Through on-going encounters with the alienworld—which has, not only differing meanings of the same objects, but differing ways of self-preservation, in their eating, their dress, in customs in general—the world as such comes to the fore as a question.[149] To be clear, however, these questions about objects and worlds are not straightaway scientific.

---

and far" of the heavens), from which there arises an intelligent ordering and measuring and a geometric method. How this relates to phenomenology, for Husserl, is especially important, as his intentionality analysis finally "goes back" to its roots, putting to question its presuppositions.

[146] A V 22/BL 27: "Er gewinnt aber Raum für eine nüchterne vom Mythischen sich ablösende Praxis und praktische Lebenswelt, in der zwar in metaphysischen: Hintergrund mythische Potenz ihre Rolle spielen..." ["But he wins space for a sober praxis and practical life-world, which is detached from the mythical and in which the mythical potency plays its role in the metaphysical background: Background mythical potency plays their role...."].

[147] Hua XXIX, p. 387: "It is nevertheless the same sun, the same moon, the same earth, the same sea and so on, which is mythologized so differently in the different peoples according to their traditionality. They are the same things that have religious meaning for the foreigner, and for the Greek in trade these pieces cost." See, again Hua Mat. Band I, p. 6, where there is a reference to Herodotus, *The Histories*, 2.41.2. See also Hua XXXVII, 16; Hua XXIX, p. 44; Hua XV, p. 432 fn. 2; and, again, in K III 3/47a. About the possibility to interpret the same object similarly which emerges here, consider A V 11/30a: "Ich kann mich in alle Zeiten versetzen, in alle historischen Zeiten, bezogen auf die generativen und kommunikativen Menschheiten in der Einheit einer Menschheit. Ich 'interpretiere' Sonne, Mond, Sterne, Milchstrassen und so on, als ferne Körper, ihre Erscheinungen als Fernerscheinungen, zu denen wie in meiner nächsten Umweltsphäre Naherscheinungen gehören müssten" ["I can transport myself to all times, to all historical times, in relation to the generative and communicative humanities in the unity of humanity. I 'interpret' the sun, moon, stars, Milky Way, and so on as distant bodies, their appearances as distant phenomena, to which, as in my immediate environment, nearby phenomena must belong."].

[148] See Hua XXIX, pp. 1–20.

[149] For some of Husserl's remarks on the encounter of normal worlds, see Hua XXIX, p. 388.

6.4 From Myth to Philosophy: A Transformation of the "Why" Question

The looking around of earlier theorist gives only a "germinating sense," as Husserl says, to scientific inquiry.[150] The early theoretical observation is still *interested* rather than *disinterested*. Indeed, this is still guided by an affective curiosity, that is, by an interest in the newness of the objects that appear within the apperceptive world. A joy of traveling for curiosity's sake is the regular appearance of objects as different than expected or anticipated: the excitation of an unfamiliar sartorial style or movement, for example, demands attention, motivates one to turn their attention to it. In this way, travel stirs curiosity and desire for the new and unexpected and leads to knowledge about it. But it is not yet *theoretical wonder*.

Once again, for Husserl, theoretical wonder is a *variation of curiosity*.[151] As a variation, they share some features. Both are, in a sense, "playful" operations: they both utilize free-phantasy and imagination without aiming toward attaining and achieving practical goals and satisfaction. But theoretical wonder does not find fulfillment in "newness" in relation to the ego, which it perpetually seeks. Rather, it varies this into a seeking for the lasting and identical, for its own sake. It is "unbounded," so to speak, from limits of *interested* perception, as it detaches from the relative striving for satisfaction of the ego, into a *disinterest* in the truth as permanent acquisition. Indeed, theory seeks to secure a structure that can be recovered repeatedly and by *everyone in each case* (*"für jedermann jeweils,"* as Husserl often says).[152]

The conflict of a presentation in the home/alien emerges from within a higher curiosity. Upon hearing the Egyptians speak about Ra, having seen the monuments which were built, the festivals which were held, the prayers which were made—all the sense, meaning, and values which emerge from the complex answers to *why*

---

[150] See Hua XXIX, p. 218: "And only in it…It is 'interested' and was historically only a preliminary stage for the breakthrough of the Greek 'Theoria,' the philosophy, but itself still germinative sense." Hua XXXIX, p. 339: "This pure interest in what really is and what it is – the theoretical in a very broad sense – is still far from that interest in the 'in itself' being, or that first in-itself is only a relative it-itself."

[151] Hua VI, p. 332: "…..curiosity, which has its original place in natural life, as an intrusion into the course of 'serious life,' as an effect of originally formed life interests or as a playful look around when the downright current needs of life have been satisfied or the working hours have expired,…".

[152] See Hua Mat VII, p. 302: "Theoretical interest means a peculiar intention that goes to true being, or first of all, as in curiosity and so also elsewhere, where it is not a matter of something new, the intention to grasp what is experienced as what it is, as an identical thing, to appropriate it permanently, to take it into one's knowledge or cognition; possibly universal as a general theoretical interest, that for a system of cognitive acquisitions, acquired identities, being, to which I can always come back, which I can always identify again and again….If I reflect on a theoretical possession, on a conviction, which I, and as a theoretical one, have already acquired by evidential reasoning, then the proposition in question, the truth in question, which, according to my conviction, is valid for everybody, is to be distinguished, on the other hand the experience, the judgment of my sense-reflection: 'I am in certainty.' I 'have' the evidential groundings." Also see Hua VIII, p. 337: "Here one saw for the first time how theoretical interest does not satisfy itself as mere curiosity about the individual and indiscriminately chases after new things, how it does not weaken in the face of the open infinities of the knowable, but rather grows, and moreover holds its own even where interests related to other areas might tempt it." Once more, Hua XXVII, p. 187: "…theoretical interest, is not a mere extended curiosity, a curiosity pouring out into the boundless, into the concrete endlessly wide environing world, to get to know this whole environing world. That was, of course, at first."

that is in their homeworld—the Greek curiosity came to ask *why that is so*. That is to say, *why is that difference which comes into conflict so*. The question can, of course, be answered by way of a transgression which says that they answer that way because they are wrong, barbarous, *alien*. But that does not really fulfill curiosity, as it neither accounts for the difference nor allows further newness. The movements of the variation of curiosity to wonder thus includes an expansion of horizon to the objective worlds. In fact, an important aspect of what Husserl calls the "revolution" of thought from curiosity to wonder is what the "astonishment" (*Verwunderung*) of, not just this or that object being different, but of the *world itself is given as being otherwise*.[153] With that astonishment comes the question about *why that is so*, now asked about the world itself.

So, in incipient theoretical wonder, conflicts between presentations appear within the conflict of worlds themselves. From these conflicts, the theorists begin to drop practical interests, in what Husserl calls a sort of ἐποχή.[154] Indeed, they begin to detach from opinions and become disinterested, gradually, to be sure, but set surely on that way of inquiry toward a truth which holds for everyone everywhere. The questions about why that is so thus varies into an attempt to determine and to differentiate these as they are "in themselves" and "between each other" rather than "to us." In other words, the answer to the *why* question becomes a *what* question, in the sense that the *what* or the *ideal* sense would explain *why that is so*. Indeed, in the differentiation of myth to science, there emerges what Husserl calls "a new idea of beings."[155] This new idea is precisely the relation of beings to each other in an *ideal* sense in order to know what they really are.

To reiterate, in the Greek world, there is not only an effort to know what this or that being is but what the world is. As such, Husserl relates the "first idealization" of the world to the "second historicity" of human beings in the world.[156] Within this, theory takes the tendency toward a universal and directs it to all beings in the

---

[153] E III 7/6b: "Eine ungebundene Neugier muss hier erwachen, das *thaumazo*, welches nicht die gemeine Neugier ist sondern die Verwunderung über die notwendig gewordene Umwälzung in der gesamten Weltvorstellung des gemeinen Lebens, der einzigen, die man bisher, wie alle Menschen, hatte" ["An unbound curiosity must awake here, the *thaumazo*, which is not the common curiosity but rather the astonishment at the revolution that becomes necessary in the whole world conception of the common life, the only one which one had till now, like all the people"]. See also Hua XXXIX, p. 308.

[154] Hua XXIX, pp. 392–333: "It is necessary to clarify the transformation from the original *theoria*, from the completely "disinterested" (taking place in the *epoché* of all practical interest) view of the world (knowledge of the world from mere universal view) to *theoria* of actual science, both mediated by the contrast of doxa and episteme."

[155] Hua XXIX, pp. 44–45: "Thus germinates a new idea of beings."

[156] Hua XXIX, p. 45: "Thus, the first discovery of the "objective" world, the one and the same for all human beings, may they belong to whatever nation, looks like the overcoming of the first, natural-naïve historicity of human existence and of the historically in him become and perpetuating world as national apperception. Thus, it is not first of all a world as a world in our sense: Idea of the scientifically true world...."

6.4 From Myth to Philosophy: A Transformation of the "Why" Question

world, thereby constituting the *Weltall* in the sense of the "world-totality."[157] The theoretical world is closely related to the mystical world, at first; and so, much of early Greek philosophy is, as Husserl points out, is "half-mythical."[158] It includes an attempt, in other words, to give answers to the questions about obscure forces and fates, though now with a decreasing subjectification or personification and an increasing "objectivity." In fact, as we have already seen, the early Greek physicists begin almost exclusively with interest in nature, calling into question the world as the objective world of a totality.[159] This objectivist inquiry continues, in some sense, unto the metaphysics and metaphysical theology of Aristotle. By then, however, there was a reflective and systematic establishment of the *theoretical attitude.*

It is illuminating that the German word for "attitude," namely, *ein-stellung* has something of an etymological parallel in the Greek ἐπί-ἵστημι. Without pushing this too far, it may be employed as a heuristic in understanding *epistēmē* as an ideal, as an attitude that one "stands in." In the case of theory, that means standing in the striving to understand true-being "in itself" and to do so *by knowing the reason why*, the *cause*, going beyond mere belief, opinion, *doxa*. In this way, the emergence of philosophy includes a sort of disruptive alteration in human development, insofar as it establishes a *new norm* of reason, and so, too, of being in the world. Historically, this occurs from personalities making the slow and gradual break from the practico-mythical attitude in which one develops.[160] A breakthrough to theory means that the philosopher itself comes to "stand in" the world in a new way.

Since the world of myth persists around these philosophical personalities, they appear strange, unfamiliar to those in the home. Nevertheless, it does not take too long for groups to form around these personalities, as others begin to admire (*Bewunder*) those in wonder (*Wunder*) and astonishment (*Verwunderung*).[161] Now, such admiration is not merely a matter of *seeing* other's different manner of being; it is, rather, a matter of reflectively taking up a possible *way of being* in accord with possibilities of *one's own being*. In short, admiration is a modification of imitation, through the reflective ideal of reason set in philosophy. There thus comes, not only a flow of philosophers, but students following after their masters. The mastery of reason itself means that they share in the ideal of reason, in seeking to determine and to differentiate being, in order to live a reasonable and responsible life.

---

[157] Hua VII, p. 311: "So universalistic tendency of theoretical interest, directed to the universe, the universe."

[158] See Hua VII, p. 289.

[159] See Hua VI, pp. 332–333.

[160] Hua VI, pp. 332–333. Also, Hua XXIX, p. 45.

[161] See, for example, Husserl's description of how the scientists of the renaissance take up the ancient view of the autonomy of reason at Hua XXIX, p. 109: "It turns against its previous, the medieval way of being, it devalues it, it wants to shape itself anew in freedom, it has its admired model in ancient humanity. It wants to imitate [*nachbilden*] this way of being in itself." I also wish to note that Husserl does, in fact, use this term to describe how people of a mythical homeworld might view the handiwork and achievements of the alienworld; for example, Hua XXIX 42: "...alien technology, alien craftsmanship excites admiration, must be recognized as superior to the home."

Moreover, while this new community works toward the building up of the reasonable world, it also *demythologizes* the world. This demythologization means a critique of the "first objective" world of myth through theory.[162] To make sense of this, recall that theory is directed toward the true world "in itself" which is accessible *by everyone in each case*. As such, it implies a critique of *doxa*, in that sense of belief which includes traditional opinions built up as myth in relation to the homeworld. For Husserl, Thales is the *Urvater* and *Urstifter*—*the primordial or original father and establisher*—of the establishment of *theoria* and so, by extension, of the movement of de-mythologizing.[163] Its reestablishment appears throughout the history of philosophy following after him. Indeed, as these philosophers put the traditional world into question, initiating a "superior survey of the world, unfettered by myth and tradition," the sufficiency of the relative truths or *myths* are continually challenged.[164] And so questions that were fulfilled by answers in the mythical world are called back into question, one by one and in an entirely new inquiring attitude.

Demythologization, for Husserl, also raises the issue of self-responsibility for making *the best possible world* overall and everywhere *through reason*.[165] A difficulty arises in the communication of this self-responsibility. Because philosophers no longer belong *simply and straightforwardly* to the normal and familiar way of being in the world, they appear as "other worldy," almost as religious figures, prophets or even dangerous charlatans, political adversaries. So, there appear the conflicting stories of Thales as the aloof philosopher and as the conniving astronomer-businessman; likewise, there are also stories of the wise Socrates on a mission from the gods, of the charlatan up in the clouds, making a fool of others for money, or of corrupting the youth for who knows what political gain. There thus comes, with the issue of demythologization, the question of how to bring others into the task of philosophical self-responsibility, wherein there are a shared ideals and values that go beyond relative interests. In short, there comes the problem of *education*, of leading others out into the light in order to experience for themselves the other possible way of being.

As such, the philosopher must also relate back to the world from which he was born and in which he was born. Thus, in a discussion of the problematic, Husserl notes the fact that Plato too used myths to convey philosophical truths, in a sort of "visualization."[166] This, he thinks, is a legitimate and, perhaps, necessary way of education. The aim was to meet people where they were in order to use their own

---

[162] Consider, for example, the manuscript at Hua XXIX, p. 4: "Demythologization and first objective. World. The critique of tradition - sprung from the intercourse of nations of a different historicity constituting their national spirituality." See also, Hua XXIX, p. 41.

[163] Hua XXIX p. 283: "Has, starting from the legendary Thales, the *Urvater* of philosophy, the original founder of the purpose idea of philosophy...."].

[164] Hua VI, p. 5: "Theoretical philosophy is the first. A superior view of the world, free from the ties of myth and tradition in general, is to be put into practice, a universal knowledge of the world and of people with absolute impartiality...."

[165] Husserl will sometimes call the relation between the original, natural attitude and the theoretical a "finitization" of science, which means it becomes a way of living. See Husserl (1970), p. 283.

[166] Hua XXIX, pp. 222–223, wherein he uses the term "*Verbildlichungen*," which is a sort of using images in order to get the idea.

spiritual resources to discover for themselves their desire for truth. This sense of philosophy begins to fragment with the development of science, however. Indeed, science fragments into apparently self-sustaining and self-enclosed, each to their own departments. In this fragmentation, philosophy loses its original place as unifying human pursuits. It is along these lines, on the *questionability of science itself* that phenomenological inquiry emerges. It emerges, short, amidst a *crisis.*

Let me say more about this process by way of a concluding overview.

Chapter 7
Concluding Overview: From Latent to Patent unto Manifest Reason

Abstract In a Concluding Overview, I provide a brief reconstruction of Husserl's account of the development of reason and inquiry (represented in the figure at the end of the main text). This places the emergence of phenomenological inquiry within generativity. It also shows that and how Husserl comes to understanding phenomenological inquiry-back into the emergence of sense, meaning, and value as bringing reason to itself and serving the endeavor to make the best possible world.

Keywords Historicity · Generativity · Interiority · Phenomenological philosophy · Theology

> But seen from the inside, philosophy is a struggle of the generations of philosophers living and surviving in spiritual community of the carriers of this development of spirit, in the constant struggle of the "awakened" reason to come to itself, to its self-understanding, to a reason which concretely understands itself in understanding the existing world, existing in its whole universal truth....[1]

If the *remote* aim of this book is to evidence the claim *that* Husserl treats an historical development of reason manifest in and through inquiry, it also does while *proximally* discovering *how* this is so. In other words, while we gathered data from his oeuvre, we also determined and differentiated possibilities of our own inquiry as it inquires-back into itself. To that end, I presented, through the chapters, four conditions of the inquiry: (1) a mode of attention and attitude which have their corresponding (2) interest and question, both of which stand in relation to (3) a mode of appropriation of the home/alienworld as a primary way their meaning is passed across generations and, finally, (4) the worldly cultural formation emergent with the question's meaningful fulfillment that sets the horizons for further questions. We then found that these conditions appear variously through three stages of reason, namely, *latent, patent, and manifest reason*. Now, let me give an overview of this process.

---

[1] Hua VI, p. 273.

In the first stage, if *instinctual* life-interests in what Husserl calls a practical "prehistory" are satisfied, there spontaneously emerges from (1) *curiosity* an originary (2) 'Why?' This question first appears as the child appropriates *practical* meanings in the homeworld via (3) imitation of others from previous generations, motivating the attempt to grasp this meaning beyond what is immediately given, to understand "*why that is so.*" Its interest is in the fulfillment of a truth relative to this home, within the means and ends of its practical, personal life. As this continues, (4) "myth" is established in a stage of *latent reason*. Here, the striving to elucidate yet obscure horizons in relation to the home occurs without critically reflecting on the role of reason in that process. Indeed, the world itself comes under a "universal myth" that guides the sense of purpose of a people, even in relation to alien-nations.

However, as the Greek world encounters alienworlds, there emerges an effort to determine the "true world." In this meeting of worlds, not only do similar objects appear as carrying different meanings, but the *world itself* appears as meaning otherwise. Thus, within this conflict between home and alien, curiosity transforms or "varies" into (1) theoretical wonder's (2) "What?" in order to determine what a particular object is or, indeed, what Every-thing is *in itself*. That is to say, the question "Why? – Why does that same object carry different meanings for them?"—varies into "What is it *really*?' or "What is the object in itself, to be known in its universality and necessity, that is, its *ideality*?"[2] The explicit tendency to the *universal* and its formulation in general concepts not only seeks to know *this* or *that being* but the Idea of the world itself and in itself, which Husserl calls it the "first objectification" and idealization of the world. Where this occurs for the Greek, they also begin to shift from a personalized Nature to an impersonal world. Indeed, Husserl finds here an emergent interest in the world as totality—τὰ πάντα, as Husserl finds the early Greeks putting it.[3] With this shift, there emerges a task of *demythologizing* the world, in which there also appears the ideal of a universal humanity, living under universal truths, rather than a homeworld of *Volk* and its relative truths and values. This appears, for these Greeks, under the name of *philosophy*. In philosophy, imitation and curiosity transform into the pairing of (3) admiration (*Bewunderung*) of exemplars and wonder (*Wunder*) at achievements in the world and the world itself. From this pairing, the ideals and values of philosophy are passed through an educational organ formed to pass on its ideal, namely, of (4) a *rigorous* science which seeks *self-justified reasons*.[4]

For Husserl, the scientific ideal is re-established in at least three main phases or moments in history, from the Greeks to the Renaissance unto modernity. Each reestablishes the ideal, according with the ideal's teleological exigencies and the factual situation. The ancient Greeks, for example, are still tied to the relativity

---

[2] Hua XXXIX, p. 339: "This pure interest in what really is and what it is – the theoretical in the very broadest sense – is still far from that interest in beings 'in themselves,' or that first in-itself is only a relative in-itself"; also see Hua VII, p. 290: "What is being? The identity of the real demands identical predicates, truths that state with eternal validity what beings are," which Husserl says in a 1925 manuscript regarding the ideal genesis of science.

[3] Husserl uses this phrase, for example, at Hua XXIX, p. 17.

[4] See Hua XLII, p. 442.

of their homeworld and its mythic imagery, despite the new call to universality. Later, in the renaissance and enlightenment, the ideal of the universality of reason becomes dogmatic, as they abstract from generativity in the overstatement of the individual's autonomy. There also came the imperialism and colonialism of the theoretical world, wherein, rather than extending an invitation to unity in a universal task for humanity, it deals in coercion, disregard, and destruction of the other's world for one's own familiar home. Amidst all this, in fact, the sciences themselves fragment from each other, not only losing the sense of their unity, but also losing the sense of science as guiding responsible action. A *crisis* appears—there emerges from the horizon a breakdown of ideals and values and so also a moment for decision. In response, the phenomenological philosopher takes up the demand for a rational humanity by turning inward, by critically *inquiring-back* into reason—*by renewing the transcendental and normative questions which move human beings in their world*.

Indeed, somewhat paradoxically, the stage of patent reason is also *problematic* or as Husserl puts it, "*questionable*."[5] In this respect, reason is a problem "internally" and "externally" to its own ideal. Internally, its demand to question everything disinterestedly nevertheless covers over the constitutive role of subjectivity *while* taking for granted the being of the world as the horizon of asking and answering questions. Externally, it fragments into many sciences, failing to account for its unity. As such, the *patency* of science may therefore be said to be *problematic*, since its demand to question everything disinterestedly nevertheless leaves the world as correlate to subjectivity unquestioned and unclarified.

From the problematic of science, the turn inward to the "how" of givenness appears in two stages of modernity. In the first stage, there emerges a rational method, represented especially by the personalities of Descartes and Kant.[6] These thinkers seek to answer the ancient transcendental question about the possiblity and actuality of cognition at all. Without an adequate answer in this first stage, the second stage of modernity emerges with the establishment of phenomenology. For phenomenology means to fulfill the scientific ideal by (1) inquiring into the "*how*" of givenness, within a phenomenological attitude that has its ideal of the principle of *presuppositionlessness*. Beginning with an analysis of (2) intentional acts and contents, it develops its *transcendental interest* and *inquiry* through an ἐποχή that suspends all positing of being and non-being. In phenomenology, (3) imitation and admiration are taken up

---

[5] See Hua VI, p. 1: "The crisis of a science means nothing less than its genuine scientific nature, that the whole way in which it set itself its task and developed its methodology for it, has become questionable."

[6] On the "first and second periods" of modernity, see Hua VI, pp. 273-276. Husserl says that the Greeks were a beginning stage (*Anfangsstadium*) and that his phenomenology is a renewed beginning (*erneute Anfang*). Descartes is, in a sense, the "*Urstifter*" of transcendental philosophy, which was renewed and reestablished by Kant. See Hua XXIX, p. 420: "So above all Descartes' original instantiation of the modern idea of philosophy (at the same time as a re-foundation of the ancient idea), pointing forward to the developments up to Kant. And Kant himself was the original founder of the new type of transcendental philosophy."

and transformed into a *methodological* invitation.[7] This invitation extends across generations, as each generation of phenomenologists reestablishes the effort to bring others into sharing the ideals and values. However, as phenomenology is not a ready-made enterprise, there is a development of its method and analyses through continued inquiry. Perhaps the most significant methodological development, in this respect, is from the "progressive-intuitive" and "regressive-inquisitive" procedures, the latter of which thematizes the norms of its own operation and, in so doing, explicitly takes content from the world and discovers its origins and roots. With this development, phenomenology makes methodologically clear how it does not proclaim its positions "from above," so to speak, but requests they be grasped from within by way of an inquiry-back into matters. The result of this is the emergence of a stage of (4) *interiority*, in which humanity appropriates themselves *as* rational and carries out their lives as rationally bound together.[8]

This threefold movement through history sketched in the above is tantamount to, as Husserl says, "reason coming to itself." Although he will, at times, call phenomenology "patent," since it *opens* the transcendental sphere of being, I prefer here his term "manifest reason" (*offenbarer Vernunft*).[9] At the stage of manifest reason, phenomenology reflects upon reason, appropriates its ideals in its own operation, and aims to guide action in the work through the appropriated rational ideal. Such an understanding and appropriation is not abstract from history but makes it understandable via an historical-teleological inquiring-back into its motivations. As such, phenomenology consciously and rationally builds upon generations of achievements as an "*Überrationalismus*." In sum, Husserl puts the process of phenomenological philosophy in the following way:

> Only in this way will we attain, not all at once, of course, but steadily and progressively, in the sense of a demand to be fulfilled and renewed step by step, the theoretical and then also the practical freedom, a completely insightful, that is, a truly philosophical science and a truly philosophical life: a life that is not merely regulated from without by a methodical but soullessly progressing science but is elucidated from within by the light of theoretical and practical insight."[10]

---

[7] Consider, for example, how Husserl describes the method of historical-teleological reflection: "...as an invitation to actually thorough exertion than as a claim of an executed performance," at Hua VII, pp. 205-206.

[8] See Hua VI, p. 258.

[9] See Hua VI, p. 13: "Humanity in general is essentially humanity in generatively and socially connected humanity, and if human being is a rational being (*animale rationale*), then he is so only insofar as his entire humanity is rational humanity – latently geared towards reason or openly geared towards reason that has come to itself, fair to itself and now in essential necessity consciously guiding human development." See also Hua XLII, pp. 246-247: "...but this becoming-patent [viz., of instinctual life-interests] is only relative, that what is already patent in a broader context prefigures something further and then makes it patents, while universal philosophy is everywhere, which in the highest form of the philosophical-phenomenological activity makes what is true in the last sense patent, the universe of relativity in its infinite formation of meaning?" For notes on transcendence as essential to subjectivity, see Hua XXXVII, pp. 89-91.

[10] Hua XXXII, p. 179.

Now, though the above gives an outline of a three-stage development of reason in history, Husserl is emphatic that the rational progression is not automatic, not without effort. As a matter of fact, there is development and disintegration, starts and restarts, continuity and crises. This occurs, in no small measure, wherever there is a breakdown of reason, a failure to allow reason to achieve that which it essentially strives to achieve. Indeed, the breakdown of reason includes the failure to ask questions and to answer objectively in order to carry out that answer reasonably and responsibly in the world. The appearance of the matter of facts of progress and decline means that there is also given to human beings a continual demand for further sense-reflection on themselves and the world. An explicit phenomenology of inquiry serves this sense-reflection by making methodological the operations by which it occurs and through which practical decisions are made. As a matter of fact, inquiry is essential to phenomenological philosophy.

What is more, though motivations are understandable in and by consciousness, generally speaking, there is also given a sphere of *mystery*. That is to say, there is not only the yet to be known—the understandable that is yet to be understood—but also the understandable that exceeds the grasp of the finite understanding. The discussion of the relation of these broaches the domain of *religion and theology*. In this respect, I have touched upon Husserl's sense of God as and understandable *entelechy* or as *a principle of development and movement*, which does not yet reach the issue of mystery and revelation in a *personal* sense. So, God as a teleological principle relates to the "methodically constructed 'Idea' of an increase of the human to the absolutely unlimited intelligence," as Husserl puts it to the Jesuit Erich Przywara.[11] To understand this principle, the phenomenologist can build from the bottom-up, as it were, moving from simpler to more complex matters: from perception and intelligence, to the subject and world, toward guiding Idea of reason, and, finally, the *Überidee* and *Überseienden* of God.[12] With this in mind, perhaps this is why he will also say: "Phenomenological philosophy as an infinite Idea is, of course, 'theology' (For me this means: real philosophy is *eo ipso* theology)."[13] Although the infinite Idea not known *per se*, it is, in some sense *understandable* as a principle. Now, at first blush, this may seem at odds with the fact that Husserl also says that his work tends to proceed as an "a-religious" path to religion and "a-theistic" path to God.[14] It makes more sense, however, upon introducing the old distinction between natural and revealed theology, which he puts thusly:

---

[11] See Appendix C.

[12] See Appendix D, below, "Husserl to Baudin, Attachment to letter from 26.6.1934."

[13] Briefwechsel, *Wissenschaftliche Korrespondenz*, p. 88; see appendix. Husserl also makes the following point in *Goettingenschule*, p. 429 to Mahnke 1921: "What you wrote in all that (also in your *Logosabhandlung*). is exactly familiar to me: these are exactly my ways! I have presented the synthesis of Fichte and of Plato's Eros theory < in > my Fichte lectures here (*Kriegsvorträge*), and they are thoughts that have moved me for decades. But I do not see in them at last. My philosophy of religion is still little developed, and I am still in the 'antechamber of truth.'".

[14] In reply to the gift of Fr. Erich Przywara's, *Analogia entis. Metaphysik*, Husserl, *Briefwechsel*, p. 237; see also Husserl, *Briefwechsel*, vol. IX, p. 124: "And for me, after all, philosophy is my a-religious path to religion, my a-theistic way to God, so to speak."

> The best of the scholastic coining the contrast between natural and supernatural light and say science is pure knowledge of the natural light. Theology is knowledge from the supernatural light and from the natural, as far as it agrees with the supernatural and has derived its rightful power from itself.[15]

Natural theology, so to speak, does not begin with the truths of revelation but proceeds to its positions only with the light of natural reason. Science may thus proceed step-wise until the principle of God appears in accord with the natural light of reason. If presuppositionless, it may begin a-religious, a-theistic, but, by natural light, come to the principle which is God. Husserl can also then mark the different, though related matter of knowledge that comes from the supernatural elevation of natural light. Here, in "supernatural revelation," there is a divine communication of mystery to natural reason which raises it up to the possibility of understanding the supernatural, in whatever aspect and measure the Divine Will deigns fitting. So, unlike the philosophical infinite Idea, which makes understandable the principle, such a revealed truth is given from that which infinitely exceeds but nevertheless touches human understanding.

Thusly, a "genuine religious" person, Husserl finds, understands and feels God in their lives.[16] Such a person communicates with God by living a prayerful life, in which their interior direction is to all as given in and through God's will.[17] As such, in what Husserl calls "manifest religion," the religious person explicitly lives "in constant, infinite striving towards God…"—a striving of the whole person, heart, soul, mind, and strength with others in the world.[18] Indeed, religion also has its history, its genetic and generative development, in which God appears as a *question* and an *answer*, that is, a call to which human beings *respond*. For the phenomenologist to get to a sense of this presence of God in religious experience and expression, it is necessary to reconstruct—and so "relive"—the experience of the religious person and persons. For that, it is necessary to inquire-back into the givenness of God in an individual's life, in the life of the community, into the development and generation of that life and that community. Of course, I have not undertaken such an inquiry-back into religious matters in this book.

So, the present study does not claim to be complete. In fact, it *cannot* be claimed to be complete, and for essential reasons: not only do more questions arise in the questionable world but mystery remains. Nevertheless, by taking Husserl as a guide and model, we shed some light on the origins of inquiry and the sense of phenomenological philosophy after him (Diagram 7.1).

---

[15] Hua XLII, p. 183.

[16] Hua XLII, p. 269: "The genuine religious is originally looking at the divine contexts that are falling into his sphere of life and in the wider circle of history, which he deeply understands from his life experience, and in his feeling, values, and willing to do so executing motivated statements."

[17] On the point, see Hua XLII, p. 269.

[18] See Hua XLII, pp. 225, 262, and 295, where Husserl speaks about ecclesial culture in "manifest religion" (*Offenbarungsreligion*).

7 Concluding Overview: From Latent to Patent unto Manifest Reason   195

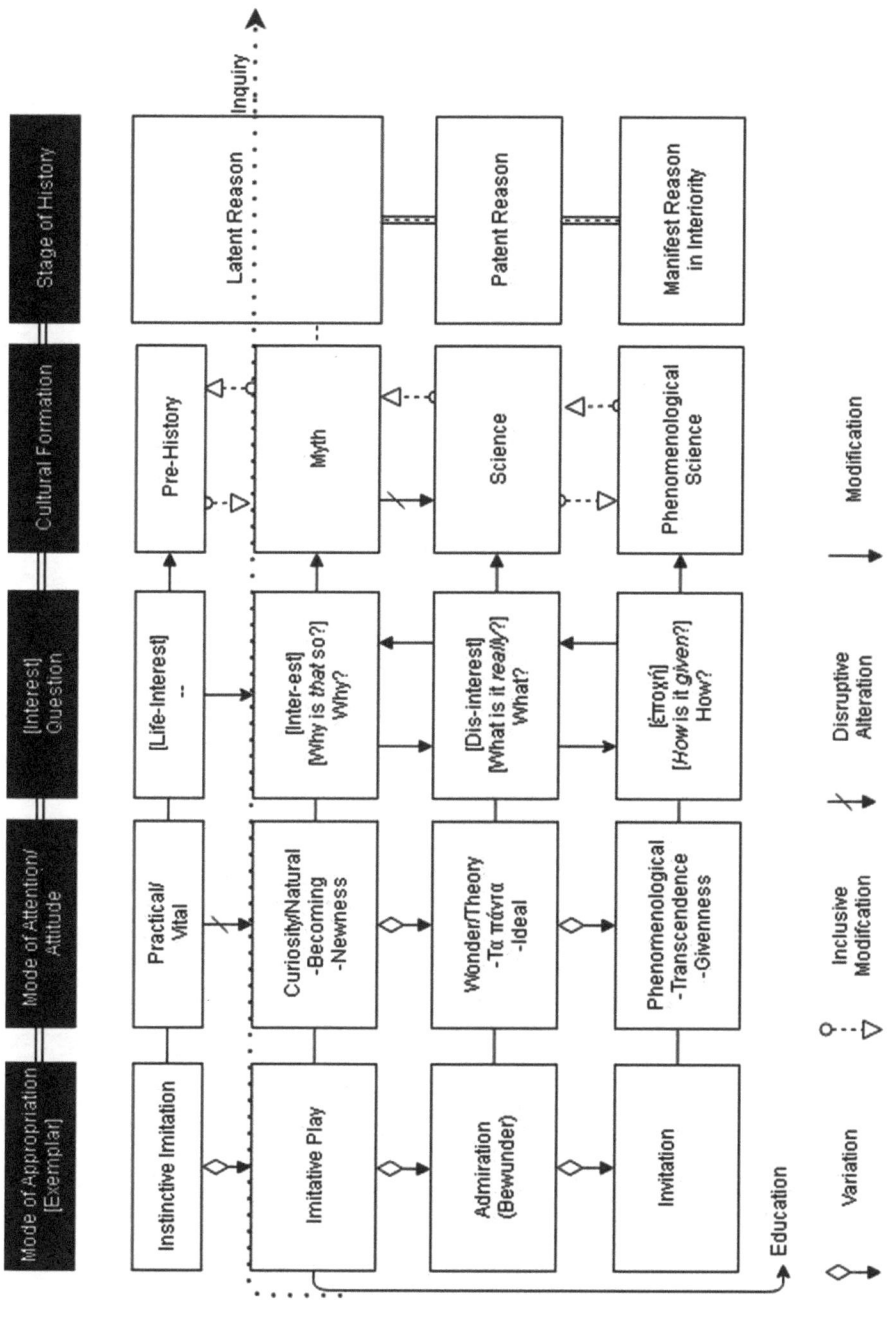

Diagram 7.1 The emergence and operation of inquiry in history

Appendices

The following appendices are a selection of letters from across Husserl's development. They were selected to elucidate some of the themes of this book. Some brief preparatory remarks to each are in order.

A. In this letter to Franz Brentano, Husserl illustrates his sense of indebtedness as well as his awareness of his departure from his teacher, relating it, in a sense, to a sort of critical *daimon* that forces him to ask ever-more further questions. This is thus also an expression of how generations of thinkers relate, namely, through a cultivation of a shared inquiring spirit. In this cultivation, indeed, Husserl expresses the joy and peace in a "like-striving" person—a friend—who encourages him to go further as he does the same in return.

B. In this letter to a colleague, George Pfeilschifter, Husserl expresses concern about the way in which philosophy is sometimes presented in relation to national concerns. Husserl reiterates the need for a method that gives a rational check—a *Hegimonikon*, he says—to the people of the nation, without reducing it to a sort of nationalism that is not philosophical. His attempt to balance his sense of a people, a nation, and the universality of science is at work here, giving a clue to the sentiment he thinks needs to be built up through philosophy.

C. In this letter to Fr. Erich Przywara, S.J., Husserl speaks to how his phenomenology relates to theology. In it, he calls his own way atheological, but also suggests that it will help theologians "someday." He gives an important clue to this help in his resistance to equating the methodologically constructed Idea of God with a genuinely phenomenological and phersonal sense of God. This expands the range of inquiry, relating, however implicitly, the philosophical, theological, and religious.

D. In this letter to Émile Baudin, Husserl gives an indication as to how he is feeling amidst the advance of the Third Reich. He emphasizes the importance of understanding the teleological sense of human being in the world in relation to a mysterious God. From this, we are given another glimpse of Husserlian speculation about what a phenomenological theology would entail, as he thinks about it in relation to the scholastic transcendentals, as well as a Platonically inspired reflection on a "beyond being," in order to try to give voice to an absolutely Transcendent Being.

E. In this letter to the longtime family friend, Gustav Albrecht, Husserl reiterates the need for phenomenological sense-reflection. He speaks of "his" Eugen Fink, expressing, not so much selfish possession, as the intertwining of generations. This letter also gives a short review of the development of philosophy through generations, and how Husserl sees the "questionability" of the sciences emerging in relation to the inquiring-back of phenomenological philosophy. On his own account, he is "overwhelmed by universal philosophical questions that are of great importance" to him.

F. In this letter to the younger colleague, Karl Löwith, which was written a little more than a year before Husserl's death, shows the elder's tentative hope for the younger generations in the wake of disappointment in his older "pupils." Setting aside whether it is fair to call Scheler and Heidegger pupils, let me underscore Husserl's insistence on bracketing one's own anthropological presuppositions to become aware of it through a sense-reflection on the self, a *Selbstbesinnung*. This follows well the notes from the letter of the previous appendix, as it shows at least one side of the method to be worked out in the *Crisis* writings.

Appendix A

Husserl to Brentano, 10.11/15.1904[1]

My most esteemed teacher!

A letter from your hand—what a great and unexpected joy! From my heart, it makes me happy to hear that you still remember me, and in such great kindness. I myself have not forgotten and will never forget how much I am indebted to you: how deeply you have influenced my philosophical development through your lectures and writings, and how many hours of noblest elevation you have granted me through personal contact. Now, of course, things have turned out differently than I thought possible at the time. I began as a young man [*Jünger*] of your philosophy (as far as you had developed it at that time) and when I had matured to independence, I could not remain with it. That was not easy for me. By nature, no need is more pronounced in me than to adore, to join in love those whom I adore and to stand up for them with zeal. But as ambivalent as my nature unfortunately is, there also lives in me an irrepressible critical sense [*unbändiger kritscher Sinn*], which, unconcerned about the inclinations of my heart [*Gemüts*], coolly dissects and ruthlessly discards what appears to it to be untenable. Bound in mind, free in intellect, so I go my way, not very happy. Always inclined to acknowledge the superiority of others in advance and to let myself be guided upward by them, I find myself compelled again and again to separate from them and to seek my own ways. Instead of continuing to build on the

---

[1] Hua, *Briefwechsel*, Band I, pp. 20–22.

foundations laid by others, as I would so much like to do, I have to work out new foundations, despairing of their solidity: a laborious, grueling work that also sticks to the ground. How I would like to live in the heights. That is where everything is going. But will I ever work my way up, just a little, so that I can gain just a bit of a clear view? I am now 45 years old and still a poor beginner. For what shall I hope? In a genius, who, in one throw, succeeds in what I long for, in whose solid spiritual structure I can settle down: climbing up to the battlements, at whose feet the world of knowledge lies clearly laid out? Or to my age and my work, which would bring me myself, if not so far, yet far enough, [21] that I could look a little way into the land of promise?—As ever, I work, and often with desperate persistence, as if to pay off something of the infinite guilt of my dullness, obscurity, and ignorance.—Useless, I think, my works are not. In the main, they are a continuation of your suggestions. How deeply I recalled your thoughts, how strongly they affected me. But they did not remain what they were, they were like living germs in me, developing following their own nature, as they had to develop on this soil: whatever I might do for or against it. But I plowed through the soil honestly, as it was my duty to do.

And the fruits? It has not exactly become so much that I could make a state with it. But, as with all honest work, it bore some fruit. Of course, it grew in straw. The straw will be threshed out for me and I myself am eager to help with it. I cannot boast of any particular success. For the older generation my investigations are inconvenient [*unbequem*], my ways too laborious. Since they are not followed, they do not see where they are going, they do not see that they aim at real and fundamental problems. Strangely, though, the young generation feels drawn to it and places its hopes on the seriousness of these efforts. They do not know (only my personal students know) that the impulses came from you. I myself think, however, how much work and perhaps also wrong ways I would have been spared if you had continued your publications!

It gives me great pleasure that you do not feel hurt by the independence with which I have continued. I am sure in advance that a great part of what I wrote is erroneous; but equally sure that they were errors that once had to be tried, had to be dared. We will not gain certain truth in the fundaments, without having seriously thought through all possibilities. But only he who believes in a possibility thinks it through seriously. In any case, my endeavor is to do solid work, and the many years of pauses between my publications, where I often work beyond my strength, show how difficult it is for me to do this. I am progressing desperately slowly. [22] May the results of your many years of research, which have certainly led you far in silence, soon come to light and help me, as well as all like-striving people! Do not believe that you forget, and even less that your effects are slight. It does not matter what you say about it or how often you speak about it in public. The facts are obvious to those who want to see them. Now that the personal antagonisms have softened, these great impulses are recognized as *Facta*, even by those who otherwise do not belong to your friends (for example, recently Windelband, *Die Philos<ophie> im Beginn d<es> XX. Jahrh<underts>*.) That the authors of the day are mentioned more is understandable. This does not exclude the possibility that their busy talk may have faded away without effect in the next generation. Their writings, according to the time, already lie quite far back, but are still very much alive and effective. What one argues against, one depends on. Certainly, also new of your writings would be strongly disputed and therefore still have a strong effect.

It would be an extraordinary pleasure for me if I could see you once again. After your extremely kind lines, I would think that a visit would not be unwelcome to you. Unfortunately, the new semester is beginning, and I must see how the next year will bring opportunities.

I greet you from the bottom of my heart and assure you once again of my unchangeable gratitude and adoration.

E. Husserl

Appendix B

Edmund Husserl to Georg Pfeilschifter, 1.10.1925
Freiburg i. B.[2]

Highly honored colleague!

I appreciate the great confidence and honor that the preparatory committee for founding a German Academy has shown me by including my name in the first list of proposed Senators. The idea of a national academy has moved me deeply. I am convinced that it is the greatest national *desideratum* at a time when the effect of the historic mission entrusted to the Germans in the world seems so threatened.

On the other hand, several phrases in the "Introduction to the Plan" fill me with serious reservations. They sound as if the German Academy should serve a national propaganda of that not exemplary kind that the French master. Can salvation for our German nation in its present distress, which is truly and above all also spiritual distress, lie in treating our ideal cultural goods like articles of industry and export, staging a kind of commercial propaganda for them? The plan of the German Academy, which Leopold von Ranke has designed and which men of your sentiment [*Gesinnung*] endeavor to put into motion, must certainly have been remote from thoughts of such nationalistic utility. For him, the idea of a national academy must have had a purely ideal meaning, in analogy with religious propaganda, as they understand the churches as an inner and outer mission. On the other hand, we live in a time in which an ingenuine nationalism (as in all nations, so, too, ours) has led us astray from that high national idealism, which belongs just to the most beautiful heritage of German philosophy.

The question now is whether the nationalistic tint, evident in the preparatory declaration, is intended to express the essence of the German Academy, or if there is a serious prospect of incorporating the purely ideal sense and bringing it to an

---

[2] Husserl, *Briefwechsel, Band VII*, 13–16. From German editors: "The German nationalist church historian Georg Pfeilschifter (1870–1936), from 1903 in Freiburg, from 1917 in Munich, initiated from there the "Academy for Scientific Research and for the Cultivation of Germanness - German Academy," which opened on May 5, 1925 (in the presence of Husserl)."

exclusively effective power through which it alone can become the blessing of the German nation newly building itself and its world mission.

What is the *unum necessarium* for our critically tested German people at this time? What kind of spiritual organ must it create as its supreme *Hegimonikon*—its German Academy?

I would think that the following guiding thoughts would come into consideration here:

1. Caught up in the process of externalization that engulfed European spiritual development at the end of the nineteenth century, and finally by the mental attrition of the war, our people [*Volk*] have forfeited the great powers of their national tradition. What was previously in mind and was practically determinative as an inherited sentiment, and which the national life of all cultural regions had given the spirit of genuineness, of selfless devotion to supra-personal ideals and the impetus of a great becoming from a great will, lost its power. Growing circles of German comrades [*deutschen Volkgenossen*], including those who are educated, are now cut off from their national history: they no longer understand anything of the greatness that has brought about national development, nothing of the historical mission, which has grown from above in the nation's historical becoming.

Here lies the first basic task of a German Academy: It should be the central organ of self-reflection and self-renewal [*Selbstbesinnung und Selbsterneuerung*] from which the nation creates itself, clarifying the original and developmentally proceeding ideal sense that has prevailed in all national cultural areas. In this newly clarified form, it should arouse new enthusiasm for the enhancement of German character [*Volkstums*], from forces of its own historical determination [*Bestimmung*] and already gained cultural achievements.

While the scientific academies treat universal and German history purely theoretically, the German Academy would have the practical task of careful advancement, living development, and internal propaganda of the vocational ideals and cultural values of every kind of those who have grown up in national life. It would have to provide for a new understanding of its meaning, for the enlightenment of its genuine value out of temporality into eternity, with a view to the reawakening of a high-minded and lofty national life. First of all, this practical goal of a *national renaissance*, an ideal self-renewal and self-enhancement of the nation would come from its own historical sources.

The mediation of the newly clarified cultural values to all politically separated and now threatened by spiritual constriction parts of the German people, which, as living, functioning members of the same, can never be abandoned, belongs as an important special region of work to this internal cultural care and cultural propaganda.

2. Germany, like any truly called nation, has a divine mission, not only for itself, but within the great context of the various nations. The highest and purest of Germany, as well as every nation, has at the same time supra-national significance; it is determined to exert ideal effects in other nations as well, and to

increase spiritually the values that have arisen in these nations. This kind of effect, which stems from the world mission of genuine national achievement and which counts on corresponding repercussions, is the sole hope of grounding a community of people rooted in mutual respect and a world culture that goes through all national cultures and links them all internally.

Here, too, economic culture, with the whole periphery of its peculiar genuine use-values, has its place. At the same time, their international exchange exercises the essential function of creating the indispensable material prerequisites for a healthy national life in general. Thus, the promotion of industry and world trade of our nation is one of the legitimate tasks of an academy supported by national idealism. From an ideal point of view, the economic aspect has its proper place in the framework of the national achievements to be promoted, in which the German nation fulfills its collective vocation for itself and for the world.

It is self-evident that an ideal sensed internal and external propaganda does not exclude struggle and under certain circumstances demands it: namely, as a defense against alien distortion and possibly conscious defamation of German essence and German spiritual achievement.

If I may hope that the German Academy, which is in the process of being founded, strives for the renewal and strengthening of German "national consciousness" in such a sense, as the consciousness of a responsible national-ethical mission, then I will gladly be its member.

But I would not be able to do it, if I had to fear that the genuine German spirit was being determined by an actually alien spirit of a nationalism directed towards outward enforcement and domination.

Forgive me, honorable colleague, for the length of this debate, which I consider necessary because it is a great and sacred thing to me. I may add the request to send me some explanatory lines. I cannot really think that we do not share principally the same sense.

E. H.

Appendix C

Letter from Edmund Husserl to Fr. Erich Przywara, SJ, 7.15.1932[3]

Reverend and honored Father Przywara!

Thank you very much for kindly sending me the first volume of your *Metaphysics*.[4]

I took it up, honestly confessed, with sinful envy and flew through it in a first survey—namely, that it is already granted to you to bring your many years of thought work to a systematic conclusion. This envy, however, does not prevent me from heartily congratulating you, as is natural in view of my old personal interest in the

---

[3] Husserl, *Briefwechsel*, Band IX, 237.

[4] In reply to Przywara's give of his book, *Analogia entis. Metaphysik*, 1: *Prinzip*, Muenchen 1930.

high-minded seriousness of your philosophical endeavors and my scientific interest in the parallelism of your theological and my atheological philosophizing. I myself am still on the way, but thank God with productive power and at the moment with the last clearing up of the sequence of the temporalities, in which the sequence of the being-for-us systematically and seen from the inside presents itself. You know that I am sure to come to the "teleological" conclusion on this transcendental-constitutive way (the expression is unfortunately dangerous) in the end; likewise also that I live in the firm conviction that my phenomenological method does enough to all genuine evidence problems, but also that it comes to a final illumination of the sense-content and the scope of these evidences by reflective clarification of the constitutive performances reflected in them. This is also true for religious evidence.

This will help the theologians one day, though it will seem at first that this will result in dire heresies. To fix me to the theism of the school tradition—in the usual interpretations of its sense—I reject decidedly. Of course, this is said against Keilbach and those "proofs of God" supposedly hoped for by me (according to alleged statements of conversation).[5] Obviously also the methodically constructed "Idea" of an increase of the human to the absolutely unlimited intelligence is not meant as an anticipation of the real phenomenological sense of "God," but only as a methodical Idea.

That you are immune to such primitivities has not only become certain to me from your work. Admittedly, by its theological-philosophical processing of the new phenomenological motifs, it will cause discomfort to those who find it more convenient to modify the traditional formulas instead of being open, like the great creators of tradition, as self-thinkers for everything self-thought of their time. Now still my sincere wishes for the satisfactory success of the new volume and for a beneficial effect of the whole work.

E. H.

Appendix D

Letters from Edmund Husserl to Émile Baudin
6.23.1934

Freiburg i. B.
Esteemed and dear Colleague!

Dr. Fink has informed me of your letter, implicitly also addressed to me, and I hasten to tell you that we have correctly received your dear, exceedingly kind letter of 8.5.33.[6] We do not doubt that we answered it then and thanked you sincerely

---

[5] Wilhelm Keilbach received his doctorate from the Gregoriana in Rome in 1935 for, *Die philosophische Problematik der Religionen. Eine religionsphilosophische Studie mit besonderer Berücksichtigung der neuen Religionspsychologie.*

[6] German editor's note: "Husserl had met the theologian Abbe Baudin in Strasbourg in March 1929. when he was on his way back from Paris to stay with Jean Hering."

for all that you, as a noble pastor and friend, expressed in heart-warming words. This letter remained unforgotten, every memory of it awakens anew the gratitude and the wish to be together with you again and to be allowed to build us up in your pure humanity. But that has its difficulties now—more for us than for you. The fact that we have no specific recollection of our answer by letter last year has its easily understandable reasons. It was, after all, the time of the first rush of the most exciting events, which had to affect us and the families of our children in ever new forms. The great rearrangement [*Umschichtung*] of the old ideas of state and people that had previously determined the meaning of "Germany"; the legal delimitation of the new concept of the German nation, defined by "blood and race," the exclusion of foreign races from all state functions, including all cultural functions—this has nationally excluded me and mine. (We do have the benefit of certain legal exceptions for the transitional period.) Facts must be accepted. This is not easy in the case of facts that so fatefully affect the whole life of the soul, right into the center of personal existence. But what God does is well done,[7] and we were given the strength to overcome interiorily, that is, to withstand. Since the end of 1932, the consumption of strength has, of course, severely hampered the extremely happy progress of my philosophical productivity in the years since my retirement (1928). I have made use of every good hour—but it is a constant struggle for the "good" hours. The role of the completely "detached spectator" is—for us, at present—all too difficult to pause. The Third Reich is still under construction and so it happens that personally attacking events break into the acquired calm attitude (and especially into the *tranquillitas animi* necessary for philosophical productivity) again and again. Nevertheless, these 1 1/2 years were not lost, they have even given the philosopher thematically great suggestions, which hopefully can still have an effect at his old age.

Whether I am *sub specie aeterni* "German," whether my philosophy can and should be called "German," that I see as a theological question, which may remain open for whoever; in itself it is decided. The only thing is, for me at least the only thing, whether I have been and still am faithful to the task—the one entrusted to me undoubtedly from above. This heaviest fate: to have to take over such a burden on such weak shoulders and to carry it as one progressing forth—this hard grace—will not let me anymore. What other bad fates may oppress me in the environing world (me through mine)[8]—I will and we will already deal with that. In sentiment, the children do not lack spirit and bravery. Nor do we lack noble friends with whom one can meet in the values of eternity. What else one has gained in human experience, how not a few old "pupils" and "friends" look now, and so on—it is a good school, and it is not too late to learn, to get rid of some hidden vanities and to laugh at oneself, even in the third decade of life.—A *most astonishing spectacle*, this hard reality of never imagined, unheard-of cruel possibilities—where one as a phenomenologist is so firm in the belief in the absolute teleology encompassing all being of every kind, of every

---

[7] German editor's note: "this is a refrain from evangelical chorals by Samuel Rodigast."

[8] German editor's note: "Husserl's son Gerhart had been "on leave" from his Kiel professorship in April 1933 and then transferred to Göttingen in December of that year and to Frankfurt in April 1934, without being able to take up either of these posts."

sense. Even if the problem and the sense of this teleology may have radically changed for the phenomenologist, it still embraces (and in infinitely superior evidence) the naively given universe, as universe of spatio-temporal realities, with all its relativities and antinomies and together with all skepticisms insurmountable in naivety.

So. in the absolute certainty of this teleology, which passes through my absolute being and which passes through "us all, as through everything intentionally implied in me and my "we all," I say to myself in the attitude of the phenomenologically contemplative spectator: what a spectacle! So now the first next to me: Heidegger! What a phenomenon in the German historical present: the shining of this inspiring comet, spellbinding the pining souls of the young generation—then the fast transformation of his originally quite unpolitical "phenomenology" (a very "contemporary" ontology of irrationalism) into a "political" phenomenology following the fast change of the spirit of the time. Moreover, the philosopher himself becomes the academic leader [*Führer*], the *rector magnificus* of the completely reorganized university! And recently: his resignation from this leading position.–[9]

But now I myself have become the curious "phenomenon": I—honored as *Erzvater* of *this* new phenomenology (and similar phenomenologies otherwise)—really: I!!,
—---

I had to break off, in the middle of the sentence, and, in the continuation, the disturbances did not cease and spoiled the well-meant into badly-said.

Now I am sending fragments, you will find this barbaric-German, beginning and end. The long middle piece—a piece of nearly a whole treatise—must be copied from the shorthand by Dr. Fink and sent to you, if I can immodestly count on you attaching value to my roughly presented thoughts.

So, for the time being this as a greeting of adoration!

E.H.

> From me the very warmest greetings!
> If only you could come with Monsieur Herring!
> Your faithful friend,
> Malvine H.

–

(Conclusion)

You remark, dear Abbé Baudin, how much transc <endental> phenomenology in its mature development could mean to me personally as a *consolatio philosophica*. Your word about the "*philosophical Sahara*" and the "*naked*" self cannot do enough to the actual sense of this philosophy. No ordinary "realist" has ever been so realistic and so concrete as I, the phenomenological "idealist" (a word which, by the way, I no longer use). The method of the phenomenological epoché and reduction presupposes the existence of the world, exactly as what it was and is valid for us in each case, and we reflecting in this method—in each case I, the reflecting—are in the fully concrete

---

[9] German editor's note that Heidegger was the rector of the University of Freiburg from April 1933 to the 27th of April 1934.

world-hood [*Welthabe*]. But this concretion we take incomparably more seriously than those who talk about the real world, but unfortunately quite abstractly about it and reality and existence. That world is constantly for us, and ultimately for me, the one that is valid for me with respective content or sense and is only as that for me—in the streaming change of subjective modes, in the individual constantly in abeyance of the modes of validity "being" and "appearance"—just that the phenomenologist takes in all his seriousness and does not let go, instead of being deceived by traditional speeches and dialectical word argumentations. An infinity of never asked questions, an exuberant infinity of experiences of a never seen dimension, comes into view with the phen<omenological> reflection in the attitude of the epoch and demands a new kind of theorizing. In a new way, the world is a constant theme, precisely as the unity of validity that constantly gives itself in the streaming life of the "ego," that shows itself in the streaming of the subjective modes of the and the contents of validity, in the and the "vague horizons," and so on.—Precisely in this concretion and intentional correlation: what is supposed, experienced, so and so valid in being valid, conscious in consciousness. Thus, phenomenology with its novel questions also encompasses everything that is naively and badly valid in the naivety of pre-scientific and scientific life, all the anonymous self-evident things that make up <the> "natural attitude." But in these all real "riddles of the world" are decided. Completely hidden in the natural attitude, they can never become maturely developed problems, the true philosophical problems, never gain conceptual form, which can have a theoretical effect in philosophical work. But now let this monstrosity of a letter really be concluded. The fact that I let myself go like this, let myself drift, may be a sign for the deep sympathy, for the veneration that I have for you. Otherwise, I am by no means an eager letter writer. Hoping to see you again, and here in Kappel.
Your warmly devoted
E. Husserl

* You will be well taken care of here! Here it is unspeakably quiet, peaceful, beautiful. It is also nicer to speak personally, from friend to friend (and "Pastor"!), in the nonchalance, but also more effective power of personal expression, instead of by letter, bound by the conventions of literary form. My wife, as well as I myself, would be heartily pleased with you and the old friend J <ean> Hering.

Husserl to Baudin, Attachment to letter from 26.6.1934

For European humanity is this actually the correct thing to do: to throw away science as an autonomous theory and science as the norm of practical autonomy, motivated by the fact that its blessing has finally also had an unpleasant effect on human existence, almost as a curse? Yet, transcendental phenomenology has the insight that it is transcendental naivety that is to blame for the unblessed historical development, and that this was but a necessary consequence of autonomy as long as naivete could not be understood and broken. This means understanding and at the same time recognizing that "decline" [*Niedergang*] or rather the bankruptcy of European culture as a culture from Greek autonomous science (universally speaking, out of "philosophy") was a teleological necessity, in order to procure for humanity *genuine* autonomy from a reform, in order to gain an absolute science, a science that overcomes all naivete, stands on absolute ground, and is of the very nature of the Absolute; that does not allow any objections and counter-arguments of science and metaphysics. Transcendental phenomenology sees itself as the necessary path of a completely transparent understanding of the self and the world, and thus as the absolutely transparent, absolutely "presuppositionless" method that ultimately proceeds in apodictic evidence, precisely this understanding systematically and concretely for the philosopher and the philosophical community (s the subjectivity of absolute sense-reflection) in a process proceeding infinitely. In her radicalism of universality, in which she is studying "world" (including all natural-naive positivity in science and every other way of norming life), she also believes in universal teleology to be assured in absolute transcendental life and give the utmost sense and ultimate legitimacy, understanding-limiting, but also legitimating to all naive worldliness and its norms directedness. Naivete is overcome, but naivete becomes also legitimated, once it is, in all its genuine evidence, overcome in the sense that its hidden "relativity" reveals its horizon of self-understanding and is grasped in its function in the totality of the constant and necessary development against a universal concordance of all relative evidences. This applies to the positive sciences, and also to religion, which, in naive religious life, where it, as in the real commandment, has the form of original evidence, always carries with it its unassailable legitimacy—even though in a sense otherwise than science. Human life runs in contradiction, in constant conflict of the evidence. It is necessary, insofar as everyone cannot leave his evidence in the self-evident nature of his situation (individual and historical), in the sense of his own apprehension, and in the misunderstanding of what others experience as their situation and in naive validity that cannot be applied to alien evidence. It is only when the totality of the transcendental life, in which all norms, all constitution, all constitution of values at all levels is carried out becomes thematic, and the universal structure of its achievements as such in a substantial relativity (and the already norm directed concordant truths from sources of evidence) become understandable, and then in the only and necessary method of transcendental research can the absolute sense of the world, including human existence, and the universe of beings, in the last and only thinkable sense can be understood absolutely.

Just then, however, the absolute teleology is understood, which is the correlate of the inseparable unity of all finite beings as merely dependent moments in the "infinite" unity of a sense out of a giving of sense that is movable into infinity, and again this teleology is understood in its relation to the absolute subjectivity as the infinite way to develop to its true being—or as the infinite achievement of the constitution of a world as nature and as the cultural world of human personal communities in ascending order, which belongs to subjectivity in its absolute and final sense, into the infinitely increasing relative concordance and truth, to which an absolute supreme Idea corresponds as ultimately sense-giving total principle for truth, for being, the first is the being of the absolute subjects and of the totality of the subjects, of the subjects that are connected with each other as a unified absolute subjectivity. The world that is uniformly valid in the infinitely flowing change of validity and which proves itself in relativity by experiencing—thinking—valuing, the world, which is necessarily as a unity of validity and probation increasing into infinity, unity in the change of world appearance; the transcendental all-subjectivity which flows into the infinite, the infinite stream of the communicated constitution of the world, and, in so doing, the infinite constitutional unification of the proving relative evidences, corresponds as an absolute ideal pole-Idea to that of an absolute in a new supra-worldly, supra-human, supra-transcendental-subjective sense: it is the *absolute Logos* that absolute truth in the full and whole sense, as the *unum, verum, bonum*, to which all finite being is directed in the unity of all and every finite being, to which lives all transcendental-subjective life as living being, constituting the truth, which every transcendental ego and each transcendental we carries in its transcendental personality as an ideal absolute norm for all its relative norms, and therewith carries in itself an ideal of its true being, to which it is applied in its factual-personal being. But this ideal is only a ray of the absolute Ideal, the Idea of an All-Personality that is infinitely superior to the factual and all becoming and development of the factual towards the ideal, lying above it as infinitely distant pole-idea of an absolutely perfect transcendental generality. This infinitely high Idea is, at the same time, the Idea of a life passing through all finiteities and factualities, which through all factual life is infinitely the ideal realization of absolutely perfect life, and is normalized as a life of absolute universality from an absolutely ideal possibility Nothing else is a unity in the totality of the absolute norms that constitute the absolute *Logos*, even possible to be explained in absolute life.

This unity of *ideas*, the highest and last, is to be seen from an evidence which implicates but also relativizes all other evidence, is an "ideal," but it obviously has an supra-reality, a supra-truth, a supra-actualitity, an supra-in-itsef [*eine Überrealität, eine Überwahrheit, eine Überwirklichkeit, ein Überansich*], which gives all relative, finite, wordly, and even transcendental-monadic being in general true sense in the first place.

Thus Plato already spoke of the Idea of the good in the form of a beyond-being [*Überseienden*], as above all in a high, and even ideal truth, but a supreme Idea which yet lies in finitude away from its equals, being a supreme idea, a supra-idea, of beyond being [*Überidee, dem Überseienden*], without which no being would be thinkable. In naivete, one has in being-certainty "the" universe, as the universe of beings, and can be and, in fact, has become of the opinion that there may be many, infinitely many possible worlds.

There are infinitely many possible worlds as descriptive variations of the respective one valid for us. But this is necessary into infinity for us and every thinkable subjectivity "appearance," and the possible worlds conceived alterations of these phenomena. In the end, however, it becomes clear that only a single, the actual world is conceivable as a world of truth—just as a *Logos* of truth is conceivable, only a God, which is an Idea, which carries an ontological uniqueness, an essence that is not eidos, but rather as an essence in absolute truth, as an essence in no relativity of situations, in no horizon, but as a true being in absolute truth in itself carrying the unique essence in absolute necessity and is reality—reality in the sense of the grounding enabling supra-reality that allows all the realities of each relative, every finite, to bear sense.

Appendix E

Husserl to Gustav Albrecht, 11.26.1934
Freiburg i. Br.[10]

Dearest friend:

Your dear letters brought us a powerful surprise. Gusti, who we cannot quite yet picture as an adult man, has entered into holy wedlock, and his bride, who has been chosen from the heart by him and all of you, is beautiful and good. What a joy. We share in his and your happiness and send our warmest congratulations. I am also delighted—and most of all—that Gusti has come into an official position, for which I did not yet dare to hope. Now, this constant care is taken from you. We are greatly embarrassed about how we should contribute to the young marriage, given this horrible hermetic sealing-off of Germany from Austria. It is difficult to think of things that, if allowed for import at all, would make custom costs. Even a money transfer has the difficulty of a bad foreign exchange for us. Only 10 m per person, which gives us a maximum of 20 M. We will send that today. In a few weeks (during the Christmas holidays), two people from Vienna (Drs. Rotter and Lassner) will come here for philosophical support. Maybe it's possible then to make a legitimate barter and give Gusti a supplement. In any case, we celebrate in the heart. We are very sorry that we cannot get to know him and his bride. A honeymoon here is probably unthinkable now. But could he give himself a holiday next year for technical purposes, to broaden his professional horizons: the Black Forest is the largest and most beautiful forest area in Germany. Freiburg lies very close to the *high* Black Forest. Here he could walk with his young wife to his heart's content and conduct studies.

Regarding your philosophical objection to my "letter," my "pessimistic" appraisal of contemporary philosophy is, unfortunately, only too well founded. Philosophy that *is* has the highest possible function for mankind. But contemporary philosophy, and not just the German, *is* not. Philosophy in its original sense, which continued until the second half of the nineteenth century, wanted to be theoretical science of the world. The world which in itself is, what it is, recognizable in systems of theoretical truth, which, as "scientific," are justified into the last—last grounds, that is, not prior convictions [*Vorüberzeugungen*] of tradition, not religious beliefs, and so on. The scientist, ideally speaking, permits neither presupposition nor naive self-evident inconspicuous yet effective conviction which he did not expressly make and recognize as apodictically valid. The novel goal of an autonomous knowledge of reason occurs in antiquity as philosophy: the conviction that the sensible [*sinnliche*] and constant traditional and mythically woven [*übersponnene*] world of everyday life ($\delta\acute{o}\xi\alpha$) is only a subjective-relative phenomenon in itself; through ($\dot{\epsilon}\pi\iota\sigma\tau\acute{\eta}\mu\eta$), that is, the attitude of the prejudice-free and of the will to the ultimate grounding in a world recognizable in itself, carried in itself. The theoretical autonomy of the human as rational which sets itself on itself and accepts nothing that is not ultimately

---

[10] *Briefwechsel. Familienbriefe*, 106–111.

grounded—that is the foundation of practical autonomy. There leads to ever-new attempts at philosophy or universal science, in which all special branches are; ever-new philosophies that never simply succeed but only continued to expand, or, better, never lead to a growing, really scientific philosophy. In a certain way, of course, the latter builds on the earlier; each refers back to the predecessor, criticizing, yet learning from them. Through the millennia, there is a continuous existence, though a transformation which preserves the core concepts, problems, methods—up to our own time. In each and every word of the generally philosophical language, there is a preserved validity. So, it was understandably the fundamental conviction of the philosophy, uninterrupted through the millennia, laying in its *Telos*, in its end-Idea [*Zweckidee*] of universal knowledge—knowledge "the" world "in itself," *idealiter* in ultimately valid theories, in an ideal system of truth, intelligible for everyone in the identical rational methodology. In the positive sciences of nature this ideal seemed undoubtedly to prove itself, though it is well-known that our physics is no longer that of Newton, and each century has its modified theories. Understandably, with the extension of the sphere of experience, they were always perfect approximations to the *physis* "in itself," or to the absolute, in itself true, ultimate physics lying at infinity. This conviction gave the Age of Enlightenment—the 17th, 18th and partly still the nineteenth century—the great momentum, the belief in progress: the belief in the vocation of the sciences (*universitas* of the same, so philosophy in the full sense), in the possibility and the necessity to make the entire human existence new and purely rational in the sense of autonomous reason; to rule over the environmental nature, as well as over human life in all its political and cultural activities in the sense of absolutely rational norms. But this belief has been lost to skepticism, especially since the war of the new generation. Rationalism has almost become a curse-word [*Schimpfwort*]. Science applies to a kind of mental technique [*geistiger Technik*] with which one can create ordinary machine technology and achieve a great deal in everyday environmental practice, but nothing less than what supposedly ought to be accomplished: recognition of truth in itself, creation [*Schöpfung*] of an autonomous and in autonomy itself increasing and satisfying humanity. The general mode is the historicist skepticism. Those of each epoch have an outlook on life, their destinies, attachments, moods, and so on, their way in the "world," of judging evidence, of norms, as is necessary. Philosophy only lays out what man implicates, what humanity actually appreciates and wants at a time, and what it is aiming for in it. Of course, this is different for the modern European people than for the ancient Egyptians or for the Chinese or the ancient Indians, and so on. We have our European logic, the primitives have their own logic, and so on. There is no mutual criticism, no common ground of validity, a truth in itself or a world being in itself, ethical-practical: unconditional, absolutely valid norms—that is a chimera. I do not want to say there is not a kernel of truth in this and in every form of skepticism accompanying the development of philosophy. But in our day, the skeptical negativism regarding the end-Idea of philosophy may have become a great and almost universal ruling current. In particular, I cannot accept your reference to the glorious history of natural science as mathematics in every sense. The accusation of the gradual transformation of knowledge really directed towards beings in themselves into a theoretical technique is rightly justified. Nowhere is one less experienced, which in the last, absolute sense is nature than in exact natural science. And it is not the case that one can accept mathematics, physics, and so on, as knowledge, and then insert a few supplementary and clarifying considerations under the title Philosophy, theory of Natural Knowledge, and so on, regarding the basic concepts that have become so questionable through paradoxes. The positive sciences are no less questionable than what, under the title "Philosophy", has in the last centuries stayed around as special disciplines (theory of knowledge, critique of practical reason, aesthetics, ethics, and so on).

In a certain manner, it is true that the entire development of science (philosophy with positive science) from Thales or Plato to the present has led to a kind of bankruptcy, to the need to stop all payments. Perhaps there are enormous *Activa* existing, but the method of doing business was false, so that the meaning and value of the change has become quite questionable. So, how to liquidate? Above all, the answer in which the end-Idea of philosophy as universal science of the "world" has been introduced into historicity and remained in continuity has an end: this theme, this end-Idea, the Idea of the world itself and wider knowledge, "We" ourselves as knowing subjects [*Erkenntnissubjekte*], has become completely unclear, or has lost its alleged clarity, and so has become a mystery.

And that is precisely my radicalism, which I have persevered from decade to decade in dogged energy, that I have grasped the idea of presuppositionlessness in unsuspected breadth and depth and have drawn the necessary consequence for a new beginning and a new method. It is in this that my philosophy is not one beside the other; between me and the others there is no critical exchange. I abolish the entire ground [*Boden*], the naive ground of validity common to all the philosophies of the past. And this ground, whose title is self-evidently being world, self-evidently given as a world of experience, self-evidently made up of recognizable realities, and so on, put in question, back into a dimension never seen, never entered, which I call transcendental subjectivity (although the word transcendental does not have the historical meaning). This leads to an abundant infinity of novel concepts, problems, and methods, from which one can have an insight that they contain all conceivable rational questions which the natural, prescientific, and positive-scientific, rational person can ask. From then on, the meaning and law and limits of the law of all historically transmitted and sciences whose work is in progress are understandable. After the "bankruptcy," it requires a radical and universal sense-reflection, and, indeed, the business must be inhibited, and the meaning and method of the business so far is now the only one demanded. Anyone who has isolated himself in this sentiment and who really has the courage of radicalism must come to the same path as me, and *then* philosophy in community is possible again. First sense-reflection, in which one stands by oneself and oversees what is present, is not yet a philosophy, not yet the universal, absolute science. As soon as it comes to definitive conclusions, there is communitization, and only in communitization does it have a fully real existence. For I, isolated in my finiteness, cannot get very far in the knowledge of the infinities. Philosophy is the task of infinite knowledge in the infinity of humanity.

You are quite right that I exaggerate my solitariness, insofar as I am not alone with my Fink. There are philosophers here and there, longing for a genuine philosophy that experiences the seriousness of my radicalism and, piece by piece, the power of my knowledge (the philosophical and psychological Abcs or the elementary grammar of the transcendental mind). But I do not have an open public, just as every philosophy has had it. But I am sure that it will be formed by a few at a time.

In these last days, I have experienced a tremendous and moving surprise. The famous Spaniard Ortega y Gasset visited me, and we spoke intensively several times. He is the authentic spiritual leader of the newly awakening Spain. I was astonished to hear that he was already living in my writings for the second decade, even though his publications do not and will not have a scientific character—he is a publicist who wants to be literary for the education of youth and can naturally only work this way. But as a professor in Madrid, he also exerts a rigorous scientific effect, and how far he himself is, we, myself and Fink, see in his questions, which reach into the finest and deepest problems of phenomenology. He is to be thanked for the Spanish translation of my three volume *Logical Investigations*, which are to have a tremendous impact. And indeed, there are (as I have already written to you) not less than four and a half thousand copies sold (much more than in Germany in the first two decades since its publication in 1900). He is about to translate my other works, in turn, first my French "Meditations" but from the German text. These are the beautiful signs of a new age, and they are piling up lately. In any case, it will take many years for phenomenology to be brought up to the height where it can be practical and worldview in general, first it must gain a large community of responsibly working people from the general praxis of peoples' lives.

Now I tell you, dear Gust, that you cannot count on such long philosophical letters so soon. You have no idea in which philosophical distress I am, now overwhelmed [überfallen] by universal philosophical questions that are of great importance to me. Unfortunately, my working time is not as good as in the "Second" Reich. The Third has cost me something.
Sincerely,
Your old and faithful
Edmund
With many greetings and congratulations on all sides.

Appendix F

Husserl to Löwith, 2.22.1937.[11]
    Dear Esteemed Colleague:

I congratulate you on your accommodation in Sendai: in the midst of my old friends![12] My return of your fr <iendly> wishes are delayed, since I had already hoped at the beginning of January to be able to send you a *Sep <aratum>* of the

---

[11] Hua, *Briefwechsel*, Band IV, 397–398.

[12] Husserl knew both Japanese students who visited Germany and Germans who moved to Japan. As German editor's note here: "At the Imperial University of Tohoku in Sendai (Japan), to which

first piece of my writing "The Crisis of the Europ <aean> Sciences and the Trans <cendental> Phenomenology." You are not yet there. Hopefully, you do not belong to the "early completers," to those who have come to a finished position, so that you still have the inner freedom to "bracket" your own anthropology and to understand, on the basis of my new, most matured exposition, why I reckon all ant <h> ropology to philosophically naive positivity and why I recognize the method of ph <enomenological> reduction as the solely philosophical one, as the only one that achieves universal knowledge of being, or universal sense-reflection on the self in real concretion. Perhaps you will understand that Scheler, Heidegger—and so all earlier "pupils"—did not understand the actual and deep sense of phenomenology—the transcendental one, as the only possible one—and how much depends on this sense. It is admittedly difficult to access, but it is worth the effort, I think.

Perhaps you will be able to understand why I, not out of obstinacy, but following on first necessities in so many years my lonely ways, which held themselves in a new dimension of questions and decisions—and why I did not understand the profound mysticism of the fashionable existential philosophies and of the so superior thinking historical philosophies. Why I had to estimate the profound mysticism of the fashionable existential philosophies and of the historical relativism, which strangely considered itself so superior, for a weak failure of a humanity that had become powerless., that avoided the enormous task that the collapse of the whole "modern age" put and still puts to it; to us all! The first piece is only slowly ascending, the next one, in the second issue—or, in the third, brings first the phenomenological reduction, unfortunately, therefore, the decisive thing comes after, in pieces, for accidental reasons.

Kindest greetings and wishes for a pure, beautiful effect of your philosophical gifts.
Yours
E. Husserl
Warmest greetings to your colleagues and friends!

Husserl's card is addressed, were the students Satomi Takahashi, Tomoye Oyama and Goichi Miyake. [Karl] Löwith had emigrated to Japan in 1936."

References

Husserliana: Edmund Husserl Gesammelte Werke (Hua)

Husserliana I: Cartesianische Meditationen und Pariser Vorträge. Edited by S. Strasser. The Hague: Martinus Nijhoff, 1973.
Husserliana II: Die Idee der Phänomenologie. Fünf Vorlesungen. Edited by Walter Biemel. The Hague: Martinus Nijhoff, 1973.
Husserliana III: Ideen zu einer reinen Phänomenologie und phänomenologischen Philosophie. Erstes Buch: Allgemeine Einführung in die reine Phänomenologie. Edited by Walter Biemel. The Hague: Martinus Nijhoff, 1950.
Husserliana III-1: Ideen zu einer reinen Phänomenologie und phänomenologischen Philosophie. Erstes Buch: Allgemeine Einführung in die reine Phänomenologie, 1. Halbband: Text der 1.-3. Auflage – Nachdruck. Edited by Karl Schuhmann. The Hague: Martinus Nijhoff, 1977.
Husserliana III-2: Ideen zu einer reinen Phänomenologie und phänomenologischen Philosophie. Erstes Buch: Allgemeine Einführung in die reine Phänomenologie, 2. Halbband: Ergänzende Texte (1912–1929). Edited by Karl Schuhmann. The Hague: Martinus Nijhoff, 1988.
Husserliana IV: Ideen zu einer reinen Phänomenologie und phänomenologischen Philosophie. Zweites Buch: Phänomenologische Untersuchungen zur Konstitution. Edited by Marly Biemel. The Hague: Martinus Nijhoff, 1952.
Husserliana V: Ideen zu einer reinen Phänomenologie und phänomenologischen Philosophie. Drittes Buch: Die Phänomenologie und die Fundamente der Wissenschaften. Edited by Marly Biemel. The Hague: Martinus Nijhoff, 1971.
Husserliana VI: Die Krisis der europäischen Wissenschaften und die transzendentale Phänomenologie. Eine Einleitung in die phänomenologische Philosophie. Edited by Walter Biemel. The Hague: Martinus Nijhoff, 1976.
Husserliana VII: Erste Philosophie (1923/24). Erste Teil: Kritische Ideengeschichte. Edited by Rudolf Boehm. The Hague: Martinus Nijhoff, 1956.
Husserliana VIII: Erste Philosophie (1923/24). Zweiter Teil: Theorie der phänomenologischen Reduktion. Edited by Rudolf Boehm. The Hague: Martinus Nijhoff, 1959.
Husserliana IX: Phänomenologische Psychologie. Vorlesungen Sommersemester 1925. Edited by Walter Biemel. The Hague: Martinus Nijhoff, 1968.
Husserliana X: Zur Phänomenologie des inneren Zeitbewusstseins (1893–1917). Edited by Rudolf Boehm. The Hague: Martinus Nijhoff, 1969.
Husserliana XI: Analysen zur passiven Synthesis. Aus Vorlesungs- und Forschungsmanuskripten, 1918–1926. Edited by Margot Fleischer. The Hague: Martinus Nijhoff, 1966.
Husserliana XII: Philosophie der Arithmetik. Mit ergänzenden Texten (1890–1901). Edited by Lothar Eley. The Hague: Martinus Nijhoff, 1970.

Husserliana XIII: Zur Phänomenologie der Intersubjektivität. Texte aus dem Nachlass. Erster Teil. 1905–1920. Edited by Iso Kern. The Hague: Martinus Nijhoff, 1973.
Husserliana XIV: Zur Phänomenologie der Intersubjektivität. Texte aus dem Nachlass. Zweiter Teil. 1921–1928. Edited by Iso Kern. The Hague: Martinus Nijhoff, 1973.
Husserliana XV: Zur Phänomenologie der Intersubjektivität. Texte aus dem Nachlass. Dritter Teil. 1929–1935. Edited by Iso Kern. The Hague: Martinus Nijhoff, 1973.
Husserliana XVI: Ding und Raum. Vorlesungen 1907. Edited by Ulrich Claesges. The Hague: Martinus Nijhoff, 1973.
Husserliana XVII: Formale und transzendentale Logik. Versuch einer Kritik der logischen Vernunft. Edited by Paul Janssen. The Hague: Martinus Nijhoff, 1974.
Husserliana XVIII: Logische Untersuchungen. Erster Teil. Prolegomena zur reinen Logik. Text der 1. und der 2. Auflage. Edited by Elmar Holenstein. The Hague: Martinus Nijhoff, 1975.
Husserliana XIX: Logische Untersuchungen. Zweiter Teil. Untersuchungen zur Phänomenologie und Theorie der Erkenntnis. In zwei Bänden. Edited by Ursula Panzer. The Hague: Martinus Nijhoff, 1984.
Husserliana XX/1: Logische Untersuchungen. Ergänzungsband. Erster Teil. Entwürfe zur Umarbeitung der VI. Untersuchung und zur Vorrede für die Neuauflage der Logischen Untersuchungen (Sommer 1913). Edited by Ulrich Melle. The Hague: Kluwer Academic Publishers, 2002.
Husserliana XX/2: Logische Untersuchungen. Ergänzungsband. Zweiter Teil. Texte für die Neufassung der VI. Untersuchung. Zur Phänomenologie des Ausdrucks und der Erkenntnis (1893/94–1921). Edited by Ulrich Melle. The Hague: Kluwer Academic Publishers, 2005.
Husserliana XXI: Studien zur Arithmetik und Geometrie. Texte aus dem Nachlass (1886–1901). Edited by Ingeborg Strohmeyer. The Hague: Martinus Nijhoff, 1983.
Husserliana XXII: Aufsätze und Rezensionen (1890–1910). Edited by B. Rang. The Hague: Martinus Nijhoff, 1979.
Husserliana XXIII: Phäntasie, Bildbewusstsein, Erinnerung. Zur Phänomenologie der anschaulichen Vergegenwartigungen. Texte aus dem Nachlass (1898–1925). Edited by Eduard Marbach. The Hague: Martinus Nijhoff, 1980.
Husserliana XXIV: Einleitung in die Logik und Erkenntnistheorie. Vorlesungen 1906/07. Edited by Ullrich Melle. The Hague: Martinus Nijhoff, 1985.
Husserliana XXV: Aufsätze und Vorträge. 1911–1921. Mit ergänzenden Texten. Edited by Thomas Nenon and Hans Rainer Sepp. The Hague: Martinus Nijhoff, 1986.
Husserliana XXVI: Vorlesungen über Bedeutungslehre. Sommersemester 1908. Edited by Ursula Panzer. The Hague: Martinus Nijhoff, 1987.
Husserliana XXVII: Aufsätze und Vorträge. 1922–1937. Edited by T. Nenon and H. R. Sepp. The Hague: Kluwer, 1988.
Husserliana XXVIII: Vorlesungen über Ethik und Wertlehre. 1908–1914. Edited by Ullrich Melle. The Hague: Kluwer, 1988.
Husserliana XXIX: Die Krisis der europaischen Wissenschaften und die transzendentale Phänomenologie. Ergänzungsband. Texte aus dem Nachlass 1934–1937. Edited by Reinhold N. Smid. The Hague: Kluwer, 1992.
Husserliana XXX: Logik und allgemeine Wissenschaftstheorie. Vorlesungen 1917/18. Mit ergänzenden Texten aus der ersten Fassung 1910/11. Edited by Ursula Panzer. The Hague: Kluwer, 1995.
Husserliana XXXI: Aktive Synthesen: Aus der Vorlesung ‚Transzendentale Logik' 1920/21. Ergänzungsband zu 'Analysen zur passiven Synthesis'. Edited by Roland Breeur. The Hague: Kluwer, 2000.
Husserliana XXXII: Natur und Geist: Vorlesungen Sommersemester 1927. Edited by Michael Weiler. Dordrecht: Kluwer Academic Publishers, 2001.
Husserliana XXXIII: Die 'Bernauer Manuskripte' über das Zeitbewußtsein (1917/18). Edited by Rudolf Bernet and Dieter Lohmar. Dordrecht: Kluwer, 2001.
Husserliana XXXIV: Zur phänomenologischen Reduktion. Texte aus dem Nachlass (1926–1935). Edited by Sebastian Luft. Dordrecht: Kluwer, 2002.

Husserliana XXXV: Einleitung in die Philosophie. Vorlesungen 1922/23. Edited by Berndt Goossens. Dordrecht: Kluwer, 2002.
Husserliana XXXVI: Transzendentaler Idealismus. Texte aus dem Nachlass (1908–1921). Edited by Robin D. Rollinger in cooperation with Rochus Sowa. Dordrecht: Kluwer, 2003.
Husserliana XXXVII: Einleitung in die Ethik. Vorlesungen Sommersemester 1920 und 1924. Edited by Henning Peucker. Dordrecht: Kluwer, 2004.
Husserliana XXXVIII: Wahrnehmung und Aufmerksamkeit. Texte aus dem Nachlass (1893–1912). Edited by Thomas Vongehr and Regula Giuliani. New York: Springer, 2005.
Husserliana XXXIX: Die Lebenswelt. Auslegungen der vorgegebenen Welt und ihrer Konstitution. Texte aus dem Nachlass (1916–1937). Edited by Rochus Sowa. New York: Springer, 2008.
Husserliana XL: Untersuchungen zur Urteilstheorie. Texte aus dem Nachlass (1893–1918). Edited by Robin Rollinger. New York: Springer, 2009.
Husserliana XLI: Zur Lehre vom Wesen und zur Methode der eidetischen Variation. Texte aus dem Nachlass (1891–1935). Edited by Dirk Fonfara. New York: Springer, 2012.
Husserliana XLII: Grenzprobleme der Phänomenologie. Analysen des Unbewusstseins und der Instinkte. Metaphysik. Späte Ethik. Texte aus dem Nachlass (1908–1937). Edited by Rochus Sowa and Thomas Vongehr. New York: Springer, 2014.
Husserliana XLIII/1: Studien zur Struktur des Bewusstseins: Teilband I Verstand und Gegenstand. Texte aus dem Nachlass (1909–1927). Edited by Ulrich Melle and Thomas Vongehr. New York: Springer, 2020.
Husserliana XLIII/2: Studien zur Struktur des Bewusstseins: Teilband II Gefühl und Wert. Texte aus dem Nachlass (1896–1925). Edited by Ulrich Melle and Thomas Vongehr. New York: Springer, 2020.
Husserliana XLIII/3: Studien zur Struktur des Bewusstseins: Teilband III Wille und Handlung. Texte aus dem Nachlass (1902–1934). Edited by Ulrich Melle and Thomas Vongehr. New York: Springer, 2020.
Husserliana XLIII/4: Studien zur Struktur des Bewusstseins: Teilband IV Textkritischer Anhang. Edited by Ulrich Melle and Thomas Vongehr. New York: Springer, 2020.

Documents and Other Editions

Husserliana Dokumente I. 1977. *Husserl-Chronik: Denk- und Lebensweg Edmund Husserls*, ed. Karl Schuhmann. Dordrecht: Springer.
Husserliana Dokumente 3: I-X. *Briefwechsel*. [Correspondence.] Edited by Karl Schuhmann. The Hague: Kluwer, 1994.
Husserliana Materialien VIII. 2006. *Späte Texte über Zeitkonstitution (1929–1934), Die C-Manuskripte.* Dordrecht: Springer.
Husserliana Materialien IX. 2012. *Einleitung in die Philosophie. Vorlesungen 1916–1919.* Dordrecht: Springer.
"Husserl an Levy-Bruhl." 1935. In *Husserliana Dokumente 3, Briefwechsel*, Vol. VII, pp. 161–64. English translation by Lukas Steinacher and Dermot Moran, *The New Yearbook for Phenomenology and Phenomenological Philosophy* VIII (2008): 1–6.

English Translations of Edmund Husserl

1960. *Cartesian Meditations.* trans. D. Cairns. The Hague: Martinus Nijhoff.
1969. *Formal and Transcendental Logic.* trans. D. Cairns. The Hauge: Martinus Nijhoff.

1970. *The Crisis of European Sciences and Transcendental Phenomenology: An Introduction to Phenomenological Philosophy*, trans. D. Carr. Evanston: Northwestern University Press.
1970a. *Logical Investigations, Volume I and II*. trans. J.N. Findlay. Cambridge: Routledge.
1973. *Experience and Judgment: Investigations in a Genealogy of Logic*, trans. J. S. Churchill and K. Ameriks. Evanston: Northwestern University Press.
1975. *Introduction to the Logical Investigations*, ed. Eugen Fink, trans. Philip Bossert and Curtis Peters. The Hague: Martinus Nijhoff.
1981. *Husserl: Shorter Works*, eds. Peter McCormick and Frederick Elliston South Bend: Notre Dame University Press.
1983. *Ideas Pertaining to a Pure Phenomenology and to a Phenomenological Philosophy. First Book: General Introduction to a Pure Phenomenology*, trans. F. Kersten. Dordrecht: Kluwer.
1989. *Ideas Pertaining to a Pure Phenomenology and to a Phenomenological Philosophy. Second Book: Studies in the Phenomenology of Constitution*, trans. R. Rojcewicz and A. Schuwer. Dordrecht: Kluwer.
1991. *On the Phenomenology of the Consciousness of Internal Time (1893–1917)*, tras. J. B. Brough. Dordrecht: Kluwer.
1997. Psychological and Transcendental Phenomenology and the Confrontation with Heidegger (1927–1931): The Encyclopedia Britannica Article, The Amsterdam Lectures, "Phenomenology and Anthropology," and Husserl's Marginal Notes in *Being and Time* and *Kant and the Problem of Metaphysics*, ed. and trans. Thomas Sheehan and Richard E. Palmer. Dordrecht: Springer.
1993. *Collected Works: Volume 5: Early Writings in the Philosophy of Logic and Mathematics*, trans. Dallas Willard. Dordrecht: Springer.
1997b. *Thing and Space: Lectures of 1907*, trans. R. Rojcewicz. Dordrecht: Kluwer.
1999. *The Idea of Phenomenology*, trans. L. Hardy. Dordrecht: Kluwer.
2001a. *Analyses Concerning Active and Passive Synthesis: Lectures on Transcendental Logic*, trans. A. J. Steinbock. Dordrecht: Kluwer.
2001b. *Logical Investigations. First Volume: Niemeyer Prolegomena to Pure Logic. Investigations I and II*, trans. J.N. Findlay. New York: Routledge.
2001c. *Logical Investigations. Second Volume: Investigations III, IV, V, VI*, trans. J. N. Findlay. New York: Routledge.
2002. "Foundational Investigations of the Phenomenological Origin of the Spatiality of Nature: The Originary Ark, the Earth, Does Not Move" in *Merleau-Ponty, Husserl at the Limits of Phenomenology*, ed. Lawlor and Bergon. Evanston: Northwestern University Press, 117–131.
2008. *Introduction to Logic and Theory of Knowledge: Lectures 1906/1907*, trans. C. O. Hill. Dordrecht: Springer.
2011. "On the Task and Historical Position of the Logical Investigations" (From the Introduction to the Lectures on "Phenomenological Psychology," Summer Semester 1925), trans. Catharina Bonnemann and Jason Bell. *Journal of Speculative Philosophy* 25 (3): 267–305.
2019. *First Philosophy: Lectures 1923/24 and Related Texts from the Manuscripts (1920–1925)*, trans. Sebastian Luft and Thane M. Naberhaus. Dordrecht: Springer.
2024. Values of Love and Ethical Reflection. eds. Sara Heinämaa and Anthony J. Steinbock, trans. Andrew D. Barrette. Cham: Springer.

Other

Aguirre, A. (1970). *Genetische Phänomenologie und Reduktion. Zur Letztbegründung der Wissenschaft aus der radikalen Skepsis im Denken E. Husserls* (Phaenomenologica 38). Den Haag: Martinus Nijhoff.

Ameriks, K. (1978). "Kant's transcendental deduction as a regressive argument." *Kant-Studien* 69: 273–287.

Benoist, J. (2002). "Non-objectifying acts." In Dan Zahavi & Frederik Stjernfelt (Eds.), *One Hundred Years of Phenomenology: Husserl's Logical Investigations Revisited*, Phaenomenologica 164. Dordrecht: Springer: 41–49.

Bernet, R. (1983). "Die ungegenwärtige Gegenwart. Anwesenheit und Abwesenheit in Husserls Analyse des Zeitbewusstseins." In *Zeit und Zeitlichkeit bei Husserl und Heidegger* (Phänomenologische Forschungen, Nr. 14): 16–57.

———. (1985). "Einleitung des Herausgebers." In *Edmund Husserl. Texte zur Phänomenologie des inneren Zeitbewusstseins (1893–1917)*. Hamburg: Felix Meiner.

———. (1994). "An intentionality without subject or object?" *Man and World*, 27, 231–255. Dordrecht: Kluwer.

———. (2002a). "Die neue Phänomenologie des Zeitbewusstseins in Husserls Bernauer Manuskripte." In H. Hüni & P. Trawney (Eds.), *Die erscheinende Welt. Festschrift für Klaus Held*. Berlin: Duncker und Humboldt: 539–555

———. (2002b). "Unconscious consciousness in Husserl and Freud." *Phenomenology and the Cognitive Sciences*, 1: 327–351.

———. (2003). "Desiring to Know through Intuition." *Husserl Studies*, 19: 153–166.

———. (2010). "Husserl's new phenomenology of time consciousness in the Bernau Manuscripts." In D. Lohmar & I. Yamaguchi (Eds.), *On time – New contributions to the Husserlian phenomenology of time* (Phaenomenologica 197): 1–19.

Bernet, R., Kern, I., and Marbach, E. (1999). *An introduction to Husserlian phenomenology*. Evanston, IL: Northwestern University Press.

Bochenski, I. M. (1961). *A History of Formal Logic*, Ivo Thomas (Trans.). Notre Dame: University of Notre Dame Press.

Boehm, R. (1968). *Vom Gesichtspunkt der Phänomenologie. Husserl-Studien* (Phaenomenologica 26). Den Haag: Martinus Nijhoff.

Boudier, C. S. (1983). "Husserl and the Logic of Questions." In A. T. Tymieniecka (Ed.), *The Phenomenology of Man and of the Human Condition*. (Analecta Husserliana, vol. 14). Dordrcht: Springer.

Brentano, F. (1952). *Grundlegung und Aufbau der Ethik. Nach den Vorlesungen uber "Praktische Philosophie" aus dem Nachlass*, hrsg. von Franziska Mayer-Hillebrand, Bern.

Breyer, T. (2015). *Verkörperte Intersubjektivität Und Empathie: Philosophisch-Anthropologische Untersuchungen*. Frankfurt am Main: Vittorio Klostermann.

Bruin, J. (2001). *Homo Interrogans: Questioning and the Intentional Structure of Cognition*. University of Ottawa Press.

Broekman, J. M. (1963). *Phänomenologie und Egologie. Faktisches und transzendentales Ego bei Edmund Husserl* (Phaenomenologica 12). Den Haag: Martinus Nijhoff.

Brough, J. B. (1991). "Translator's introduction." In E. Husserl (Ed.), *On the phenomenology of the consciousness of internal time (1893–1917)*. J. B. Brough (Trans.). Dordrecht: Kluwer.

Brough, J. B. (2010). "Notes on the absolute time-constituting flow of consciousness." In D. Lohmar & I. Yamaguchi (Eds.), *On time – New contributions to the Husserlian phenomenology of time* (Phaenomenologica 197). Dordrecht: Springer: 21–49.

Brough, J. B. (2011). "The most difficult of all phenomenological problems." *Husserl Studies*, 27: 27–40.

Brudzinska, J. (2005).*Assoziation, Imaginäres, Trieb. Phänomenologische Untersuchungen zur Subjektivitätsgenesis bei Husserl und Freud*. Universität zu Köln.

Byrne, P. (1997). *Analysis and Science in Aristotle*. Albany: SUNY Press.

Cairns, D. (1972). *The many senses and denotations of the word Bewusstsein ("Consciousness") in Edmund Husserl's writings, lifeworld and consciousness: Essays for Aron Gurwitsch*. Evanston: Northwestern University Press: 19–31.

———. (1976). *Conversations with Husserl and Fink* (Phaenomenologica 66). The Hague: Martinus Nijhoff.

Casey, E. (2000). *Remembering: A Phenomenological Study*. Bloomington: Indiana University Press.

Caminada, E. (2014). *Joining the background: Habitual sentiments behind we-intentionality. Institutions, emotions, and group agents: Contributions to social ontology*, in Institutions, Emotions, and Group Agents, A Konzelmann Ziv and H.B. Schmid (Eds.): 195–212.

———. (2019). *Das Manuskript Gemeingeist I. Vom Gemeingeist zum Habitus: Husserls Ideen II: Sozialphilosophische Implikationen der Phänomenologie*, (Phenomenologica 25) Dordrecht: Springer.

Cavallaro, M. (2016). "Das 'Problem' der Habituskonstitution und die Spätlehre des Ich in der genetischen Phänomenologie E. Husserls." *Husserl Studies*, 32: 237–261.

Charles, P. (1930). "La philosophie du primitif." *Nouvelle Revue Théologique*, 57 (2): 110–126.

Chrudzimski, A. (2001). *Intentionalitätstheorie beim frühen Brentano* (Phaenomenologica 159). Dordrecht: Springer.

Davidson, L. (2021). *Overcoming Psychologism: Husserl and the Transcendental Reform of Psychology*. Cham: Springer Nature.

De Warren, N. (2009). *Husserl and the promise of time: Subjectivity in transcendental phenomenology*. Cambridge: Cambridge University Press.

Depraz, N. (1998). "Can I anticipate myself? Self-affection and temporality." In D. Zahavi (Ed.), *Self-awareness, temporality, and alterity: Central topics in phenomenology* (Contributions to Phenomenology 34). Dordrecht: Kluwer: 83–97.

DeRoo, N. (2011). "Revisiting the Zahavi-Brough/Sokolowski debate." *Husserl Studies*, 27: 1–12.

DeRoo, N. (2013). *Futurity in phenomenology. Promise and method in Husserl, Levinas, and Derrida*. New York: Fordham University Press. Derrida, J. (1973). *Speech and phenomena and other essays on Husserl's theory of signs*. D. B. Allison & N. Garver (Trans.). Evanston: Northwestern University Press.

Drummond, J. J. (2006). "The case(s) of (self-)awareness." In U. Kriegel & K. Williford (Eds.), *Self-representational approaches to consciousness*. Cambridge: MIT Press, 199–220.

Džanic, D. (2023). *Transcendental Phenomenology as Human Possibility: Husserl and Fink on the Phenomenologizing Subject*. Cham: Springer.

Ferencz-Flatz, C. (2014). "Husserls Begriff der Kinästhese und seine Entwicklung." *Husserl Studies*, 30: 21–45.

Ferrer, G. (2015). *Protentionalität und Urimpression. Elemente einer Phänomenologie der Erwartungsintentionen in Husserls Analyse des Zeitbewusstseins* (Orbis Phaenomenologicus, Studien 36). Würzburg: Königshausen & Neumann.

Fink, E. (1966). *Studien Zur Phänomenologie* (Phaenomenologica 21). The Hague: Martinus Nijhoff.

———. (1981). "Operative concepts in Husserl's Phenomenology," William McKenna (Trans), in William Mckenna, Robert M. Harlan, & Laurence E. Winters (Eds.), *Apriori and world. European Contributions to Husserlian Phenomenology*. The Hague: Martinus Nijhoff: 56–70.

———. (1988a). *VI. Cartesianische Meditation. Teil 1. Die Idee einer Transzendentalen Methodenlehre* (Husserliana Dokumente. Bd. II/1). Dordrecht: Kluwer.

———. (1988b). *VI. Cartesianische Meditation. Teil 2. Ergänzungsband* (Husserliana Dokumente. Bd. II/2). Dordrecht: Kluwer.

———. (2004). *Nähe und Distanz. Phänomenologische Vorträge und Aufsätze*. Freiburg/München: Karl Alber.

———. (2006). *Die Doktorarbeit und erste Assistenzjahre bei Husserl* (Phänomenologische Werkstatt Bd. 1). Freiburg/München: Karl Alber.

———. (2008). *Bernauer Zeitmanuskripte, Cartesianische Meditationen und System der phänomenologischen Philosophie* (Phänomenologische Werkstatt Bd. 2). Freiburg/München: Karl Alber.
Fréchette, G. (2017). "Brentano on time-consciousness." In U. Kriegel (Ed.), *The Routledge handbook of Franz Brentano and the Brentano school*. New York: Routledge: 75–86.
Føllesdal, D. (1982). "Husserl's conversion from psychologism and the Vorstellung-meaning-reference distinction: Two separate issues." In Dreyfus & Harrison Hall (Eds), *Husserl, intentionality and cognitive science*. Cambridge: MIT Press: 52–56.
Heidegger, M. (1962). *Being and Time*. John Macquarrie & Edward S. Robinson (Trans.). New York: Harper.
———. (1985). *History of Concept of time*. Theodore Kisiel (Trans.). Bloomington: Indiana University Press.
———. (2000). *Supplements: From the Earliest Essays to Being and Time and Beyond*. John Van Buren (Ed). Albany: SUNY Press.
———. (2008). *Toward the Definition of Philosophy*. Ted Sadler(Trans.) Continuum.
Held, K. (1966). *Lebendige Gegenwart* (Phaenomenologica 23). Den Haag: Martinus Nijhoff.
———. (2010). "Phenomenology of 'authentic time'." In D. Lohmar & I. Yamaguchi (Eds.), *On time – New contributions to the Husserlian phenomenology of time* (Phaenomenologica 197). Dordrecht: Springer: 91–114.
Henry, M. (2008). *Material phenomenology*. S. Davidson (Trans.). New York: Fordham University Press.
Herrmann, F.-W. v. (1992). *Augustinus und die phänomenologische Frage nach der Zeit*. Frankfurt am Main: Vittorio Klostermann.
Heumer, W. (2004). "Husserl's Critique of Psychologism and his Relation to the Brentano School." In Arkadiusz Chrudzimski & Wolfgang Huemer (Eds.), *Phenomenology and Analysis: Essays on Central European Philosophy*. Frankfurt: Ontos.
Holenstein, E. (1972). *Phänomenologie der Assoziation* (Phaenomenologica 44). Den Haag: Martinus Nijhoff.
Hopp, Walter. (2010). "How to think about nonconceptual content." *New Yearbook for Phenomenology and Phenomenological Philosophy* 10: 1–24.
———. (2020). *Phenomenology: A contemporary introduction*. Routledge.
Hopkins, B. C. (2015). "Phenomenologically pure, transcendental, and absolute consciousness." In A. Staiti (Ed.), *Commentary on Husserl's ideas I*. Berlin/Boston: De Gruyter: 119–131.
Hubick, Joel. (2024). *The Phenomenology of Questioning: Husserl, Heidegger and Patočka*. London: Bloomsbury Academic.
Ingarden, R. (1975). *On the Motives which led Husserl to Transcendental Idealism*. The Hague: Springer.
Kern, I. (1962). "Die drei Wege zur transzendental-phänomenologischen Reduktion in der Philosophie Edmund Husserls." In *Tijdschrift voor Filosofie* (24ste Jaarg., Nr 2). Leuven: Peeters: 303–349.
Klein, J. (1979). *A Commentary on Plato's Meno*. Chapel Hill: The University of North Carolina Press.
Kneale, W. and M. (1971). *The Development of Logic*. Oxford: Oxford University Press.
Kohák, E. (1978). *Idea and Experience: Husserl's Project of Phenomenology in Ideen I*. Chicago: University of Chicago Press.
Kortooms, T. (2002). *Phenomenology of time. Edmund Husserl's analysis of time-consciousness* (Phaenomenologica 161). Dordrecht: Kluwer.
Kraus, O. (1919). *Franz Brentano. Zur Kenntnis seines Lebens und seiner Lehre*. München: C.H. Beck'sche Verlagsbuchhandlung Oskar Beck.
Künne, W. (1997), "Propositions in Bolzano and Frege." *Grazer Philosophische Studien* 53 (1): 203–240.
———. (2003). "Are Questions Propositions?" *Revue Internationale de Philosophie* 57 (224 (2)): 157–168.

Landgrebe, L. (1954). "Prinzipien der Lehre vom Empfinden." *Zeitschrift für philosophische Forschung*, VIII (2), 195–209. Meisenheim/Glan: Westkultur Verlag Anton Hain.

———. (2010). *Der Begriff des Erlebens. Ein Beitrag zur Kritik unseres Selbstverständnisses und zum Problem der seelischen Ganzheit*. Würzburg: Könnigshausen & Neumann.

Lear, J. (1980). *Aristotle and logical theory*. Cambridge: Cambridge University Press.

Lee, N.-I. (1993). *Edmund Husserls Phänomenologie der Instinkte* (Phaenomenologica 128). Dordrecht: Springer.

Levinas, E. (1987). *Time and the other, and additional essays*. R. A. Cohen (Trans.). Pittsburgh: Duquesne University Press.

———. (2000). *Discovering existence with Husserl*. R. Cohen & M. Smith (Trans.). Evanston: Northwestern University Press.

———. (2003). *On escape*. B. Bergo (Trans.). Stanford: Stanford University Press.

Lohmar, D. (1993). "Grundzüge eines Synthesis-Modells der Auffassung: Kant und Husserl über den Ordnungsgrad sinnlicher Vorgegebenheiten und die Elemente einer Phänomenologie der Auffassung." *Husserl Studies*, 10: 111–141.

Lohmar, D. (1998). *Erfahrung und kategoriales Denken. Hume, Kant und Husserl über vorprädikative Erfahrung und prädikative Erkenntnis* (Phaenomenologica 147). Dordrecht: Springer.

———. (2002a). "What does protention 'protend'? Remarks on Husserl's analyses of protention in the Bernau manuscripts on time-consciousness." *Philosophy Today*, 28/5, 154–167. SPEP Supplement 2002. Charlottesville: Philosophy Documentation Center.

———. (2002b). "Die Idee der Reduktion. Husserls Reduktionen – und ihr gemeinsamer, methodischer Sinn." In H. Hüni & P. Trawney (Eds.), *Die erscheinende Welt. Festschrift für Klaus Held*. Berlin: Duncker und Humboldt: 751–771.

———. (2003). Über phantasmatische Selbstaffektion in der typisierenden Apperzeption und im inneren Zeitbewusstsein. Leitmotiv (ledonlin.it), 3/2003, 67–80. https://www.ledonline.it/leitmotiv-2001-2006/allegati/leitmotiv030304.pdf.

———. (2005). "Die phänomenologische Methode der Wesenschau und ihre Präzisierung als eidetische Variation." In *Phänomenologische Forschungen*. Hamburg: Felix Meiner: 65–91.

———. (2009). "Eine Geschichte des Ich bei Husserl." In M. Pfeifer & S. Rapic (Eds.), *Das Selbst und sein Anderes*. Freiburg/München: Karl Alber: 162–180.

———. (2010). "On the constitution of the time of the world: The emergence of objective time on the ground of subjective time." In D. Lohmar & I. Yamaguchi (Eds.), *On time – New contributions to the Husserlian phenomenology of time* (Phaenomenologica 197). Dordrecht: Springer: 115–136.

———. (2011). "Genetic phenomenology." In S. Luft & S. Overgaard (Eds.), *The Routledge companion to phenomenology*. New York/London: Routledge: 266–275.

———. (2012a). "Zur Vorgeschichte der transzendentalen Reduktion in den Logischen Untersuchungen. Die unbekannte 'Reduktion auf den reellen Bestand'." *Husserl Studies*, 28: 1–24.

———. (2016). *Denken ohne Sprache: Phänomenologie des nicht-sprachlichen Denkens bei Mensch und Tier im Licht der Evolutionsforschung, Primatologie und Neurologie*. Germany: Springer International Publishing.

Lotz, C. (2007). *From affectivity to subjectivity. Husserl's phenomenology revisited*. New York: Palgrave Macmillan.

Luft, S. (2002). *"Phänomenologie der Phänomenologie". Systematik und Methodologie der Phänomenologie in der Auseinandersetzung zwischen Husserl und Fink* (Phaenomenologica 166). Dordrecht: Kluwer.

———. (2011). "Husserl's method of reduction." In S. Luft & S. Overgaard (Eds.), *The Routledge companion to phenomenology*. London/New York: Routledge: 243–253.

Marbach, E. (1974). *Das Problem des Ich in der Phänomenologie Husserls* (Phaenomenologica 59). Den Haag: Martinus Nijhoff.

Melle, U. (2007). "Husserl's personalist ethics." *Husserl Studies* 23 (1): 1–15.

———. (2020). "Objectifying and non-objectifying acts." In John J. Drummond & Otfried Höffe (Eds.), *Husserl: German Perspectives*. Fordham University Press: 193–208.

Mensch, J. (1999). "Husserl's concept of the future." *Husserl Studies*, 16: 41–64.
———. (2010a). *Husserl's account of our consciousness of time*. Milwaukee, WI: Marquette University Press.
———. (2010b). "Retention and the schema." In D. Lohmar & I. Yamaguchi (Eds.), *On time – New contributions to the Husserlian phenomenology of time* (Phaenomenologica 197). Dordrecht: Springer: 153–168.
Micali, S. (2008). *Überschüsse der Erfahrung. Grenzdimensionen des Ich nach Husserl* (Phaenomenologica 186). Dordrecht: Springer.
———. (2010). "The temporalizations of the absolute flow." In D. Lohmar & I. Yamaguchi (Eds.), *On time – New contributions to the Husserlian phenomenology of time* (Phaenomenologica 197). Dordrecht: Springer: 169–185.
Mohanty, J. (1974). "Husserl and Frege: A new look at their relationship." *Research in Phenomenology* 4 (1): 51–62.
Montagova, K. S. (2013). *Transzendentale Genesis des Bewusstseins und der Erkenntnis* (Phaenomenologica 210). Dordrecht: Springer.
Natorp, P. (1977). "On the question of logical method in relation to Edmund Husserl's Prolegomena to pure logic." In J. N. Mohanty (Ed.), *Readings on Edmund Husserl's logical investigations*. The Hauge: Martinus Nijhoff.
Orth, E. W. (2002). "Die Pluralität der transzendental phänomenologischen Reduktion und das Problem des Reduktionismus." In H. Hüni & P. Trawney (Eds.), *Die erscheinende Welt. Festschrift für Klaus Held*. Berlin: Duncker und Humboldt: 737–749.
Picardi, Eva, and Annalisa Coliva (2022). "Sigwart, Husserl, and Frege on truth and logic, or is psychologism still a threat?" In Annalisa Coliva (Ed.), *Frege on Language, Logic, and Psychology: Selected Essays*. Cambrdge: Oxford University Press.
Picolas, C., and Soueltzis, N. (2019). "Bodily and temporal pre-reflective self-awareness." *Phenomenology and the Cognitive Sciences*, 18/3, 603–620. Cham: Springer.
Plotka, Witold (2012). "Husserlian phenomenology as questioning: An essay on the transcendental theory of the question." *Studia Phaenomenologica* 12 (-1): 311–329.
Ricoeur, P. (1967). *Husserl: An analysis of his phenomenology*. Edward Ballard & Lester Embree (Trans.). Evanston: Northwestern University Press.
———. (1988). *Time and narrative*. Vol. 3. K. Blamey & D. Pellauer (Trans.). Chicago: The University of Chicago Press.
———. (2004). *Memory, history, forgetting.* K. Blamey & D. Pellauer (Trans.). Chicago: The University of Chicago Press.
Rodemeyer, L. M. (2003). "Developments in the theory of time-consciousness: An analysis of protention." In D. Welton (Ed.), *The new Husserl. A critical reader*. Bloomington: Indiana University Press: 125–154.
———. (2006). *Intersubjective temporality – It's about time* (Phaenomenologica 176). Dordrecht: Springer.
Römer, I. (2010). *Das Zeitdenken bei Husserl, Heidegger und Ricoeur* (Phaenomenologica 196). Dordrecht: Springer.
Sakakibara, T. (2010). "Refection upon the living-present and the primal consciousness in Husserl's phenomenology." In D. Lohmar & I. Yamaguchi (Eds.), *On time – New contributions to the Husserlian phenomenology of time* (Phaenomenologica 197). Dordrecht: Springer: 251–271.
Schnell, A. (2002). "Das Problem der Zeit bei Husserl. Eine Untersuchung über die husserlschen Zeitdiagramme," in *Husserl Studies*, 18: 89–122.
Schuhmann, K. (1987). "Questions: An essay in Daubertian phenomenology." *Philosophy and Phenomenological Research* vol.47 (3): 353–384.
———. (2005). "Against idealism: Johannes Daubert vs. Husserl's Ideas I." In K. Schuhmann and B. Smith (Eds.), *Selected papers on Phenomenology*: 35–59.
Sobota, D. R. (2020). "The law and question. The phenomenon of question as a possible point of departure for the phenomenologico-genetic theory of law." *Acta Universitatis Lodziensis Folia Iuridica* 90: 105–117.

---. (2021). "The question of reality. A postscript to Schuhmann and Smith on Daubert's response to Husserl's Ideas I." In *The idealism-realism debate among Edmund Husserl's early followers and critics.* (Contributions to Phenomenology 112.) Dordrecht: Springer.

Sokolowski, R. (1970). *The formation of Husserl's concept of constitution* (Phaenomenologica 18). The Hague: Martinus Nijhoff.

Spiegelberg, H. (1984). "Three types of the given: The encountered, the search-found and the striking." *Husserl Studies*, 1: 69–78. St. Augustine. (1912). *Confessions II.* W. Watts, (Trans.). London/New York: The Loeb Classical Library.

Staiti, A. (2014). *Husserl's transcendental phenomenology: Nature, spirit, and life.* Cambridge: Cambridge University Press.

Steinbock, A. J. (1995). *Home and beyond. Generative phenomenology after Husserl.* Evanston: Northwestern University Press.

---. (2002). „Affektion und Aufmerksamkeit." In H. Hüni & P. Trawney (Eds.), *Die erscheinende Welt. Festschrift für Klaus Held*. Berlin: Duncker und Humboldt: 241–273.

---. (2017). *Limit-phenomena in Phenomenology and Husserl.* UK: Rowman & Littlefield.

Ströker, E. (1987). *Phänomenologische Studien.* Frankfurt am Main: Vittorio Klostermann.

---. (1997). *The Husserlian Foundations of Science.* Dordrecht: Springer.

Stumpf, C. (1919). "Erinnerungen an Franz Brentano." In O. Kraus (Ed.), *Franz Brentano. Zur Kenntnis seines Lebens und seiner Lehre.* München: C.H. Beck'sche Verlagsbuchhandlung Oskar Beck: 87–149.

Taguchi, S. (2006). *Das Problem des 'Ur-Ich' bei Edmund Husserl. Die Frage nach der selbstverständliche 'Nähe' des Selbst* (Phaenomenologica 178). Dordrecht: Springer.

Theodorou, P. (2015). *Husserl and Heidegger on reduction, primordiality and the categorial. Phenomenology beyond its initial divide* (Contributions to Phenomenology 83). Dordrecht: Springer.

Varga, P.A. (2013). "The missing chapter from the logical investigations: Husserl on Lotze's formal and real significance of logical laws." *Husserl Studies* 29: 181–209.

Vassiliou, F. (2013). Primordial perception, linguistic thematization and scientific idealization in Husserl's phenomenology (Dissertation, in Greek). https://thesis.ekt.gr/thesisBookReader/id/40109#page/1/mode/2up.

Zahavi, D. (1999). *Self-awareness and alterity. A phenomenological investigation.* Evanston: Northwestern University Press.

---. (2003). "Inner time-consciousness and pre-reflective self-awareness." In *The New Husserl: A critical reader.* Bloomington: Indiana University Press: 157–180

---. (2004). "Time and consciousness in the Bernau Manuscripts."*Husserl Studies*, 20, 99–118. Dordrecht: Kluwer.

---. (2005). *Subjectivity and selfhood. Investigating the first-person perspective.* Cambridge: MIT Press.

---. (2011a). Objects and levels: "Reflections on the relation between time-consciousness and self-consciousness." *Husserl Studies*, 27: 13–25.

---. (2011b). "The experiential self: Objections and clarifications." In M. Siderits, E. Thompson, & D. Zahavi (Eds.), *Self, Nno Self? Perspectives from Analytical, Phenomenological, and Indian traditions.* Oxford: Oxford University Press: 56–78.

---. (2015). "Phenomenology of reflection." In A. Staiti (Ed.), *Commentary on Husserl's ideas I*. Berlin/Boston: De Gruyter: 177–193.

Index

A
Act phenomenology, 62

C
Curiosity, 8, 165, 169–174, 176, 178, 179, 183, 184, 190

D
Development, 5, 7, 8, 10, 11, 13, 18, 19, 25, 39, 42, 52, 76, 82, 83, 85, 92, 94, 95, 118, 139, 142, 149, 150, 152, 154, 155, 158–164, 166–170, 173, 174, 178, 180, 181, 185, 187, 189, 191–196, 199, 203–206, 208, 209
Disinterest, 108–110, 116, 183

E
Ἐποχή, 2, 7, 16, 42, 49, 56–60, 62, 71, 184, 191
Ethics, 8, 115–118, 121, 123–126, 132, 134, 138, 209

F
Facticity, 7, 52, 83, 84, 95, 150, 151

G
Generative phenomenology, 2, 146, 156
Generativity, 115, 142, 143, 146, 148, 155, 156, 159, 166–168, 170, 171, 176, 180, 181, 191
Genetic phenomenology, 92

H
Historicity, 155, 156, 165, 178–180, 184, 186, 209
Horizon, 2, 3, 5, 7, 39, 42, 44, 48, 52, 54, 55, 59, 62, 64, 66, 84, 85, 98–101, 104, 107, 108, 110, 111, 115, 124, 128, 137, 143–146, 148, 152, 153, 156, 160, 165, 166, 168, 170, 172, 173, 176, 178–182, 184, 189–191, 204–207

I
Inquiring-back, 87, 111, 127, 144, 147, 148, 152, 154–156, 164, 191, 192, 196
Inquiry, 1–10, 12, 16, 19, 24, 25, 30, 32, 34–39, 42, 43, 45–49, 52–61, 63–66, 70, 71, 73, 75–78, 85, 92, 94–100, 102–104, 106, 107, 109–112, 114, 115, 117–123, 126, 127, 132, 134, 138, 140, 141, 143, 147, 148, 150, 151, 153, 156, 160–162, 165, 176, 178, 183–185, 187, 189, 191–195
Instinct, 132, 148, 156, 160–165, 168–170, 173, 176, 178
Intentionality, 7, 24, 25, 28, 29, 43, 55, 72, 82, 87, 141, 182
Interest, 5, 7, 17, 20, 37, 52, 54, 60, 68, 69, 78, 92, 95, 100, 101, 104, 105, 107–110, 116, 117, 125, 141, 148, 155, 162, 164–166, 169–174, 176, 183–186, 189, 190, 192, 200
Interiority, 27, 51, 130, 151, 160, 192

L

Logic, 7, 9, 10, 13–19, 24, 25, 32, 33, 37, 39, 75–77, 80, 82, 86, 93, 96, 118, 123, 154, 208

M

Motivation, 30, 31, 35, 39, 45–48, 60, 87, 90, 101, 109, 111, 114, 126–128, 131–133, 136, 140, 142, 148, 151, 162, 176, 192, 193

N

Natural Inquiry, 7, 42, 43, 64, 65, 71
Normativity, 46, 92, 93, 144

O

Origins, 5, 7, 21, 24, 26, 42, 59, 64, 65, 76, 85–88, 90, 95, 108, 127–129, 141–143, 147, 156, 181, 192, 194

P

Phenomenological philosophy, 3, 5, 110, 114, 130, 137, 140, 146, 148, 149, 192, 193, 196
Pure phenomenology, 13, 76

S

Source, 5, 7, 30, 36, 42, 49, 56, 62–65, 71, 75, 76, 78, 80, 81, 91, 110, 143, 145, 147, 160, 161, 163, 168–170, 199, 205

T

Theology, 185, 193–195
Transcendental, 3, 7, 9–13, 15, 17, 24, 25, 27, 30, 39, 42, 43, 48–50, 52, 53, 55, 57, 59, 60, 62–65, 71–73, 75, 76, 79, 80, 86, 87, 93, 110, 114, 125, 132, 140–143, 145, 146, 150, 152, 153, 156, 160, 161, 163, 166, 191, 192, 201, 204–206, 209–211

V

Values, 2, 3, 7, 8, 26, 31, 33, 39, 67, 71, 76, 84, 85, 87, 88, 103, 112, 117–126, 128, 129, 133–136, 138, 143, 144, 148, 151, 152, 154, 155, 157, 159, 162, 163, 166, 168, 169, 174–178, 180, 182, 183, 186, 190, 192, 194, 199, 200, 202, 203, 205, 209

W

Wonder, 1, 8, 169, 170, 181, 183–185, 190